DISCOVERING A VOICE:
A RHETORIC FOR WRITERS

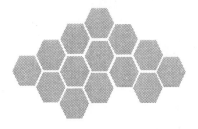

Robert Miller   **Cher Brock**   **Steve Sansom**

FOUNTAINHEAD
PRESS

Books may be purchased for educational purposes.

For information, please call or write:

1-800-586-0330

Fountainhead Press
Southlake, TX. 76092

Web site: www.fountainheadpress.com

Email: customerservice@fountainheadpress.com

Second Edition

ISBN 978-1-59871-361-9

Printed in the United States of America

ACKNOWLEDGMENTS

So many of our colleagues at Lone Star College–North Harris have generously assisted us in the preparation of this text. We are indebted to them all for their encouragement and support. To our distant colleague Dr. Matthew Batt at University of St. Thomas in St. Paul, Minnesota, we owe a special debt for his contributions and patient assistance. Felix Frazier and the staff at Fountainhead Press have been most helpful and accommodating in bringing this project to its completion. A very special thanks to Joann Engallina, whose expertise got us through the whole ordeal. Finally, we thank our friends and loved ones for their suggestions, inspirations, and tolerance. Whatever success this text enjoys, we share with all these folks. Whatever shortcomings it contains are ours alone.

R. M.
C. B.
S. S.

Houston, Texas
August 2008

CONTENTS

PART ONE: A Guide to Writing

PART TWO: Exposition and Argumentation

PART THREE: Further Readings

Student Models:

THEMATIC GUIDE TO THE CONTENTS

Family Relationships

"Once More to the Lake" by E. B. White

"Digging" by Andre Dubus

"Why We Fall in Love" by M. Scott Peck

"Why Men Marry" by George Gilder

"Sex, Lies, and Conversation" by Deborah Tannen

Race and Culture

"Letter from Birmingham Jail" by Martin Luther King, Jr.

"Just Walk on By: A Black Man Ponders His Power
to Alter Public Space" by Brent Staples

"None of this is Fair" by Richard Rodriguez

"On Being Black and Middle Class" by Shelby Steele

"Just Be Nice" by Stephen L. Carter

"Declaration of Independence" by Thomas Jefferson, et al.

"In Defense of Prejudice" by Jonathan Rauch

"The Tyranny of the Majority" by Lani Guinier

"Lessons from Lockdown" by Matthew Batt

Language and Education

Ethics

History and Politics

PART I

A GUIDE TO WRITING

The Elements
of Rhetoric

From the time of the ancient Greeks and Romans to our present day, someone has always attempted to alter the lives of others through words; witness the eloquent phrases in the Declaration of Independence, Lincoln's "Gettysburg Address," Martin Luther King's "I Have a Dream" speech, John F. Kennedy's inaugural address, even the demagoguery of Adolph Hitler and Saddam Hussein. The major power of their words is the power of rhetoric, the art or discipline of writing effectively and persuasively, used to inform or motivate an audience. While Aristotle defined rhetoric as discovering the best means of persuasion in any given situation, this definition might include not only the argumentative but the expository or informative mode of discourse as well. In fact, rhetoric operates in almost every form of writing we find. For this reason, rhetoric is still an important concern of each of us today, primarily because none of us can escape it—not the lawyer, the teacher, the politician, the computer analyst, or the student. We all indulge in and are exposed to rhetoric daily. Therefore, the goal of the class in which you are enrolled and the goal of this text are to raise your awareness of the rhetorical components all around you so you might be more effective in expressing your own ideas as well as more alert to others' use and misuse of rhetoric. This text, through its instructions and exercises, can serve as a guide for you in your move toward communicating your thoughts and feelings through words.

Your tasks as a writer can range from giving the directions for planting a garden to persuading an audience that capital punishment should or should not be abolished. Whether you choose to use the expository or persuasive method, you should understand and be able to use certain rhetorical elements in order to make your ideas more convincing or persuasive. These elements include the writer's purpose, audience, voice, and the situation. While all four elements play a role in every composition, they do not always have equal roles. For example, audience would obviously assume a

FIGURE 1-A

Rhetorical Elements

greater place in process analysis and persuasive essays than in a comparison and contrast essay, and voice might play a minimal role in definition and a major role in narration and description. Nevertheless, each principle must be present for you to achieve your goal of communicating your ideas. However varying their presence in an essay, all four elements must be included.

PURPOSE

Writing always has a purpose. Every writer must have a reason for writing, and that reason, or purpose, determines which of the other three elements of rhetoric will be emphasized. The general purpose of various writing methods is to know what we think and how best to communicate those thoughts. Therefore, we must always determine what particular message we want to convey and what method would likely be most effective. Do we wish simply to report or inform, to explain, or to persuade? During your college career and afterwards, you might be required to report on a given project or to inform your audience as to the progress of a particular project. In addition, you might be expected to explain to a co-worker the step-by-step procedure for seeking advancement in the company, or you may wish to persuade your supervisor that your particular ideas warrant attention over the proposals of a co-worker. Whichever rhetorical mode you select to write your essay, it must have a purpose, and the purpose must be clearly evident to the reader. The rhetorical purpose is sometimes determined by the specific assignment. If a topic is assigned, your task of deciding on a purpose may already have been done for you. However, often you will have to determine the purpose yourself. If it cannot be discovered immediately, the purpose can emerge from your preliminary brainstorming of the assigned general topic and from the early stages of organizing your random thoughts. Until a purpose is clearly in your mind, though, it is best not to begin writing the essay, else you will likely waste time and effort. Time spent in determining your purpose is far better used than time spent in wandering from point to point without direction. Knowing your purpose helps you sharpen your focus. Make certain, too, that your goals are reasonable and that you can manage what you tell your audience you will accomplish in your statement of purpose, or your thesis. Then you can decide which method of presentation is the most efficient and can best accomplish your purpose. These rhetorical methods are discussed in specific detail in Chapters 4 through 11.

AUDIENCE

Your audience is your intended listener or reader. Every word we utter is directed toward something or someone, even if we are only talking to ourselves. When we speak to someone, we have the advantage of immediate feedback, of noting the reaction, either verbal or nonverbal, and so we are able to determine whether or not he understands us. When speaking, therefore, we can adjust our voice, gestures, or language to accommodate our listener, thus increasing our chances of being understood. In writing, however, the advantages of instant feedback and subsequent adjustments are not available to us. Therefore we must be more aware of who our audience is and what he or she knows. If we want to achieve an intended effect (purpose), we must be able to make certain assumptions about our audience. In adapting your ideas to meet your particular audience, you must bear in mind the interests and values of those you want to reach. Estimate what their backgrounds are, their education, age, sex, political and religious inclinations, and experiences. What can they expect to gain by reading your ideas? These concerns help you establish which approach to use in presenting your ideas and what to stress or to omit in your essay. Identifying the audience will assist you in anticipating questions and in being prepared to address those questions in your essays. This procedure is not unlike a job applicant's research into a company with whom he intends to interview.

Students are correct in assuming their audience is their instructor. But most writing instructors will want you to specify a variety of audiences, real or imagined, in order to sharpen your rhetorical skills to meet the demands of different situations. This task is not always easy. Addressing a variety of audiences in a variety of essays places restraints on students, but these situations more than likely reflect the situations you may encounter in life. You will always be confronted with different audiences, different situations, and different subjects. It is best, then, to keep in mind that you will likely have more than one audience for your essay—your instructor and some other designated audience. This dual audience requires you to adapt to each one's needs and expectations, just as a newspaper reporter must write a news item with his editor as well as the general reading public in mind. Knowing your audience and writing to them does not mean you have to sacrifice your own beliefs in order to accommodate those of your audience. You must not feel you have to choose between your integrity and reader appeal. If you are skillful in the use of rhetoric, you can maintain an honest and authentic voice and at the same time still be a successful strategist.

VOICE

Having defined your audience, you must now determine the role that you want to assume with your audience. This stance, or voice, that you must assume is much like the different masks you prepare daily. You present yourself one way when attending class, and you present yourself quite differently when you are on a date or visiting your in-laws. While these masks are different, your identity is still the same. Each role is sincere, but each allows you the flexibility to select the appropriate demeanor and words for a specific occasion and audience. This role-playing is similar to the role you assume in presenting your ideas in your essay to a given audience. Consider how you would express yourself in a personal letter to a friend as compared to how you would express yourself in a letter of application for scholarship funds. Authenticity and sincerity are imperative. They guide the voice in its attempt to demonstrate you are serious about your subject and respectful of your audience. Be genuine in whatever voice you assume. You can be sympathetic, neutral, angry, or humorous, but most of all be yourself. What you say and how you say it, therefore, are determined by your purpose, audience, and subject matter.

SITUATION

The fourth element of the rhetorical process is the situation. It is the most important of all four elements because without it you would have no basis for an essay. The remainder of this text is concerned with the steps in putting together your ideas and deciding on the appropriate method of presenting those ideas to a designated audience in a given situation. Which arrangement to use in presenting your essay depends upon the situation, your audience, your voice or the stance you take in offering your ideas, and your purpose. The rules for the art and craft of rhetoric are not written in stone, nor are they "writ in water." A great deal of rhetorical flexibility in regard to these rules is available to writers of compositions, but sometimes the refusal to concern yourself with these rules can have disastrous consequences. In the classroom the results can be an inferior grade, while in the marketplace they can mean unemployment. The rules that are discussed in the following pages represent the methods of writing that are time-proven, that have served people in almost every endeavor—mostly, but not always, for good purposes. We can only hope that you use your rhetorical skills for the general good, never to be abused or misused.

So now we arrive at our starting place; through language and the expression of ideas we begin to understand our world and ourselves.

ON THE NET

How Audience and Purpose Affect Focus. Colorado State University.
<http://writing.colostate.edu/guides/processes/focus/list4.cfm>

Audience and Purpose. State University of New York at Geneseo.
<http://writingguide.geneseo.edu/?pg=topics/audiencepurpose.html>

A Word About Style, Voice, and Tone. Online Guide to Writing and Research. University of Maryland University College.
<http://www.umuc.edu/ewc/onlineguide/chapter3/chapter3-21.shtml>

Tone: A Matter of Attitude. Capital Community College.
<http://grammar.ccc.commnet.edu/grammar/composition/tone.htm>

Tone in Business Writing. The OWL at Purdue.
<http://owl.english.purdue.edu/owl/resource/652/01/>

2 The Writing Process

The first rule of writing a composition is "Don't panic." The task of writing does not have to be a dreadful undertaking, but neither should it be taken too casually. Instead, view it as an opportunity to express your ideas. Even if you presently lack the confidence to take on such a task comfortably, you will discover that it is within your abilities if you understand the general principles of what constitutes good, effective writing. Most of your assignments will require observations, feelings, or opinions. This explanation is the general substance of expository writing. In addition, you may be asked to defend your opinions or observations or to attempt to convince your readers of your opinions, that is, to use persuasive writing. Knowing the fundamental components of each of these types of composition will reduce much of your tendency toward panic and will, at the same time, provide you with the proper tools to begin your writing assignment. Finally, you may be asked to write a critical analysis, i.e., your interpretation or observations about an essay. This project, too, requires the basic components of expository and persuasive writing.

Writing is a recursive process: each step overlaps another step. You may begin and proceed through the process in several ways. However, a logical approach is to follow certain prewriting steps to get started.

THE BEGINNING

Finding a Topic

Beginning an essay can be extremely frustrating when you have the freedom to choose your own topic. Coming up with a fresh, original subject and having something unique to say about it can be overwhelming. Finding a topic does not have to be stressful, however; it can be turned to your advantage. It will allow you to focus on what you know, what you have experienced, and what you would prefer to discuss. Your own experiences are your best sources, whether you decide to write a narrative of your harrowing experiences during registration or you have to argue your views on the irrelevancy of the grading system.

No matter what the assignment is, first consider what you know the most about—yourself. Your own experiences and perceptions will always play a major part in your writing. Maybe your career or studies toward a career can provide some interesting topics. Perhaps you have just read a book or seen a play or movie that deals with a subject that intrigues you. Perhaps you want to make known your views about a particular controversial issue that is important to you. Sources for potential topics are all around you, but you must be observant. Many instructors prefer that you keep journal entries to record your experiences as they occur. This practice not only provides you with personal explorations and possible source material for your essays, but it also affords you the chance to practice your writing skills. Finally, your general reading and research will provide supplementary information for your opinions and observations. Your preparation for writing depends on how involved you are with the world around you.

Brainstorming/Gathering Details

Whether your topic is assigned or you have a choice of subjects, you should first brainstorm to help you determine what you want to say about your subject. First, select a topic you find interesting or one with which you are most familiar. If you are undecided as to what to write about, brainstorm two or three possible topics and then see which subject generates the most ideas. One advantage of brainstorming is that it is graphic: it reveals to you the topic about which you know the most. Once you have settled upon a topic and a general approach, determine for whom you will be writing your essay—your audience. This decision is crucial before you brainstorm further because it will determine what to include in and exclude from your discussion.

An essay about the benefits of attending college that is to be read by a college professor will include quite different information than would the same essay aimed at an audience of graduating high school seniors. Be aware of your audience: it determines your approach. In a writing course, however, you must realize that you are writing for two audiences: your designated reader and your instructor. Therefore, even though your designated reader may vary with each assignment, you always have to keep in mind the requirements of your other reader—your instructor.

Finally, clarify your purpose. Ask yourself, "What do I want to accomplish?" "What do I want my audience to do or to understand?" Purpose is largely dependent upon audience. If you are discussing the advantages of attending college for an instructor, chances are your purpose is to inform. But if the essay will be read by a high school senior, your purpose is probably to persuade. Without knowing your purposes before you organize your ideas, you risk misdirection and increased frustration, not to mention the loss of precious time and energy.

Once you have gone through this initial exercise, begin brainstorming. Brainstorm alone or with others and write down as quickly as you can anything—any random fragments, words, or sentences—that relate even remotely to your subject. Do not pause to consider the relevance of any item that surfaces, its spelling, grammar, or level of importance; that step will come later. Anything jotted down at this stage is relevant and valid and, even though you might ultimately reject some ideas, they might possibly generate other useable thoughts. The example below is a brainstorming exercise on the assigned topic "The Qualities of a Good Teacher." The student determined that his audience would be a group of his peers on the occasion of a teacher awards ceremony, and his purpose would be to inform them of what he believes constitutes excellence in teaching.

Qualities of a Good Teacher

has high expectations of students
competent
shows relevance of field of study
patience w/students
stimulates interest
prepared and organized
accessible after class
rarely absent
fair, unbiased
flexible
doesn't patronize
doesn't speak down
loves subject & enjoys it
considerate
clear instructions
asks questions
interested in students' ideas
keeps up to date in field
never uses yellow lecture notes
no favorites
never embarrasses students
variety of teaching styles
can answer any question
can "tell stories"
Mr. Carver's stories
drives a Corvette
young

wide knowledge, not just of
    subject
no spoonfeeding
praises good work
not monotone
encourages critical
    thinking
organized notes
command of language
creative
enthusiastic
open-minded
brings ideas to discussion not
    in textbook
tactful
listens to opposing views
clear expectations
grades consistently / fairly
interesting lectures
doesn't repeat readings
values student contributions
motivates, inspires
prompt
fair tests
Mrs. Jones—history
attractive
single

Obviously not everything from this list will make its way to the final draft of the essay. Much will be cut and much will be incorporated into more general topics. You can see from this list that "good teachers" is a topic that produces a wealth of material.

Once your brainstorming session seems to have exhausted itself, group together those items that share some common characteristics. After forming these tentative groups, eliminate everything that does not fit into any of these groups. Now these groups and the details that remain should help shape an approach that will eventually become the focus of your thesis. Notice how the details from our original brainstorming of "good teachers" are grouped in the following example:

I. Relationships with students

has high expectations of students
no spoonfeeding
praises good work
patience with students
doesn't patronize
doesn't speak down
considerate
tactful
listens to opposing views
interested in students' ideas
provides additional help if needed
accessible after class
fair, unbiased
flexible
open-minded
values student contributions
motivates, inspires
no favorites
doesn't ridicule or embarrass students

II. Style of teaching

sense of humor
loves subject and enjoys it
stimulates student interest
asks questions
not a monotone
encourages critical thinking
creative
clear expectations & instructions
grades consistently
interesting lectures
doesn't repeat readings
fair tests
enthusiastic
variety of teaching styles
can adapt methods spontaneously

III. Knowledge of subject

competent
prepared and organized
command of language
brings ideas to discussion not in text
keeps up to date in field
doesn't lecture from yellow notes
wide knowledge, not just of subject
shows relevance of field of study
can "tell stories"
knows incidental information
can answer almost any question

Grouping shows that the details we save can be sorted into three general groups: relationship with students, teaching style, and knowledge of the subject matter. However, if we had to deal with all three subtopics, we would have quite a long essay, much longer than what is required for a typical writing assignment. We can pick any of these three groups and use it alone as the topic for our essay. Since most of our brainstorming ideas fall into the category of relationships with students, we choose that as the narrowed topic of our essay.

At this point in the writing process you have a specific subject, an audience, a purpose, and a general idea of what you want to discuss. The next step is to construct a statement that will incorporate your primary ideas into a workable thesis.

Formulating a Thesis Statement

Many beginning writers make the mistake of underestimating the importance of a thesis statement or of confusing it with the topic or a statement of purpose of the essay. The thesis is an explicit statement, usually a single sentence that expresses the central point the writer wishes to make. It is the summary of all the individual elements in your paper that relate to your topic. The thesis is what holds the essay together and gives it direction. Without a good thesis you will likely have a poorly organized essay. The steps suggested below should help you formulate a thesis statement that will work to your advantage by giving focus, coherence, and organization to your essay.

Step One

After you have discovered your topic and have brainstormed it thoroughly, as in the earlier exercise regarding good teachers, you now must state what is a key component of the thesis statement—the subject. The subject of your thesis sentence states the narrowed, restricted topic of your essay. It tells what your essay will be about. The subject part of the thesis sentence says, simply, that you will discuss, not just "teachers," but "good teachers." Putting a subject in a thesis statement is easy by now since by brainstorming you have already arrived at a fairly restricted subject. However, that is not to say that you cannot further revise the subject at this stage. Remember that we limited our topic further to "the relationship good teachers have with their students." Be sure that the subject you choose is restricted enough to give the reader a clear and thorough treatment of it in the length of the essay required. Too broad a subject will result in a discussion that is too general and superficial, while too narrow a subject will leave you with nothing to say after one or two sentences.

Step Two

The other key component of a thesis statement, the focus, is usually the predicate portion of your sentence, that portion which asserts exactly what you intend to say about your subject. The focus is not as easy to formulate as the subject, and many beginning writers tend to neglect it. This oversight is a fatal mistake. Imagine an essay that begins, "There are many good teachers at my school." The reader, right before falling asleep or throwing the paper into the trash, will reply, "So what?" It is not enough to say that there are good teachers out there; you must be able to say something about them: "The best teachers have three qualities in common," or, "Mrs. Jones, the best teacher I ever had, cared about her students both in and out of the classroom."

To arrive at a focus, let's take another look at our subtopic "Relationship with students" and see how we can group the details there.

Motivation/Inspiration

has high expectations of students
no spoonfeeding
praises good work
motivates, inspires
makes class interesting

Respect for students

patience with students
doesn't patronize
doesn't speak down
considerate
tactful
listens to opposing views
fair, unbiased
flexible
open-minded
values student contributions
no favorites
doesn't ridicule or embarrass students

Personal interest in students

provides additional help if needed
accessible after class
interested in extra-curricular activities

As well as helping to restrict your subject, the groupings furnish you the specific terms with which to compose a tentative thesis statement. From the groupings above we can formulate the following thesis sentence: *A good teacher respects students, has a personal interest in them, and motivates them to do their best.* Now that you have a specific subject and a clearer focus in front of you, you are better prepared to organize and present your material. You have taken your random thoughts and formed them into a cohesive whole.

Step Three

Because you have identified a specific audience that may not be easy to convince, make certain your thesis is precise, concise, and unified. By being precise, you make certain that no word is ambiguous or unclear. Say clearly what you mean and what you intend to discuss. Don't tell your reader that "Mrs. Jones, my favorite teacher, was interesting and nice," although she probably was both. Even if your audience is the least bit interested in this insightful observation, the point will be almost impossible to prove. How does one define "nice"? Was she friendly? polite? cheerful? caring? "Nice" means all of these things and none of them. And the word "interesting" runs the gamut from being able to tell the best jokes of anyone on the faculty to having an extensive collection of World War II artillery shells. Use specific, concrete words rather than vague general terms. Being concise comes from taking the time to choose the most precise words and phrases, those that say exactly what you want to say and that will be easy to develop in the body of the essay. In addition, you must state succinctly what your intention is and no more. Consider this thesis sentence: "Mrs. Jones was the best teacher I ever had because she cared for her students; that is, she always had a kind word for everyone and she helped us study for the tests." After a thesis like that, there will be little left to discuss in the rest of the paper. Remember, although your purpose in the essay is to present, explain, or argue an idea, the thesis statement is not the place to begin your argument or explanation. It is only to sum up or to defend your position, sometimes referred to as the "method of approach." "Mrs. Jones was the best teacher I ever had because she cared for her students" indicates what you are going to discuss, but does not reveal the whole essay in the opening paragraph.

Finally, unless your essay is a lengthy one, make certain your thesis statement contains a single issue or idea; otherwise, the scope of your essay will be too broad and your supporting examples too general to be convincing. A unified thesis statement reduces the possibilities of unity violations in the body of the essay. "Mrs. Jones, the best teacher I ever had, cared about her students: that is, she always had a kind word for everyone, even though she never had much to say to my friend Hortense." Aside from being wordy and too precise, this sentence violates unity in that it wanders off to the subject of Hortense. A well-focused thesis statement reduces the ever-present potential for violations of unity in the body of the essay.

A final word about the thesis statement.

Here are a few suggestions to make your thesis sentence work for you and not against you:

1. Avoid the obvious. While you want to make it clear to your audience what you intend to do, never say, "In this paper I will …." Statements like this are dull, plodding, and unsubtle. Make your wording original and fresh.

2. Be direct and forceful in stating your opinion without alienating the reader. Make it clear that you are taking a stand and are allied with a certain position.

3. Do not, however, say, "It is my opinion that …." The reader will know that the opinions in the essay are yours. Phrasing a sentence thus only makes for another dull and plodding sentence. If the ideas are not yours, they must be correctly documented.

4. Make sure that your thesis sentence indicates the organization of your paper. If you have three characteristics of excellence in teachers to discuss, mention each briefly in the thesis sentence and mention them in the order you wish to discuss them in the body of the paper. This method of organization creates confidence in the reader regarding your ability to be clear, logical, and organized from the outset.

5. Make certain the length of your sentence is appropriate for the length of your paper. A 45-word thesis statement is too long for a 600-word essay. Your introductory paragraph should not consist only of a thesis. This paragraph introduces your thesis as well as the entire essay.

6. The thesis statement should be ONE SENTENCE ONLY. A compound sentence is okay, but do not make it merely a string of independent clauses. Selective wording will eliminate a "rambling" sentence.

7. Finally, never hesitate to revise your thesis statement at any stage in drafting your essay if you feel you can improve it. Even though it may mean additional adjustments in the body of the essay, your extra effort will usually pay off. You should make at least two revisions.

THE MIDDLE

Now that you have a thesis statement to control the essay, you must organize the body of your discussion. To begin this process, look back at your notes from your brainstorming once again and notice the way you grouped the details. Why did you group certain things together? What did they have in common? What "heading" could you give each group? Each of the groupings that you made in your brainstorming now will become a main element in the body of your essay and will be mentioned in your thesis statement. Next, formulate the ideas generated in each of the brainstorming categories into a working statement that summarizes all the ideas in the category. This sentence will serve as your topic sentence for each category; it will be formed eventually into a paragraph composed of subtopics and examples. This topic sentence functions as the controlling idea of the paragraph. Just as your thesis statement states your purpose for the entire essay, your topic sentence directs your audience's attention to the single idea you will discuss in each particular paragraph. Each topic sentence, just like the thesis statement, has a subject and a focus. This focus will signal to the reading audience precisely what you intend to illustrate in the course of that paragraph and how it relates to the thesis. The same rules of clarity, conciseness, and unity required of your thesis statement apply to the topic sentence as well, for, regardless of its length and complexity, the paragraph should contain only one central idea.

Outlining/Developing a Plan

While the word outline itself provokes scurrilous mutterings and utter contempt from most composition students, it need not be treated as an adversarial force to be conquered or endured. It must, however, be done before you write the essay, not after. Once you become familiar enough with the benefits of outlining, you may discover it is the most critical step in all the pre-writing stages. The outline functions much like the blueprints of an architectural project. It is the framework on which to build your essay. You must overcome the tendency to resist this key step in the stage of writing, for, regardless of which rhetorical mode you select for your essay, good planning is essential. Likewise, poor planning is quickly evident. The value is endless for the writer as well as the reader. Consider the following advantages:

1. For the writer, the outline encourages brevity.

2. It can keep you from violating unity by indicating that an idea does not belong. At the same time, the outline will often suggest that some additional idea might be included.

3. The outline can ensure that important ideas are placed in the appropriate places according to relative value.

4. Its format allows you to check for stylistic consistency, continuity, and clarity.

5. It keeps you focused on the separate ideas and lets you actually **visualize** the level of generality among your ideas. Your ideas in the outline format are simply easier to see.

6. Finally, the outline will provide you with a psychological boost. Having succeeded in organizing your ideas logically, you enjoy a sense of accomplishment that should allow you to move on to the next writing stage with increased confidence.

There are two basic outline forms—the topic outline and the sentence outline. Regardless of the assignment, you will want to consider using both forms at strategic stages in the prewriting phase. Now that your purpose is clear, your audience is designated, and you have a workable thesis clearly in mind, it is time to impose the standard outline system of organization on your thoughts. The following system is the universal format for outlining ideas:

THESIS

I. [First topic related to discussion of thesis]
  A.
    1.
      a.
      b.
      c.   (Note: the old adage "If you have a 1,
    2.   you must have a 2" is a valid point.
      a.   The same holds true of any subhead-
      b.   ing or level of development. A good
      c.   rule to remember is that a pair is the
  B.   required minimum.)
    1.
      a.
      b.
      c.
    2.
      a.
      b.
      c.

II. [Second topic related to thesis statement]
  A. [etc.]

Each Roman numeral is a major division of the thesis of the essay, and each of the subheadings, capital letters, Arabic numerals, and lower case letters are more specific information that develop each division (paragraph).

Topic Outline

The topic outline is helpful in the preliminary organization of the essay when you want to determine the main points of your discussion and the order in which you will discuss them. Each entry in a topic outline is just what the term implies: a topic heading, much like a title, not a complete sentence, but a "bare bones" phrase. The topic outline delineates the areas to be discussed but does not yet deal with what specifically will be said about them. Even at the topic outline level, however, you should be grammatically consistent. If you want to use nouns, nouns plus a verb form, or prepositional phrases, make certain you use them at each letter or number level in order to create a parallel structure. This consistency will assist you later when transforming your topic outline to the body paragraphs of the essay.

GOOD TEACHERS

Thesis: A good teacher respects students, has a personal interest in them, and motivates them to do their best.

I. Respect for students

    A. Considerate

        1. Tactful

        2. Non-ridiculing

        3. Patient

        4. Non-patronizing

    B. Fair

        1. Flexible

        2. Fair in testing

        3. Objective in grading

        4. No favoritism

    C. Values students' contributions

        1. Compliments students' work

        2. Praises student involvement

Sentence Outline

Whether it is used initially or instead of the topic outline, the sentence outline requires more effort. You will still be required to list, categorize and order your ideas by relative importance. This time, however, you must write your thoughts in **complete sentences.** The first stage of a sentence outline might look like this:

GOOD TEACHERS

Thesis: A good teacher respects students, has a personal interest in them, and motivates them to do their best.

I. A good teacher respects her students.
   A. She is considerate of her students.
      1. She criticizes them tactfully.
      2. She does not ridicule them or embarrass them.
      3. She is patient with them.
      4. She never patronizes her students.
   B. She treats her students fairly.
      1. She is flexible and open-minded.
      2. Her tests are fair.
      3. She grades objectively and consistently.
      4. She does not have favorites.
   C. She shows that she values the contributions of everyone in the class.
      1. She compliments her students on their work.
      2. She praises them for their involvement even when she disagrees with them.

II. (etc.)

A hint about outlining. Regardless of which outline form you use, it is a good idea to write down all the headings/sentences for the Roman numerals before going on to the capital letters and all the capital letter headings before going on to the next level. Doing so helps keep the levels of development, the subtopics and details, clear. With this systematic organizational plan behind you, you can now concentrate on the next phase: development.

The Paragraph

The standard paragraph is made up of a topic sentence, subtopic headings, and various levels of specific examples. The topic sentence functions in the paragraph just as the thesis statement functions in the essay. The topic sentence also supports the thesis statement by offering a main point in the discussion and announces what specifically will be discussed in the paragraph. Likewise, each subtopic heading (the A, B, etc., of the outline) will support the specific focus of the paragraph.

Finally, the examples under each subtopic heading offer illustrations that support the assertions of the subheading. Thus, in a well-organized paragraph, the relationship of every detail to the topic sentence is obvious, and, in turn, the connection with the thesis is obvious. Remember that the paragraph is a miniature essay. Mastering the principles of paragraph form offers greater assurance toward mastering the essay. This mastery involves being familiar with unity, development, coherence, and continuity within the paragraph.

Paragraph Unity

For a paragraph to have unity, each sentence in a body paragraph must directly relate to the purpose indicated in the topic sentence. The paragraph must hang together as a whole, creating an unmistakable sense of oneness. Any departure from the single purpose of the paragraph violates paragraph unity. For example, if you were to bring into your discussion of good teachers the idea that teachers' salaries need to be raised, you would be shifting the focus away from the main idea, thus breaking the unity in the paragraph. Stick to your topic sentence! Keep in mind that a paragraph is, by definition, a unified statement of a particular idea. A way to test paragraph unity is to try to link each sentence to a word or phrase in the topic sentence. Draw lines and arrows if you must. Any sentence that you cannot obviously link to the topic sentence is probably irrelevant and, therefore, will undermine the effectiveness of your paper.

Paragraph Development

Just because you have said in your thesis statement that a good teacher respects her students, shows interest in them, and motivates them, that does not mean that your readers have to accept your viewpoint automatically. You must convince your audience that what you have to say is sound, sensible, and well-supported. In other words, even if you are informing, you are still persuading your readers. You must explore your main idea explicitly, concretely, and thoroughly, and you must strive to include enough supporting evidence in each paragraph to present your point convincingly. *Inadequate paragraph development is one of the most serious weaknesses of beginning writers.* No matter how organized and unified your ideas are, if they are not developed fully, you will have failed to communicate to your audience. Supporting evidence or examples come from your own experiences, from hypothetical examples, research material, authoritative evidence, facts, or from just about any sound, reliable source.

Many students ask, "What is enough support?" The answer is arbitrary, but some general guidelines apply. You want enough support to convince your audience of the soundness of your argument. Whose opinion, for example, is more likely to be accepted in a court of law: a defense attorney's claim that her client is innocent because the defendant's family and friends know he is innocent or the prosecuting attorney's claim that the defendant is guilty because of fourteen eyewitnesses and extensive forensic evidence? Valid evidence is convincing and supports opinions and observation. The same is true of paragraph development. You must provide enough information to convince them of the soundness of your argument. As a rule, the average length of a paragraph in a college-level essay might run approximately three-fourths of a typed page. While striving arduously for quantity, however, NEVER forget that quality is more important. The fact that Aunt Zona Gail believes men make better teachers than women is not the strong evidence you want to support your contentions about good teachers. But surveying students or speaking with teachers who have won awards or recognition for excellence in teaching would serve as appropriate proof. In moving from topic sentence to supporting evidence in a paragraph, you are moving from general to specific. The order and progression of this movement is essential to effective paragraphs, and the outline is the most efficient method of making certain this progression occurs logically. This order ranks and demonstrates the levels of generality in a paragraph. For example:

Thesis: Igor often failed to live up to his expectations. LEVEL ONE

I. [topic sentence—general statement] Igor was a poor student. LEVEL TWO

    A. [subtopic—less general] He was not conscientious. LEVEL THREE

        1. [example—specific] He never handed in assignments on time. LEVEL FOUR

            a. [more specific] He handed in his first English composition two weeks late. LEVEL FIVE

These levels constitute the arrangement of ideas in the paragraph, from general statement to specific examples. Always develop your ideas in the outline of your paragraph at least to level four. The logic behind this recommendation is that you most likely will have to reach level three before you can provide examples that are specific and concrete enough to persuade your readers of your general assertion (level one). In addition, the ideal number of level two or level three statements is three; that is, A, B, C and 1, 2, and 3. If you offer only two examples, you could risk sounding dogmatic and inflexible. Four or more examples under the same subtopic, however, suggests you wish to appeal emotionally to your readers. Some readers might cry out "Enough already!" There is such a thing as overkill, especially if your examples tend to be repetitious. You will not always be able to provide three examples, but the goal is a worthy one. Make sure you understand and can recognize the different levels so you can create good, effective outlines and, consequently, good paragraphs.

Thesis: Good teachers have certain qualities in common. LEVEL ONE

I. A good teacher respects her students. LEVEL TWO

A. She is considerate of her students. LEVEL THREE

   1. She criticizes them tactfully. LEVEL FOUR

      a. She always tells them something positive about their work along with suggestions on how to improve it. LEVEL FIVE

Finally, if your paragraph is a long one, you might consider including a summary sentence, a "clincher," to close your paragraph. The inclusion of such a sentence serves at least two purposes. First, it brings closure to the main idea of the paragraph, especially if you have provided extensive examples. Closure helps your audience by returning them to your central idea and reminding them of your specific intention in the paragraph. Second, the summary sentence is on the same level of generality as your topic sentence; therefore, it will make your task of bridging the connection between this paragraph and the next easier than it would be if you had to move from a very specific level of generality, a minor support statement, to a new topic sentence in a new paragraph. This final summary sentence "clinches" the discussion and emphasizes the main idea. Some writers prefer to provide in this final sentence some notion of what is to come in the next paragraph through some kind of transition device.

Continuity in the Paragraph

Continuity means literally "holding together." It is achieved through good organization and unity, as we have seen, and also by the language you use to illustrate to your readers how your ideas fit together. The language you use will serve as transitions, devices that link sentences to each other. Transitions are also used to connect paragraphs, thus linking your ideas together in a smooth, logical order.

Transitional devices include pronouns and demonstrative adjectives, repetition of key words, the use of synonyms, transitional expressions, and parallel construction.

   1. Pronouns and demonstrative adjectives—When their antecedents are clearly understood, pronouns (they, it, she, he) help the reader recognize that the phrase or sentence in which they appear is linked to the preceding idea. Example: "Steinbeck is fascinated by the animal motivation behind human behavior. Frequently in his fiction, he equates human and animal conduct to show their similarities."

     Demonstrative adjectives also clearly link the sentence containing them with the preceding sentences. These adjectives are words like *that, this, these,* and *those.* Notice how the demonstrative adjective links the following two sentences: "Recognition of the unity of all life is the basis for John Steinbeck's artistic use of nature. One of the major expressions of this unity is the kinship that man feels with the land."

2. Repetition of key words and use of synonyms. The important rule here is to repeat key words, those words that keep your focus in the minds of your audience. Notice how the word unity is repeated in the example above. Be careful, however, that you do not rely too heavily on this transitional technique; too much repetition becomes monotonous. If you feel you are repeating the same word too often, substitute a synonym. Instead of unity, try *oneness* or harmony occasionally if it fits the context of your meaning.

3. Transitional words—The most recognizable and most effective transitional words include "furthermore," "moreover," "likewise," "similarly," "nevertheless," "on the other hand," "conversely," "first," "second," "third" and so on. Each of these words has a definite function, whether it is to show logical order or to indicate logical relationships between ideas and sentences. Without these expressions, your sentences would make little sense and certainly would not fit together to develop your idea. A word of caution, however: be sure the transitional expression you choose does precisely what you want it to do. Do not simply close your eyes and select a transitional word from the list. Use an appropriate term for the meaning or connection you wish to convey. Never use "furthermore" when "however" is what you need to alter the direction or to qualify a statement.

Consult your handbook or thesaurus for additional help.

4. Parallel construction—This transitional device links your sentences and ideas by repeating a grammatical structure, thereby forcing your audience not only to keep the focus in mind but to realize fully the connection between your ideas. Note, for example, President Lincoln's use of parallel construction in his famous "Gettysburg Address" and the power of its connected ideas to hold his audience:

> *It is rather for us to be here dedicated to the great task remaining before us; that from these honored dead we take increased devotion to that cause for which they gave the last full measure of devotion; that we here highly resolve that these dead shall not have died in vain; that this nation, under God, shall have a new birth of freedom, and that government of the people, by the people, for the people, shall not perish from the earth.*

All transitional devices assist you, the writer, in avoiding dull repetition by making the expression of your ideas more interesting and more varied. These devices keep you and your reader from having to leap from one idea to another because they offer convenient and persuasive bridges which add to the coherence and logic of your ideas. Most writers find that they naturally include the transitional devices within paragraphs, but additional editing might be required during revising to make certain that there is adequate bridging between paragraphs.

The following excerpt is written with the transitional devices italicized. Notice how the transitional devices make the argument easy to follow and make the writing style more fluid.

> Kinship between man and the land is only one aspect of Steinbeck's celebration of the unity of all life. *As man* is one with the *land,* so is *he one* with the *animal life* that inhabits the *land. Man* is part of nature, and *his* social and biological behavior is not unlike the lower forms of *animal life. Furthermore,* the *biologist* who observes the living habits of animals can correctly apply *his observations* to human nature. Steinbeck the *biologist* is fascinated by the *animal* motivation behind *human behavior.* Frequently in *his* fiction, *he* equates *human and animal conduct* to show *their* similarities.
>
> Steinbeck uses *animal life* symbolically in three ways. *First,* he frequently describes the *human community* with the image of a many-celled organism, a "group-man" whose individual cells contribute to *his* total function. *This image* is a basic one and it's the foundation of much of Steinbeck's social theorizing. *Second,* many of his individual characters display obvious *animal* characteristics and are closely associated with, and often symbolized by, particular *animals. Third,* he uses animals to *symbolize* many of the human problems, emotions, and activities appearing in the novels and the short stories. Both the *human community* and the *individual, then,* are related to *animal life.*

From Paragraph to Essay

When you understand the principles that constitute a good paragraph, you will understand the general organization of the essay. Remember that a paragraph is a miniature essay. Only the scope of a paragraph changes to meet the requirements of the following essay. The system remains the same, but the form expands. Consider the diagram below and note the simple changes that occur when the components of the paragraph are converted to the essay.

I. Topic sentence	*becomes*	Thesis statement
A. Subtopic	*becomes*	I. Topic sentence
1. Example	*becomes*	A. Subtopic
2. Example	*becomes*	B. Subtopic
B. Subtopic	*becomes*	II. Topic sentence
1. Example	*becomes*	A. Subtopic
2. Example	*becomes*	B. Subtopic
C. Subtopic	*becomes*	III. Topic sentence

What is needed now in the essay is an additional level of development. Under the subtopics in the above essay format, you would add specific, supporting examples to complete the essential skeleton of the essay (i.e., add 1., 2., 3. under A. and B., etc.). In general, most of your writing will have an introductory paragraph, usually three or more body paragraphs, and a concluding paragraph. Regardless of the length of the essay, the principles of organization remain the same.

The End

Now you are ready to conclude the writing process by putting the finishing touches on your essay. This stage of your writing actually includes several steps. Not only does it involve the concluding paragraph, but it also includes constructing the introductory paragraph and a title for the essay. Having completed the heart of your thoughts in your body paragraphs (the middle), you now need to introduce those thoughts in an opening paragraph that includes your thesis and to conclude your discussion by offering closure. Although the techniques vary considerably regarding these two paragraphs, the primary function is to provide the framework for the ideas you convincingly present to your audience. This stage completes the writing phase.

Introductory Paragraph

Because the opening paragraph is the audience's first contact with you and with what you have to say, it is of utmost importance. Traditionally, however, writers have discovered that this paragraph is the most difficult to write, perhaps because of its importance and uniqueness or perhaps because of the "mental block" associated with the dreaded "blank page syndrome." There are at least two options in putting your introductory paragraph together. Some writers prefer to write their opening paragraph first, knowing what they intend to discuss in the body paragraphs and what their thesis statement is. If they feel that the introductory paragraph needs to be altered after having written the essay, they simply revise it accordingly. However, some writers prefer to wait until the essay is complete before they tackle this paragraph. Perhaps it is easier to explain to someone where you are going if your have already been there. Since you have had your thesis in mind throughout the organizing and writing stages, and since you now know what ground you have traveled in your body discussion, you can more confidently address the issue of putting an introduction of your ideas together, capped, of course, by your thesis statement. You now must show your audience precisely which path you will travel together.

To begin, you must keep in mind the four primary functions of the introductory paragraph:

1. To get the reader's attention;

2. To set the tone for the rest of the essay;

3. To show the audience why they should continue to read your essay;

4. To make a commitment, to take a stand that tells the audience what to expect from your discussion in the essay.

To help you determine what kind of opening paragraph you need, you must remind yourself of your audience and purpose. When you write an essay, you make a commitment to your audience. You are obligated to live up to your commitment; therefore, you want to fulfill that obligation by explaining and supporting your ideas with as much information as you can. By learning what your commitment and purpose are in your opening paragraph, your readers know what to expect. If you fail to interest them in the introductory paragraph or renege on your obligation, your audience might decide to read no further. In short, you want your audience to read all the way through your discussion; therefore, you want to do what you said you would do.

The opening paragraph also sets the tone for the rest of the essay. If your topic is a serious one, the opening paragraph should be sufficiently serious. Conversely, if your essay is humorous, the opening should establish a light tone. Nothing is more disconcerting to a reader and self-defeating to a writer than inconsistency in tone.

The introductory paragraph for an average college-level essay usually will require no more than five or six sentences, depending upon how specific you are in your opening comments. The paragraph moves from a general statement introducing the subject to a specific thesis statement. The organization might be diagrammed as an inverted pyramid, thus:

FIGURE 11-A

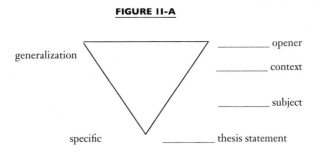

The thesis is the most specific statement in the paragraph and generally will appear as the last sentence of the paragraph. In the following introductory paragraph, notice how the writer moves from a general statement about the treatment of minor medical emergencies, to the independent emergency clinic, to her own experiences with such a clinic, to her thesis that the independent clinic will soon replace the hospital emergency ward:

In the past several years, a new concept in the treatment of minor medical emergencies has emerged. The independent emergency clinic is devoted to the patient with minor problems. In the past, I have had the misfortune of seeking minor emergency care in the hospital emergency ward. Even though I always received excellent medical care, I did encounter some disadvantages. Upon visiting this new type of facility as both observer and patient, I found the medical care equal to the hospital without many of the disadvantages. The independent clinic may very well replace the hospital emergency ward in the treatment of minor medical emergencies in the future.

Even though you will move in the paragraph from general to specific, you should avoid beginning with too broad a generalization. The more general you are at first, the longer it will take you to get around to your thesis and the more you risk losing your audience's attention. A first sentence about the quality of health care in the United States today would have been much too broad for the introductory paragraph on independent clinics.

Begin with a sentence that is not so general that it fails to get the readers' attention but that gets them involved in your discussion. There are several effective methods of achieving this goal:

1. Use a relevant anecdote or personal narrative. The writer of the paragraph on independent clinics could have had a much more compelling introduction if she had recounted one of the times when she had to go to an emergency ward. The anecdote might include the "attention-getter" sentence, or it can follow a separate "attention-getter" sentence.

2. Ask a question. "In this day of rising medical costs, what can the consumer do to get the best emergency health care at the best price?"

3. Offer a startling opening statement: "Medical technology has advanced as never before, yet more than 20% of Americans cannot afford even the most basic health care."

4. Use an analogy or comparison. "Many health care professionals scornfully refer to the independent clinic as 'Doc-in-the-Box' or 'Quack Shack.'"

5. Offer an informal definition. Without referring to the dictionary (denotative) definition, state your own meaning of a term that will allow you to introduce your subject and its discussion.

No matter which of these methods you select, make certain your beginning is interesting and says something important and relevant to your subject. Make sure that your opening anecdote, analogy, or startling statistic fits smoothly into the rest of your introductory paragraph and leads logically to your thesis statement. Too many beginning writers come up with an attention-getting first sentence but then fail to tie it in smoothly to the rest of the opening paragraph; such a failure stops the reader cold.

The suggestions listed above certainly do not exhaust the possibilities. As you develop as a writer, you will discover other methods of introduction that might be even more suitable to your own taste, style, or technique. But never lose sight of the general purpose and function of the introductory paragraph.

Concluding Paragraph

While your final paragraph is not as important as your introductory paragraph, it is vital to your purpose because it is your last chance to make an impression on your audience. This paragraph should achieve at least the following goals:

1. Restate the thesis but reword it this time;

2. Summarize the key topics presented in the discussion (This goal is optional. Inquire about your instructor's preference.);

3. Suggest larger implications than you could have offered before you presented all your evidence, especially in persuasive writing;

4. Give the audience a sense of closure. Do not just stop writing!

FIGURE II-B

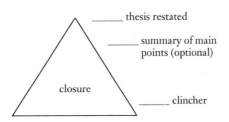

You want to realize that much of what your readers will remember about your discussion is what you present in your concluding paragraph. You have kept their attention long enough to bring them to your closing remarks; don't lose them now! Offer something that is memorable. What you have said in the body paragraphs has surely taken your readers beyond the boundaries of your thesis statement. Now you must relate to your audience what your purpose and thesis imply. Do not, however, claim more than your presentation justifies or you can deliver. Make your point and close. Never give the impression that you have simply stopped writing. The readers desire and expect a sense of closure—an end or conclusion. Never mention a new idea in your conclusion that could or should have been discussed earlier in the essay. Not much can be added at this point that might convince readers if it has not already been said in the body paragraphs. Close while you still have their attention, avoiding platitudes, overused generalities, or noble-sentiment endings. Sometimes the methods suggested earlier for opening your introductory paragraph can work for the closure of your final paragraph as well. Do not, however, merely repeat your opening sentence or your thesis. Make your closure interesting, provocative, informative, or inspiring. Whatever works for you, use it.

Titles

Most writers prefer to consider a title after they have completed their entire draft. Now that your subject and focus, your tone, and your audience and purpose are all clearly determined and you have the full picture of what you have said in the essay, you might try to capture the essence of this writing in a few words. After all, the title is the first thing your audience sees of your essay; therefore, why not establish an initial greeting that captures your whole discussion? Be accurate and specific in your title, providing more than the mere subject of your essay. The title should let the reader see the link between what it promises and what the essay delivers. You might include a key word from the focus of your discussion, but never let a sentence be your title. Be consistent with the tone; a serious essay is undermined by a flippant title. In short, use your imagination and be creative; strive to get the attention of your audience. Instead of titling your essay "Good Teachers," why not "How Good Teachers Treat their Students," or better yet, "Good Teachers: Respect Begetting Respect."

Revising the Draft

Revision is the third and final phase of constructing a good essay. Its importance lies in the fact that it is your final involvement with the essay; therefore, you need to make sure you have corrected all the problems and put the finishing touches to your draft. Many students neglect this "polishing" step for one reason or another, but the difference between an excellent essay and a mediocre one can depend on how thoroughly you proofread and revise your ideas.

Once you have completed your first draft, you should allow some time to pass before you begin to revise it. If you wait until you are fresh and a bit removed from your essay, you will be able to detect the problems in it more easily. Some writers have found that if they transfer their hand-written draft to a typed or printed form (or from screen to hard copy), they can more readily recognize and correct their errors. Typing allows you to view the essay more objectively. Because there are so many areas to be reviewed, you should plan to read your draft several times, determining in advance what specific potential problems you are searching for and correcting. You should also consider reading the draft aloud. You will be surprised to discover that your ears will detect an awkward sentence or phrase that your eyes overlooked.

Next, proofread your essay with the following checklist in mind. Examine your draft for effectiveness in these four areas: (1) subject matter, (2) organization, (3) style, and (4) mechanics and grammar.

◆

CHECKLIST

1. Subject matter
   a. Are your examples valid? Do they contribute to the validity of your opinions?
   b. Have you provided an adequate number of examples to develop each topic sentence?
   c. Does each topic sentence directly relate to the thesis statement?
   d. Do your paragraphs maintain unity? Have you taken out any material that is irrelevant, unnecessary, or vague?

2. Organization
   a. Is your purpose clearly implied, and is your thesis statement specifically stated?
   b. Are your paragraphs in logical order?
   c. Do your transitions function effectively? Do your ideas flow smoothly and logically from one sentence to the next? from one paragraph to the next? Do your transitional devices eliminate vagueness?
   d. Does your introductory paragraph get the readers' attention, does it establish the context for your subject, and does your thesis statement have a limited subject and a restricted focus?
   e. Have you summarized your main points (if you are required to do so) and provided effective closure in your final paragraph?

3. Style
   a. Have you offered a variety of sentence constructions (i.e., simple, compound, complex sentences)? Could some sentences be combined through modification or subordination for more effective expression? Can you improve sentence structure for better emphasis or focus?
   b. Are your language and examples appropriate for your specified purpose and audience? Have you selected the best word for the meaning you wish to convey?
   c. Have you removed all "deadwood," those phrases or words that are unnecessary or fail to contribute directly to your purpose? Remember that more is not always better. For example, rather than saying "Due to the fact that," simply say "Because."
   d. Is your diction consistent with the tone you want to convey? Have you avoided jargon and slang expressions?
   e. Are your ideas clear, appropriate, and interesting?

4. Mechanics and Grammar
   a. Always check for the following:
      1. spelling errors
      2. subject-verb agreement errors
      3. sentence fragments
      4. fused sentences
      5. comma splices
      6. punctuation errors
      7. pronoun reference agreement errors
      8. dangling or misplaced modifiers
      9. verb tense inconsistencies
      10. clichés
         Make minor corrections in the text of your draft if they can be done neatly; otherwise, retype or rewrite the essay.
   b. Is your handwritten draft legible? Is it neat? If not, make it so.
   c. If your essay is a research assignment, have you complied with the MLA style form? Consult your handbook for specific guidelines and procedures.
   d. Are you convinced that this essay represents you and your best ideas? Can you submit it to your instructor with pride and certainty? Remember that the final draft suggests to your reader that it is the best you can do. Is it? If not, revise further. Rumor has it that when asked why he revised the last page of his novel *A Farewell to Arms* thirty-nine times, Ernest Hemingway replied "Getting the words right." This many revisions might be a little extreme for a freshman essay. Nevertheless, when you are satisfied with the essay and you feel you cannot improve upon it any more (and by now you are probably sick of the whole thing anyway), turn it in for evaluation, and feel confident that you have accomplished what you set out to do in the beginning.

ON THE NET

The Writing Process. MIT (The Massachusetts Institute of Technology). Sections on Prewriting, Drafting, Revising, and Editing.
<http://web.mit.edu/writing/Writing_Process/writingprocess.html>

The Writing Process. Cleveland State University. The Writing Center.
<http://www.csuohio.edu/writingcenter/writproc.html>

Starting the Writing Process. The On Line Writing Lab at Purdue.
<http://owl.english.purdue.edu/owl/resource/587/01/>

Principles of Composition: The Writing Process. Capital Community College.
<http://grammar.ccc.commnet.edu/GRAMMAR/composition/composition.htm>

EXERCISES

Outlining Exercise

Arrange the following sentences in order by putting the number of the sentence in the proper place in the outline. Remember to look specifically for levels of generality.

(1) When a real rape occurs, she should report it to the police.

(2) Colleges must alert incoming students to the problems and dangers of adulthood and then stand back and get out of the sex game.

(3) The only solution to date rape is female self-awareness and self-control.

(4) They are not equipped or trained for legal inquiry.

(5) Complaining to college committees because the courts "take too long" is ridiculous.

(6) A woman's number one line of defense is herself.

(7) College administrations are not a branch of the judiciary.

I. Topic sentence:_____

A. _____

    1. _____

    2. _____

B. _____

    1. _____

    2. _____

Paragraphing Exercise

Consider the topic of "Jobs for Teenagers." Brainstorm this topic for a few minutes. Next, write THREE sentences that best support the view presented in the topic sentence below. These three sentences will serve as your subtopics A, B, and C (major supports) for the paragraph. Finally, offer at least two examples in complete sentences that specifically develop each of the three subtopic statements.

Jobs for Teenagers

Thesis: (Level One)Teenagers need part-time jobs for a number of reasons.

I. **Topic sentence:** (Level Two) A teen needs a job to meet the expenses of dating.

A. (Level three)_____

    1. (Level four)_____

    2. _____

    3. _____

B. (Level three) _____

    1. (Level four)_____

    2. _____

    3. _____

C. (Level three)_____

    1. (Level four)_____

    2. _____

    3. _____

Topic Sentences Exercise

Construct an appropriate sentence based on the evidence given:

I. Topic sentence: _____

_____

A. Kate's toys always seem to be misplaced.

B. She is usually late for dinner.

C. She sometimes forgets her homework assignments.

D. Her room, despite her mother's pleadings, is a mess.

II. Topic sentence: _____

_____

A. Colleen is always available to talk to about one's problems.

B. Colleen never judges anyone.

C. She is dependable and reliable.

D. Colleen is very trustworthy.

III. Topic sentence: _____

_____

A. I once forgot to feed my kids' parakeet and it died.

B. One rainy day I accidentally ran over my dog Fido.

C. Even goldfish turn white and float on their backs at my house.

D. My pet iguana jumped off the roof and impaled himself on a metal rod.

IV. Topic sentence: _____

_____

A. Bubba dips snuff and wears boots and tight Wrangler jeans.

B. He drives an extended cab pick-up truck.

C. Bubba's belt buckle is larger than his truck's chrome rims.

D. He has nothing but contempt for any kind of music other than country and western.

V. Topic sentence: _____

_____

A. Thirty-seven percent of all traffic accidents are linked to drivers' negligence while talking on their cell phones.

B. Cell phones unleash low levels of electromagnetic radiation waves which are believed to cause brain tumors.

C. Cell phones constantly ring at inappropriate times and disturb other people in public places.

D. Nextel two-way cell phones double the annoyance factor for bystanders.

VI. Topic sentence: _____

_____

A. Mrs. Bone lies about insignificant things.

B. Mrs. Bone never lets her friends lead their own lives without offering some form of advice.

C. She has a volatile temper and has never learned to discuss problems without shouting at the top of her voice.

D. She expects more from others than she is capable of giving herself.

E. She likes to pit her friends against one another.

VII. Topic sentence:_____

_____

A. Mr. Legree requires every employee to present a doctor's note for each absence.

B. In a dispute between a supervisor and an employee, he always takes sides with the supervisor.

C. The last time he recommended anyone for a raise in salary was ten years ago.

D. Mr. Legree was recognized by the President of the company for leading the firm in productivity and cost control.

VIII. Topic sentence:_____

_____

A. Many Americans support stricter gun control laws.

B. They feel that stricter laws are needed to keep guns out of the hands of children.

C. Others feel that the existing gun laws are adequate, but need to be more strictly enforced.

D. Still others feel that the Second Amendment gives citizens the unlimited right to own a gun.

IX. Topic sentence:_____

_____

A. The radioman on the ship *Carpathia* was not on duty to hear the *Titanic's* distress signals.

B. There were enough lifeboats for only half the passengers on the *Titanic*.

C. Passengers from first class were allowed to board the lifeboats first.

D. Many passengers ignored the crews' warnings, thinking that the ship could not possibly be sinking.

X. Topic sentence: _____

_____

A. Geoffrey's apartment is completely without dust.

B. He cannot tolerate dirty dishes in the sink.

C. He vacuums his apartment every day.

D. All the canned goods in his pantry are neatly arranged.

Paragraph Development Exercise

Complete each of the sections below by providing appropriate subtopics and examples (appropriate levels) to support the topic sentence given.

I. College registration is often a frustrating process.

A. The amount of time it takes to register is discouraging.

    1. _____

    2. _____

B. The student often cannot get the courses he desires.

    1. _____

    2. _____

C. The registrant often finds he does not have all the necessary paperwork.

    1. _____

    2. _____

    3. _____

Clincher: _____

II. One of the disadvantages of living in a large city is the traffic problem.

A. _____

    1. There often are bottlenecks on major thoroughfares that have no apparent cause.

    2. _____

    3. _____

B. _____

    1. _____

    2. _____

    3. _____

C. _____

    1. _____

    2. The Interstate has been under construction since the 1950s.

    3. _____

Clincher: _____

_____

III. Working while attending college creates several hardships for the student.

A. Budgeting and allotting time for everything is a problem.

    1. _____

    2. _____

    3. _____

B. _____

    1. _____

    2. _____

    3. _____

C. The most severe hardship is_____.

    1. _____

    2. _____

    3. _____

Clincher: _____

_____

Topic Sentences Exercise

Narrow the subject and limit the focus of each of the following general statements so they could serve as effective topic sentences for paragraphs.

1. Stella is a fascinating young woman.

_____

_____

2. City drivers are bad.

_____

_____

3. My friend Juan is weird.

_____

_____

4. Teens today face many challenges.

_____

_____

5. My parents' taste in music sucks.

_____

_____

6. I need a new car.

_____

_____

7. Computer labs are quite helpful.

_____

_____

8. High school, when compared to college, was a real drag.

_____

_____

9. A girlfriend/boyfriend can be expensive.

_____

_____

10. Living in an apartment is more fun than living at home.

_____

_____

Brainstorming Exercise

I. Brainstorm two of the following topics, listing everything that comes to mind, as in the example of "Good Teachers" earlier in this chapter. Your brainstorming should suggest ways to narrow the topics.

Topics: High school graduation night, Family life, The anxieties of social dating,

Advantages of a community college, Peer pressure, TV commercials, Careers, Sports, Love, Death.

Topic #1:_____

Topic #2:_____

GROUPING AND OUTLINING

II. Choose one of the topics you brainstormed in the previous exercise and group the details into three major groups. Then organize the details within those three groups.

THESIS SENTENCE AND OUTLINE

III. Now, write a thesis sentence for an essay about the topic you have chosen. Make sure your thesis sentence deals with the three major headings in your outline. Below the thesis sentence, write an outline for an essay on your topic.

Thesis sentence: _____

_____

3 Textual Analysis

You probably have already read, and written, a number of essays, and you have probably had occasion throughout your career in school to read numerous short articles in magazines and newspapers or on your computer. In its broadest sense, the word *essay* can cover everything from a short report to a lengthy, technical article. The motives behind essays are also varied. Essays are written to entertain, to explain, to persuade, to justify one's actions, to beg for support or money, to sell, to condemn some person or action, to report on what has been done in an experiment or accomplished on a job, to encourage patriotism, to inflame one group of people against another, to deceive, to express adoration and love—the possibilities are myriad. In addition to essays, authors compose literary works of all sorts—short stories, novels, poems, and plays—to accomplish all of the same ends.

Teachers of rhetoric use the more inclusive term *text* to cover such variety, and they add oral communication to the list. Modern critics engage in analyses of such divergent texts as Fourth-of-July speeches, campaign addresses, parking regulations, and recipes. They analyze novels, short stories, and poems. Modern critics also approach their texts from an astonishing variety of perspectives: there are sociological critics, feminist critics, historical critics, psychological critics, Marxist critics, cultural critics, post-modern critics. A text to contemporary critics is anything but a group of words whose meaning is carved in stone, and just as there are common elements of fiction that help us to understand and analyze short stories, so are there, though perhaps less standardized than in fiction, elements common to all prose texts.

COMMON RHETORICAL ELEMENTS

As **Chapter One** of this book explains, all written texts—whether they are essays or handwritten notes—contain certain common, rhetorical elements. As you read and analyze an essay, you should examine and identify each of the following:

Audience

The intended audience of an essay may be identified by looking at the author's style (his diction and sentence structure), the complexity and type of ideas discussed, the essay's length, its purpose and situation, and the persona adopted by the writer.

Where an essay is published, in *Time, Field and Stream,* or *Scientific American,* is also a clue to the educational level and interests of the audience. The intended audience is discovered inductively; for example, we might determine that the 5:30 evening news is aimed toward an older, conservative, affluent audience by noting the number of advertisements shown during the half-hour for such things as denture cream, investment opportunities, and luxury automobiles.

Purpose

What does the writer want the reader to understand, to feel, to do? Writers want to change their readers' beliefs or attitudes, make them laugh, make them cry, make them understand a complex issue. A list of purposes would be very long: to entertain, to persuade, to explain, to frighten, to teach, to anger, to placate.

Situation

All discourse is constrained by the situation in which it appears. Situation, loosely defined, is the context in which a particular text appears or the occasion on which a discourse is delivered. For example, the following are different situations with different contexts: you are required to write a ten-page report on the causes of the American Civil War in history class; you volunteer to speak to your younger brother's scout troop on *tae kwon do*; you write a letter applying for a summer job at Yellowstone National Park. Each situation or context demands a different response. In analyzing an essay, you should try to determine the situation or context in which the essay was written and the specific constraints such a situation places on what the writer says. Keys to context or situation for published essays include when it was published, in what magazine or journal it was published, and the tone and language employed by the writer.

Voice and Tone

The writer reveals his personality, his attitudes, his prejudices and desires through what he says and the way he says it. Just as there is a narrator who tells a story from a particular point of view, just as there is a "voice" in poetry, so there is a speaker in an essay, a **persona** (in Latin, literally "actor's mask"). A writer may unconsciously reveal the kind of person he is through what he writes. We may determine that he is arrogant, friendly, aloof, narrow-minded, or flippant. More often the writer's purpose, his audience, and the writing situation cause him to assume or adopt a persona. Aristotle says, for example, that when trying to persuade an audience we should present ourselves as honest, open-minded, and knowledgeable, with the *best interests of our audience in mind.* The persona a writer adopts may also reflect his social or cultural role. For example, we expect a priest and a movie critic to write in certain ways reflecting their different roles and positions in society.

Finally, the tone of an essay is closely connected to **persona.** Writers may adopt tones that are serious, playful, ironic, antagonistic, or passionate, among others. In writing a critical analysis of an essay, you should determine the persona and tone of the writer. Whether consciously or unconsciously revealed, tone is crucial to the total effect a text has on its audience.

THE RATIONAL APPEAL

Because persuasion is an attempt to make ideas and proposals attractive to an audience, you should become familiar with the methods writers and speakers use to appeal to their audience. Aristotle identified these appeals as the rational appeal (*logos*), the ethical appeal (*ethos*), and the emotional appeal (*pathos*). These three appeals are generally interwoven throughout an essay, but you must understand how each works to analyze that essay effectively.

Aristotle believed that what separated mankind from other animals was the ability to reason. Many writers thus employ rational appeals in an attempt to convince their audiences to accept or reject particular beliefs, claims, or courses of action. When a scientist writes a paper claiming to have discovered a new sub-atomic particle, when a biotechnology lab claims to have discovered the gene that causes Huntington's disease, when an engineer claims that a system of mass-transit will solve a city's transportation problems—all support their claims with evidence and logic. If a writer provides little or no proof for the claims he or she makes, you should be wary of accepting those claims, even though the claims might seem to be true. Further, in writing an analysis of an essay that focuses on its rational appeal, you will first need to review **Chapter Twelve,** "Constructing an Argument," which defines *logic* and *argument.* In addition, you should consider the following:

Burden of Proof

A basic principle of reason, as of law, is that the burden of proof rests with the person making a claim. A claim is a proposition, a statement about what is or is not true. If the state claims that Joe Smith murdered his wife, for instance, then the state must prove beyond a reasonable doubt that Joe is guilty; Joe does not have to prove that he did *not* murder his wife. Careful writers will not make claims that they cannot back up. Thus, when you read essays, always look to see what **evidence and support** the writer provides to back up her claims. Further, be wary of non-testable claims. A non-testable claim is set up in such a way that no possible evidence or change in circumstances could render it false. As Stephen Jay Gould writes in *Evolution as Fact and Theory:* "A set of ideas that cannot, in principle, be falsified is not science. [. . .] Unbeatable systems are dogma. [. . .]" For example, if someone argues that people *always* act from selfish motives, and no counter example you come up with, no action or set of circumstances you devise, is ever accepted as an example of an unselfish action, it is a non-testable claim; that is, it is an assertion of belief. Beliefs are strongly held attitudes involving judgments about the world and are often accepted as articles of faith, beyond the realm of rational inquiry.

Fallacies

Logicians have identified a number of common fallacies (faulty reasoning that may appear to be good); you need to look for them when you analyze a writer's argument. Refer to **Chapter Twelve**, "Constructing an Argument," for a list of the most common fallacies.

Toulmin Analysis

In an *Introduction to Reasoning* (1984), Steven Toulmin presents a simple, practical method for analyzing an argument. He divides his analysis into an attractive scheme of three primary parts—claim, data (grounds), and warrant. To begin with, one must determine the claim the author is making. There are several types of claims on which to base one's argument.

CLAIMS. A **factual claim** is a declarative sentence that asserts something is or is not the case, was or was not the case, or will or will not be the case. "Denver is the capital of Colorado" is a claim about reality. "Dallas is the largest city in Texas" is also a claim about reality. "The Chicago Cubs will win the pennant" is a claim about the future. (One must wait until October for verification of it!) "Socrates lived in ancient Athens" is a claim about the past which can be verified by reading accounts of his contemporaries. Thus, claims of fact can be **verified or falsified.** That is, a factual claim is **true** if it corresponds to reality—or is a **tautology** (something true by definition, such as "A bachelor is an unmarried man.").

A **value claim** is a declarative sentence that asserts something is good or bad, right or wrong. Some value claims are merely **expressions of personal taste,** of liking or disliking: "Broccoli tastes bad." "I prefer living in the city to living in the country." "I feel hot." Such claims cannot be disputed.

Other value claims are **moral or aesthetic judgments:** "Stealing is wrong." "A liberal education is better than a technical one." "Andrew Wyeth is a better painter than Jackson Pollock." Such value claims are supported by reference to a code of values, an accepted ideal, or a set of criteria the arguer uses as the basis of his claim. The Christian *Bible* might be the basis for the first claim, the Humanist ideal for the second, and standards of realist painting for the third.

A **causal claim** is a declarative sentence that asserts something is, or was, the cause of something else. "Smoking is a major cause of cancer" is a causal claim. "Slavery was a major cause of the American Civil War" is another.

A **definitional claim** is a declarative sentence that asserts something is just like, or is exactly the same as, something else. "Keeping animals in cages is just like keeping slaves in shackles" is such a claim. "Abortion is murder" is another.

A **deliberative claim** is a declarative sentence that asserts that something should or should not be done. These are sometimes called **claims of policy.** "You should quit smoking" is a deliberative claim. "The state of Utah should adopt a law making English its official language" is another deliberative claim.

Following Toulmin's system, first find the **claim,** the conclusion of the argument or the thesis of the essay. Make sure that the claim is a testable-claim (that it is possible to support the claim by evidence), and that it is not preposterous or whimsical. For example, the following claim was made by a student in a paper on women in the military: *Women should not be allowed in ground combat units in the army.*

GROUNDS. Next look for the data that support that claim, that is, the evidence the writer gives in support of his proposition. For example, the student supported the above claim with the following evidence: *The fact that a woman can get pregnant may keep her from performing her task, thus rendering the squad ineffective to perform in a combat situation. An example of this situation occurred when I was stationed at Ft. Rucker, Alabama; in my squad there were four men, and each of us was assigned a different task: machine gunner, sniper, squad leader, and Dragon gunner. We went on an exercise and the machine gunner became ill. He was rushed to the hospital, and I had to take over his task. The result of his illness was a catastrophe. When we attacked the enemy we were slower because I had to perform the jobs of two men. Therefore, the squad lost the battle, which not only had an effect on the squad but produced a chain reaction and destroyed the whole company. Thus, if a woman were to be assigned to a combat unit and she became pregnant, it would have a negative influence on the whole company.*

WARRANT. Third, look for any support that the writer gives to show that the evidence is relevant to the claim. For example, if the writer cites the statement of an authority, does he or she give the credentials of the authority? Is the authority speaking in his own field of expertise? If a major scientific study is discussed as evidence, are other confirming studies also cited? For example, the student writing on women in combat added the following to the evidence given above: *More than 1,200 pregnant women were evacuated from the Gulf region during the Gulf War; that is the equivalent of two infantry battalions. If the loss of one man from a squad can cause a company's performance to drop, how much more harm would there be with the loss of two battalions of soldiers? It would have a devastating effect.*

BACKING. Fourth, look for information that gives added support to the Warrant. For example, our student next added the following sentence to the above warrant: *The statistics on the number of women evacuated from the Gulf War were released in a report by the Pentagon.*

Rebuttal. Finally, check to see if the writer has acknowledged counter claims and arguments; that is, has he mentioned and then refuted claims that contradict his own? Also see if the writer has explained apparent exceptions to his evidence or mitigated the force of counter claims in some way. For example, our student included the following in a refutation section: *Some women argue that many other countries use women in combat roles. This statement is not altogether true. There are very few countries that have women in combat roles. Israel was one of those countries who tried to put women in combat, but they quickly stopped the program because it was a catastrophe. Israel still uses women in its military, but does not allow them in combat.*

Using Toulmin's scheme will help you recognize the structure of the argument you are analyzing and the strengths and weaknesses of that argument; however, simply because a writer supplies a warrant and backing for a claim does not mean that his argument is sound or cogent. Be sure to apply the standards of appropriate evidence and reasoning to the argument. Finally, remember that arguments are made to be convincing and that we are daily inundated by the mass media with hundreds of claims. The only rational stance to adopt in a world such as ours is one based on a respect for truth and an attitude of skepticism. In his essay "Of Cannibals," Montaigne says, "We should be on our guard against clinging to vulgar opinions and [. . .] we should judge things by light of reason, and not from common rumor."

The Emotional Appeal

If all people were as dispassionate as Mr. Spock or Data on the old *Star Trek* television series, then an account of the argument of an essay, of its rational appeal, would be the only analysis we would need to make. Yet while all people may be born with the capacity to reason, reasoning well requires knowledge, training, and practice. However, to echo the French eighteenth-century writer Jean Jacques Rousseau, we *felt* before we *thought*. Feeling, Rousseau said, is primary; it, not reason, makes us human. Further, as Antonio R. Damasio, Professor of Neuroscience at the University of Southern California, has pointed out, "emotions [...] inform the deployment of logic."

Therefore, when we want to persuade an audience, we often find it necessary to appeal to the personal nature of our topic. People are generally more interested in those matters that touch their hearts than in statistics or logic. The writer of a persuasive argument cannot ignore the fact that much of our identity resides in our emotions and imaginations. If we are to convince readers, we must appeal to their emotions, attempting to ascertain which of our emotions they will accept or approve. The skillful writer can then use certain associations which will elicit the desired emotional response in his audience. For instance, if he is addressing a religious group, he might associate the idea of human leadership or fellowship with Christ. This reference links the writer's own propositions to what the audience already identifies with and respects. Sometimes a well-placed word or phrase will enhance the emotional appeal of an argument, as when a writer of an essay against pornography mentions "innocent" children. Conversely, writers know, because they know the emotional character of their audience, what not to use in their appeal.

Thus, emotions are powerful forces in humans, and while we might think of some people as "lacking feeling," most people are strongly affected by their emotions. In Part II of *The Art of Rhetoric*, on "Emotion and Character," Aristotle lists ten emotions. The first four are positive—calm, friendship, favor, and pity; the next six are negative—anger, fear, shame, indignation, envy, and jealousy. In his 1872 book, *The Expression of the Emotions in Man and Animals*, Charles Darwin began the modern discussion of the nature and origin of emotions. More recent investigators have emphasized the neurological basis of emotions and have listed eight basic emotions—anger, fear, joy, sadness, acceptance, disgust, surprise, and interest or curiosity. Others have divided emotions into "primary" and "secondary" emotions. Robert Plutchik, late professor at the Albert Einstein College of Medicine, lists the eight basic emotions as fear (terror, shock, surprise), anger (rage), sorrow (sadness), joy (happiness, glee), disgust, acceptance, anticipation, and surprise. In an article in *American Scientist* in 2001, he gave a three-dimensional "color wheel" model of the emotions. From "outside-in" the opposed emotions on the wheel are:

> Pensiveness, Sadness, Grief—Ecstasy, Joy, Serenity
> Boredom, Disgust, Loathing—Admiration, Trust, Acceptance
> Distraction, Surprise, Amazement—Vigilance, Anticipation, Interest
> Annoyance, Anger, Rage—Terror, Fear, Apprehension

Finally, while we consider our emotions *natural*, we know that these emotions are conditioned by our culture, our social background, and our individual upbringing. Writers appeal to their particular audience's emotions in order to motivate them to action or to gain their commitment to a belief or a group. For example, writers are well aware that people respond emotionally to words and images that appeal to certain deep-seated human desires, such as love, sex, nourishment, and pleasure. Conversely, people respond emotionally to what they fear: rejection, privation, pain, and death. On the one hand, writers appeal to their audience's sense of comfort which they derive from belonging to a group such as a family, city, state, or country, or their affiliation with a certain ethnic or linguistic group, economic class, or political party; on the other hand, writers play on their audience's fear and distrust of things or people who are strange or foreign to them.

The language used in emotional appeals can be direct or subtle. Writers can use words that have an obvious and immediate emotional impact on their audience and that are calculated to provoke a strong and predictable response. For instance, how do you react to the following words: *jerk, extremist, atheist, bubba, dumb blonde;* or to *peace, patriot, Christian, Muslim, entrepreneur, mother?* For example, note Richard Nixon's use of emotionally charged language in the following paragraph, the conclusion to a famous speech he made on television in September of 1952; at the time many people were calling for his resignation as candidate for vice-president under Dwight Eisenhower because of allegations of misappropriation of campaign funds:

> *But just let me say this last word. Regardless of what happens, I am going to continue this fight. I am going to campaign up and down America until we drive the crooks and the communists and those that defend them out of Washington, and remember, folks, Eisenhower is a great man, and a vote for Eisenhower is a vote for what is good for America.*

The words used in this passage depict two contrasting sets of images. The first set creates the image of a man battling against the forces of evil: "I am going to continue this *fight* [. . .] until *we* [Note the shift in person. He is one of us.] drive the *crooks* and the *communists* and *those that defend them* out of *Washington* [. . .]." Here is the image of a man trying to drive out evil from one of our political holy places, perhaps like as Jesus drove the moneychangers out of the Temple. The second set of words—"*Eisenhower is a great man*" and "*what is good for America*"—evokes the feelings of pride we have in a renowned military leader and associates those feelings with our feelings of patriotism. These feelings of greatness, goodness, and loyalty to our homeland are linked to the lonely fight against evil conducted by this man on our behalf.

In another example, in 2008 as the war in Iraq entered its sixth year and the number of United States troop deaths rose to over 4,000, President George W. Bush continued to defend the righteousness and necessity of the war. Speaking of those who had given their lives, he said, "one day people will look back at this moment in history and say, 'Thank God there were courageous people willing to serve, because they laid the foundation for peace for generations to come.'" Bush here uses the words "God," "courageous," "serve," and "peace" to evoke religious and patriotic emotions. He further intimates that history, "one day," will ultimately be on his side in judging the morality of the war, and that the future, "generations to come," will praise those who, under his leadership and command, gave their lives for the benefit of their countrymen. With this statement, President Bush both aligns his policies in Iraq with God, country, and history, and implies that those who oppose the war and want to withdraw U. S. forces lack courage, foresight, and backbone.

The emotion of a passage may also arise naturally from the writer's subject and the intensity of the writer's engagement with that subject. For example, few would question the sincerity of the emotion expressed in the following sentences by the Russian writer Leo Tolstoy who, at the peak of his career as a writer, with fame, wealth, an interesting circle of friends, a family—all that a person might desire—suddenly experienced a terrible, gripping sense of the utter futility of life. He wrote of this life-altering experience in *Confession* (here translated by David Patterson):

If not today, then tomorrow sickness and death will come (indeed, they were already approaching) to everyone, to me, and nothing will remain except the stench and the worms. My deeds, whatever they may be, will be forgotten sooner or later, and I myself will be no more. Why, then, do anything? How can anyone fail to see this and live? That's what is amazing! It is possible to live only as long as life intoxicates us; once we are sober we cannot help seeing that it is all a delusion, a stupid delusion! Nor is there anything funny or witty about it; it is only cruel and stupid.

The intensity of feeling in this passage arises from the writer's emotional involvement with his subjects—death and the meaning of life. Tolstoy conveys his fear of death and his sense of the utter meaninglessness of life in such phrases as "sickness and death will come," "the stench and the worms," and "I myself will be no more." These words are simple, direct, and unadorned. Tolstoy also employs an everyday image of a drunk versus a sober man to convey his feelings about every man's blindness to the reality of his own death. The emotions we feel when we read such a passage arise directly from the subject and the writer's engagement with it. Tolstoy's primary purpose is to convey his feelings, to make us feel what he himself feels.

In writing a critical analysis of an essay that focuses on its emotional content, therefore, you will need to look carefully for any emotionally charged words used by the writer, at any images the writer creates through description, and at any figurative language the writer uses (see the section on analysis of style later in this chapter). In addition, ask yourself the following questions:

- What emotion is the writer trying to make the reader feel?
- Is the writer's use of emotion consistent with his purpose?
- Is the writer's use of emotion appropriate to his subject, his audience, and the occasion?
- Does the writer's use of emotionally charged language dominate the essay, or is it subordinated to more rational arguments?

Answering these questions will also help you decide what the writer's attitude is toward his material and his audience. For example, is the writer asking the reader to sympathize or be outraged? Is the writer being satiric or ironic?

Finally, what can an analysis of the emotional appeals made in an essay tell us? First, it can clarify a complex argument by helping us separate the emotional appeals from the logical ones. Focusing on the language and metaphors employed by the writer in developing his emotional appeal can help us gain emotional distance, and thus objectivity. Therefore we may begin to notice that the writer gives little solid evidence to support his claims and essentially begs the question he is trying to prove. Or we may find that the emotional language drives home a point supported abundantly by evidence and reason. Second, an analysis of the emotional language and appeals in a speech or an essay can sensitize us to the sometimes subtle assault on our emotions made in newspapers and magazines, or over television and radio, by politicians, preachers, teachers, and radio talk show hosts (and overwhelmingly in advertisements). Studying the emotional appeals made even in a single essay can help us to understand and to arm ourselves against such assaults. Emotions are very powerful; be wary of allowing yours to be manipulated.

THE ETHICAL APPEAL

Besides being rational and emotional creatures, humans are also moral beings. We like to think of ourselves as "being good" and "doing what is right." We are, therefore, more willing to believe those people who we think are honest, upright, fair, and knowledgeable. The ethical appeal is, according to Aristotle, the most potent of all the means of persuasion. For writers' arguments to be effective, their ethos must be apparent in their work and realized by their readers. Simply because a writer presents an argument does not mean that he or she can expect the reader's assent, or even attention; nor can the mere presence of sincerity or emotion bring about the desired assent. To determine the nature of the ethical appeal, one must understand that the writer's words have emotional associations as well as definite meanings. Although the ethical appeal is not restricted by any given specific rules or qualities, certain components can be discussed. For example, three major qualities of the ethical appeal illustrate how writers can reveal their character, their authenticity, through the words they choose.

For a writer or speaker to be convincing, he must make apparent to the audience his **good sense, good will,** and **good moral character. Good sense** suggests that the writer is capable of making practical decisions and choosing the proper means to achieve an end. It must be apparent to the reader that the writer is confident in his argument and that it is, in fact, correct and that he views his topic in the proper perspective. Very simply, **good will,** the second component, consists in the writer's making clear to his audience that he has nothing but good will towards them. He must demonstrate that he shares their good intentions and basic aspirations and that he shares, too, some of their biases and prejudices, if necessary. The third component, **good moral character** is successfully presented if the writer convinces his audience that he would not deceive them and that he genuinely knows right from wrong. To acquire this trust, the writer must be sincere and believable.

Good writers and speakers will attempt to present themselves as reasonable and trustworthy. They do this, first, by showing that they know a lot about the subject they are discussing. They may reveal their credentials (their college degrees, their current position in government or at a university for example), they may discuss the research they themselves have done or discuss a wide range of research conducted by others (up-to-date research, of course), or they may provide convincing examples and other support for their generalizations and conclusions. Second, they may show their thoroughness by their consideration of all relevant material and points of view that have a bearing on their subject. Finally, they may show their fairness by considering opposing points of view and differing interpretations of the facts, by discussing those other positions courteously, and by acknowledging the strengths of those positions where reason demands they should. Ultimately, they want their readers or listeners to believe that they, themselves, are upstanding and creditable people who can be believed and who have the welfare of their audience at heart.

Keep in mind that the ethical appeal emerges throughout the essay. It is not something a writer merely inserts in his introduction or between paragraphs. A writer's ethos develops as he or she makes clear to the reader the possession of all three of the components: the heart is genuine, the intentions good, and the recommendations worthy of the reader's attention.

Writers, like trial lawyers, must convince their audience. While it is a popular cliché that "facts speak for themselves," we should be mature enough to realize that they don't; they must be given a voice and a context by a speaker or a writer, and that voice shapes the way we understand the facts.

ANALYSIS OF STYLE

Jonathan Swift described style as proper words in proper places. Today the word *style* is used in a number of different ways to describe such things as fashion, written formats (as in letter style), and the way people live (as in lifestyle). Written prose style reflects the education, experience, and habits of thought of the writer as well as the basic elements of rhetoric: purpose, audience, voice, and situation. Style is also part of the argumentative and emotional design of an essay. The clarity and force of an argument depend as much on style as on logic; likewise, the emotional impact of an essay depends heavily on style.

To analyze a writer's style you must focus on the words a writer uses and the way those words are arranged in phrases, clauses, sentences, and paragraphs. The purpose of a stylistic analysis is to show how a writer's language, sentence structure, and imagery contribute to his overall purpose and design (or how they contradict it) as well as the way they reveal the writer's attitude toward his subject matter and audience. You can approach a stylistic analysis in one of two ways:

1. You can take one element of style, say the writer's use of figurative language, and analyze the entire essay in terms of this one element alone.

2. You can examine a single paragraph, or several related short paragraphs, and do a more complete analysis of several elements of style.

In general, a writer's style depends on the way he uses the following:

Diction

The kinds of words writers choose, their *diction*, depend upon their educational and linguistic background and upon the audience and purpose of their essay. We can arrange words along a scale based upon an analogy with social custom. For example, just as men wear suits and ties on solemn and formal social occasions, so writers use formal diction on solemn occasions and for serious purposes.

FORMAL DICTION. Formal diction is characterized by polysyllabic words, many with Latin and Greek roots (*transference, multidimensional, orthodox*), abstract words (*cognitive, affective, discipline*) and words specific to a particular science or profession (medical terminology or legalese, for example). Formal diction contributes to a formal style, which is also characterized by its objectivity and the writer's use of the third person, both of which distance the writer from the reader. Formal diction is often used in college textbooks, scientific journals, and philosophical essays; formal style is standard for exposition of serious subjects directed to educated audiences.

INFORMAL DICTION. At the other end of the scale, comparable to men wearing T-shirts, cut-off shorts, and flip-flops, is highly informal diction. Informal diction is characterized by monosyllabic words, many with Anglo-Saxon roots (short, familiar words, such as *man, run, fish, speak*), colloquialisms, dialect (*"y'all"*), slang, contractions, and non-standard usage (*"ain't"*). Informal diction more closely copies everyday speech and contributes to an informal style, characterized by its subjectivity and the writer's use of first person, which attempts to bring the writer and the audience closer together. Informal diction is used in texting, e-mails, personal letters, the personal essay, and all sorts of short, written communication. As always, audience and purpose are important in the degree of informality of one's diction and style. Between these two poles (say, a man wearing loafers, slacks and an untucked shirt) is a broad range of diction that incorporates words from both ends to a greater or lesser degree.

Besides the degree of formality or informality of the diction of an essay, you can also look at whether the words a writer chooses tend to be more abstract or more concrete, more general or more specific, or more dependent on denotation or connotation.

CONCRETE AND ABSTRACT WORDS. Concrete words stand for items that you can touch and see, such as *book, desk, cat,* and *fireplace*. Writers use concrete words to help us visualize what we read. Abstract words, such as *honor, justice, love,* and *peace* do not call up specific images; nevertheless, we have some way of visualizing them: we can picture a child in the arms of its mother when we read the word *love,* for example. Even more removed from our ability to visualize, however, are certain super-abstract words generally deplored by most good writers as **jargon;** *factor, case, condition, thing,* and *degree* are examples. It is very hard to visualize a *factor.* Concrete diction contributes to a more familiar style and brings us closer to the writer: we see what the writer has seen; we feel what the writer has felt.

SPECIFIC AND GENERAL WORDS. Likewise, specific words create specific images, while general words help us to group classes of items. Again, we can set up a scale with very general words on one end and very specific ones on the other: *creature, animal, human, male, boy, son, Daniel.* Good writers are always moving between the general and the specific, going from one end of the scale to the other as they move between broad statements of ideas and issues and specific, detailed examples. Specific language helps us see how large philosophical, moral, or political issues affect us on a personal level. We want a wide-angle lens to show us the big picture; we need a telephoto lens to show us the details.

DENOTATIONS AND CONNOTATIONS. Finally, writers use words for their limited, denotative meaning or for their emotional associations, their connotations. Think of another scale with scientists on one end using words for their specific meanings and poets on the other end using words that have multiple meanings and wide associations. A writer's purpose and audience are again extremely important. A politician at a political rally, for example, may use such evocative words as *freedom, democracy, free enterprise, village,* and *family.* A scientist at the other extreme may use words like *dorsal, ventral,* and *suture* that have precise meanings. Scientists want to communicate their ideas directly and clearly; they want neither the confusion that might arise from using words that have multiple meanings nor the emotional reactions that highly connotative words might create.

Syntax

Syntax designates the way words are arranged to form phrases, clauses, and sentences. One way to analyze a writer's prose style is to look at the sentences he habitually uses. For example, some writers use longer sentences than others, piling up phrases and clauses within a single sentence. Others prefer short, more direct sentences. The sentences of the American authors William Faulkner and Ernest Hemingway provide a classic example of this contrast:

> *The boy, crouched on his nail keg at the back of the crowded room, knew he smelled cheese, and more: from where he sat he could see the ranked shelves close-packed with the solid, squat, dynamic shapes of tin cans whose labels his stomach read, not from the lettering which meant nothing to his mind but from the scarlet devils and the silver curve of fish—this, the cheese which he knew he smelled and the hermetic meat which his intestines believed he smelled coming in intermittent gusts momentary and brief between the other constant one, the smell and sense just a little of fear because mostly of despair and grief, the old fierce pull of blood* ("Barn Burning").

The girl stood up and walked to the end of the station. Across, on the other side, were fields of grain and trees along the banks of the Ebro. Far away, beyond the river, were mountains. The shadow of a cloud moved across the field of grain and she saw the river through the trees ("Hills Like White Elephants").

The first passage from Faulkner shows his preference for complex sentences with clauses embedded within clauses. The sentence is evocative and rich with emotional overtones. The second passage from Hemingway, however, shows his preference for short, simple sentences. The prose is direct and disarmingly simple.

What can we learn from an analysis of the sentence structure of such writers? First, we can gain insight into what might be called the "world view" or the psychological perspective of the writer. Faulkner's complex sentences reflect the complex world portrayed in his novels—a world where narrators try to recapture the past in recursive attempts to understand and reinterpret the present. Hemingway's habitual use of short, simple, subject-verb-object sentences reflects his belief, also portrayed in his fiction, that life is lonely and harsh and must be confronted directly with simple dignity. Second, a study of sentence structure can help us understand the power, effectiveness, and emotional impact of writing as well as learn, through an understanding of such techniques as repetition and parallelism, how to replicate such effects in our own sentences.

In your own analysis, to determine sentence length, for example, count the number of words in each sentence in several paragraphs and divide by the number of sentences to get an average word length per sentence. (Count all the words, including function words, such as articles and prepositions.) You might also count the number of very short sentences, say those under eight words, and the number of very long sentences, say those over thirty words. Again, to determine the frequency of the different types of sentences, count the number of sentences by type in several paragraphs. Determining sentence length and type, for example, tells us how well writers develop their topics, how detailed their explanations are, and how much they qualify their generalizations. Some writers hammer home their points with short, direct blows; others allow us to follow the chain of reasoning that leads them to subtle and complex truths. One benefit of an analysis of this sort is that you can compare the length and type of your author's sentences to your own; you may find that clarity is not necessarily the result of short, simple sentences, nor is brevity always the soul of wit. To convey the richness and complexity of an imagined world, or the intricacies of a subtle argument, a writer may need the flexibility of a wide range of syntactic structures.

Sentences are defined as being **loose**—where the main clause or idea comes first and qualifying statements and dependent clauses are tacked on, or **periodic**—where the dependent clauses and qualifying statements come first and the main clause comes at the end. For example, consider the following two sentences:

I waited three long days in your outer office, continually embarrassed by the number of people who came, waited a short while, and went in, smirked at by secretaries traipsing in and out, and feeling degraded by the position of beggar I had to assume.

Continually embarrassed by the number of people who came, waited a short while, and went in, smirked at by secretaries traipsing in and out, and feeling degraded by the position of beggar I had to assume, I waited three long days in your outer office.

The first sentence trails off after the main clause about waiting for three days in an outer office by simply adding details, one after the other. The reader focuses on each added detail but in the process relegates the earlier ones to the back of the mind. By the end of the sentence, the importance of the three-day wait has waned. In the second sentence, however, tension and suspense are built up as we add one detail to the next because we don't know what they refer to. The answer explodes at the end, and we feel the frustration and sense of indignity the writer has had to endure for three long days. We usually write words one after the other, adding details, descriptions, and explanations as we think of them, following the normal subject-verb-object pattern of English. Loose sentences are thus the workhorses of prose; periodic sentences add drama, suspense, and intensity.

There are other qualities of syntax that are important in analyzing prose style. Books on rhetoric devote much time to such qualities, including the methods writers use to expand and collapse sentences, the way they use particular punctuation marks to achieve certain effects, and their methods of opening and closing sentences. Prominent among these other qualities are the ways writers employ **parallel sentence structure, antithesis,** and **repetition:**

PARALLEL SENTENCE STRUCTURE. English demands that parallel or equal grammatical structures be used on either side of a coordinating conjunction: *"cat and dog," "running and playing," "jump and shoot,"* but not *"running and jump."* English also demands parallel grammatical structures in series: *"books, magazines, newspapers, and television,"* but not *"books, magazines, and decided to leave."* Writers employ more elaborate schemes of parallelism to develop parallel ideas and to give force to them. Consider the emotional impact of the following two sentences:

But, in a larger sense, we cannot dedicate—we cannot consecrate—we cannot hallow—this ground. (Lincoln's *Gettysburg Address*). In this justly famous sentence, Lincoln emphasizes his inability to say anything that could remotely capture the sacrifice and heroism of the men who fought at Gettysburg. By repeating the same phrase, "we cannot," three times, and by raising the importance and force of the verb each time—going from the rather mundane "dedicate" to the more spiritual "consecrate," and finally to the holy and sanctified "hallow"—Lincoln's sentence does what he says he cannot do.

Now consider this sentence: *In such condition, there is no place for industry, because the fruit thereof is uncertain: and consequently no culture of the earth; no navigation, nor use of the commodities that may be imported by sea; no commodious building; no instruments of moving, and removing, such things as require much force; no knowledge of the face of the earth; no account of time; no arts, no letters; no society; and which is worst of all, continual fear, and danger of violent death; and the life of man, solitary, poor, nasty, brutish, and short.* (Thomas Hobbes's *Leviathan*). In this loose sentence, Hobbes describes man in a state of nature, before the advent of civilization. The sentence builds on a series of parallel "no" clauses indicating the bareness and harshness of man's condition without the rules and laws of society. It ends in a climax of short, parallel adjectives that have the rapid-fire force of machine gun bullets.

Sentences employing **antithesis** balance contrasting ideas in parallel structures. We use *but* or *or* instead of *and* many times to signal a contrasting idea. In the following opening lines (the sentence continues), from *A Tale of Two Cities*, Charles Dickens expresses the glaring contradictions in French society on the eve of the French Revolution: *It was the best of times, it was the worst of times, it was the age of wisdom, it was the age of foolishness, it was the epoch of belief, it was the epoch of incredulity, it was the season of Light, it was the season of Darkness, it was the spring of hope, it was the winter of despair [. . .] .*

REPETITION. Repetition of words, phrases, and sometimes whole sentences is used to drive home a point or build suspense or tension within a paragraph or essay. A famous example is the speech of Marc Antony in Act III, scene ii, of Shakespeare's *Julius Caesar*, where Antony repeats the ironic phrase "Brutus is an honourable man" four times in a short speech to the Roman mob. Look at the repetition in the following lines by Martin Luther King:

> *I have a dream that one day on the red hills of Georgia, sons of former slaves and sons of former slave-owners will be able to sit down together at the table of brotherhood.*

> *I have a dream that one day, even the state of Mississippi, a state sweltering with the heat of injustice, sweltering with the heat of oppression, will be transformed into an oasis of freedom and justice.*

> *I have a dream my four little children will one day live in a nation where they will not be judged by the color of their skin but by the content of their character. I have a dream today!*

The repetition of the phrase "I have a dream" emphasizes the fact that freedom, equality, and justice for African-Americans are still *only* dreams. Yet the repetition also affirms Dr. King's belief in change and the ultimate goodness and brotherhood of all men. The phrase, repeated a number of times in the entire speech, rings in the ear like the repetitions in a prayer.

FIGURES OF SPEECH. Finally, writers many times use figures of speech to shock or surprise their readers, to emphasize a point, or to clarify their ideas. For example, Jane

Goodall, in "The Exploitation of Non-Human Animals," uses simile and metaphor when she speaks of laboratories that are "not unlike concentration camps," and when she says that many people remain "largely ignorant" of what goes on in laboratories "rather as the German people were mostly uninformed about the Nazi concentration camps." She further says that chimpanzees "live out their lives as prisoners, in bondage to man." These two comparisons equate animals first with the victims of Nazi genocide and second with slaves. The figures of speech are used to transfer our emotional revulsion against these historical atrocities to the current treatment of lab animals.

In analyzing the style of an essay, you should not simply *point out* parallel sentence structures or figures of speech; you should explain how such elements of style contribute to the clarity, purpose, or force of the essay as a whole. For example: Does the writer use specific and concrete diction to help us visualize his ideas? Parallel sentence structure to help us grasp equal points? Repetition to help us keep complicated discussions in order? Further, does the style of the essay fit the purpose, voice, and situation of the essay? Does the writer use a formal style for a serious subject or formal occasion, or a formal, perhaps inflated style, for a trivial subject? (Sometimes a contrast between style and subject is a deliberate attempt to create humor or satire.) Finally, do the stylistic features of the essay contribute to or detract from the force or emotional impact of the essay? Is the writer deliberately trying to arouse our emotions with the choice of diction and sentence structure, or simply trying to convey his or her own feelings? Is the writer teaching us or preaching to us? As you can see, style is a complicated, integral part of all writing that directly creates meaning in an essay, not just a flourish added by a writer to make his prose "pretty" or "important."

Organization

Writing a rhetorical analysis of an essay is not an easy task, but it can be made easier if you follow a plan and avoid some common mistakes. Keep in mind that your general purpose in writing a critical analysis is to explain and evaluate what the author has written.

First, follow a logical plan in preparing and writing your essay:

1. Read the essay to gain a general understanding of its purpose and meaning, underlining and writing notes in the margin to mark important passages.

2. Outline the essay, focusing on the thesis and the major supports of that thesis (evidence, examples, explanations, extended arguments, causes, effects, and so on). If the writer fails to support his or her claims, or if he or she uses colorful, emotional language, be sure to note these facts. Making this outline will give you a much clearer idea of the structure and scope of the essay.

3. Make a decision about what critical approach to take in analyzing your chosen essay. You might want to focus on the writer's use of the rational, emotional,

or ethical appeals, or perhaps you might do an analysis of the author's style as it is exhibited in a single paragraph or several related paragraphs.

4. Now that you have chosen an approach, read the essay again, listing or otherwise noting examples of the types of support, instances of sound or cogent (or of specious) reasoning, or emotive language you want to emphasize in your essay.

5. Organize the material you have isolated, draw your conclusions, set up a thesis, and write your paper, providing copious examples from the essay to support general observations.

6. Be sure to mention the author's full name and the complete title of the essay in your introduction.

7. Finally, be sure you give your essay a precise, descriptive title such as "Audience Appeal In 'Letter from Birmingham Jail.'"

Second, avoid the following mistakes in writing your rhetorical analysis:

1. Be sure that you have a **critical** thesis and not a **descriptive** one. A critical thesis is one that states an evaluation or judgment of an essay based on your analysis of it. For example: *In "Some Thoughts on the Exploitation of Non-Human Animals," Jane Goodall mounts a strong emotional appeal by using highly connotative language, vivid figures of speech, and an effective moral analogy.* A descriptive thesis, however, merely summarizes what the author says in the essay: *In "Some Thoughts on the Exploitation of Non-Human Animals," Jane Goodall says that experimenting on animals, even if it benefits humans, is morally wrong.* This thesis will lead the writer merely to summarize what Goodall says in her essay; it provides no **analysis** of what she says or direction the critical analysis will take.

2. Keep in mind that assertions are not arguments but judgments; they must be supported with details and examples drawn from the essay. For example, if you say that Goodall engages in fallacious reasoning, you must name the fallacies she uses and give examples of them drawn from the text. You must also tie in what the author says to the point you are making. Don't say merely that "Goodall uses emotionally charged words, such as 'concentration camps,' 'suffering,' and 'heartless monsters.'" Instead, for example, say that "Goodall's use of words and phrases such as 'concentration camps,' 'suffering,' and 'heartless monsters' helps to develop her emotional appeal by causing the reader to think of scientists as cruel and inhuman."

3. Never use such phrases as "It is my opinion that [. . .]" or "I believe that [. . .]." A critical analysis is written from a third-person, objective point of view.

4. Do not write about your chosen essay in the past tense; use the historical present: not "Goodall *said* [. . .]" but "Goodall *says* [. . .] ."

✦

CHECKLIST

1. Have you read the essay you are analyzing a second time, looking up all the words and allusions you are unfamiliar with?
2. Have you annotated the essay, underlining important points and making marginal notations?
3. Have you established the author's intended audience, her purpose, the situation, if possible,and the tone of the essay?
4. Have you decided on a focus, either the rational, emotional, or ethical appeal?
5. If you are focusing on the rational appeal, have you employed Toulmin analysis to find the claim, listed the amount and types of evidence, looked for warrants and backing, and found refutation of counter claims? Has the author employed any fallacious types of reasoning?
6. If you are focusing on the emotional appeal, have you determined which emotion(s) the author is trying to arouse? Have you looked for examples of loaded language, striking images, and rhetorical figures of speech?
7. If you are focusing on the ethical appeal, have you determined how the author presents himself or herself? For example, has he given his credentials, taken an objective tone, used neutral and non-biased language, appealed strictly to evidence, avoided colorful figures, and admitted counter claims?
8. Have you stated a clear, defendable thesis that can be supported by your analysis?
9. Have you started with an interesting lead-in and mentioned the author, title, and date of the essay you are analyzing?
10. Did you edit your paper carefully, checking for major grammatical and spelling errors?

TEXT FOR STUDY

The "Letter from Birmingham Jail," by the Reverend Martin Luther King, Jr., is a classic example of argumentative and persuasive writing. It was written in response to a statement by eight clergymen who were urging withdrawal of support for the civil rights' movement orchestrated by King and other leaders. When you read King's letter, pay close attention to his use of the ethical, emotional, and logical appeals. Also consider the four elements of rhetoric—situation, voice, purpose, and audience. You should discover through your examination of this letter why King is considered one of America's foremost orators. First, here is the statement by the clergymen that prompted King's famous reply.

PUBLIC STATEMENT
BY EIGHT ALABAMA CLERGYMEN

April 12, 1963

We the undersigned clergymen are among those who, in January, issued "An Appeal for Law and Order and Common Sense," in dealing with racial problems in Alabama. We expressed understanding that honest convictions in racial matters could properly be pursued in the courts, but urged that decisions of those courts should *in the meantime be obeyed.*

Since that time there had been some evidence of increased forbearance and a willingness to face facts. Responsible citizens have undertaken to work on various problems which cause racial friction and unrest. In Birmingham, recent public events have given indication that we all have opportunity for a new and constructive and realistic approach to racial problems.

However, we are now confronted by a series of demonstrations by some of our Negro citizens, directed and led in part by outsiders. We recognize the natural impatience of people who feel that their hopes are slow in being realized. But we are convinced that these demonstrations are unwise and untimely.

We agree rather with certain local Negro leadership which has called for honest and open negotiation of racial issues in our area. And we believe this kind of facing of issues can best be accomplished by citizens of our own metropolitan area, white and Negro, meeting with their knowledge and experience of the local situation. All of us need to face that responsibility and find proper channels for its accomplishment.

Just as we formerly pointed out that "hatred and violence have no sanction in our religious and political traditions," we also point out that such actions as incite to hatred and violence, however technically peaceful those actions may be, have not contributed to the resolution of our local problems. We do not believe that these days of new hope are days when extreme measures are justified in Birmingham.

We commend the community as a whole, and the local news media and law enforcement officials in particular, on the calm manner in which these demonstrations have been handled. We urge the public to continue to show restraint should the demonstrations continue, and the law enforcement officials to remain calm and continue to protect our city from violence.

We further strongly urge our own Negro community to withdraw support from these demonstrations, and to unite locally in working peacefully for a better Birmingham. When rights are consistently denied, a cause should be pressed in the courts and in negotiations among local leaders, and not in the streets. We appeal to both our white and Negro citizenry to observe the principles of law and order and common sense.

LETTER FROM BIRMINGHAM JAIL

Martin Luther King, Jr.

April 16, 1963

My Dear Fellow Clergymen:

WHILE CONFINED here in the Birmingham city jail, I came across your recent statement calling my present activities "unwise and untimely." Seldom do I pause to answer criticism of my work and ideas. If I sought to answer all the criticisms that cross my desk, my secretaries would have little time for anything other than such correspondence in the course of the day, and I would have no time for constructive work. But since I feel that you are men of genuine good will and that your criticisms are sincerely set forth, I want to try to answer your statement in what I hope will be patient and reasonable terms.

I think I should indicate why I am here in Birmingham, since you have been influenced by the view which argues against "outsiders coming in." I have the honor of serving as president of the Southern Christian Leadership Conference, an organization operating in every southern state, with headquarters in Atlanta, Georgia. We have some eighty-five affiliated organizations across the South, and one of them is the Alabama Christian Movement for Human Rights. Frequently we share staff, educational, and financial resources with our affiliates. Several months ago the affiliate here in Birmingham asked us to be on call to engage in a nonviolent direct-action program if such were deemed necessary. We readily consented, and when the hour came we lived up to our promise. So I, along with several members of my staff, am here because I was invited here. I am here because I have organizational ties here.

But more basically, I am in Birmingham because injustice is here. Just as the prophets of the eighth century B.C. left their villages and carried their "thus saith the Lord" far beyond the boundaries of their home towns, and just as the Apostle Paul left his village of Tarsus and carried the gospel of Jesus Christ to the far corners of the Greco-Roman world, so am I compelled to carry the gospel of freedom beyond my own home town. Like Paul, I must constantly respond to the Macedonian call for aid.

Moreover, I am cognizant of the interrelatedness of all communities and states. I cannot sit idly by in Atlanta and not be concerned about what happens in Birmingham. Injustice anywhere is a threat to justice everywhere. We are caught in an inescapable network of mutuality, tied in a single garment of destiny. Whatever affects one directly, affects all indirectly. Never again can we afford to live with the narrow, provincial "outside agitator" idea. Anyone who lives inside the United States can never be considered an outsider anywhere within its bounds.

You deplore the demonstrations taking place in Birmingham. But your statement, I am sorry to say, fails to express a similar concern for the conditions that brought about the demonstrations.

I am sure that none of you would want to rest content with the superficial kind of social analysis that deals merely with effects and does not grapple with underlying causes. It is unfortunate that demonstrations are taking place in Birmingham, but it is even more unfortunate that the city's white power structure left the Negro community with no alternative.

In any nonviolent campaign there are four basic steps: collection of the facts to determine whether injustices exist; negotiation; self-purification; and direct action. We have gone through all these steps in Birmingham. There can be no gainsaying the fact that racial injustice engulfs this community. Birmingham is probably the most thoroughly segregated city in the United States. Its ugly record of brutality is widely known. Negroes have experienced grossly unjust treatment in the courts. There have been more unsolved bombings of Negro homes and churches in Birmingham than in any other city in the nation. These are the hard, brutal facts of the case. On the basis of these conditions, Negro leaders sought to negotiate with the city fathers. But the latter consistently refused to engage in good-faith negotiation.

Then, last September, came the opportunity to talk with leaders of Birmingham's economic community. In the course of the negotiations, certain promises were made by the merchants—for example, to remove the stores' humiliating racial signs. On the basis of these promises, the Reverend Fred Shuttlesworth and the leaders of the Alabama Christian Movement for Human Rights agreed to a moratorium on all demonstrations. As the weeks and months went by, we realized that we were the victims of a broken promise. A few signs, briefly removed, returned; the others remained.

As in so many past experiences, our hopes had been blasted, and the shadow of deep disappointment settled upon us. We had no alternative except to prepare for direct action, whereby we would present our very bodies as a means of laying our case before the conscience of the local and the national community. Mindful of the difficulties involved, we decided to undertake a process of self-purification. We began a series of workshops on nonviolence, and we repeatedly asked ourselves: "Are you able to accept blows without retaliating?" "Are you able to endure the ordeal of jail?" We decided to schedule our direct-action program for the Easter season, realizing that except for Christmas, this is the main shopping period of the year. Knowing that a strong economic-withdrawal program would be the by-product of the direct action, we felt that this would be the best time to bring pressure to bear on the merchants for the needed change.

Then it occurred to us that Birmingham's mayoral election was coming up in March, and we speedily decided to postpone action until after election day. When we discovered that the Commissioner of Public Safety, Eugene "Bull" Connor, had piled up enough votes to be in the run-off, we decided again to postpone action until the day after the run-off so that the demonstrations could not be used to cloud the issues. Like many others, we waited to see Mr. Connor defeated, and to this end we endured postponement after postponement. Having aided in this community need, we felt that our direct-action program could be delayed no longer.

You may well ask: "Why direct action? Why sit-ins, marches and so forth? Isn't negotiation a better path?" You are right in calling for negotiation. Indeed, this is the very purpose of direct action. Nonviolent direct action seeks to create such a crisis and foster such a tension that a community which has constantly refused to negotiate is forced to confront the issue. It seeks so to dramatize the issue that it can no longer be ignored. My citing the creation of tension as part of the work of the nonviolent-resister may sound rather shocking. But I must confess that I am not afraid of the word "tension." I have earnestly opposed violent tension, but there is a type of constructive, nonviolent tension which is necessary for growth. Just as Socrates felt that it was necessary to create a tension in the mind so that individuals could rise from the bondage of myths and half-truths to the unfettered realm of creative analysis and objective appraisal, so must we see the need for nonviolent gadflies to create the kind of tension in society that will help men rise from the dark depths of prejudice and racism to the majestic heights of understanding and brotherhood.

The purpose of our direct-action program is to create a situation so crisis-packed that it will inevitably open the door to negotiation. I therefore concur with you in your call for negotiation. Too long has our beloved Southland been bogged down in a tragic effort to live in monologue rather than dialogue.

One of the basic points in your statement is that the action that I and my associates have taken in Birmingham is untimely. Some have asked: "Why didn't you give the new city administration time to act?" The only answer that I can give to this query is that the new Birmingham administration must be prodded about as much as the outgoing one, before it will act. We are sadly mistaken if we feel that the election of Albert Boutwell as mayor will bring the millennium to Birmingham. While Mr. Boutwell is a much more gentle person than Mr. Connor, they are both segregationists, dedicated to maintenance of the status quo. I have hope that Mr. Boutwell will be reasonable enough to see the futility of massive resistance to desegregation. But he will not see this without pressure from devotees of civil rights. My friends, I must say to you that we have not made a single gain in civil rights without determined legal and nonviolent pressure. Lamentably, it is an historical fact that privileged groups seldom give up their privileges voluntarily. Individuals may see the moral light and voluntarily give up their unjust posture; but, as Reinhold Niebuhr has reminded us, groups tend to be more immoral than individuals.

We know through painful experience that freedom is never voluntarily given by the oppressor; it must be demanded by the oppressed. Frankly, I have yet to engage in a direct-action campaign that was "well timed" in the view of those who have not suffered unduly from the disease of segregation. For years now I have heard the word "Wait!" It rings in the ear of every Negro with piercing familiarity. This "Wait" has almost always meant "Never." We must come to see, with one of our distinguished jurists, that "justice too long delayed is justice denied."

We have waited for more than 340 years for our constitutional God-given rights. The nations of Asia and Africa are moving with jet-like speed toward gaining political independence, but we still creep at horse-and-buggy pace toward gaining a cup of coffee at a lunch counter. Perhaps it is easy for those who have never felt the stinging darts of segregation to say, "Wait." But when you have seen vicious mobs lynch your mothers and fathers at will and drown your sisters and brothers at whim; when you have seen hate-filled policemen curse, kick, and even kill your black brothers and sisters; when you see the vast majority of your twenty million Negro brothers smothering in an airtight cage of poverty in the midst of an affluent society; when you suddenly find your tongue twisted and your speech stammering as you seek to explain to your six-year-old daughter why she can't go to the public amusement park that has just been advertised on television, and see tears welling up in her eyes when she is told that Funtown is closed to colored children, and see ominous clouds of inferiority beginning to form in her little mental sky, and see her beginning to distort her personality by developing an unconscious bitterness toward white people; when you have to concoct an answer for a five-year-old son who is asking: "Daddy, why do white people treat colored people so mean?"; when you take a cross-country drive and find it necessary to sleep night after night in the uncomfortable corners of your automobile because no motel will accept you; when you are humiliated day in and day out by nagging signs reading "white" and "colored"; when your first name becomes "nigger," your middle name becomes "boy" (however old you are), and your last name becomes "John," and your wife and mother are never given the respected title "Mrs."; when you are harried by day and haunted by night by the fact that you are a Negro, living constantly at tiptoe stance, never quite knowing what to expect next, and are plagued with inner fears and outer resentments; when you are forever fighting a degenerating sense of "nobodiness"—then you will understand why we find it difficult to wait. There comes a time when the cup of endurance runs over, and men are no longer willing to be plunged into the abyss of despair. I hope, sirs, you can understand our legitimate and unavoidable impatience.

You express a great deal of anxiety over our willingness to break laws. This is certainly a legitimate concern. Since we so diligently urge people to obey the Supreme Court's decision of 1954 outlawing segregation in the public schools, at first glance it may seem rather paradoxical for us consciously to break laws. One may well ask: "How can you advocate breaking some laws and obeying others?" The answer lies in the fact that there are two types of laws: just and unjust. I would be the first to advocate obeying laws. Conversely, one has a moral responsibility to disobey unjust laws. I would agree with St. Augustine that "an unjust law is no law at all."

Now, what is the difference between the two? How does one determine whether a law is just or unjust? A just law is a man-made code that squares with the moral law or the law of God. An unjust law is a code that is out of harmony with the moral law. To put it in the terms of St. Thomas Aquinas: An unjust law is a human law that is not rooted in eternal law and natural law. Any law that uplifts human personality is just. Any law that degrades human personality is unjust. All segregation statutes are unjust because segregation distorts the soul and damages the personality. It gives the segregator a false sense of superiority and the segregated a false sense of inferiority. Segregation, to use the terminology of the Jewish philosopher Martin Buber, substitutes an "I-it" relationship for an "I-thou" relationship and ends up relegating persons to the status of things. Hence, segregation is not only politically, economically, and sociologically unsound, it is morally wrong and sinful. Paul Tillich has said that sin is separation. Is not segregation an existential expression of man's tragic separation, his awful estrangement, his terrible sinfulness? Thus it is that I can urge men to obey the 1954 decision of the Supreme Court, for it is morally right; and I can urge them to disobey segregation ordinances, for they are morally wrong.

Let us consider a more concrete example of just and unjust laws. An unjust law is a code that a numerical or power majority group compels a minority group to obey but does not make binding on itself. This is difference made legal. By the same token, a just law is a code that a majority compels a minority to follow and that it is willing to follow itself. This is sameness made legal.

Let me give another explanation. A law is unjust if it is inflicted on a minority that, as a result of being denied the right to vote, had no part in enacting or devising the law. Who can say that the legislature of Alabama which set up that state's segregation laws was democratically elected? Throughout Alabama all sorts of devious methods are used to prevent Negroes from becoming registered voters, and there are some counties in which, even though Negroes constitute a majority of the population, not a single Negro is registered. Can any law enacted under such circumstances be considered democratically structured?

Sometimes a law is just on its face and unjust in its application. For instance, I have been arrested on a charge of parading without a permit. Now, there is nothing wrong in having an ordinance which requires a permit for a parade. But such an ordinance becomes unjust when it is used to maintain segregation and to deny citizens the First-Amendment privilege of peaceful assembly and protest.

I hope you are able to see the distinction I am trying to point out. In no sense do I advocate evading or defying the law, as would the rabid segregationist. That would lead to anarchy. One who breaks an unjust law must do so openly, lovingly, and with a willingness to accept the penalty. I submit that an individual who breaks a law that conscience tells him is unjust, and who willingly accepts the penalty of imprisonment in order to arouse the conscience of the community over its injustice, is in reality expressing the highest respect for law.

Of course, there is nothing new about this kind of civil disobedience. It was evidenced sublimely in the refusal of Shadrach, Meshach, and Abednego to obey the laws of Nebuchadnezzar, on the ground that a higher moral law was at stake. It was practiced superbly by the early Christians, who were willing to face hungry lions and the excruciating pain of chopping blocks rather than submit to certain unjust laws of the Roman Empire. To a degree, academic freedom is a reality today because Socrates practiced civil disobedience. In our own nation, the Boston Tea Party represented a massive act of civil disobedience.

We should never forget that everything Adolf Hitler did in Germany was "legal" and everything the Hungarian freedom fighters did in Hungary was "illegal." It was "illegal" to aid and comfort a Jew in Hitler's Germany. Even so, I am sure that, had I lived in Germany at the time, I would have aided and comforted my Jewish brothers. If today I lived in a Communist country where certain principles dear to the Christian faith are suppressed, I would openly advocate disobeying that country's antireligious laws.

I must make two honest confessions to you, my Christian and Jewish brothers. First, I must confess that over the past few years I have been gravely disappointed with the white moderate.

I have almost reached the regrettable conclusion that the Negro's great stumbling block in his stride toward freedom is not the White Citizens' Counciler or the Ku Klux Klanner, but the white moderate, who is more devoted to "order" than to justice; who prefers a negative peace which is the presence of tension to a positive peace which is the presence of justice; who constantly says: "I agree with you in the goal you seek, but I cannot agree with your methods of direct action"; who paternalistically believes he can set the timetable for another man's freedom; who lives by a mythical concept of time and who constantly advises the Negro to wait for a "more convenient season." Shallow understanding from people of good will is more frustrating than absolute misunderstanding from people of ill will. Lukewarm acceptance is much more bewildering than outright rejection.

I had hoped that the white moderate would understand that law and order exist for the purpose of establishing justice and that when they fail in this purpose they become the dangerously structured dams that block the flow of social progress. I had hoped that the white moderate would understand that the present tension in the South is a necessary phase of the transition from an obnoxious negative peace, in which the Negro passively accepted his unjust plight, to a substantive and positive peace, in which all men will respect the dignity and worth of human personality. Actually, we who engage in nonviolent direct action are not the creators of tension. We merely bring to the surface the hidden tension that is already alive. We bring it out in the open, where it can be seen and dealt with. Like a boil that can never be cured so long as it is covered up but must be opened with all its ugliness to the natural medicines of air and light, injustice must be exposed, with all the tension its exposure creates, to the light of human conscience and the air of national opinion before it can be cured.

In your statement you assert that our actions, even though peaceful, must be condemned because they precipitate violence. But is this a logical assertion? Isn't this like condemning a robbed man because his possession of money precipitated the evil act of robbery? Isn't this like condemning Socrates because his unswerving commitment to truth and his philosophical inquiries precipitated the act by the misjudged populace in which they made him drink hemlock? Isn't this like condemning Jesus because his unique God-consciousness and never-ceasing devotion to God's will precipitated the evil act of crucifixion? We must come to see that, as the federal courts have consistently affirmed, it is wrong to urge an individual to cease his efforts to gain his basic constitutional rights because the quest may precipitate violence. Society must protect the robbed and punish the robber.

I had also hoped that the white moderate would reject the myth concerning time in relation to the struggle for freedom. I have just received a letter from a white brother in Texas. He writes: "All Christians know that the colored people will receive equal rights eventually, but it is possible that you are in too great a religious hurry. It has taken Christianity almost two thousand years to accomplish what it has. The teachings of Christ take time to come to earth." Such an attitude stems from a tragic misconception of time, from the strangely irrational notion that there is something in the very flow of time that will inevitably cure all ills. Actually, time itself is neutral; it can be used either destructively or constructively. More and more I feel that the people of ill will have used time much more effectively than have the people of good will.

We will have to repent in this generation not merely for the hateful words and actions of the bad people but for the appalling silence of the good people. Human progress never rolls in on wheels of inevitability; it comes through the tireless efforts of men willing to be co-workers with God, and without this hard work, time itself becomes an ally of the forces of social stagnation. We must use time creatively, in the knowledge that the time is always ripe to do right. Now is the time to make real the promise of democracy and transform our pending national elegy into a creative psalm of brotherhood. Now is the time to lift our national policy from the quick-sand of racial injustice to the solid rock of human dignity.

You speak of our activity in Birmingham as extreme. At first I was rather disappointed that fellow clergymen would see my nonviolent efforts as those of an extremist. I began thinking about the fact that I stand in the middle of two opposing forces in the Negro community. One is a force of complacency, made up in part of Negroes who, as a result of long years of oppression, are so drained of self-respect and a sense of "somebodiness" that they have adjusted to segregation; and in part of a few middle-class Negroes who, because of a degree of academic and economic security and because in some ways they profit by segregation, have become insensitive to the problems of the masses. The other force is one of bitterness and hatred, and it comes perilously close to advocating violence. It is expressed in the various black nationalist groups that are springing up across the nation, the largest and best-known being Elijah Muhammad's Muslim movement. Nourished by the Negro's frustration over the continued existence of racial discrimination, this movement is made up of people who have lost faith in America, who have absolutely repudiated Christianity, and who have concluded that the white man is an incorrigible "devil."

I have tried to stand between these two forces, saying that we need emulate neither the "do-nothingism" of the complacent nor the hatred and despair of the black nationalist. For there is the more excellent way of love and nonviolent protest. I am grateful to God that, through the influence of the Negro church, the way of nonviolence became an integral part of our struggle.

If this philosophy had not emerged, by now many streets of the South would, I am convinced, be flowing with blood. And I am further convinced that if our white brothers dismiss as "rabble-rousers" and "outside agitators" those of us who employ nonviolent direct action, and if they refuse to support our nonviolent efforts, millions of the Negroes will, out of frustration and despair, seek solace and security in black-nationalist ideologies—a development that would inevitably lead to a frightening racial nightmare.

Oppressed people cannot remain oppressed forever. The yearning for freedom eventually manifests itself, and that is what has happened to the American Negro. Something within has reminded him of his birthright of freedom, and something without has reminded him that it can be gained. Consciously or unconsciously, he has been caught up by the *Zeitgeist*, and with his black brothers of Africa and his brown and yellow brothers of Asia, South America, and the Caribbean, the United States Negro is moving with a sense of great urgency toward the promised land of racial justice. If one recognizes this vital urge that has engulfed the Negro community, one should readily understand why public demonstrations are taking place. The

Negro has many pent-up resentments and latent frustrations, and he must release them. So let him march; let him make prayer pilgrimages to the city hall; let him go on freedom rides—and try to understand why he must do so. If his repressed emotions are not released in nonviolent ways, they will seek expression through violence; this is not a threat but a fact of history. So I have not said to my people: "Get rid of your discontent." Rather, I have tried to say that this normal and healthy discontent can be channeled into the creative outlet of nonviolent direct action. And now this approach is being termed extremist.

But although I was initially disappointed at being categorized as an extremist, as I continued to think about the matter I gradually gained a measure of satisfaction from the label. Was not Jesus an extremist for love: "Love your enemies, bless them that curse you, do good to them that hate you, and pray for them which despitefully use you, and persecute you." Was not Amos an extremist for justice: "Let justice roll down like waters and righteousness like an ever-flowing stream." Was not Paul an extremist for the Christian gospel: "I bear in my body the marks of the Lord Jesus." Was not Martin Luther an extremist: "Here I stand; I cannot do otherwise, so help me God." And John Bunyan: "I will stay in jail to the end of my days before I make a butchery of my conscience." And Abraham Lincoln: "This nation cannot survive half slave and half free." And Thomas Jefferson: "We hold these truths to be self-evident, that all men are created equal. . . ." So the question is not whether we will be extremists, but what kind of extremists we will be. Will we be extremists for hate or for love? Will we be extremists for the preservation of injustice or for the extension of justice? In that dramatic scene on Calvary's hill three men were crucified. We must never forget that all three were crucified for the same crime—the crime of extremism. Two were extremists for immorality, and thus fell below their environment. The other, Jesus Christ, was an extremist for love, truth and goodness, and thereby rose above his environment. Perhaps the South, the nation and the world are in dire need of creative extremists.

I had hoped that the white moderate would see this need. Perhaps I was too optimistic; perhaps I expected too much. I suppose I should have realized that few members of the oppressor race can understand the deep groans and passionate yearnings of the oppressed race, and still fewer have the vision to see that injustice must be rooted out by strong, persistent, and determined action. I am thankful, however, that some of our white brothers in the South have grasped the meaning of this social revolution and committed themselves to it. They are still all too few in quantity, but they are big in quality. Some—such as Ralph McGill, Lillian Smith, Harry Golden, James McBride Dabbs, Ann Braden, and Sarah Patton Boyle—have written about our struggle in eloquent and prophetic terms. Others have marched with us down nameless streets of the South. They have languished in filthy, roach-infested jails, suffering the abuse and brutality of policemen who view them as "dirty nigger-lovers." Unlike so many of their moderate brothers and sisters, they have recognized the urgency of the moment and sensed the need for powerful "action" antidotes to combat the disease of segregation.

Let me take note of my other major disappointment. I have been so greatly disappointed with the white church and its leadership. Of course, there are some notable exceptions. I am not unmindful of the fact that each of you has taken some significant stands on this issue. I commend you, Reverend Stallings, for your Christian stand on this past Sunday, in welcoming Negroes to your worship service on a non-segregated basis. I commend the Catholic leaders of this state for integrating Spring Hill College several years ago.

But despite these notable exceptions, I must honestly reiterate that I have been disappointed with the church. I do not say this as one of those negative critics who can always find something wrong with the church. I say this as a minister of the gospel, who loves the church; who was nurtured in its bosom; who has been sustained by its spiritual blessings and who will remain true to it as long as the cord of life shall lengthen.

When I was suddenly catapulted into the leadership of the bus protest in Montgomery, Alabama, a few years ago, I felt we would be supported by the white church. I felt that the white ministers, priests, and rabbis of the South would be among our strongest allies. Instead, some have been outright opponents, refusing to understand the freedom movement and misrepresenting its leaders; all too many others have been more cautious than courageous and have remained silent behind the anesthetizing security of stained-glass windows.

In spite of my shattered dreams, I came to Birmingham with the hope that the white religious leadership of this community would see the justice of our cause and, with deep moral concern, would serve as the channel through which our just grievances could reach the power structure. I had hoped that each of you would understand. But again I have been disappointed.

I have heard numerous southern religious leaders admonish their worshipers to comply with a desegregation decision because it is the law, but I have longed to hear white ministers declare: "Follow this decree because integration is morally right and because the Negro is your brother." In the midst of blatant injustices inflicted upon the Negro, I have watched white churchmen stand on the sideline and mouth pious irrelevancies and sanctimonious trivialities. In the midst of a mighty struggle to rid our nation of racial and economic injustice, I have heard many ministers say: "Those are social issues, with which the gospel has no real concern." And I have watched many churches commit themselves to a completely otherworldly religion which makes a strange, un-Biblical distinction between body and soul, between the sacred and the secular.

I have traveled the length and breadth of Alabama, Mississippi, and all the other southern states. On sweltering summer days and crisp autumn mornings I have looked at the South's beautiful churches with their lofty spires pointing heavenward. I have beheld the impressive outlines of her massive religious-education buildings. Over and over I have found myself asking: "What kind of people worship here? Who is their God? Where were their voices when the lips of Governor Barnett dripped with words of interposition and nullification? Where were they when Governor Wallace gave a clarion call for defiance and hatred? Where were their voices of support when bruised and weary Negro men and women decided to rise from the dark dungeons of complacency to the bright hills of creative protest?"

Yes, these questions are still in my mind. In deep disappointment I have wept over the laxity of the church. But be assured that my tears have been tears of love. There can be no deep disappointment where there is not deep love. Yes, I love the church. How could I do otherwise? I am in the rather unique position of being the son, the grandson, and the great-grandson of preachers. Yes, I see the church as the body of Christ. But, oh! How we have blemished and scarred that body through neglect and through fear of being nonconformists.

There was a time when the church was very powerful—in the time when the early Christians rejoiced at being deemed worthy to suffer for what they believed. In those days the church was not merely a thermometer that transformed the mores of society. Whenever the early Christians entered a town, the people in power became disturbed and immediately sought to convict the Christians for being "disturbers of the peace" and "outside agitators." But the Christians pressed on, in the conviction that they were "a colony of heaven," called to obey God rather than man. Small in number, they were big in commitment. They were too God-intoxicated to be "astronomically intimidated." By their effort and example they brought an end to such ancient evils as infanticide and gladiatorial contests.

Things are different now. So often the contemporary church is a weak, ineffectual voice with an uncertain sound. So often it is an arch-defender of the status quo. Far from being disturbed by the presence of the church, the power structure of the average community is consoled by the church's silent—and often even vocal—sanction of things as they are.

But the judgement of God is upon the church as never before. If today's church does not recapture the sacrificial spirit of the early church, it will lose its authenticity, forfeit the loyalty of millions, and be dismissed as an irrelevant social club with no meaning for the twentieth century. Every day I meet young people whose disappointment with the church has turned into outright disgust.

Perhaps I have once again been too optimistic. Is organized religion too inextricably bound to the status quo to save our nation and the world? Perhaps I must turn my faith to the inner spiritual church, the church within the church, as the true *ekklesia* and the hope of the world. But again I am thankful to God that some noble souls from the ranks of organized religion have broken loose from the paralyzing chains of conformity and joined us as active partners in the struggle for freedom. They have left their secure congregations and walked the streets of Albany, Georgia, with us. They have gone down the highways of the South on tortuous rides for freedom. Yes, they have gone to jail with us. Some have been dismissed from their churches, have lost the support of their bishops and fellow ministers. But they have acted in the faith that right defeated is stronger than evil triumphant. Their witness has been the spiritual salt that has preserved the true meaning of the gospel in these troubled times. They have carved a tunnel of hope through the dark mountain of disappointment.

I hope the church as a whole will meet the challenge of this decisive hour. But even if the church does not come to the aid of justice, I have no despair about the future. I have no fear about the outcome of our struggle in Birmingham, even if our motives are at present misunderstood. We will reach the goal of freedom in Birmingham and all over the nation, because the goal of America is freedom. Abused and scorned though we may be, our destiny is tied up with America's destiny. Before the pilgrims landed at Plymouth, we were here. Before the pen of Jefferson etched the majestic words of the Declaration of Independence across the pages of history, we were here. For more than two centuries our forebears labored in this country without wages; they made cotton king; they built the homes of their masters while suffering gross injustice and shameful humiliation—and yet out of a bottomless vitality they continued to thrive and develop. If the inexpressible cruelties of slavery could not stop us, the opposition we now face will surely fail. We will win our freedom because the sacred heritage of our nation and the eternal will of God are embodied in our echoing demands.

Before closing I feel impelled to mention one other point in your statement that has troubled me profoundly. You warmly commended the Birmingham police force for keeping "order" and "preventing violence." I doubt that you would have so warmly commended the police force if you had seen its dogs sinking their teeth into unarmed, nonviolent Negroes. I doubt that you would so quickly commend the policemen if you were to observe their ugly and inhumane treatment of Negroes here in the city jail; if you were to see them slap and kick old Negro men and young boys; if you were to observe them, as they did on two occasions, refuse to give us food because we wanted to sing our grace together. I cannot join you in your praise of the Birmingham police department.

It is true that police have exercised a degree of discipline in handling the demonstrators. In this sense they have conducted themselves rather "nonviolently" in public. But for what purpose? To preserve the evil system of segregation. Over the past few years I have consistently preached that nonviolence demands that the means we use must be as pure as the ends we seek. I have tried to make clear that it is wrong to use immoral means to attain moral ends. But now I must affirm that it is just as wrong, or perhaps even more so, to use moral means to preserve immoral ends. Perhaps Mr. Connor and his policemen have been rather nonviolent in public, as was Chief Pritchett in Albany, Georgia, but they have used the moral means of nonviolence to maintain the immoral end of racial injustice. As T.S. Eliot has said: "The last temptation is the greatest treason: To do the right deed for the wrong reason."

I wish you had commended the Negro sit-inners and demonstrators of Birmingham for their sublime courage, their willingness to suffer and their amazing discipline in the midst of great provocation. One day the South will recognize its heroes. They will be the James Merediths, with the noble sense of purpose that enables them to face jeering and hostile mobs, and with the agonizing loneliness that characterizes the life of the pioneer. They will be old, oppressed, battered Negro women, symbolized in a seventy-two-year-old woman in Montgomery, Alabama, who rose up with a sense of dignity and with her people decided not to ride segregated buses, and who responded with ungrammatical profundity to one who inquired about her weariness: "My feets is tired, but my soul is at rest." They will be the young high school and college students, the young ministers of the gospel and a host of their elders, courageously and nonviolently sitting in at lunch counters and willingly going to jail for conscience' sake. One day the South will know that when these disinherited children of God sat down at lunch counters, they were in reality standing up for what is best in the American dream and for the most sacred values in our Judaeo-Christian heritage, thereby bringing our nation back to those great wells of democracy which were dug deep by the founding fathers in their formulation of the Constitution and the Declaration of Independence.

Never before have I written so long a letter. I'm afraid it is much too long to take your precious time. I can assure you that it would have been much shorter if I had been writing from a comfortable desk, but what else can one do when he is alone in a narrow jail cell, other than write long letters, think long thoughts, and pray long prayers?

If I have said anything in this letter that overstates the truth and indicates an unreasonable impatience, I beg you to forgive me. If I have said anything that understates the truth and indicates my having a patience that allows me to settle for anything less than brotherhood, I beg God to forgive me.

I hope this letter finds you strong in faith. I also hope that circumstances will soon make it possible for me to meet each of you, not as an integrationist or a civil-rights leader but as a fellow clergyman and a Christian brother. Let us all hope that the dark clouds of racial prejudice will soon pass away and the deep fog of misunderstanding will be lifted from our fear-drenched communitites, and in some not too distant tomorrow the radiant stars of love and brotherhood will shine over our great nation with all their scintillating beauty.

Yours for the cause of Peace and Brotherhood,
Martin Luther King, Jr.

STUDENT ANALYSIS

The following rhetorical analysis of King's letter was written by Julie Sculley, a student. She writes an analysis of King's skillful rhetorical appeal to his audience, one of the four elements of persuasive discourse.

AUDIENCE APPEAL IN "LETTER FROM BIRMINGHAM JAIL"

Julie Sculley

In any piece of persuasive writing an author uses specific language and references designed to win over his intended audience. In "Letter From Birmingham Jail," Martin Luther King, Jr., tailors his writing to appeal to the clergymen who have expressed their disapproval of both King's actions and their timing. Some of the more important methods King uses to achieve his purpose are his referral to church ideology, his historical references, and his use of religious metaphors.

Since King is directing his letter to clergymen, he makes many references to church ideology. He does this for two reasons; he wants to evoke a sense of moral right and wrong in his audience, and he wants to point out the hypocrisy often shown by the actions, or lack thereof, of the church. At one point in his essay, for example, King states directly what he would like to hear from white ministers and their followers on the subject of compliance with desegregation: "Follow this decree because integration is morally right and because the Negro is your brother," King says (70). Clearly, his purpose here is to induce feelings of guilt in those members of clergy who have made similar dismissive statements.

As students and teachers of theology, clergymen are expected to be well-versed in the history of the Bible, the people of that time, and religious figures in general. With this in mind, King makes several religious and historical references in his letter. Most of these are presented to support his beliefs and actions. He compares his role as a minister, for example, to that of the ancient prophets and the apostle Paul who traveled far in order to spread the word of God. He defends his civil disobedience by referring to biblical law-breakers, such as Shadrach, Meshach, and Abednego, who refused to submit to Nebuchadnezzar for moral reasons, and to early Christians who died grisly deaths instead of complying with Roman law. King also seeks to remind the clergymen that early Christians were often perceived as "outside agitators" because of their adherence to their beliefs. By doing this, he hopes to cause the ministers to question their own passivity.

King also employs religious metaphors to sway his audience in much of his writing. To defend his decision to act, as well as to further illustrate the inactivity of the church, King asks: "Where were their voices of support when bruised and weary Negro men and women decided to rise from the dark dungeons of complacency to the bright hills of creative protest?" (70). "Their voices of support" refers to members of the church and is another swipe at the clergy. The current passive states of many Negroes are described as "dark dungeons," while the protestations of King and other like-minded individuals are termed "bright hills." The criticism of the timing of King's actions is defended with a metaphorical reference, which serves to emphasize the need to make changes and act now: "But the judgment of God is upon the church as never before. If today's church does not recapture the sacrificial spirit of the early church, it will lose its authenticity, forfeit the loyalty of millions, and be dismissed as an irrelevant social club with no meaning for the twentieth century" (71). Metaphorically reducing the church to the level of a social club makes a powerful statement designed to undermine the very thing the clergymen value most. Further, King hopes that his stinging words of criticism will serve to refocus the clergymen on what the church is all about.

King's essay, written in the form of a letter, is a masterful blend of words, phrases, and ideas whose purpose is to appeal to his intended audience, the clergymen. As a member of the clergy himself, King skillfully selects and weaves these examples into his writing in a most persuasive manner.

ON THE NET

College and university-sponsored sites on the internet cover almost every topic related to rhetoric. You will find more detail about each topic discussed in this chapter at the following sites:

Aristotle's Rhetoric: A Hypertext Resource, Compiled by Lee Honeycutt. This translation of *Aristotle*, by W. Rhys Roberts, is conveniently divided into three books and features a keyword search box. Sponsored by Iowa State University.
<http://www.public.iastate.edu/~honeyl/Rhetoric/>

An Introduction to Rhetorical Style. Robert N. Gaines lists and gives examples of different prose styles as well as their components, such as comparison, personification, hyperbole, and antithesis.
http://www.wam.umd.edu/~gaines/style.html

A Glossary of Rhetorical Terms with Examples. Sponsored by the Division of Classics at the University of Kentucky; this is a list of terms from Alliteration to Zeugma.
<http://www.uky.edu/AS/Classics/rhetoric.html>

Silva Rhetoricae: The Forest of Rhetoric. This online guide is provided by Dr. Gideon Burton of Brigham Young University. The site is divided into two panels. On the left is the "Forest," with sections on the appeals, the branches of oratory, and the canons of rhetoric. On the right is the "Flowers," with definitions of all the key rhetorical terms.
<http://humanities.byu.edu/rhetoric/silva.htm>

Rational Appeal: Logos. The HyperText Books. Composition 1101. Daniel Kies, College of DuPage, has an extensive site with discussion of logic, syllogisms, and enthymemes, as well as *Pathos* and *Ethos*.
<http://papyr.com/hypertextbooks/comp1/logos.htm>

Writing A Rhetorical Analysis. Sponsored by the University of British Columbia Writing Centre, this site breaks the process of writing a rhetorical analysis into Critical Reading and Critical Writing, followed by a sample text and an analysis of that text.
<http://www.writingcentre.ubc.ca/workshop/tools/rhet1.htm>

Color Coded Rhetorical Analysis of Letter from Birmingham Jail. As the title states, this analysis, by Mary Schultz of DeAnza College, puts in different colors the different appeals employed by Dr. King in his famous letter.
<http://faculty.deanza.fhda.edu/schultzmary/stories/storyReader$884>

EXERCISES

I. Read the following two passages, both from famous speeches. In each, certain words are placed in bold print. Determine which of these words are concrete and which are abstract, which are specific and which are general. Next, determine what connotations the words have. Finally, determine whether the passage is formal or informal. When you have finished this exercise, write a short paragraph discussing the author's use of diction in each passage.

A. "I say to the House as I said to ministers who have joined this **government**, I have nothing to offer but **blood, toil, tears,** and **sweat.** We have before us an **ordeal** of the most grievous kind. We have before us many, many months of **struggle** and **suffering.** You ask, what is our **policy**? I say it is to wage **war** by **land, sea,** and **air.** War with all our **might** and with all the **strength God** has given us, and to wage war against a **monstrous tyranny** never surpassed in the **dark** and **lamentable catalogue** of human **crime.** That is our policy." Winston Churchill. May 13, 1940.

B. "Men, this **stuff** some sources **sling** around about America wanting to stay out of the war and not wanting to **fight** is a lot of **baloney!** Americans love to fight, **traditionally.** All **real Americans** love the **sting** and **clash** of battle. America loves a **winner.** America will not **tolerate** a **loser.** Americans **despise** a **coward**; Americans play to **win.** That's why America has never lost and never will lose a war." George S. Patton. May 17, 1944.

II. In the following passages each sentence is numbered. Determine which of the following syntactic schemes—repetition, parallelism, and antithesis—are employed in each passage and then write a short paragraph discussing the emotional impact of the use of these schemes.

A. **1.** "There are many people in the world who really don't understand, or say they don't, what is the great issue between the free world and the Communist world. **2.** Let them come to Berlin. **3.** There are some who say that communism is the wave of the future. **4.** Let them come to Berlin. **5.** And there are some who say in Europe and elsewhere we can work with the Communists. **6.** Let them come to Berlin. **7.** And there are even a few who say that it is true that communism is an evil system, but it permits us to make economic progress. **8.** *Lass' sie nach Berlin kommen.* **9.** Let them come to Berlin." John F. Kennedy. June 26, 1963.

B. **1.** "What constitutes an American? **2.** Not colour nor race nor religion. **3.** Not the pedigree of his family nor the place of his birth. **4.** Not the coincidence of his citizenship. **5.** Not his social status nor his bank account. **6.** Not his trade nor his profession. **7.** An American is one who loves justice and believes in the dignity of man. **8.** An American is one who will fight for his freedom and that of his neighbor. **9.** An American is one who will sacrifice property, ease and security in order that he and his children may retain the rights of free men. **10.** An American is one in whose heart is engraved the immortal second sentence of the Declaration of Independence." Harold Ickes. May, 1941.

PART II

EXPOSITION AND ARGUMENTATION

4 Description *and* Narration

In any writing you do, you must determine who your audience is, what your purpose is, what the situation is, and what voice you will use to meet the challenges established. In order to write well, you will need to consider the best possible organizational plan to communicate clearly. In exposition, there are several useful rhetorical strategies, including description and narration, profiles or memoirs, process analysis, definition, illustration/exemplification, comparison/contrast, classification/division, and causal analysis.

In the following pages these rhetorical strategies will be discussed as separate units. Each will be presented as a means to an end, but in actual writing situations, you will find that you must use multiple strategies. In almost any essay you write, your purpose will be served by paying attention to specific details in order to describe, by exemplifying and illustrating any generalizations you make, by keeping in mind that all writing is an on-going process, and by keeping cause-effect relationships clear. You may need to develop each paragraph using one or the other of the rhetorical strategies while your overall purpose calls for a broader organizational plan.

You will find that your understanding of these rhetorical strategies, sometimes called modes, will assist you in developing your ideas clearly, whether for an essay, an essay exam, or some other purpose. Your thesis, in any case, will be determined by the situation, your audience, and your particular purpose.

DESCRIPTION

In nearly every essay-writing situation, we use description, especially in providing vivid examples. When we describe, we try to recreate for the audience the sensations we may have felt in a similar situation. The basis of any good description is, of course, close observation and a careful consideration of the audience and purpose. Remember the last time you were asked where you had parked your car and you had to rely on description to explain exactly what your car looked like and generally how to get there? Unless you observe the details, explaining anything clearly for your audience is difficult.

Implementation

Description is used in almost any rhetorical mode. It is often not an end in itself. It clarifies your point in narration, explains in comparison and classification, makes definition interesting, and creates strong emotional appeals in persuasive writing.

Strategy

In addition to observing closely, choosing the right word is an essential feature of any writing experience. When we use any word in context, we must take several different things into consideration, including the degree of specificity and the nuances of the words. Beginning any discussion with a generalization or an abstraction is entirely possible. However, leaving the subject at that level does not create a very clear image or impression for the audience. In order to write evocatively, the writer must aim toward the specific rather than the general and the concrete rather than the abstract. Introducing an abstraction like *loyalty* is a beginning; however, describing the black and white terrier named Scotty sleeping on his master's grave in the cemetery night after night becomes more specific. Certain techniques help create vivid writing.

Attention To Diction

Every writer understands the differences between denotation and connotation. Denotation is the dictionary definition of a particular word. If you look up *mother* in the dictionary, you find it means "female parent"—no real surprise. The connotational value of a word, however, includes the associations our experience brings to that word. For some, the connotations of mother bring images of hot dogs, SUVs, and apple pie while for others it connotes a busy, organized woman with a briefcase. Connotations can be positive, neutral, or negative as well. If we refer to a person as obstinate or principled, we mean that person has a tendency to stick tenaciously to convictions. A person with conviction might also be called stubborn or, in some contexts, pig headed: in each case the connotations become progressively more negative. Our choices of words indicate how we want the reader to understand what we mean. Using the wrong word in certain contexts communicates something to the reader that we never meant! Suppose you were writing about water pollution, for instance, and you found yourself repeating "pure" over and over again in the conclusion. You might open your thesaurus to find another word to vary the way you present your summation of evidence. Among the synonyms, you will find "chaste." Now, chaste does mean purity in some contexts, but it would give your reader an unusual perception of water! Diction—your choice of the right word in the right place—makes a major difference in how your audience understands your point.

Comparisons

Communicating means putting yourself in the place of the audience well enough for you to figure out what the audience knows and to fill the gaps so you can get your point across. One way to do so is to use literal comparisons. That is, by comparing an unfamiliar thing to a familiar one, one the audience understands, you can clarify the unfamiliar. The literal comparison usually requires finding likenesses in two things that are basically similar in nature. Have you ever eaten fried alligator? What does it taste like? Chicken? Your answer is an example of a literal comparison: two things of like nature (sources of protein) compared in order to make the unfamiliar more familiar.

Another kind of comparison used in description is the figurative comparison. Figures of speech usually compare two things of essentially unlike nature. Common figures of speech include some of the following:

simile: a comparison of two essentially unlike things using words that make the comparison clear ("like," "as," "resembles," "than," and similar words). When you say that a certain child eats like a horse, you are using a simile to indicate a single aspect of the two subjects where the qualities of one make the qualities of the other vivid or interesting by comparison.

metaphor: a comparison of two essentially unlike things not using words that emphasize the comparison. The metaphor is a more implicit comparison. When we say a person turns beet red or is a mad dog when he is angry, we are using metaphor.

personification: a comparison of two essentially unlike things in which inanimate objects are given human or animal characteristics, abstractions are given qualities of humans or animals, animals are given human characteristics, and so forth. People who give their cars a name are personifying. If your car coughs and dies, you have given it (a machine with internal problems) human characteristics.

synecdoche: a comparison of two unlike things, in this case a part with the whole. If a farmer hires extra help during harvest, he may say he hires four hands. He actually hires four people with eight hands, but the essential aspect of his help is their ability to work with their hands, of course. In class it does not take you long to figure out which students are quick to catch on or which students have come to class well prepared. You may call those students "brains" to indicate their essential characteristics. You do not mean that they sit in the back of the class in a beaker.

Rhetorical Devices

Closely allied to figurative language, these devices are often included in descriptions. They are often examples of verbal irony, a discrepancy between what we say and what we mean.

hyperbole: a deliberate exaggeration for a particular effect. Anyone who lives in Texas understands the basic focus of hyperbole (pronounced hi per' bo le, not "hyper bowl"—which sounds like a game played between two champion teams who have had too much sugar). When we say a mountain of dirty dishes is in the sink, we are using hyperbole. No matter where you park on campus, your car is 7000 miles from any class you have—truth or hyperbole?

understatement: a deliberate undercutting or downplaying of importance to create a particular effect. If the rain begins unexpectedly during class, catching you unprepared, and if it rains forty days and forty nights in an hour and a half (hyperbole), and if your car is 7000 miles from any shelter near a parking lot, and some character wanders past you in a yellow slicker, an umbrella, and hip boots and says, "Damp out, isn't it?" he is understating the situation.

paradox: an apparent contradiction that proves to be true upon reflection. Wordsworth's statement that the "child is father of the man" seems backwards but says something about the relative understanding of the two generations. *Everything I Needed to Know I Learned in Kindergarten* would seem to operate upon the same paradox. An *oxymoron* is a paradox in which the seeming contradiction is contained within a single phrase. The usual examples are "jumbo shrimp" and "sophomore" ("wise fool"). Some more literary references to "darkness visible," a "terrible beauty," and "wintry fever" also fit the definition.

Imagery

Imagery appeals to the senses. Obviously you must describe sensory impressions if you are to involve the reader in the point you are trying to make. The five kinds of sensory appeals include visual imagery (appeals to the way things look), tactile imagery (the way things feel), auditory/aural imagery (the way things sound), gustatory imagery (the way things taste), and olfactory imagery (the way things smell). In English there are more words to describe the way things look than to describe any other single image. Usually, the first three kinds of images are used more often in expository writing, but every once in a while, you may be called upon to use all the senses to vivify your writing. While you may start a discussion by saying that something looks good or that it sounds great, you really have not told the audience anything to expand understanding. You must use specific adjectives to create particular images to evoke corresponding sensations in the audience, to recreate for them the same sensations that you as the writer experienced.

Organization

No descriptive passage exists in a vacuum: it is designed to fit your audience and your purpose. Therefore, most descriptions are used within examples to support whatever point you are making. Descriptions usually support a dominant impression you are trying to convey in your discussion and are organized to present the information in the most clearly logical way for your audience: *spatially* or emphatically. You may choose to arrange according to where things are in space or how they relate to each other (spatial). You may choose, on the other hand, to arrange your description according to the relative importance of your details (emphatic). No matter what the arrangement, the details you select will communicate your point to the reader. In certain circumstances you may want to present an objective description, trying to be as complete and unbiased in your presentation as possible. In other cases, your dominant impression may be subjective. You will want to involve your audience emotionally in your subject. Although the following passage deals with fiction, the same literary devices can be used in expository writing. Consider the following description from Michael McFarland's short story "The False Country":

> *The center stripe was the bright line to which the dark world vibrated. It was the flashing middle marker stretching all the way from the horizon of the flat farmland. Far off at its origin was a point that Stephen aimed his car toward. Although it was night, he could see many other dimmer lines—made by the freeway's painted edge, the ditches, the endless fences, even the horizon, and—above the horizon—the tree line. They all seemed to begin at this central point and they came toward him at different speeds—sadly, slowly. Finally, reaching him, they slipped by until they were no longer in sight but probably converged at some equidistant point behind. The painted lines were the most dramatic, especially the center one. It constantly started up slowly and crept towards him, gathering speed until it flashed under. Finally it gave itself to the roar of the engine. The car seemed almost to be running on this energy like the toy cars he had played with as a boy. He had pushed them along the floor hard, until the momentum gave them life and they whirred off under their own power.*

You will quickly notice the vivid auditory and visual images he creates. Comparison—literal and figurative—and rhetorical devices also contribute to the effect McFarland seeks to convey. At least one comparison appears as he likens the car to "the toy cars he had played with as a boy," and he personifies the lines as "[creeping] towards him," moving toward Stephen "sadly, slowly," examples of alliteration. The fences are called "endless"—a hyperbole, of course. The engine roars and the lines whir onomatopoetically: the evocative language involves the reader in the description. The dominant impression is subjective. From Stephen's point of view there is much movement and the lines are the central focus.

◆

CHECKLIST FOR DESCRIPTION ESSAY

1. Is your point-of-view appropriate for you audience? Can you identify your audience?
2. What is your purpose in the essay? Are you informing or attempting to provide a specific response?
3. Did you include a dominant impression in your description? Is it explicitly stated or implied?
4. Did you check to make certain your details are concrete and supportive of the dominant impression?

5. Is your essay arranged emphatically, spatially, or chronologically?
6. Did you include more than just sensory impressions?
7. Does your figurative language offer fresh images and not just clichés?
8. Did you edit your paper carefully, checking for major grammatical and spelling errors?

In the following descriptive narrative, student Kathleen Looper recounts her childhood home, recollecting nostalgically her earlier surroundings and family. Notice how she moves spatially through her description. What examples of figurative language can you find?

GOING HOME

Kathleen Looper

My parents' home is located on three-and-a-half acres south of Akron, Ohio. The area used to be a farming community as recently as the early 1950s. The house faces Pickle Road, which is a combination of tar and gravel. The best time for surfacing the road, in the county's opinion anyway, is the middle of summer when the high humidity and the blazing sun keeps the tar the consistency of melted caramel; it continues to ooze up through the gravel long after the workmen have finished. The edges of the road are always more tar than gravel, and it sticks to shoes and feet. Tires fling the hot sticky mess onto the wheel wells and rocker panels of the cars as they hurry by. The aroma that rises from the hot tar is barely noticeable when compared to the smell of burning rubber that pours from the tire factories in town. There was a time when Akron, Ohio, was known as the "Rubber Capital of the World"; those who lived and worked in the area were used to the smell of burning rubber and therefore did not mind the insignificant fragrance of melting tar, which saturated the air on a hot summer day. From the road the house looks like a picture one might find on an old calendar, the kind of picture a mother takes, not framed especially well, but pleasing to the eye. The house is old. My father and his father built it in 1949. Actually, they started it then, and now, decades later, it is still not quite finished. It is red with a large front porch of concrete with four large square wooden pillars. Dad also built the porch himself and believed that everything that is required to stand up must be set in concrete. Once my brother Richard misjudged the driveway and ran into the porch with Dad's van. One of the pillars broke off, flew into the air, and crashed down on the roof of the van. It popped out of its place like a child's broken tooth, leaving the rest of the porch intact. Because the remaining three pillars were also set in cement, Richard would have had to run into each one separately before the roof would have budged. Richard's accident was merely one more inconvenience to Dad; it only presented a new challenge—to reconstruct a pillar that could be anchored somehow in the same spot and reset in cement.

The original garage, now Dad's shop, is attached to the house by a small enclosed breezeway. Everybody had breezeways back in the '50s. I don't know why; it's not as if there was ever a breeze—except during the winter. One Christmas when there were presents for eight to fit around a tree, someone thought it would be a good idea to set up Christmas in the breezeway. "Christmas" meant a live, pine-forest-smelling evergreen, which occupied most of the room, and a cardboard fireplace. We did not have a real fireplace, and Mom thought it would save the woodwork if we could hang our stockings somewhere besides the painted windowsills. It was pretty realistic looking, too, with cardboard logs and a bright cellophane fire, which seemed to flicker when lit from behind with yellow and red electric lights. But, cozy as it may sound, December in Ohio is not the perfect season for relaxing on the breezeway. So, from then on, the live pine and the fake cardboard fireplace were allowed to remain in the house. Dad's shop in the garage is larger than the house, with two front windows like large rectangular eyes staring at the road, as if to watch for customers. The house also has two eyes, two large picture windows through which we could watch the world go by. And those on the outside can look into the rooms behind the windows, like children peering into a dollhouse. The living room and kitchen lie behind these windows. The house was built this way intentionally because Mother wanted to be able to see what was happening outside. The front door sits quietly between them like the nose on our faces: it seems to do nothing but is vital to our existence. The two bedroom dormers upstairs seem to peek over the roof of the porch like raised eyebrows, to indicate approval or disapproval as the house watches all who travel on Pickle Road.

The house and garage sit back from the road, a distance which allowed us to use the front lawn for a baseball diamond. Mom always preferred that we play at home. There were five maple trees my dad dug out of the woods, and he and Grandpa planted them three in a row along the yard and two in a second row right behind them. When one of the trees died in the back row, it left one lone maple tree looking rather out of place. But during our baseball games it was in the perfect place to serve as first base, and the tree directly across from it was third base. We had to improvise for second base with a rock, an old chair cushion from the shop, someone's shirt, or an extra mitt; we grabbed whatever was available at the time and only had a problem if the mitt was needed for play or the owner of the shirt wanted it back. Dad had not envisioned the baseball diamond in his plan for the yard, for if he had, I know he would have planted a tree for second base.

I visited the old home this past summer, the first summer visit in five years, and the house seemed smaller than I remembered. We usually visit at Christmas when it's cold and the snow covers the ground and house with a white blanket and there are no leaves on the trees. But this visit there was no snow to hide the changes. The trees are larger now, and the house seems small. The house used to stand out and the trees were merely ornaments on the lawn, but now the house seems to be slipping into the greenery. Where the house once stood on flat ground, it is now hidden in a jungle of maple trees and weeping willows. The flat spot of dirt that we knew as Home Plate has disappeared and has been replaced by thick green grass that perfectly matches the rest of the yard and is slowly creeping into the gravel and dirt driveway, crowding it out of its due space. The trees on either side of the house used not to make such a thick wall. Where they used to give only the impression of a fence, they now form a barrier heavy enough to make one forget that there are houses on the other side.

A row of pine trees on the right of the house overlooks a bank and separates Dad's home from that of the neighbors on the hill. Mr. and Mrs. Scott have lived there many years now, but it is still the Weavers' place to us. On the left edge of the property, a white cross-rail fence separates the grounds from a piece of land Dad sold unwillingly when he needed money to pay my sister's hospital expenses. Weeping willow trees flank the fence from the road to the top of the drive and around to the back of the house. The drive forms a horseshoe around the house, fitting neatly between the two sets of trees. The weeping willows form the left top of the horse-shoe down to the road while the maple trees line up across the front yard; then on the right the row of pine trees stand. The trees seem to form a wall around the house, making it look as though it is sinking into a great hole, or maybe that it's the ripe red tomato in a large salad.

The house seems now, many years later, to be sinking out of sight, engulfed in plant life, just barely able to peek out through the trees. I fear I will come home one summer day and the place where the house once stood will have disappeared into the trees and there will be no voices to lead the way. I will go "home again," but there will be nothing there.

Read E. B. White's essay "Once More to the Lake." As you read, note the descriptive techniques he uses, paying particular attention to the figures of speech and vivid images. Consider White's dominant impression and how it ties together his descriptive link between the past, the present, and the future

ONCE MORE TO THE LAKE

E. B. White

August 1941

One summer, along about 1904, my father rented a camp on a lake in Maine and took us all there for the month of August. We all got ringworm from some kittens and had to rub Pond's Extract on our arms and legs night and morning, and my father rolled over in a canoe with all his clothes on; but outside of that the vacation was a success and from then on none of us ever thought there was any place in the world like that lake in Maine. We returned summer after summer—always on August 1 for one month. I have since become a salt-water man, but some-times in summer there are days when the restlessness of the tides and the fearful cold of the seawater and the incessant wind that blows across the afternoon and into the evening make me wish for the placidity of a lake in the woods. A few weeks ago this feeling got so strong I bought myself a couple of bass hooks and a spinner and returned to the lake where we used to go, for a week's fishing and to revisit old haunts.

I took along my son, who had never had any fresh water up his nose and who had seen lily pads only from train windows. On the journey over to the lake I began to wonder what it would be like. I wondered how time would have marred this unique, this holy spot—the coves and streams, the hills that the sun set behind, the camps and the paths behind the camps. I was sure that the tarred road would have found it out, and I wondered in what other ways it would be desolated. It is strange how much you can remember about places like that once you allow your mind to return into the grooves that lead back. You remember one thing, and that suddenly reminds you of another thing. I guess I remembered clearest of all the early mornings, when the lake was cool and motionless, remembered how the bedroom smelled of the lumber it was made of and of the wet woods whose scent entered through the screen. The partitions in the camp were thin and did not extend clear to the top of the rooms, and as I was always the first up I would dress softly so as not to wake the others, and sneak out into the sweet outdoors and start out in the canoe, keeping close along the shore in the long shadows of the pines. I remembered being very careful never to rub my paddle against the gunwale for fear of disturbing the stillness of the cathedral.

The lake had never been what you would call a wild lake. There were cottages sprinkled around the shores, and it was in farming country although the shores of the lake were quite heavily wooded. Some of the cottages were owned by nearby farmers, and you would live at the shore and eat your meals at the farmhouse. That's what our family did. But although it wasn't wild, it was a fairly large and undisturbed lake and there were places in it that, to a child at least, seemed infinitely remote and primeval.

I was right about the tar: it led to within half a mile of the shore. But when I got back there, with my boy, and we settled into a camp near a farmhouse and into the kind of summertime I had known, I could tell that it was going to be pretty much the same as it had been before—I knew it, lying in bed the first morning smelling the bedroom and hearing the boy sneak quietly out and go off along the shore in a boat. I began to sustain the illusion that he was I, and therefore, by simple transposition, that I was my father. This sensation persisted, kept cropping up all the time we were there. It was not an entirely new feeling, but in this setting it grew much stronger. I seemed to be living a dual existence. I would be in the middle of some simple act, I would be picking up a bait box or laying down a table fork, or I would be saying something and suddenly it would be not I but my father who was saying the words or making the gesture. It gave me a creepy sensation.

We went fishing the first morning. I felt the same damp moss covering the worms in the bait can, and saw the dragonfly alight on the tip of my rod as it hovered a few inches from the surface of the water. It was the arrival of this fly that convinced me beyond any doubt that everything was as it always had been, that the years were a mirage and that there had been no years. The small waves were the same, chucking the rowboat under the chin as we fished at anchor, and the boat was the same boat, the same color green and the ribs broken in the same places, and under the floorboards the same fresh water leavings and debris—the dead hellgrammite, the wisps of moss, the rusty discarded fishhook, the dried blood from yesterday's catch. We stared silently at the tips of our rods, at the dragonflies that came and went. I lowered the tip of mine into the water, tentatively, pensively dislodging the fly, which darted two feet away, poised, darted two feet back, and came to rest again a little farther up the rod. There had been no years between the ducking of this dragonfly and the other one—the one that was part of memory. I looked at the boy, who was silently watching his fly, and it was my hands that held his rod, my eyes watching. I felt dizzy and didn't know which rod I was at the end of.

We caught two bass, hauling them in briskly as though they were mackerel, pulling them over the side of the boat in a businesslike manner without any landing net, and stunning them with a blow on the back of the head. When we got back for a swim before lunch, the lake was exactly where we had left it, the same number of inches from the dock, and there was only the merest suggestion of a breeze. This seemed an utterly enchanted sea, this lake you could leave to its own devices for a few hours and come back to, and find that it had not stirred, this constant and trustworthy body of water. In the shallows, the dark, water-soaked sticks and twigs, smooth and old, were undulating in clusters on the bottom against the clean ribbed sand, and the track of the mussel was plain. A school of minnows swam by, each minnow with its small individual shadow, doubling the attendance, so clear and sharp in the sunlight. Some of the other campers were in swimming, along the shore, one of them with a cake of soap, and the water felt thin and clear and unsubstantial. Over the years there had been this person with the cake of soap, this cultist, and here he was. There had been no years.

Up to the farmhouse to dinner through the teeming dusty field, the road under our sneakers was only a two-track road. The middle track was missing, the one with the marks of the hooves and the splotches of dried, flaky manure. There had always been three tracks to choose from in choosing which track to walk in; now the choice was narrowed down to two. For a moment I missed terribly the middle alternative. But the way led past the tennis court, and something about the way it lay there in the sun reassured me the tape had loosened along the backline, the alleys were green with plantains and other weeds, and the net (installed in June and removed in September) sagged in the dry noon, and the whole place steamed with midday heat and hunger and emptiness. There was a choice of pie for dessert, and one was blueberry and one was apple, and the waitresses were the same country girls, there having been no passage of time, only the illusion of it as in a dropped curtain—the waitresses were still fifteen; their hair had been washed, that was the only difference—they had been to the movies and seen the pretty girls with the clean hair.

Summertime, oh, summertime, pattern of life indelible with fade-proof lake, the wood unshatterable, the pasture with the sweetfern and the juniper forever and ever, summer without end; this was the background, and the life along the shore was the design, the cottages with their innocent and tranquil design, their tiny docks with the flagpole and the American flag floating against the white clouds in the blue sky, the little paths over the roots of the trees leading from camp to camp and the paths leading back to the outhouse and the can of lime for sprinkling, and at the souvenir counters at the store the miniature birch-bark canoes and the postcards that showed things looking a little better than they looked. This was the American family at play, escaping the city heat, wondering whether the newcomers in the camp at the head of the cove were "common" or "nice," wondering whether it was true that the people who drove up for Sunday dinner at the farmhouse were turned away because there wasn't enough chicken.

It seemed to me, as I kept remembering all this, that those times and those summers had been infinitely precious and worth saving. There had been jollity and peace and goodness. The arriving (at the beginning of August) had been so big a business in itself, at the railway station the farm wagon drawn up, the first smell of the pine laden air, the first glimpse of the smiling farmer, and the great importance of the trunks and your father's enormous authority in such matters, and the feel of the wagon under you for the long ten-mile haul, and at the top of the last long hill catching the first view of the lake after eleven months of not seeing this cherished body of water. The shouts and cries of the other campers when they saw you, and the trunks to be unpacked, to give up their rich burden. (Arriving was less exciting nowadays, when you sneaked up in your car and parked it under a tree near the camp and took out the bags and in five minutes it was all over, no fuss, no loud wonderful fuss about trunks.)

Peace and goodness and jollity. The only thing that was wrong now, really, was the sound of the place, an unfamiliar nervous sound of the outboard motors. This was the note that jarred, the one thing that would sometimes break the illusion and set the years moving. In those other summer times all motors were inboard; and when they were at a little distance, the noise they made was a sedative, an ingredient of summer sleep. They were one-cylinder and two-cylinder engines, and some were make-and-break and some were jump-spark, but they all made a sleepy sound across the lake. The one-lungers throbbed and fluttered, and the twin cylinder ones purred and purred, and that was a quiet sound, too. But now the campers all had outboards. In the daytime, in the hot mornings, these motors made a petulant, irritable sound; at night in the still evening when the afterglow lit the water, they whined about one's ears like mosquitoes. My boy loved our rented outboard, and his great desire was to achieve single-handed mastery over it, and authority, and he soon learned the trick of choking it a little (but not too much), and the adjustment of the needle valve. Watching him I would remember the things you could do with the old one-cylinder engine with the heavy flywheel, how you could have it eating out of your hand if you got really close to it spiritually. Motorboats in those days didn't have clutches, and you would make a landing by shutting off the motor at the proper time and coasting in with a dead rudder. But there was a way of reversing them, if you learned the trick, by cutting the switch and putting it on again exactly on the final dying revolution of the flywheel, so that it would kick back against compression and begin reversing. Approaching a dock in a strong following breeze, it was difficult to slow up sufficiently by the ordinary coasting method, and if a boy felt he had complete mastery over his motor, he was tempted to keep it running beyond its time and then reverse it a few feet from the dock. It took a cool nerve, because if you threw the switch a twentieth of a second too soon you would catch the flywheel when it still had speed enough to go up past center, and the boat would leap ahead, charging bull-fashion at the dock.

We had a good week at the camp. The bass were biting well and the sun shone endlessly, day after day. We would be tired at night and lie down in the accumulated heat of the little bedrooms after the long hot day and the breeze would stir almost imperceptibly outside and the smell of the swamp drift in through the rusty screens. Sleep would come easily and in the morning the red squirrel would be on the roof, tapping out his gay routine. I kept remembering everything, lying in bed in the mornings—the small steamboat that had a long rounded stern like the lip of a Ubangi, and quietly she ran on the moonlight sails, when the older boys played their mandolins and the girls sang and we ate doughnuts dipped in sugar, and how sweet the music was on the water in the shining night, and what it had felt like to think about girls then. After breakfast we would go up to the store and the things were in the same place—the minnows in a bottle, the plugs and spinners disarranged and pawed over by the youngsters from the boy's camp, the Fig Newtons and the Beeman's gum. Outside, the road was tarred and cars stood in front of the store. Inside, all was just as it had always been, except there was more Coca-Cola and not so much Moxie and root beer and birch beer and sarsaparilla. We would walk out with the bottle of pop apiece and sometimes the pop would backfire up our noses and hurt. We explored the streams, quietly, where the turtles slid off the sunny logs and dug their way into the soft bottom; and we lay on the town wharf and fed worms to the tame bass. Everywhere we went I had trouble making out which was I, the one walking at my side, the one walking in my pants.

One afternoon while we were at that lake a thunderstorm came up. It was like the revival of an old melodrama that I had seen long ago with childish awe. The second-act climax of the drama of the electrical disturbance over a lake in America had not changed in any important respect. This was the big scene, still the big scene. The whole thing was so familiar, the first feeling of oppression and heat and a general air around camp of not wanting to go very far away. In mid-afternoon (it was all the same) a curious darkening of the sky, and a lull in everything that had made life tick; and then the way the boats suddenly swung the other way at their moorings with the coming of a breeze out of the new quarter, and the premonitory rumble. Then the kettledrum, then the snare, then the bass drum and cymbals, then crackling light against the dark, and the gods grinning and licking their chops in the hills. Afterward the calm, the rain steadily rustling in the calm lake, the return of light and hope and spirits, and the campers running out in joy and relief to go swimming in the rain, their bright cries perpetuating the deathless joke about how they were getting simply drenched, and the children screaming with delight at the new sensation of bathing in the rain, and the joke about getting drenched linking the generations in a strong indestructible chain. And the comedian who waded in carrying an umbrella.

When the others went swimming my son said he was going in, too. He pulled his dripping trunks from the line where they had hung all through the shower and wrung them out. Languidly, and with no thought of going in, I watched him, his hard little body, skinny and bare, saw him wince slightly as he pulled up around his vitals the small, soggy, icy garment. As he buckled the swollen belt, suddenly my groin felt the chill of death.

NARRATION

Description is often used in conjunction with narrative. Every time you tell your friends and family about a particular event in your day, you use narration. Any time you tell a story to answer, "What happened?" you use narration. Usually, there is a point to the details you choose to include in your recitation. Your details support a central idea. If the day was horrendous, your details turn into a long whine; if the day was wonderful, your details bolster the effect. A joke, a journal entry, a story, an historical perspective—all require narrative.

Implementation

Narration may be used any number of ways:

1. as an introductory or concluding technique to gain the reader's interest and create a vivid beginning or ending for the essay.

2. as an essay in itself to explain an event, a process, or to make a point.

3. throughout an essay to provide personal examples.

Strategy

The sequence of events, called plot in fiction, indicates the order in which events happen. You may want to use chronological order to show how events unfold. Begin with the setting and situation and proceed to tell the story from first to last. In the process you will pay attention, again, to logical details necessary to fulfill your purpose. Narrative should usually develop causally: an event should follow any preceding one logically. You may want to present events out of their normal order to emphasize an important effect you are trying to create. Be careful with this kind of development, however. No matter what order you choose, you must describe the beginning, middle, and end to make causal relationships clear. As you present your narrative, you will find that some kind of conflict is intrinsic to your discussion.

Conflict. This is, of course, a clash of wills, characters, or forces. It can be internal (within you or the central character you are presenting) or external (between two people or forces). Presenting conflict in an extended narrative creates an essential tension necessary to good narrative writing. Unless there is conflict, there really is not much suspense—or interest—generated in the reader.

Setting. For the most part, setting establishes where and when the events take place. It may be used straightforwardly to emphasize your point or it may be used ironically.

Selection of details. In a narrative the author chooses details that create the illusion of reality for the reader, verisimilitude. Your selection of details helps you make your point and create vivid impressions for the audience. The point of your story will be emphasized by your handling of setting, sequence, and people or characters.

Characters. These are the people involved: how you introduce and describe them gives the reader an understanding of your point. They may be described physically or psychologically or both, but the effect is much more vivid if you do not tell the reader how to feel. Instead you need to describe the character in such a way that the reader knows what kind of person he or she is. Mark Twain once said that it is not enough to tell about an old lady who shows up and is unhappy; "bring her on and let her scream" her head off.

Time. When you describe, you are probably more interested in spatial relationships, but in narrative the important relationships are most concerned with time. You will use chronological order most of the time to indicate the beginning, middle, and end of the incident, but as a writer you must decide whether to compress time or to emphasize or de-emphasize certain aspects. Sometimes, you will want to start *in medias res*, in the midst of the action, to vivify the events and put the reader into the action. No matter which kind of sequence you choose, be particularly careful with verb tenses. In most cases *present tense* makes sense unless you are referring to incidents which occur in the past of the characters.

Dialogue. Another way to make your narrative vivid and immediate is to use direct dialogue rather than referring to conversation indirectly. In other words, you must check your handbook for the proper use of quotation marks and punctuation to allow your characters to speak for themselves.

Point of view. While you often use third person ("she," "he") in academic writing, in personal narrative, especially, you may be told to use first person ("I") in order to create immediacy and interest. All your choices in any kind of writing are determined by your audience and your particular purpose, which are essential to the way you present your point. Keep your readers firmly in mind and present significant details in descriptive language tailored to them.

Organization

Narration, whether used to relate incidents in fiction or sequences in non-fiction, will always move your reader through situations and processes in time. Therefore you must have a clear idea of the progression of events through time that you are going to convey. You might, for example, want to set up a timeline on a sheet of paper with the major events in your sequence placed alongside it. You will also want to be extremely careful with the tenses you use so as not to confuse your reader. While many narratives, such as memoirs, are recalled from the past and require the use of past and past perfect tenses, careful use of the present tense can give immediacy to your narrative. For example, notice the shifts in tense (highlighted in bold) in the following passage from the opening of John Updike's short story, "A&P," which is being retold by Sammy after the event:

> In **walks** these three girls in nothing but bathing suits. I**'m** in the third check-out slot, with my back to the door, so I **don't** see them until they**'re** over by the bread. The one that **caught** my eye first **was** the one in the plaid green two-piece. She **was** a chunky kid, with a good tan and a sweet broad soft-looking can with those two crescents of white just under it, where the sun never **seems** to hit, at the top of the backs of her legs. I **stood** there with my hand on a box of HiHo crackers **trying** to remember if I **rang** it up or not. I **ring** it up again and the customer **starts** giving me hell. She**'s** one of these cash-register-watchers, a witch about fifty with rouge on her cheekbones and no eyebrows, and I **know** it made her day to trip me up. She**'d been watching** cash registers forty years and probably never **seen** a mistake before.

Sammy begins his story *in medias res* and places us in the checkout stand with him as he watches three girls enter the grocery store. The dramatic use of present tense captures our attention, just as the three girls earlier captured his. He then switches to past tense as he describes the girls and his own frozen attention: he can't remember if he **rang** up the crackers or not. He switches again to present tense as he focuses on the old lady in front of him, and then switches to past perfect in describing her probable previous cash-register-watching activity.

In non-fiction narrative, particularly if you are explaining a process, you must pay close attention to your audience and your purpose. How much can you assume your audience knows? How much detail will be needed to convey the process or events? The following paragraph explains—narrates—the operation of Darwinian natural selection in creating the giraffe's long neck. It was published in *Natural History*, the monthly magazine of the American Museum of Natural History in New York City. The magazine is written for non-specialists interested in science:

> A Darwinian explanation [of the giraffe's long neck] assumes that the neck length has always varied among the individuals in a giraffe population. In the past, the giraffes with the longest necks reached the highest leaves, which were more abundant, and may have held more nutrients than the lower leaves, but were inaccessible to shorter-necked giraffes. Overall, then, the longest-necked animals were the best-fed members of the population. Better nutrition translated into longer or healthier lives, and so longer-necked giraffes produced more offspring than shorter-necked giraffes. With time, differential rates of survival and reproduction skewed the giraffe population toward animals with elongated necks. The key to the mechanism of Darwinian evolution is natural selection.

Here the authors, Luis and Monika Espinasa, keep their audience firmly in mind. The diction is simple and straightforward, although they assume their audience will know such words and terms as "nutrients" and "differential rates of survival." They stay in the past tense and include such transitions as "In the past," "Overall, then," and "With time" to move the narrative along.

✦

CHECKLIST FOR NARRATION ESSAY

1. What is the overall purpose of your narrative? Is it clear? Is the mood appropriate for your purpose?
2. Is the setting included in your narrative?
3. What is your narrative's conflict? Is the conflict dramatic enough?
4. If you use dialogue, does it enrich or detract from your purpose or character portrayal?
5. If a flashback or flash-forward is used, does it highlight the purpose and help create the effect of the overall essay?
6. Do all the characters you include contribute significantly to the essay's rhetorical situation and purpose?
7. Is your point-of-view clear and consistent throughout the essay?
8. Have you included enough transitional devices to create fluidity in your narrative?
9. Have you avoided the commonplace and clichés?
10. Did you edit your essay carefully, checking for major grammatical and spelling errors?

The following student narrative describes a memorable time in her past that has since altered the way she views nature, particularly the threat of turbulent weather.

A SEASONAL TWIST

Tammy Bogs

When I was five years old, my grandparents owned a large ranch in Marquez, Texas, about 150 miles north outside of Houston. My parents, aunts, uncles, and other family members usually went up on weekends. We had cows, horses, chickens, and pigs there, as well as a garden for growing different vegetables. That made for quite a bit of work, but it was fun, too. Our favorite time of year was spring because the pastures were alive with color. Bluebonnets, Indian Paintbrushes, and other types of beautiful wildflowers grew there and thrived on the seasonal showers.

One spring, my grandfather invited his sister and brother-in-law, who lived in Maryland, to come visit for the weekend. They usually visited us every year, but only in Houston. My great-uncle Will did not really care for the country much, having lived his whole life in the city. But for some reason that year he and my great-aunt Virginia agreed to come to the ranch for the weekend. Because of this, the main house was full, so my parents offered to stay in the bunkhouse. There was no way any of us could have predicted that our choices could have had dangerous consequences because the following morning after we had all arrived, just after breakfast, a tornado swept through, sweeping away our plans for a relaxing weekend with it.

Since they had planned for us to go horseback riding that morning and had even talked Uncle Will into joining us, my dad and uncles had gone down to the stables to saddle the horses. My mom and I had returned to the bunkhouse to change into jeans and grab a few things. We noticed on the walk over that what had begun as a breezy but sunny spring day had changed dramatically since we had walked over to the main house for breakfast. The sky had darkened considerably, and there was a definite threat of rain in the air. I can remember my mother telling me that we should hurry, but I loved picking the wildflowers so much that our progress was slow at first. As the rain started to fall and the wind increased, my mom suddenly grabbed my hand and we began to run. At the time I thought it was so we would not get wet, and I even giggled when she suddenly swept me up in her arms and ran. You see, while my attention had been on the ground, my mother's had been focused on the sky and the clouds that had begun to swirl in a circular pattern a good distance away. I can remember thinking how pretty it was, all the different shades of gray swirling together in the sky above. I started to wiggle in my mother's arms, wanting her to put me down so I could watch, but she yelled at me to stop, and honestly it was not her yelling at me that made me stop; it was the fear in her voice. This was the first clue I had that something was very wrong, because I think it was the first time I had ever seen my mother afraid. We got to the bunkhouse and ran straight for the small bathroom at the front of the house—the one with no windows. We huddled together on the bathroom floor, me in my mother's lap while she said the "Our Father" over and over. Soon I could not really hear the words because the wind was so loud, along with the rain falling heavily overhead on the tin roof. The next sound I could hear, but only faintly, was my dad shouting for us as he came through the door. My mom called out to him, saying that we had to get out of there and back to the main house, and he yelled back that it was too late; we would never make it in time because the tornado was headed straight for us. I can remember wondering briefly what a tornado was exactly, but then a sound of devastation I will never forget seemed to fill the world.

My father grabbed us up and we stepped into the walk-in shower. Since the shower pipe was on the outside of the wall, he gathered my mother and me into his arms and then held on to the pipe. As the wind roared deafeningly, suddenly a sound like a skill saw laboring through metal roared above the wind and the roof of the house was completely ripped off. Then, in an instant, it was over, and what had once been a house was now rubble with only three of the four main walls still standing.

Luckily for us, it was not a particularly large tornado, nor had it hit the house directly, or else my family and I could have been seriously injured or killed. It had come close enough to cause serious damage, but other than some scratches and bruises and my father's arm being dislocated from holding my mother and me and the pipe, we were safe.

Meanwhile, my grandfather and uncles had taken shelter in the barn, which had been spared along with the main house, and everyone else was safe. But all they could see from their angle was only two standing walls left of the bunkhouse, so they were terrified that something horrible had happened to us. They jumped into the truck and raced over to what was left of the bunkhouse, praying that we were still alive. They managed to help us out of the debris, and I recall vividly my grandfather pulling me up and holding me close, as if he never wanted to let me go. They got us all out safely, but when we returned to the main house, things were in a bit of an uproar. My grandmother and aunts were arguing with my great uncle, who had his suitcases in hand and was headed for their car. This angered my grandmother because she felt that he should have been a little less concerned with himself, and more concerned about everyone else. Nevertheless, he and my great-aunt were in the car and gone before anyone had the chance even to say goodbye, to which my grandmother said we were probably well rid of them anyway.

My father told me later that the tornado was similar to how life could be in a way because one has to endure the bad and to be able to enjoy the good things in life. What I got out of this experience is that one should always have a healthy respect for the weather, its beauty as well as its destructive power, especially tornadoes. To this day, when the clouds start to gather and the weather appears ominous, I always head indoors to check the Weather Channel to make sure that there is nothing more than a rainstorm on the way.

DIGGING

Andre Dubus

That hot June in LaFayette, Louisiana, I was sixteen, I would be seventeen in August, I weighed one hundred and five pounds, and my ruddy, broad-chested father wanted me to have a summer job. I only wanted the dollar allowance he gave me each week, and the dollar and a quarter I earned caddying for him on weekends and Wednesday afternoons. With a quarter I could go to a movie, or buy a bottle of beer, or a pack of cigarettes to smoke secretly. I did not have a girlfriend, so I did not have to buy drinks or food or movie tickets for anyone else. I did not want to work. I wanted to drive around with my friends, or walk with them downtown, to stand in front of the department store, comb our ducktails, talk, look at girls.

My father was a civil engineer, and the district manager for the Gulf States Utilities Company. He had been working for them since he left college, beginning as a surveyor, wearing boots and khakis and, in a holster on his belt, a twenty-two-caliber pistol for cottonmouths. At home he was quiet; in the evenings he sat in his easy chair, and smoked, and read: *Time, The Saturday Evening Post, Collier's, The Reader's Digest*, detective novels, books about golf, and Book of the Month Club novels. He loved to talk, and he did this at parties I listened to from my bedroom, and with his friends on the golf course, and drinking in the clubhouse after playing eighteen holes. I listened to more of my father's conversations about politics and golf and his life and the world than I ever engaged in during the nearly twenty-two years I lived with him. I was afraid of angering him, seeing his blue eyes, and reddening face, hearing the words he would use to rebuke me; but what I feared most was his voice, suddenly and harshly rising. He never yelled for long, only a few sentences, but they emptied me, as if his voice had pulled my soul from my body. His voice seemed to empty the house too and, when he stopped yelling, the house filled with silence. He did not yell often. That sound was not part of our family life. The fear of it was part of my love for him.

I was shy with him. Since my forties, I have believed that he was shy with me too, and I hope it was not as painful for him as it was for me. I think my shyness had very little to do with my fear. Other boys had fathers who yelled longer and more often, fathers who spanked them or, when they were in their teens, slapped or punched them. My father spanked me only three times, probably because he did not know of most of my transgressions. My friends with harsher fathers were neither afraid nor shy; they quarreled with their fathers, provoked them. My father sired a sensitive boy, easily hurt or frightened, and he worried about me; I knew he did when I was a boy, and he told me this on his deathbed, when I was a Marine captain.

My imagination gave me a dual life: I lived in my body, and at the same time lived a life no one could see. All my life, I have told myself stories, and have talked in my mind to friends. Imagine my father sitting at supper with my mother and two older sisters and me: I am ten and small and appear distracted. Every year at school, there is a bully, sometimes a new one, sometimes the one from the year before. I draw bullies to me, not because I am small, but because they know I will neither fight nor inform on them. I will take their pushes or pinches or punches, and try not to cry, and I will pretend I am not hurt. My father does not know this. He only sees me at supper, and I am not there. I am riding a horse and shooting bad men. My father eats, glances at me. I know he is trying to see who I am, who I will be.

Before my teens, he took me to professional wrestling matches because I wanted to go; he told me they were fake, and I did not believe him. We listened to championship boxing matches on the radio. When I was not old enough to fire a shotgun, he took me dove hunting with his friends: we crouched in a ditch facing a field, and I watched the doves fly toward us and my father rising to shoot; then I ran to fetch the warm, dead, and delicious birds. In summer, he took me fishing with his friends; we walked in woods to creeks and bayous and fished with bamboo poles. When I was ten, he learned to play golf and stopped hunting and fishing, and on weekends I was his caddy. I did not want to be, I wanted to play with my friends, but when I became a man and left home, I was grateful that I had spent those afternoons watching him, listening to him. A minor-league baseball team made our town its home, and my father took me to games, usually with my mother. When I was twelve or so, he taught me to play golf, and sometimes I played nine holes with him; more often and more comfortably, I played with other boys.

If my father and I were not watching or listening to something and responding to it, or were not doing something, but were simply alone together, I could not talk, and he did not, and I felt that I should, and I was ashamed. That June of my seventeenth year, I could not tell him that I did not want a job. He talked to a friend of his, a building contractor, who hired me as a carpenter's helper; my pay was seventy-five cents an hour.

On a Monday morning, my father drove me to work. I would ride the bus home and, next day, would start riding the bus to work. Probably my father drove me that morning because it was my first day; when I was twelve, he had taken me to a store to buy my first pair of long pants; we boys wore shorts and, in fall and winter, knickers and long socks till we were twelve; and he had taken me to a barber for my first haircut. In the car, I sat frightened, sadly resigned, and feeling absolutely incompetent. I had the lunch my mother had put in a brown paper bag, along with a mason jar with sugar and squeezed lemons in it, so I could make lemonade with water from the cooler. We drove to a street with houses and small stores and parked at a corner where, on a flat piece of land, men were busy. They were building a liquor store, and I assumed I would spend my summer handing things to a carpenter. I hoped he would be patient and kind.

As a boy in Louisiana's benevolent winters and hot summers, I had played outdoors with friends: we built a clubhouse, chased one another on bicycles, shot air rifles at birds, tin cans, bottles, trees; in fall and winter, wearing shoulder pads and helmets, we played football on someone's very large side lawn; and in summer we played baseball in a field that a father mowed for us; he also built us a backstop of wood and chicken wire. None of us played well enough to be on a varsity team; but I wanted that gift, not knowing that it was a gift, and I felt ashamed that I did not have it. Now we drove cars, smoked, drank in nightclubs. This was French Catholic country; we could always buy drinks. Sometimes we went on dates with girls, but more often we looked at them and talked about them; or visited them, when several girls were gathered at the home of a girl whose parents were out for the evening. I had never done physical work except caddying, pushing a lawn mower, and raking leaves, and I was walking from the car with my father toward workingmen. My father wore his straw hat and seersucker suit. He introduced me to the foreman and said: "Make a man of him."

Then he left. The foreman wore a straw hat and looked old; everyone looked old; the foreman was probably thirty-five. I stood mutely, waiting for him to assign me to some good-hearted Cajun carpenter. He assigned me a pickax and a shovel and told me to get into the trench and go to work. In all four sides of the trench were files of black men, swinging picks and shoveling. The trench was about three feet deep and it would be the building's foundation; I went to where the foreman pointed, and laid my tools on the ground; two black men made a space for me, and I jumped between them. They smiled and we greeted one another. I would learn days later that they earned a dollar an hour. They were men with families and I knew this was unjust, as everything else was for black people. But on that first morning, I did not know what they were being paid, I did not know their names, only that one was working behind me and one in front, and they were good to me and stronger than I could ever be. All I really knew in those first hours under the hot sun was raising the pickax and swinging it down, raising it and swinging, again and again till the earth was loose; then putting the pick on the ground beside me and taking the shovel and plunging it into dirt that I lifted and tossed beside the trench.

I did not have the strength for this: not in my back, my legs, my arms, my shoulders. Certainly not in my soul. I only wanted it to end. The air was very humid, and sweat dripped on my face and arms, soaked my shirt and jeans. My hands gripping the pick or shovel were sore, my palms burned, the muscles in my arms ached, and my breath was quick. Sometimes I saw tiny black spots before my eyes. Weakly, I raised the pick, straightening my back, then swung it down, bending my body with it, and it felt heavier than I was, more durable, this thing of wood and steel that was melting me. I laid it on the ground and picked up the shovel and pushed it into the dirt, lifted it, grunted, and emptied it beside the trench. The sun, always my friend till now, burned me, and my mouth and throat were dry, and often I climbed out of the trench and went to the large tin water cooler with a block of ice in it and water from a hose. At the cooler were paper cups and salt tablets, and I swallowed salt and drank and drank, and poured water onto my head and face; then I went back to the trench, the shovel, the pick.

Nausea came in the third or fourth hour. I kept swinging the pick, pushing and lifting the shovel. I became my sick, hot, tired, and hurting flesh. Or it became me; so, for an hour or more, I tasted a very small piece of despair. At noon in Lafayette, a loud whistle blew, and in the cathedral the bell rang. I could not hear the bell where we worked, but I heard the whistle, and lowered the shovel and looked around. I was dizzy and sick. All the men had stopped working and were walking toward shade. One of the men with me said it was time to eat, and I climbed out of the trench and walked with the black men to the shade of the toolshed. The white men went to another shaded place; I do not remember what work they had been doing that morning, but it was not with picks and shovels in the trench. Everyone looked hot but comfortable. The black men sat talking and began to eat and drink. My bag of lunch and jar with lemons and sugar were on the ground in the shade. Still I stood, gripped by nausea. I looked at the black men and at my lunch bag. Then my stomach tightened and everything in it rose, and I went around the corner of the shed where no one could see me and, bending over, I vomited and moaned and heaved until it ended. I went to the water cooler and rinsed my mouth and spat, and then I took another paper cup and drank. I walked back to the shade and lay on my back, tasting vomit. One of the black men said: "You got to eat."

"I threw up," I said, and closed my eyes and slept for the rest of the hour that everyone—students and workers—had for the noon meal. At home, my nineteen-year-old sister and my mother and father were eating dinner, meat and rice and gravy, vegetables and salad and iced tea with a leaf of mint; and an oscillating fan cooled them. My twenty-two year-old sister was married. At one o'clock, the whistle blew, and I woke up and stood and one of the black men said: "Are you all right?"

I nodded. If I had spoken, I might have wept. When I was a boy, I could not tell a man what I felt, if I believed what I felt was unmanly. We went back to the trench, down into it, and I picked up the shovel I had left there at noon, and shoveled out all the loose earth between me and the man in front of me, then put the shovel beside the trench, lifted the pick, raised it over my shoulder, and swung it down into the dirt. I was dizzy and weak and hot; I worked for forty minutes or so; then, above me, I heard my father's voice, speaking my name. I looked up at him; he was there to take me home, to forgive my failure, and in my great relief I could not know that I would not be able to forgive it. I was going home. But he said: "Let's go buy you a hat."

Every man there wore a hat, most of them straw, the others baseball caps. I said nothing. I climbed out of the trench and went with my father. In the car, in a voice softened with pride, he said: "The foreman called me. He said the Nigras told him you threw up, and didn't eat, and you didn't tell him."

"That's right," I said, and shamefully watched the road, and cars with people who seemed free of all torment, and let my father believe I was brave, because I was afraid to tell him that I was afraid to tell the foreman. Quietly, we drove to town and he parked and took me first to a drugstore with air conditioning and a lunch counter, and bought me a 7 UP for my stomach, and told me to order a sandwich. Sweet-smelling women at the counter were smoking. The men in the trench had smoked while they worked, but my body's only desire had been to stop shoveling and swinging the pick, to be, with no transition at all, in the shower at home, then to lie on my bed, feeling the soft breath of the fan on my damp skin. I would not have smoked at work anyway, with men. Now I wanted a cigarette. My father smoked, and I ate a bacon and lettuce and tomato sandwich.

Then we walked outside, into humidity and the heat and glare of the sun. We crossed the street to the department store, where, in the work-clothes section, my father chose a pith helmet. I did not want to wear a pith helmet. I would happily wear one in Africa, hunting lions and rhinoceroses. But I did not want to wear such a thing in Lafayette. I said nothing; there was no hat I wanted to wear. I carried the helmet in its bag out of the store and, in the car, laid it beside me. At that place where sweating men worked, I put it on; a thin leather strap looped around the back of my head. I went to my two comrades in the trench. One of them said:

"That's a good hat."

I jumped in.

The man behind me said: "You going to be all right now."

I was; and I still do not know why. A sandwich and a soft drink had not given me any more strength than the breakfast I had vomited. An hour's respite in the car and the cool drugstore and buying the helmet that now was keeping my wet head cool certainly helped. But I had the same soft arms and legs, the same back and shoulders I had demanded so little of in my nearly seventeen years of stewardship. Yet all I remember of that afternoon is the absence of nausea.

At five o'clock, the whistle blew downtown and we climbed out of the trench and washed our tools with the hose, then put them in the shed. Dirt was on my arms and hands, my face and neck and clothes. I could have wrung sweat from my shirt and jeans. I got my lunch from the shade, my two comrades said: "See you tomorrow," and I said I would see them. I went to the bus stop at the corner and sat on the bench. My wet clothes cooled my skin. I looked down at my dirty tennis shoes; my socks and feet were wet. I watched people in passing cars. In one were teenaged boys, and they laughed and shouted something about my helmet. I watched the car till it was blocks away, then took off the helmet and held it on my lap. I carried it aboard the bus; yet all summer I wore it at work, maybe because my father bought it for me and I did not want to hurt him, maybe because it was a wonderful helmet for hard work outdoors in Louisiana.

My father got home before I did and told my mother and sister the story, the only one he knew, or the only one I assumed he knew. The women proudly greeted me when I walked into the house. They were also worried. They wanted to know how I felt. They wore dresses, they smelled of perfume or cologne, they were drinking bourbon and water, and my sister and father were smoking cigarettes. Standing in the living room, holding my lunch and helmet, I said I was fine. I could not tell the truth to these women who loved me, even if my father were not there. I could not say that I was not strong enough and that I could not bear going back to work tomorrow, and all summer, any more than I could tell them I did not believe I was as good at being a boy as other boys were: not at sports, or with girls; and now not with a man's work. I was home, where vases held flowers, and things were clean, and our manners were good.

Next morning, carrying my helmet and lunch, I rode the bus to work and joined the two black men in the trench. I felt that we were friends. Soon I felt this about all the black men at work. We were digging the foundation; we were the men and the boy with picks and shovels in the trench. One day, the foundation was done. I use the passive voice, because this was a square or rectangular trench, men were working at each of its sides, I had been working with my comrades on the same side for weeks, moving not forward but down. Then it was done. Someone told us. Maybe the contractor was there, with the foreman. Who dug out that last bit of dirt? I only knew that I had worked as hard as I could, I was part of the trench, it was part of me, and it was finished; it was there in the earth to receive concrete and probably never to be seen again. Someone should have blown a bugle; we should have climbed exultant from the trench, gathered to wipe sweat from our brows, drink water, shake hands, then walk together to each of the four sides and marvel at what we had made.

On that second morning of work, I was not sick, and at noon I ate lunch with the blacks in the shade; then we all slept on the grass till one o'clock. We worked till five, said good-bye to one another, and they went to the colored section of town, and I rode the bus home. When I walked into the living room, into cocktail hour, and my family asked me about my day, I said it was fine. I might have learned something if I had told them the truth: the work was too hard, but after the first morning I could bear it. And all summer it would be hard; after we finished the foundation, I would be transferred to another crew. We would build a mess hall at a Boy Scout camp and, with a black man, I would dig a septic tank in clay so hard that the foreman kept hosing water into it as we dug; black men and I would push wheelbarrows of mixed cement; on my shoulder I would carry eighty pound bags of dry cement, twenty-five pounds less than my own weight; and at the summer's end, my body would be twenty pounds heavier. If I had told these three people who loved me that I did not understand my weak body's stamina, they might have taught me why something terrible had so quickly changed to something arduous.

It is time to thank my father for wanting me to work and telling me I had to work and getting the job for me and buying me lunch and a pith helmet instead of taking me home to my mother and sister. He may have wanted to take me home. But he knew he must not, and he came tenderly to me. My mother would have been at home that afternoon; if he had taken me to her, she would have given me iced tea and, after my shower, a hot dinner. When my sister came home from work, she would have understood, and told me not to despise myself because I could not work with a pickax and a shovel. And I would have spent the summer at home, nestled in the love of the two women, peering at my father's face, and yearning to be someone I respected, a varsity second baseman, a halfback, someone cheerleaders and drum majorettes and pretty scholars loved; yearning to be a man among men, and that is where my father sent me with a helmet on my head.

ON THE NET

Writing Descriptions. Purdue University Online Writing Lab.
    <http://owl.english.purdue.edu/handouts/general/gl_describe.html>

Descriptive Essays. LEO: Literacy Education Online. St. Cloud State University.
    <http://leo.stcloudstate.edu/acadwrite/descriptive.html>

How to Write a Description. Northern Illinois University English Department
    <http://www.engl.niu.edu/wac/descr_how.html>

Narrative and Descriptive. Capital Community College.
    <http://grammar.ccc.commnet.edu/grammar/composition/narrative.htm>

Descriptive Writing. Steve Campsall. English & English Literature: Coursework, Homework, and Exam Help. englishbiz.co.uk.
    <http://www.englishbiz.co.uk/mainguides/describe.htm>

A Brief Guide to Writing Narrative Essays. Roane State Community College Online Writing Lab.
    <http://www.rscc.cc.tn.us/owl&writingcenter/OWL/Narration.html>

Narrative Writing. The Writing Site.org.
    <http://www.thewritingsite.org/resources/genre/narrative.asp>

EXERCISES

Descriptive I Exercise

1. Go somewhere on campus. The place may be inside or outside. Make yourself comfortable for a minute and decide whether the place impresses you favorably or unfavorably. On this sheet jot down as many specific details, observations, and ideas as you can in ten minutes or so. Focus on your senses, what can you see, touch, taste, hear, or smell?

2. Go somewhere else where you have a good writing surface, space, and quiet. Review your list. Now go through your jottings and make a specific figure of speech of at least ten of them. Create at least ten vivid images of at least ten other details. Do not use clichés.

3. Now write your subjective dominant impression of the place to describe it to your audience.

4. Next choose specific details, images, and figures of speech to support your dominant impression.

5. Finally, write a paragraph in which you allow your audience to perceive a place on campus the way you do. Include your dominant impression, specific details, vivid language, logical transitions, and a clincher to emphasize your purpose.

Descriptive II Exercise

Here is a simple declarative sentence:

The man and his daughter walked through the shopping mall.

Fill in the blanks in the sentences below with descriptive words, phrases, and clauses.

You will want to consider what the man and his daughter look like (How old are they? What are they wearing? Who are they?), how they are walking (Are they striding? lolling? Are they happy? upset? afraid?), and what the mall looks like? (What will happen at the end of their shopping trip?).

1. The _____ man and his _____ daughter walked through the shopping mall.

2. The _____ and his _____ were

   walking through the shopping mall.

3. The _____ man and _____ were

   _____through the _____shopping mall

   _____.

4. _____ the _____man and his

   _____daughter were _____ly through the

   shopping mall_____and _____.

Descriptive Techniques Exercise

Identify and underline the descriptive devices E. B. White uses in this paragraph
from "Once More to the Lake."

> One afternoon while we were at that lake a thunderstorm came up. It was like the
> revival of an old melodrama that I had seen long ago with childish awe. The second-
> act climax of the drama of the electrical disturbance over a lake in America had not
> changed in any important respect. This was the big scene, still the big scene. The
> whole thing was so familiar, the first feeling of oppression and heat and a general air
> around camp of not wanting to go very far away. In midafternoon (it was all the same)
> a curious darkening of the sky, and a lull in everything that had made life tick; and then
> the way the boats suddenly swung the other way at their moorings with the coming
> of a breeze out of the new quarter, and the premonitory rumble. Then the kettle
> drum, then the snare, then the bass drum and cymbals, then crackling light against the
> dark, and the gods grinning and licking their chops in the hills. Afterward the calm,
> the rain steadily rustling in the calm lake, the return of light and hope and spirits,
> and the campers running out in joy and relief to go swimming in the rain, their bright
> cries perpetuating the deathless joke about how they were getting simply drenched,
> and the children screaming with delight at the new sensation of bathing in the rain,
> and the joke about getting drenched linking the generations in a strong indestruc-
> tible chain. And the comedian who waded in carrying an umbrella.

1. To what does he compare the storm? Is the comparison literal or figurative?

2. What images does he use?

3. Which figures of speech are employed?

4. What transitional devices does he use in this paragraph? Why does he repeat
   "then" in sentence 7?

5 Profiles *and* Memoirs

PROFILES

Profiles are used in many different academic and professional arenas. We most commonly expect to see them in celebrity magazines and Sunday newspapers or frequently in video or audio interviews with famous or otherwise noteworthy people; however, nearly all good writing includes the use of profiles. From describing the qualifications of an author you quote in your paper to full-blown stand-alone biographies, profiles play a tremendous role in our literate lives. Essentially the story of a person from an objective point of view, the profile is arguably the best narrative venue for personifying an idea, argument, or situation.

A profile is often a detailed story of a person. Depending on the purpose for the profile, the person may or may not be famous. Profiles use similar details for good descriptive and narrative writing, such as comparisons, physical details, exposition, and dialogue.

The structure of a profile is generally less rigid and formal than other academic writing. Whether or not the writer chooses to include herself as a character in the profile, audiences tend to appreciate profiles that feel like the result of a conversation. The questions may have been planned well ahead of time, but in the final draft most profiles tend toward an organic development and a deepening of conversation instead of a more traditional structure of plot or argument development.

Part of the reason profiles are so popular is that readers love feeling as though they've gained access to an otherwise restricted world. Most good profiles are intimate and sympathetic toward their subject. The object of a profile is not judgment but understanding.

Strategy

Different modes of profile writing have somewhat different demands. If your goal is to write a stand-alone profile for, say, publication in the school newspaper or a local magazine, your audience is accordingly different than if you are using profile writing to enhance the strength of your research in a literature essay or in a case study for a psychology paper. The principles are more or less the same, however, so we'll look first at the writing of a stand-alone profile.

Occasion

In monthly periodicals, daily newspapers, as well as on TV and radio shows, profiles are generally produced about a figure reaching a certain prominence in her field. Whether it's a quarterback achieving a milestone number of receptions, a dancer having performed in her hundredth *Nutcracker*, or a politician having made the same election reform promise more than anyone before him, we usually seek out profiles about individuals who have recently found a way to distinguish themselves in the public eye. The purpose of a profile of these people is not so much to introduce them to the public as to shed more focused light on someone with whom we are already familiar. To interview a person of this stature, the writer is usually already a professional journalist.

Less common, but at least as compelling, are profiles of people known (or even unknown) to the writer but not the public at large. The purpose of interviewing folks such as a local alderman fighting to build a new leash-free dog park or an ice cream truck owner/proprietor who is finally retiring at age 94 is less immediately evident. Chances are there is an occasion known only to a few that has put these people briefly in the spotlight, and the purpose of the profile is to widen that light just a bit so that we the readers can identify with this lifelong neighbor in a new and more enriched way.

Perhaps the most prevalent form of the profile you'll encounter as a student is that of the case study. The profile will be used inside a larger rhetorical structure—probably an ethnographic essay—which is driven not so much by characterization and empathy but rather by thesis and argument. In this case the person profiled will likely be someone who personally is affected by or otherwise bears out a claim you seek to support. Bear in mind this is at once a very effective strategy but also one which is almost entirely based on the emotional appeal. In other words, a single person can't represent a whole group of people for very long. To better understand this, make a list of the qualities that categorize you. To what extent would you want to represent all female, Korean students, psychology majors, drivers of Yugoslavian cars and so on? Part of what makes profiles most compelling is also what makes them inherently flawed: we love learning about what makes people unique.

Stance

Depending on the goals you have established for your profile, you need to situate yourself to your subject. If you're coming at your profile from the point of view of a scientist, you'll need to maintain an objective detachment from your subject. Similarly, you'll need to document all aspects of your profile, especially the conversation and other research methods used to get the material for the interview.

Hard scientific evidence, however, is not always the goal in research. If your profile goals are to elicit a more personal and subjective interview, it won't do to treat your subject with clinical precision. Most subjects appreciate someone who is genuinely interested in their story and asks honest if sometimes challenging questions. Digital recorders can make otherwise chatty people clam up, so some subjects might do better if you use a simple pad and pencil to document the highlights of your conversation.

Depending on which approach you choose, you'll need also to figure out for yourself where your point of view is situated in your essay. If you want absolute scientific anonymity, you will likely omit the use of the first person point of view entirely. If you seek to write a warm, moving, more pathos-based profile, you might allow yourself to enter into the conversation from time to time through the use of your personal impressions of the subject, the feel of the room, the direction of the day, and your own hopes and goals for the interview.

Goals

A prepared interviewer is likely to be a successful one. However, sometimes success is found where it cannot be made. You should plan on the interview going in one direction, but not so much so that if it takes off in another, or if your line of inquiry is met with indifference or outrage on the part of the subject, you can change direction and salvage the interview. Similarly, even though you pick your subject, try to inject as few of your own specific expectations as possible. Remember that your job is to ask good questions, not ask questions that are thinly veiled comments.

Organization

When preparing to write your profile, you should research your subject and make yourself as informed as possible. Subjects can be put off by interviewers who know nothing of their area. However, you will rarely encounter a subject who enjoys looking down his nose at his interviewer. More often than not, your interview will go well in proportion to your interest and preparedness. And no matter how purportedly obscure you might think your subject's area of expertise, bear in mind that he has likely spent a great portion of his days and nights doing that very thing, whether it's working on carburetors or beekeeping. If you're interviewing a typewriter repairman and don't even know that IBM was once the king of typewriters or that the gun maker Remington also once made typewriters and sewing machines, you're not likely to earn your subject's trust and confidence.

Make your contact with your subject friendly but also clear and easy to read so that nothing gets in the way of a good interview. Be on time and be prepared to do the interview; and even if you plan to use a digital recorder, an intrepid journalist will always have a back up machine and spare batteries and will still take notes during the interview. This kind of triple redundancy may initially seem tedious and unnecessary, but when it comes time to write your profile you will find that the notes you take help organize themes or significant parts of the interview you might choose to use as directly quoted matter.

If you record your interview, you will find it useful (if not immensely time consuming) to make a transcript of your recording. It will make writing your profile much easier to work with even though it will take a good bit of time.

As we mentioned in the Strategy section, when you write your profile for a broad or general audience, you should appeal to most readers' fondness for good stories. Begin with the scene: describe the day, the place, the time … all the physical details that only someone present that day would notice.

Finally, bring an open and eager mind to your interview. Expect to be wrong about some of your assumptions on the subject and welcome the unusual or unexpected when it comes up. Part of what makes profiles one of the most compelling modes of writing is that even the most unwilling subject will usually spill his guts if you're interested and patient enough.

CHECKLIST FOR PROFILE ESSAY

1. Choose a person to interview who fits in the parameters of your assignment.

2. Contact your subject to arrange an interview.

3. Find out as much as you can about the subject and her relevant work.

4. Make a list of questions you would like to ask. It should be twice as long as you think you'll need. Commit as many to memory as you can.

5. Decide how you're going to document the interview. If by taking notes, make sure you have lots of paper and several pens. You'll have to write more than you think, and you don't want anything to stop the interview. If you'll record it, make sure you have tested your device and have backup batteries; take some notes during the interview, too, to record the time and topic or question. For example: 3:25, art and religion. 3:40, painting and faith.

6. Transcribe your interview and organize your notes.

7. You're in business. Time to write your profile. Don't forget to be a good storyteller as well as a journalist, anthropologist, psychologist, and poet.

8. Send your subject a thank you note. You probably won't interview her again, but it's just good form.

9. Did you edit your paper carefully, checking for major grammatical and spelling errors?

MALLORY

Baylee Reagan

One time I picked my nose and stuck a fantastic booger on the hallway light switch. This wasn't recent, but it was a time when I was old enough to know that boogers don't go on light switches, and my mother automatically blamed one of my younger sisters. I did, too, obviously, because Mom would not have been happy to know her seven-year-old daughter was a booger-smearer, let alone still actually picked her nose.

I remember perfectly my mother's stance right after she made her discovery; she stood in the middle of the hallway with her right hand on her hip and her left index finger pointing at the huge, crusted yellow glob. Her lips were pursed so that her cheek bones were accented and her wide eyes bulged from their sockets. Mom was pissed. She had just called the three of us upstairs and was ready to unleash her anger on the culprit responsible for the smearing. I can just imagine her thoughts upon first noticing the booger: *What the hell is this? A booger? Who the hell did this? And what have I done wrong in rearing my children?* She stood in the hallway, feet firmly planted, pointing precisely at the dirty deed. "Which one of you wiped a booger on my light switch?" "Not I," said the little pig. The three of us shook our heads and remained silent. When no one came clean, Mom decided that it was Mallory's booger.

"Mallory! You did this, didn't you?"

"No, Mom!" she said. I don't even think I was questioned—I was too old to do such a thing. And McKenna was only two and too short; an electrical socket would have been more in her range. Naturally, Mallory smeared the booger on the light switch. "I swear I didn't do it, Mom!"

"Don't you lie to me, missy. Now do you know what you're gonna do? You're going to go downstairs and get a paper towel with some soap and water and come back up here and clean this up." Mal looked at me; I shook my head and shrugged. There was no more questioning for Mom; her mind was made up that Mallory had committed the crime, and now she was going to pay. The five-year-old hung her head to her feet, trudged her way down to the kitchen, and returned with wet paper towels in hand.

Perhaps the reason to blame Mallory had something to do with her history of wrongdoing. I was an angel in class; Mallory was continually sent home from school because she was biting her classmates. I was good at playing the piano and Mallory was not; I could play Beethoven's "Fur Elise" and Joplin's "The Entertainer," and one day my dad flipped out and said Mallory had played "Take Me Out to the Ballgame" too many times and was no longer allowed to play the piano until she learned a new song. Once, when a friend of hers from kindergarten showed up at our house with his dad in order to discuss pee-wee soccer sign-up, she hacked a loogie and spat it on his car window, for absolutely no reason. We all knew she had a crush on the little boy, so it was odd that Mal found loogies to be some sort of sign of affection. Mallory had a criminal record in the Reagan family household; therefore, *she* wiped boogers on walls.

Born just two years apart, Mal and I had a strong relationship as kids, despite Mallory's getting in trouble for my dirty deeds. I still have the writing journals that I collected in my first grade class, and repeatedly throughout the notebooks I have inserts that say something to the effect of, "I luv my Malory. She is my bes frend." Throughout our childhood, we entertained ourselves with playing school (I was always the teacher, she the pupil), and with little Playmobile people and American Girl Dolls. Mallory was definitely a more daring child; just a few months after we received our American Girl Dolls, each costing about $100, Mallory chopped the hair off her doll, Addy. Once again, my mom was not too happy with Mal, and I believe she was relieved of the doll for weeks.

We were definitely close as children, but very much opposites. Mal always had something to say and was always a true ham in front of the camera. I, on the other hand, was a little more shy and reserved. Mal tried her best to be an athlete but, unfortunately, was not blessed with athletic coordination, whereas I excelled in sports. In school she struggled with math but eventually became a very avid reader; math and science were my strongest subjects, and I found no joy in reading books. Our physical nature differed, too. She grew up with a dark bowl-cut and brown eyes, and I had long scraggly blond hair, green eyes, and freckles. The only clue to our sisterhood was our mouths; we both had big, messy, jagged teeth that eventually needed braces (though my front two flared out, hers flared in).

When I was about twelve and she ten, our once-close relationship had dwindled, as most sibling relationships do at that age. We had very different personalities and interests, and her constant babble easily got on my nerves. When Mal and I would get into fights, my mom had two specific ways of making us resolve the issue. First, we had to "mate the socks" in the sock-box (our family never got the system down to simply matching the socks out of the dryer), or, alternatively, we had to stand in the living room with our foreheads together until we each said five nice things about each other. Usually, we'd get the sock box first but this only led to more fighting, which always resulted in the "All right you two, heads together!" from Mom. We'd stand there in front of the fireplace, our two foreheads touching and our arms crossed, eyes diverted elsewhere. Eventually, though, my mom's plan always worked, and after a few minutes the two of us would start laughing and we would be pals again.

It is only now that I recognize Mallory's admiration for me growing up. I wonder how many times I got her into trouble and she would just take it. One particular instance comes to mind when I think of Mal covering up for me. When we moved out of Omaha to the suburb of Elkhorn, I was eight and Mallory six. Though Mal was of age to defend her rights before the court, I still tried to cover up my mischief. Our current spare bedroom was then unfinished, and the rafters in the ceiling made for brilliant climbing and daring adventure. An old rotting couch sat against the wood wall, and behind it a queen-size mattress had been stored, pinned between the couch and the wall in a horizontal position. The mattress was my way of getting up to the rafters, where I had begun placing all of the alien head stickers I had been collecting from the bowling alley. And I didn't just decorate the rafters; I also used them as support beams for the mock-hammock I had created out of an old soccer net and two jump ropes. However, the rafters had been forbidden by both my mother and father, as they were an area of danger and not a place for small children to be crawling around.

One day I dared Mallory to join me up in the ceiling—she refused. She actually had grown into quite the Miss Prissy, which *really* got on my nerves. After much persuading that she wasn't going to fall, wasn't going to hurt herself, I convinced her to join me. She climbed onto the back of the old couch, and with her puny arms she reached up to the top of the mattress and hoisted herself up so that she could stand on top of it. I had already made my way up and was waiting for her to join me when the mattress bent forward. She lost her balance and fell backward, landing behind the mattress and in between the wall, and ultimately onto the hard wood floor. She immediately shrieked bloody murder, and I, too, was scared for a second that I might have had a broken neck to deal with. But, when I climbed down to her and realized that she could move her limbs, just not her pinky finger, I got upset at her for screaming so loud. As she sat there holding her crooked finger and trying to mask her sobs, I looked into her tear-filled eyes and told her, "Don't you dare tell Mom or Dad about this."

To Mal's credit, she did a wonderful job that day of concealing that her finger was broken. That is, until Dad made us get in the car to go up to Shadow Ridge and hit some golf balls. I did not especially enjoy hitting balls. But his ability to make me feel terrible for not ever wanting to golf worked magic in convincing me. Since Mallory loved spending time at the driving range, and though still in (secret) pain, she decided to join as well. It didn't take *too* long for my dad to realize something wasn't perfect with her grip. "No, Mal, you're holding the club wrong, it's like this ...." He demonstrated how to grasp the pinky of his right hand with the forefinger of the other. To my surprise, Mal gave it a shot, lips sealed and all. I questioned myself on what I had ever done to make her want to cover my back. I knew that her giant zig-zagged right pinky finger was not normal, and I had no idea how she was hiding the pain. That is, until she took her first swing with Dad's new hand position.

Upon slicing the ball nine feet to the right, Mallory threw down her four iron and grasped her hand in pain as tears began to stream down her cheeks. "What happened, Mal?" my father asked. "Do you need a glove? Sometimes those help take away the shock from the club...."

"It's my piiiinky!!" Mal shrieked.

"Your pinky? Well what the hell did you do to your pinky?"

"I fell. In the attic room. I fell from the rafters."

"The what?!" For once, my father's face immediately shot to mine, for he knew the little monkey in me would be the only culprit behind the rafter scheme. "Did you take your sister up to the beams, Baylee?" I stood motionless, as if I were about to be eaten.

"Yes."

"Yes WHAT!"

"Yes, sir!" Sometimes, when my dad was really mad, it made him feel better to pretend he was a sergeant.

"I didn't hear you!"

"Yes, SIR!" I yelled, standing straight up on my driving range pad. Yes sir, I had done it. I had taken my younger sister up to the forbidden rafters, and for once I was convicted of my crime. Mallory was rushed to EmergiCare where she received a splint for the broken bone, and I was rushed to my bedroom. I was allowed up to the rafters once more, but only to remove my alien stickers from the wood planks

Though I was caught, the fact that she had covered up a twisted finger for me was a true demonstration of Mal's huge heart and her admiration for her family. Today we still have our little differences, as our personalities remain different and our interests opposite. However, nothing will ever come between the bond we share built on love. Mallory still gets in trouble at the age of twenty, especially at the dinner table when my mom snaps at her to take smaller bites and my dad yells at her when she spits her milk everywhere after I make her laugh. And though I was a terrible human being for constantly blaming Mallory for the mischief in our childhood, today the boogers, the sock box head-locks, and the rafter schemes are now only subjects of our dinner table laughter.

OBJETS D'ART

Matthew Batt

Bradford Overton sits in his sunny, downtown Salt Lake loft, stirring coffee in a French press with a Japanese chef's knife. His coffee maker broke, and as I'll find out through our conversations, it's the breakdown of the conventional that more often than not leads Overton to heed Ezra Pound's modernist mantra, "make it new."

Overton's phone, set on vibrate, has been skittering across the table for some time. "It's my wife," he says. He's a tall, pony-tailed man who is immediately as striking in appearance as he is complicated: playfully serious, childishly mature, dynamically simple … a man on whom nothing is lost. "T.S. Eliot once wrote that he measured his life in coffee spoons," Overton says, after hanging up the phone. "My wife says I measure mine with Calistoga bottles." It's not just coincidence that Overton's art is as affected by objects both real and imagined as he is with such objects as Calistoga bottles.

Overton's paintings are rife with enticing objects that seem to do far more than make for happy art. Origami folding monkeys, antique kids' cars, wooden skateboards, even reproductions of other art populate his paintings with a surpassing wit. In one of his most challenging and yet touching pieces, Go Play Outside, a dog-eared image of Adam and Eve getting expelled from the Garden of Eden is thumb-tacked above a toy zebra hanging-ten (or four?) on an old roller skate, while a tiger figurine plays with the string of a yo-yo. The respective orientation of toys and biblical figures, the bright color palettes, the implication of light from left of the frame, puts theology into conversation with childhood and, in doing so, takes viewers along for a ride.

Born the oldest of six children in Escondido, California, to a sculptor mother and an insurance salesman father, Brad didn't get a lot of TV as a kid. "Go make something," his mom would say. And so he did. "A few years ago, I was painting these abstract things in a shed behind our place in Sugar House," he says, cradling his coffee cup with both hands. "I was refurbishing furniture for money, and I realized it wasn't making me happy."

While his work in visual art has spanned his lifetime, Overton found his true subject matter after receiving his master of fine arts degree from the University of Utah. He has since immersed himself in the playful, intriguing, and chromatically evocative still-lifes filled with equal parts Americana junk store and Arabian bazaar. Such works have brought him regional and national acclaim—including a recent feature in Southwest Art magazine and numerous commissions by Nordstrom department stores.

But when asked about reviewers labeling his recent still-lifes as allegorical or symbolic, Overton shrugs. "I definitely have an idea behind each one of my paintings," he says. "But it's more like a starting point than a destination." Still, viewers find their own attachment to Overton's paintings. His painting *Star Fighter*, for example, took on a life of its own.

While staying with his wife in Santa Fe, a sculptor friend gave him a toy soldier wrapped in purple tissue paper. Add a yellow paper, crescent moon, some gold foil stars—and some realistically rendered Scotch tape—and before he knew it, Overton had the makings for a sublime amalgamation of objects, chroma, and emotional texture. But the real story, Overton insists, is in the interplay of interpretation that comes later.

When recently visiting the home of the couple who purchased *Star Fighter*, Overton was pleasantly surprised to find it hanging next to the front door. The couple considered it a guardian, a sort of protector. " I never even thought about it like that, but it's brilliant," says Overton. "How can I touch that, and why would I want to? That's what I love about art. It's not about closing curtains or putting things into cans. It's about making something beautiful— something that opens a door to a new world and says, 'Come on in.'"

And it's that dynamism between what Overton sees, how he portrays it, and what his viewers interpret that explains why Bradford Overton is such a hot commodity these days. From a market of art that has been over-ripe with ironically blank canvases and barb-wired installations, Overton's work hints toward a new mode of painting where truth and beauty are as they should be: expressive, current, and timeless.

Reflecting on what it's like to be an artist in an "up-and-coming" market like Salt Lake City, Overton admits many of his friends have left for the coasts to seek richer though more saturated markets. But he sees a real potential here. From the faculty and student artists at the University of Utah and hard-working gallery owners, to the growing population of eager collectors, Overton insists things are brewing in Utah. "l remember reading something Emerson wrote about how Rome wasn't built by people who left, and thinking, 'Yeah, this is my city and I'm gonna make it happen'"

And a key feature of Overton's determination has a lot to do with his recently becoming a father. He tells the story of his 18-month-old son, Noah—named, he says, not just for a guy from the Bible, but for somebody who dared to do something crazy that ended up saving civilization. "It's like you nurture kids and try to give them everything they need to be all they can be, and you're expecting them to just become little versions of yourself," says Overton. "But then they're totally themselves, this magically unique thing that is at once you and perfectly separate." For Bradford Overton, art and life are not that much different.

An hour after our interview, Overton calls with a clarification. "The Calistoga bottles? I thought you might like to know," he says. "My wife, she brings me a bottle of water home from work each day. So there are all these Calistoga bottles in the fridge, and that's why I measure my life by them, day by day."

After we hang up, I wonder if there isn't some painting-in-the-making of a refrigerator overflowing with bottles of sparkling water—if there isn't something *meaningful* about those objects—but I realize I'm missing the point. So long as Bradford Overton keeps finding ways to tell the stories behind the things of his life, it looks as though he will continue to transform the way we see the beauty of the image, the art of the object, and the live nature of the still-life.

EXERCISES

1. Find a member of your local community (feel free to interpret "community" literally or figuratively) with whom you are familiar. Interview him/her in a general way, though toward the end of your interview work in Anna Deavere Smith's questions: Have you ever been close to death? Do you know the circumstances of your birth? Have you ever been accused of a crime you didn't commit? Clearly, these difficult questions will require sensitive introduction and should be delivered with respect. (See Memoir section "Prompts" below).

2. Find a member of your local community (feel free to interpret "community" literally or figuratively) with whom you are not personally familiar. Interview him/her with the goal of writing a brief profile such as might be published in a local magazine featuring interesting members of a given community.

Memoirs

Blessed and cursed as the go-to genre of the "me generation," memoir is a dynamic, popular and contentious form. Once upon a time it was thought that only captains of industry, assassins of presidents, and presidents themselves were significant enough to record the stories of their lives into the history of nations because, well, they already had. Despite the fact that memoirs have been written in every form from sketches on cave walls to diaries to eleven volume, shelf-breaking tomes, as a genre it has very much come into its own in the last twenty years. The academic application of memoir seems slight, but actually when a writer is able to intertwine her emotional and intellectual lives by committing them to an autobiographical essay she has begun a practice of thoughtful, reflective, and conscientious living and thinking that will benefit her for the rest of her life.

Distinguishing Features

There are almost more words to describe various kinds of memoir than there are kinds of memoirists. The word *memoir* comes from the French via the Latin word for *memory*. The novelist and memoirist Gore Vidal described the difference between autobiography and memoir as a distinction of degree, rather than kind: "a memoir is how one remembers one's own life, while an autobiography is history, requiring research, dates, facts double-checked." A memoir might be cast therefore as the personal story of one's life whereas an autobiography is more the public record. Many people disagree with this, however, and so it's useful to expect an argument depending on what you want to call your work.

For the most part, you will be writing your memoirs via the essay. That form, too, has an interesting etymology. It also comes from the French, as a verb or a noun (*essai*, a try, an attempt, to endeavor.) In English, especially in high school, we all too frequently think of essays as trials rather than adventures. Historically, however, the form goes back thousands of years to the so-called "pillow books" of those educated and well-off enough not only to learn to read and write but to be able to afford paper and writing utensils. Suffice it to say that the essay is the classic academic and intellectual opportunity to test one's emotional limits, brave one's candor, and seek knowledge that one does not already possess.

One of the hallmarks of the essay in general and the memoir in particular is its opportunity to wander and wonder. Digressions, tangents, philosophical musings, anecdotes, portraits—just about anything you can think of to include in a memoir can find a way to matter in the overarching narrative. Art has been argued to be the amalgamation of disparate elements. With the right treatment and sensibility, no two elements can be so different as not to be connected through a vivid memoir.

The best memoirs are often those that follow in the tradition of the 16th-century writer Michel de Montaigne, who demanded that "we must remove the mask." In other words, a common assumption and expectation for readers of memoir is that no matter whether the writer is a war criminal or a saint, a philanthropist, or Gene Simmons, when we read their memoirs we expect full backstage access. A memoir should not merely be the parade of one's successes but rather the story of one's ups and downs, strengths and weaknesses. Ultimately the balance will tip in the favor of one or the other, but the best memoirs seek to tell their stories at any cost. No matter what, be honest with your story, your readers, and yourself, and you're bound to succeed.

Strategy

Because the house of memoir and autobiography is technically about half of any given bookstore, it's important to clarify your reasons for writing early in the process. Even if your urge or prompt is as broad as "Write a memoir," you'll want to begin thinking about a central event or events so you have a dramatic focus around which to construct your essay. Trying to tell your life story from beginning to middle to end will be, to say the least, a daunting work and one that won't be finished until, well, you know. Much better, especially for the purposes of an essay to be written for a class, is to focus your creative and intellectual powers on something specific and concrete that you experienced that has stayed with you for some time. Try to think of something distant enough in time that you can still feel shadowed by it but mostly out from under it. If you're still in the throes of some challenge or difficulty, trying to write about it is going to be a great way to work your way through it, but not in an academic setting. Save that for your journal or for later. The American short story writer Flannery O'Connor said that "anyone who has survived childhood has enough information to last him the rest of his days." Go back a few years and mine your past for the wonders and mysteries it offers.

Prompts

In his philosophical memoir, *Zen and the Art of Motorcycle Maintenance*, Robert Pirsig describes how, when one is faced with the daunting task of writing about one's life, she becomes hopelessly hobbled. When given the opportunity, however, to write about not just one's home town, or its main street, or a favorite building but rather just one brick from that building she will virtually never run out of things to say. In other words, choke up on your subject so that you can better hit it out of the park. The playwright and performer Anna Deavere Smith used a linguist's technique to do first-hand research when writing some of her finest work, such as *Twilight: Los Angeles, 1992*, a performance about the aftermath of the Rodney King trial. Here are her questions:

1. Have you ever come close to death?

2. Do you know the circumstances of your birth?

3. Have you ever been accused of something you didn't do?

Those ought to keep you going for years if not at least a solid essay or two.

After having begun an essay and gotten caught, try the novelist and short-story writer Melanie Rae Thon's fantastic exercise. The ideal circumstances would be when you have written the bare bones of a scene from your memory but aren't satisfied with its depth or sophistication. Do this: make two lists, one titled "I Remember," the other "I Don't Remember." With your sticking point in mind, make twenty entries in each list. Allow yourself to go back and forth. "I remember," for example, "the feel of my father's stubble when he tucked me in and kissed me goodnight, but I don't remember ever seeing him at the dinner table." It might seem silly to include these in a memoir, a bunch of things that you don't remember. But think about it as the negative image of a photo or all the white space around any given black letter on your paper. Negative space gives shape to our thoughts and hearts, whether or not the thing we long for was ever there in the first place.

Goals

If you're writing a memoir simply to trot out that which you already know and have just been waiting for the right occasion to write, you'll be in crowded company with all the celebrity tell-alls that choke the bestsellers lists. If, however, you seek a more challenging story to tell—a story from your life that hasn't yet completely resolved itself—something that happened that you think about as you fall asleep—something that you did or didn't do that you can neither undo nor forget—if you choose that road it'll doubtless take you to higher, more rarified elevations where the writing will be more difficult but also more rewarding. Embrace the memoir for what it is: an opportunity for memory to tell its own story.

Organization

Organizing a memoir is often a practice that comes better in revision than in pre-drafting or early draft stages. When we come to memoirs or otherwise personal essays, we don't expect a lot in the way of contrivances or superstructures the way we sometimes do with other formal, academic, or highly stylized modes of writing. Rather, we expect the memoir essay to reflect the writer's subject dealing with life as it happened, not life as we would like to reconstruct it so as to tidily shoehorn it into a story. There will be narrative cul-de-sacs and plot dead ends. We expect that you will not have thought of the perfect retort to that bully's comment or made precisely the smoothest move when trying to woo that childhood sweetheart. In other words, don't try to force your essay. Let it tell you what it wants to say and then try to strike up a conversation with it. As you revise, there will be plenty of opportunities to go back and reconfigure sections that are entirely unnecessary or otherwise superfluous, and the feedback from your peers and other readers will help you continue to maximize the form of the essay until it has best suited its content.

Allow yourself plenty of time, however, to work through various drafts. Because a reader cannot know what else you might include or discover through future drafts, she will likely make hypothetical suggestions *(Was there more to this conversation? I'd really like to hear what your mother said in response to that tow-truck driver.)* which may or may not be useful. Nonetheless, you need to take all responses to your work as constructive and helpful, whether they literally are or are not. If someone asks, for example, *Did that really happen? Man, I wouldn't know what to say if a guy mugged me for my socks!*, your job is not to shrug that reader off as incredulous, but rather to hear her disbelief as something that needs to work itself into your own narrative by registering a reader's potential disbelief. *If I had fallen asleep and woken up in a reed basket floating on the Nile I wouldn't have been as surprised as I was when the mugger prodded me with his .38 and said, "Your socks or your life, Sparky."*

Use exercises, journaling, and even research to enhance your work where it might have hit a dry spot. Though memory might be the predominant source for material, don't limit yourself to a static body of remembrances. Re-interview the significant players in your story. Track down relevant newspaper articles or your own journals or diary entries. Find out precisely what kind of station wagon that might have been or exactly how your mother made that brisket so amazingly smoky despite your brother's severe hickory allergy.

If, on the other hand, your writing seems to show a "hot spot" where it doesn't need to—if your writing gets really lively and vivid at some point despite the fact that you're lost somewhere in what you thought was a tangent—you should listen to that excitement. If you don't, you would hope your readers will and will tell you where it got really compelling even though maybe it took away from the supposed story at hand. Like a miner panning for gold who keeps coming up with these huge pesky chunks of silver, you may have struck upon something that you didn't go looking for but nonetheless found. Go with it for a few paragraphs and see where it takes you. You may just strike it rich.

Lastly, don't leave yourself alone in the past to deal with your past self. Whenever we write essays about our former selves, we often feel obliged to deny our present selves have any communication with them. Rather, interrogate your past self from the safety of your present desk. Let yourself wonder how the smart, talented and savvy you-of-the-present could possibly be related to that stubborn, foolish and ham-hearted you-of-the-past. Don't forget: it won't be all that long when the next you-of-the-present is asking the same question. That's why we'll always have something to write about.

◆

CHECKLIST FOR MEMOIRS ESSAY

1. Give yourself plenty of time to draft through this process, allowing for some events or memories to simply not sustain an entire essay so you can start from scratch. The only time that's a problem is when you don't allow enough drafting time in your schedule.
2. When drafting through exercises and prompts, always try to focus your writing on the most concise and concrete experiences. An event is not the summer when you were thirteen working as a sorter in your uncle's jelly bean factory. An event is the day you got your ponytail caught in the augur. If there's any doubt, ask yourself whether you could take a picture of the event in question. If yes, then you're in business. If no, keep narrowing down your search. Broad memories are fine for books, but they tend to make for lousy essays.
3. Forego the temptation to use the old tried-and-true (and boring) five paragraph essay here. You don't need an introduction to tell a story, nor do you need to have a grand conclusion in the form of a caboose paragraph. Get right to business, make every paragraph fight for its life, and try to get yourself to be a better, more honest and creative writer with every next word. Good work will follow.
4. Experiment with different aspects of your story (point of view, voice, tone, stance, even genre) so that you can get at the real story that might be hiding from your conscious self. We all have secrets—especially from ourselves—and trying to root them out for our own edification can make for some of the most compelling reading in any genre.
5. That said, bear in mind your audience and their responsibilities. Unless you're writing specifically to a priest or a psychiatrist, there's no patient/client privilege when it comes time to testify in court. In other words, don't write about any pending crimes or anything else you wouldn't want to be brought before judgment.
6. Above all, be brave and be honest. If you tackle material that's slightly more challenging than you think you can handle but do so in a courageous, forthright, and generally self-effacing fashion, you will always earn the respect and admiration of your audience and, quite deservedly, yourself. Putting the right words in the right order, as the poet says, may not grant you absolution, but knowing that you've reached something true about yourself and your people is certainly something that rarely happens, as the Southern writer Harry Crews put it, by going to the zoo and eating cotton candy.
7. Did you edit your paper carefully, checking for major grammatical and spelling errors?

HER HAIR

Baylee Reagan

In an old family home-video, my mom kneels on the ground watching her daughters play Pogs, her hair barely fitting into the clip she has used to put it up. Mallory introduces her sisters with a toothless grin and an inability to say her 'R's while I brush my long scraggly hair off my face and onto the shoulder of my oversized Herby Husker t-shirt. McKenna shows off how old she is by holding up the number three as she twirls around in her Cinderella dress, and in the background my father's voice booms, "Honey, have you seen my checkbook?" It's my mother's hair I'm thinking about here.

I don't even remember being scared. I don't remember how sick the chemo made her. I just think about the hair.

Ever since we dug up the 13-year-old video from the piles of unlabeled VHS tapes, every one of us girls has, at some time or another, quoted our dad's infamous "checkbook" line. We all look ridiculous in the tape; Mal has a bowl-cut, and McKenna's hair is in a hideous up-do for which I apparently was proudly responsible. My own thin, ratted hair is down to my waist and there is absolutely no reason why my mother should ever have allowed me to have such a thing. It resembled the tangled hair of a Barbie lost in the basement toy-box for five years. It's easiest, though, to laugh at my dad, who appears at the end of the film as the camera pans up from his tapered wrangler blue jeans to his hands on the hips of his green-trimmed jean jacket, to a double chin (poor angle, he would say), and finally his over-sized tinted glasses on his bald head. Earlier in the tape you hear the "checkbook" line and no one answers. At the end, I am holding the camera videotaping, and Mallory asks, "Now, who's that fine young gentleman behind you?" My father answers Mal's question, much angrier this time, as the camera pans up to his body as he releases one arm from his hip in front of him: "Someone who wants to know ... Have you SEEN my CHECKBOOK?"

My mom, though, looks beautiful. She's been cleaning all day and has somehow managed to put her short dark hair up into a clip off her neck. The clip is long, silver, and slender, and it holds her hair up and flat to her head, leaving just a few short strands behind. It's always kind of funny when my mom does this; for as long as I can remember she's had hair to her chin or above. Every once in a while, she gets sick of it and attempts to put it up on her head like the rest of her daughters do, though she would never leave the house with the image. Usually someone makes a comment and she takes it down, although it never looks bad—we're just not used to it.

I still feel so guilty about the day they told us. My parents sat on the couch opposite their three girls, my dad with his arm around my mom's shoulder, stroking it. I can't remember if she said anything at all; I just know tears welled in her eyes, and it was the first time I heard my dad's voice quiver. Mal and McKenna both sobbed as they got up to hug my mom, and as I headed over to her I had to turn my head away so she wouldn't see that I wasn't crying.

It is an odd scene—walking into your parents' bathroom to find your own father with Fiskers in his hand, trying his best to artistically sculpt a decent haircut on his wife. My dad was no hairdresser; when I was young and Mom would leave for the weekend, my dad would drive me over to my grandma's for a ponytail before school. It was out of place to see him behind my mother, trying so hard to gracefully craft something she would like for the next few days, a towel draped around her thinning shoulders, the shears with the orange handle and that terrible slicing sound they made on thick hair. He just kept cutting, cutting, and to make amusement of the situation my mother pulled a strand from her head and held it up: "Look, Baylee, it just comes right out!"

McKenna and Mal were already there, too, and both were doing a great job of comforting my mom, making light of what was finally happening, helping my dad with the sculpting. I just stood there. A bout of nausea rolled in. I shook my head when my mom asked if I wanted to help, and I fought back tears as I left the bathroom, my family still in there together trying their best to be strong for my mom. Now, I can't even imagine what it must have felt like for *her*, a woman able to pull the hair from her own head, strands that seemed to be giving up. It was the first time I cried.

She had been sick for a month. We had had multiple family meetings, and she had gone through surgery, but I hadn't been able to cry. You would think that a sophomore in high school at risk of losing her mother would have at least shed a tear on the day her mom was diagnosed. For God's sake, I cry at every sad story in the world—I'll read the newspaper and cry at any car accident, and I still fight back the tears when I watch *The Lion King* and Mufasa dies. I cry at every mention of cancer in someone I know, but not my own mother's? Sometimes I wonder if I had a premonition, if somehow I knew that in the end of it all she would be okay. Or, maybe I just needed the physical reality of the hair to prove what was happening, what was at stake.

Eventually, my mom had a synthetic wig made. It actually looked pretty similar to her hair before it was gone: light brown, slightly wavy, and right above the ears. She hated it. She said it was itchy. I would sit on her bathtub and watch her put it on as she would try to readjust it on her scalp. It didn't feel right to watch a head of hair move around, something that is supposed to be so firmly in place. Each time, tears would flood into her eyes until she would get so worked up she'd scream "I *hate* this thing!"

Right when she first got the wig, I made the mistake of forgetting my basketball jersey at home on the day of a home game. Just fifteen minutes after I called, my mom was up at school and found me outside the locker room. It was her first appearance in public with the wig. Her hands were fidgety and she kept fixing the little chunks of hair behind her ears. I remember noticing how nervous her face looked, her lips curled into themselves and her eyes big, moving quickly. She handed me my jersey and leaned into my ear, "Can you tell?" she said. "No, Mom, you look great," I said, and after she turned to leave I stood outside the locker room door, fighting off the tears again.

When she got a little more comfortable with her appearance, she nixed the wig and switched to hats—just ball caps, in every color. No matter what she wore, she would dig through a drawer filled with cotton baseball caps for one to match. On Mother's Day that year, four months after her diagnosis, we asked her what she wanted for a gift. "More caps," she said. My dad gave us fifty dollars. We went to Target and came home with a bouquet of caps in every color she didn't already have: sky blue, dark brown, bright pink, lime green. On Mother's Day, when she opened her gifts from us, she was so excited about the new colors. "Oh! Lime green! I'll have to get a shirt to wear with this one! Thank you girls," she said. I cried that day, too.

It's the story I always tell, the hair is what got me.

After she completed the eight months of chemo, the hair came back. It came back in dark little curls, tight to her head, like a nicely-done eighties perm. It was gorgeous. She had always wanted curly hair and said that when she was younger my grandma would tell her that eating bread crusts would give her curls, though it never worked. It's almost as if the coarse nest of curls was the body's apology for taking the breast, a little miracle at the end of an illness to resurrect confidence and beauty. A new *look*.

At the beginning of the video, my mom's voice provides an introduction to our game, "It is March, 1995, and the girls are playing Pogs, the game of the future!" I try to explain what a Slammer is before Mallory cuts me off with her introductions. When my dad comes in at the end, repeating his furious question, all four of us girls burst out laughing. Holding the camera, I zoom in to my mom's face. She readjusts the clip holding up her hair, tries to hold the laughter behind her smirked lips, and stands up to help my father find his checkbook.

LESSONS FROM LOCKDOWN:
Sometimes Inmates Make the Best College Students

Matthew Batt

Some 90 miles north of Madison, a brown wood sign the size of a man's forearm directs me off County Trunk B to "FCI Oxford." It's the kind of hand-carved sign that you'd usually find in a state park bearing the word "Latrines," the kind of sign you'd miss unless you were looking for it. After passing a few farms, mobile homes and wary herds of deer, I crest a hill and there it is: Oxford Federal Corrections Institute, unnaturally lit like a college campus but fortressed like few things are.

The sign at the entrance, in English and Spanish, warns me that all vehicles and persons are subject to search and seizure. A white F-150 patrols slowly, like a carnivore, assuring me the warning is literal. Inside, I inspect the lacquered wood plaque commemorating a "fallen officer," and before I can get my mind around that—that people die working here—I hear my name barked out in military precision.

"With that hair, I knew it had to be the new English teacher," says a short, flat-topped man wearing both a belt and suspenders. He squeezes my hand until he can see pain in my face, then leads me into a generic boardroom for an interview with the assistant warden and the director of human resources. There, I'm grilled about various scenarios, none of which appear to be scripted.

"What if you were at a picnic, and your wife wanted to know if you had met the ... the senator's son's brother-in-law who was in Oxford for ... for... it doesn't matter. What would you say?"

My response time lags as I wonder why I would need to be at a picnic to be talking to my wife.

"So let's say," the interrogation continues, "you get a phone call, and it's an inmate's sister and she wonders if maybe you couldn't take him a little package for her. What would you do?"

We're talking about criminals, of course—why would I fall for that? But I am the only one laughing when the assistant warden reminds me: "Regardless of his name, Warden Dick Stiff is not known for his sense of humor."

Before I'm taken inside the prison proper for a drug test, the warden adds: "And by the way, when you teach here, try not to dress like the inmates." He gestures at my jeans and green button-down. "Makes things difficult, shall we say, in a crisis situation—to tell you from them."

As a faculty member of the University of Wisconsin at Baraboo/Sauk County, I have the option to teach at Oxford, where inmates can sign up for—and pay their own tuition for, incidentally—college courses. David Cole, a 30-year-plus veteran of Boo-U, encourages me to teach there as soon and as often as possible: "Like one of my former Oxford students put it: 'When I'm in college, I ain't in prison.'"

Teaching four sections of freshman and sophomore college composition is the rough equivalent of hazing junior faculty members, but there's no Everclear or livestock involved. Only fleet after fleet of vigorously uninterested teenagers, stupefied by words like "verb" and "noun." And so, after a few years of such a fate and untold scores more, I seize the opportunity to teach at Oxford.

Two interviews, a training session, a fingerprinting, a urinalysis, a background check, and a photographing later, I find myself alone in the lobby at Oxford, waiting for the guard in Control to open the first of seven gates between me and my classroom.

Fifteen minutes later I stand in front of my class: 13 men, fanned out racially across the room. Young black men in the rear left. Older black men in front. Whites, young and old, in the right rear. A couple of older Latinos at right front. The seating arrangement will remain the same throughout the semester.

"So what you think of Camp Mickey Mouse?" one student asks, a white man in his mid-30s with narrow eyes and bad posture.

"Don't know," I say. "Is that what you think of it? Disneyland?"

A sophisticated black man wearing filligreed, gold-rimmed glasses answers, "Compared to real prisons, yeah. This is kindergarten." He holds up his pint of Ben & Jerry's as proof.

I don't know whether to take this as a bluff or not until two weeks later, when I lose the first of six students to the Special Housing Unit (SHU), or solitary confinement.

Oxford is a medium- to maximum- security Federal prison where, from what I can unofficially gather, men are sent to serve on average, 10- to 20- year bids for non-violent (or at least non-fatal) drug, firearm, robbery or fraud convictions. But despite the apparent lack of "violent felons," it is always a prison; my students, no matter how I regard them, always inmates.

The class is Business Communication: a fluff class that neither English nor Business faculty are eager to teach since it's basically a résumé writing workshop that supposedly looks good on transcripts for future employers. During my semester at Oxford, one question is never very far from my mind: How good will this class look to my students' (future ex-cons) would-be employers?

It's the second week, and we're working on résumés. The examples from the book seem generous enough. One is from an up-and-comer MBA type. Another from a silver-spooner who never had more than a summer job. Both make good use of Internships and traditional educations as well as life-guarding experience.

One of my students, a huge black man known as "Heavy," breaks in: "Yeah, but Teach. I mean, what if we *never* had a job?"

I shrug and refer him to the dressed-up lifeguard's résumé and how he emphasizes his education before his work experience.

Heavy is clearly unsatisfied. "Yeah, but I mean come on. We felons, man. What we gonna put?"

It's the first of many questions to which I have no response.

What do you say to a 30-year-old black man (with another 10 years on his sentence) who has never held a legitimate job and wants to know what kind of future he's got in store for himself? What do you say to a 50-year-old Mexican-American who wants to be a dental prosthetic technician but will be 60 before his time is served? What do you say to a brilliant young white man, who held up a bank with a note but would just as soon talk about *The Odyssey* as *Monday Night Football*, when he tells you he wants to teach literature in high school?

How do you tell these men that employers cannot legally discriminate against them for their convictions so long as they disclose their criminal histories, when, of course, they can and do? How do you tell these men that washing dishes, slinging hash browns or digging ditches is satisfying, well-paying work?

How do you lie to these men when you know the truth—that their sentences will never be served—that they will always be convicts? Or rather, how do you tell them the truth without locking up your own heart?

In my orientation/training, where all contract workers and volunteers are initiated into the wily ways of the prison, various corrections officers and administrators warn us that inmates are manipulators. "They've got nothing but time on their hands," one red-scalped lieutenant promises. "Twenty-four-seven they're trying to figure out how to get what they want from you and me."

And indeed, there are some manipulators. One is known mockingly as "The Toolbox." A 20-something, sunglasses-at-night-wearing white man makes an early habit of standing too close to me during breaks and bragging about how, back in Topeka, he'd had a couple of hot chicks dragging around in his convertible Ferrari with him most nights.

The third week of class he's in the SHU, and not long after, I learn that his fate is left to "Diesel Therapy"—they'll bus him from one Federal pen after the other so he can never get settled, never make any friends, never be close to family, never feel like anything more than cargo.

But most of my Oxford students are bright and congenial beyond all reasonable expectation. As diverse and gifted—and as challenging—as an inner-city honors class.

At UW-Baraboo, we work almost exclusively from the textbook, using its safe, tidy examples, learning its safe, tidy lessons. These rarely, if ever, fit at Oxford. Trying to get a bunch of docile, hard-working but unacademic central Wisconsinites to develop a sales letter for a lemonade stand is fairly cut-and-dried work. Trying to get Federal convicts from all parts of the world to do so is the pedagogical equivalent to suicide. Instead, I ask them what they want to sell.

After a few off-hand, bragging comments from around the room about how successful at sales they all were before getting brought up on Federal charges, we take a straw poll. Sporting goods, auto care, and bagels all lose out to cologne. But not just any cologne. No. The cologne we develop isn't your standard over-the-counter fare. This is Stud II G: a pheromone-enhanced spray that will "turn Herman the Herb into Hermano the Hulk."

By evening's end, we've devised a logo, a distribution plan, a price point, and a focus market. Before we know it, truck stops and strip clubs nationwide will offer Stud II G, a scent that will turn B.O. into an aphrodisiac.

Granted, it's not the kind of product that's liable to go off well in a politically correct, mixed-gender classroom, but this is as far from that as the Kitty Kat's men's room.

Trying to reach my students at Oxford on their terms, I decide to include a bit of my personal experience in the business world. After discussing résumés, I tell them about how I have just applied for a job as a waiter in Madison. I describe how I was the only applicant, among five other (much more attractive) applicants, who had arrived, with a résumé in hand.

But before I can make good on my little lesson, Heavy cries out from the back corner: "You *what?* What kind of job? A restaurant?"

I pause. I don't understand his line of questioning.

"You mean you gots—what?—two or three degrees and shit, and you applying to be a waiter? A waiter! Aw, Batt, say it ain't so! Say it ain't so."

I can't.

At first I try to convince him that I actually like waiting tables, that it's a nice change from the academic junk, and that it keeps me honest. It's not until I am dodging deer on the drive back to Madison that I realize what a jerk I've been. What I said was the equivalent of "I like going to Cabrini Green because it's like a real live ghetto."

To my students at Oxford, working in a restaurant—no matter how many college degrees they amass in prison or afterwards—might be the best they can hope for in the next decade. To me, it's just "fun."

By the time we get halfway into most of our three-hour classes, most of the material has been covered. What matters in business, after all, is not florid prose but a black bottom line. There is no *Best American Business Writing of 2002* due out any time soon.

To fill the time before the guard escorts me out, my students and I do a lot of gabbing. It's a heady environment for a teacher used to being ignored or merely tolerated on a traditional campus. To the inmates, I'm the educational equivalent of a celebrity.

Lest you think I'm overstating my case, walk the hall with me after class while 100-some inmates are waiting for the college doors to he unlocked so they can return to their cells. Inmates I have never met call me by name—and pronounce it correctly (unlike the administrators).

One of my students—the one with the fancy gold glasses—asks me why I wear my ring on a different finger. Another asks why I don't wear a watch: Am I afraid it'll get stolen? Still another suggests I get some "bling-bling"—a Rolex or a Tag, something flashy.

Little goes unnoticed here, but much goes unsaid.

Later in the semester, I encourage my students to personalize their cover letters, to make them the catalyst for an interview. "Think of your résumé as the basketball," I tell them, "the cover letter as Michael Jordan." (It's just my luck that they are collectively far more interested in wrestling than basketball.)

And so one of my students—the older man hoping to work in dentistry—shows me a polished revision of his letter and asks for feedback. I make a few notations in the margins as I read and think I'll have to send him back to the drawing board (again) when I notice something off-key in his closing line: "I am available for an interview anytime on or after January 1, 2009."

I tell him everything looks fine.

At every traditional campus where I've taught, a college education is by and large taken absolutely for granted. Except for the few non-traditional students, college is what you do when you finish high school so that you can get a job that pays better than Taco Bell. It's a pain in the ass, but it's pretty easy, and there's a lot of time to meet members of the opposite sex and drink ridiculous amounts of cheap beer with them. Going to college is part of our economy. It's a rite, a test, an initiation, a standard.

In prison, your status isn't based on your SATs or your note-taking proficiency but rather on your gang affiliation or your benching max. Your status is based on the sharpness of your shiv; how many pushups or pull-ups you can do, how much wine you can brew or how many stamps or cigarettes you can garner without getting caught

It's true: Almost all of my students at Oxford have been bad men. Men who have corrupted, stolen from, hurt or killed other men and women. There's no getting around that. They are men who have broken the rules, let down their parents and teachers and loved ones (if they have had any).

But what I discover—as cheesy as it sounds—is that my Oxford students are the best students I've ever had. They are sweethearts, most of them, who have done something profoundly regrettable and, at least to me, they show no signs of having forgotten their mistakes.

Halfway through the semester, I cancel class in order to be with my mother while she undergoes a brief hospitalization. When I return the following week, one of my students, nicknamed "Sweets," hands me an envelope. It's a Hallmark card signed by the whole class with their prayers and best wishes.

As if the card and their blessings aren't enough, figure in the fact that inmates at Oxford make $5.25 a month for working full-time jobs within the prison and that any goods they purchase are only to be had from the prison's commissary. Imagine working a week-and-a-half—60 hours—in a prison factory to buy a card for your Business Communication teacher's mother.

On the second to last day of class, a spring storm tears through Adams County, and when lightning strikes the fence at Oxford, all inmates are recalled to their cells. Contract workers (like me) are required to leave the grounds immediately. I stand by the steel-enmeshed window with one of my students, a guy nicknamed "'Toro," while the others gather their books.

"Can you see it?" he asks, "The deer?"

We both stare out the window toward where the woods border the razor wire fence. Black clouds are rolling over the trees and guard towers. The grate on the window is too dense to see very clearly, but Toro seems to see just fine.

"I used to hunt deer down near Laredo on my uncle's farm," Toro says. "He had this exotic wildlife preserve and got all these crazy animals from everywhere in the world. It was beautiful, man. Like the whole world on this one little farm."

The lesson seems too obvious, the analogy too apt for either of us to bear. We laugh, and he winks at me, then continues: "Yeah, but he let all these stupid rich guys from Dallas come in and shoot the place up. They were mostly fat and drunk and didn't hit shit. Because I kept everything clean, and cooked for the gringos and gutted whatever they managed to kill, my uncle, he let me hunt whatever I wanted. I've bagged gazelles, lions, elk, all kinds of deer, man—even the ones with those spiral antlers."

Toro glances down the hall, shoulders his bag and tells me to have a safe trip home.

As I pass through the seven gates to leave Oxford, I think of my colleague's former inmate/student who said that when he was in college, he wasn't in prison. I try to figure out how that notion applies to me. When I am in college, am I in prison? When I am in prison, aren't I in college? The truth is somewhere in the messy middle, of course. Education—and incarceration—thrives on both sides of the bars.

ON THE NET

How to Write a Profile Feature Article. Student Voices. New York Times On the Web.
   <http://www.nytimes.com/learning/students/writing/voices.html>

How to Report and Write a Tough but Fair Profile. No Train, No Gain: Training for Newspaper Journalists.
   <http://www.notrain-nogain.org/list/prof.asp>

On Memoir, Truth and 'Writing Well.' Interview with William Zinsser. National Public Radio. April 13, 2006. Excerpt "How to Write a Memoir."
   <http://www.npr.org/templates/story/story.php?storyId=5340618>

Sixties Personal Narrative Project. University of Virginia Institute for Advanced Technology in the Humanities.
<http://www2.iath.virginia.edu/sixties/HTML_docs/Narrative.html>

The Personal Essay. Capital Community College.
<http://grammar.ccc.commnet.edu/grammar/composition/personal.htm>

This I Believe. National Public Radio.
<http://www.npr.org/templates/story/story.php?storyId=4538138>

The Personal Essay. Mr. Bauld's English.
< http://www.mrbauld.com/essays.html>

EXERCISES

In his book *Writing Life Stories,* Bill Roorbach suggests the following exercise for all writers of memoir and autobiography as a great starting place, as well as a touchstone exercise that can be repeated over and over with slight variations. It has two parts:

1. Draw a map of your earliest childhood home. Interpret "map" and "home" to mean whatever seems useful to you. Interpret "draw" to be literal: get the Crayons out and a big piece of butcher paper and have at it. Be as detailed as possible.

2. As you're drawing, make a list of events that happened in any given place on your map. Don't stop drawing, though, until you've finished the map or you've come up with a hefty list of twenty events. Then you'll be able to pick the one or two that seem most compelling, challenging, and rewarding to tell.

6 Process Analysis

We use process analysis all the time. When we read and follow the directions on a pay telephone or a self-service gas pump, we are using process. Process is a habit of mind involving ideas in logical sequences. There is an orderly and efficient way to do almost everything, although nearly everyone thinks his or her way is best. Basically there are two kinds of processes: directional and informational. The directional process explains how to do something so that the reader can duplicate the action suggested while the informational process explains how a more complicated process is done but not with the intent of duplication. You do not have to be a miner to understand how strip mining works, nor are you expected to run right out and create a strip mine in your back yard if you read about how the process is done.

Process analyses are used in almost anything that requires a step-by-step explanation. When you explain the steps of a chemistry experiment, you are presenting a directional process. You use informational processes every time you explain how the Native Indians were disenfranchised, how a bill becomes law, or how the writing process works. Chapter Two in this book specifically discusses the writing process, for instance.

Strategy

When you explain a process, particularly a directional one, you should take several things into consideration.

1. Provide an overview of general principles. Give your reader an understanding of the way you intend to develop your plan.

2. Provide complete details. All the techniques you use in describing anything will, of course, be applicable to describing how to do a process or how a particular process is done.

3. Define any technical terms. Keep your audience in mind and try to make your explanation clear enough to communicate effectively.

4. Provide reasons for the steps you include. You should tell why it is important to include certain elements of the process as well as how to do them.

5. Include negative directions as well as the reasons for doing things a certain way in a certain order. You must warn the reader in key places about what

not to do. Since cyanide is difficult to remove from all kinds of surfaces, including glass, it is probably better not to mix Kool-Aid for the neighborhood kids in a beaker you usually use for cyanide experiments.

6. Illustrate your process using descriptive techniques. Normally, you will not have diagrams or other visual aids in your writing; therefore, you need to create images to make your process clear.

7. You will have noticed in the course of this discussion that its point of view violates the rules you may have been told about using second person and shifting points of view. Since this book is designed as a set of directions or instructions for the reader, it often uses second person. The purpose and audience determine the point of view you will use in your writing. Sometimes your instructor will insist that you use third person ("one," "he," "she") in order to practice appealing to certain audiences of the type you will write for in many academic settings. One way to implement the consistent use of third person in a process is to introduce an actor—someone who is logically involved in the process—early in your discussion. If you are describing how to bake bread, the person involved in the process is the baker. When you refer to the baker as the actor in the process, you refer to him or her in the third person. Sometimes you may be asked to use the imperative: a command or request who's implied subject is "you." An old Paul Simon song advises the audience about "fifty ways to leave a lover" and uses the imperative: "Get on the bus, Gus" "Make a new plan, Stan;" "No need to be coy, Roy." Likewise, the directions on the service station gas pump are consistently imperative:

1. Select octane grade; 2. Lift handle; 3. Insert nozzle and pump.

No matter what the assignment requires, you must maintain a consistent point of view. Do not shift from "I" to "you" to "he" and back again. Keep your audience firmly in mind.

Organization

In writing process papers, the same general steps that apply to all writing situations are also important. As you outline, you should group steps logically. You will not put each step in a single short paragraph. The reader should be aware that you have a plan, an outline, but it should not be intrusive. Your outline is the skeleton of your essay; the essay should flesh out that skeleton. Be sure you choose a process which is a suitable length for the paper required, and organize logically, usually chronologically. The thesis statement should indicate the specific groups of steps you will discuss, corresponding to the paragraphs you develop. Throughout the paper, keep your reader firmly in mind: the audience and the purpose will determine your tone, your techniques, and your direction. Do not condescend to or patronize your audience; explain clearly. In a directional process you may want to use personal narrative, especially in the introduction to indicate how you became familiar with the process or why you think knowing about this process is important or worthwhile. Transitions are particularly important in process, usually indicating that the steps are chronological for a reason. Generally you will use transitions like "first," "next", "then," "additionally," and "finally" in addition to any devices you need to make your ideas clearly logical for your reader. You may want to include phrases like "Be sure to ___ before you try to ___" or "Under no circumstance should you do ___ before doing ___." In your conclusion, you should indicate the results of the procedure—a fluffy soufflé, a law, a well-written essay, an embalmed corpse—and their significance.

◆

CHECKLIST FOR PROCESS ESSAY

1. Did you list all the necessary steps?
2. Is each step explained thoroughly, offering specific, vivid details?
3. Did you define any terms that might be unfamiliar to your audience?
4. Did you provide clear connective words to indicate the sequential nature of the process described?
5. Did you vary your sentences enough to avoid monotony?
6. Is your purpose clear, either to inform and entertain or to help someone duplicate a step-by-step process?
7. Did you edit your paper carefully, checking for major grammatical and spelling errors?

As you read the following student essay, pay particular attention to the structure and organization. Both elements take the audience through a step-by-step process for duplicating the task at hand.

PLANTING A VEGETABLE GARDEN

There are three major steps in planting a summer vegetable garden. Besides being good exercise, gardening can bring pleasant family activity to the back yard for a nominal investment. Many a backyard gardener has become addicted after his first harvest. With a little planning and preparation, as is described below, one may enjoy the fruit of his labor for several weeks during the picking season.

The first major step is preparation. As the gardener begins to prepare for his garden, he needs to be aware of the last predicted date for frost in his area. Also, he should consider the types of crops which would likely flourish in his region. Other considerations are the proper spot, in terms of size, for projected yield, location for a minimum of six hours of sunlight daily, and elevation of the plot for purposes of drainage. Once these factors have been decided, he must gather the proper tools and supplies. These may include gloves, a garden hoe, rotary tiller, water hose, prepared commercial fertilizer of a five-ten-five ratio, previously composted material, seeds and plants, such as tomatoes to be set, and, perhaps, some bottomless paper cups for use as support collars.

The second major step to vegetable gardening is that of action. First, the soil must be prepared. This is done by tilling the desired area to remove grass and weeds and to loosen the dirt. Once the grass and weeds are loose, they may be manually picked up and discarded. At this time the gardener should add four pounds, per one hundred square feet, of commercially prepared fertilizer of a five-ten-five ratio. Also, it is helpful to add three to four inches in depth of composted matter, for richness and moisture retention. Re-tilling this mixture into the soil will insure proper blending. At this stage, the furrows may be formed by using a hoe and burrowing along in the fluffy ground. The excess dirt may be lightly tossed to each side to form the mounds for planting. When shallow trenches are made in the furrows, the seeds may be planted. Three seeds at a time may be sown at specified intervals noted on the envelope in which they were packaged. When the seeds are planted, the trench may be closed up by pinching the soil back in place over the mound. This is when young seedlings are to be set in the remaining garden area, at one foot intervals.

Now that the actual planting is done, the finishing stage remains. One final touch might be to cover weak or spindly seedlings with inverted paper cups, which are bottomless. Also, the gardener should quench this thirsty new crop with the water hose before spraying clean the tiller blades and hoe. The implements may be put away along with the gloves, unused fertilizer, leftover paper cups, remaining seeds, and the recoiled water hose. Of course, any trash generated by the project needs to be discarded at this time.

The original planning and maintaining of a vegetable garden are a lot of work and not very cost effective for the average family's consumption. Most backyard gardens are small and puny in comparison to amber waves of grain. However, the sore back, the callused hands, and the hours of pulling weeds are usually forgotten with the first juicy bite of a "Big Boy" variety tomato picked from the vine only minutes ago.

DESPERATION WRITING

Peter Elbow

I know I am not alone in my recurring twinges of panic that I won't be able to write something when I need to, I won't be able to produce coherent speech or thought. And that lingering doubt is a great hindrance to writing. It's a constant fog or static that clouds the mind. I never got out of its clutches till I discovered that it was possible to write something—not something great or pleasing but at least something usable, workable—when my mind is out of commission. The trick is that you have to do all your cooking out on the table: your mind is incapable of doing any inside. It means using symbols and pieces of paper not as a crutch but as a wheel chair.

The first thing is to admit your condition: because of some mood or event or whatever, your mind is incapable of anything that could be called thought. It can put out a babbling kind of speech utterance, it can put a simple feeling, perception, or sort-of-thought into understandable (though terrible) words. But it is incapable of considering anything in relation to anything else. The moment you try to hold that thought or feeling up against some other to see the relationship, you simply lose the picture—you get nothing but buzzing lines or waving colors.

So admit this. Avoid anything more than one feeling, perception, or thought. Simply write as much as possible. Try simply to steer your mind in the direction or general vicinity of the thing you are trying to write about and start writing and keep writing.

Just write and keep writing. (Probably best to write on only one side of the paper in case you should want to cut parts out with scissors—but you probably won't.) Just write and keep writing. It will probably come in waves. After a flurry, stop and take a brief rest. But don't stop too long. Don't think about what you are writing or what you have written or else you will overload the circuit again. Keep writing as though you are drugged or drunk. Keep doing this till you feel you have a lot of material that might be useful; or, if necessary, till you can't stand it any more—even if you doubt that there's anything useful there.

Then take a pad of little pieces of paper—or perhaps 3 x 5 cards—and simply start at the beginning of what you were writing, and as you read over what you wrote, every time you come to any thought, feeling, perception, or image that could be gathered up into one sentence or one assertion, do so and write it by itself on a little sheet of paper. In short, you are trying to turn, say, ten or twenty pages of wandering mush into twenty or thirty hard little crab apples. Sometimes there won't be many on a page. But if it seems to you that there are none on a page, you are making a serious error—the same serious error that put you in this comatose state to start with. You are mistaking lousy, stupid, second-rate, wrong, childish, foolish, worthless ideas for no ideas at all. Your job is not to pick out good ideas but to pick out ideas. As long as you were conscious, your words will be full of things that could be called feelings, utterances, ideas—things that can be squeezed into one simple sentence. This is your job. Don't ask for too much.

After you have done this, take those little slips or cards, read through them a number of times—not struggling with them, simply wandering and mulling through them; perhaps shifting them around and looking through them in various sequences. In a sense these are cards you are playing solitaire with, and the rules of this particular game permit shuffling the unused pile.

The goal of this procedure with the cards is to get them to distribute themselves in two or three or ten or fifteen different piles on your desk. You can get them to do this almost by themselves if you simply keep reading through them in different orders; certain cards will begin to feel like they go with other cards. I emphasize this passive, thoughtless mode because I want to talk about desperation writing in its pure state. In practice, almost invariably at some point in the procedure, your sanity begins to return. It is often at this point. You actually are moved to have thoughts or—and the difference between active and passive is crucial here—to *exert* thought; to hold two cards together and *build* or *assert* a relationship. It is a matter of bringing energy to bear.

So you may start to be able to do something active with these cards, and begin actually to think. But if not, just allow the cards to find their own piles with each other by feel, by drift, by intuition, by mindlessness.

You have now engaged in the two main activities that will permit you to get something cooked out on the table rather than in your brain: writing out into messy words, summing up into single assertions, and even sensing relationships between assertions. You can simply continue to deploy these two activities.

If, for example, after that first round of writing, assertion- making, and pile-making, your piles feel as though they are useful and satisfactory for what you are writing—paragraphs or sections or trains of thought—then you can carry on from there. See if you can gather each pile up into a single assertion. When you can, then put the subsidiary assertions of that pile into their best order to fit with that single unifying one. If you *can't* get the pile into one assertion, then take the pile as the basis for doing some more writing out into words. In the course of this writing, you may produce for yourself the single unifying assertion you were looking for; or you may have to go through the cycle of turning the writing into assertions and piles and so forth. Perhaps more than once. The pile may turn out to want to be two or more piles itself; or it may want to become part of a pile you already have. This is natural. This kind of meshing into one configuration, then coming apart, then coming together and meshing into a different configuration—this is growing and cooking. It makes a terrible mess, but if you can't do it in your head, you have to put up with a cluttered desk and a lot of confusion.

If, on the other hand, all that writing *didn't* have useful material in it, it means that your writing wasn't loose, drifting, quirky, jerky, associative enough. This time try especially to let things simply remind you of things that are seemingly crazy or unrelated. Follow these odd associations. Make as many metaphors as you can—be as nutty as possible—and explore the metaphors themselves—open them out. You may have all your energy tied up in some area of your experience that you are leaving out. Don't refrain from writing about whatever else is on your mind: how you feel at the moment, what you are losing your mind over, randomness that intrudes itself on your consciousness, the pattern on the wallpaper, what those people you see out the window have on their minds—though keep coming back to the whateveritis you are supposed to be writing about. Treat it, in short, like ten-minute writing exercises. Your best perceptions and thoughts are always going to be tied up in whatever is really occupying you, and that is also where your energy is. You may end up writing a love poem—or a hate poem—in one of those little piles while the other piles will finally turn into a lab report on data processing or whatever you have to write about. But you couldn't, in your present state of having your head shot off, have written that report without also writing the poem. And the report will have some of the juice of the poem in it and vice versa.

ON THE NET

Process Analysis Essay. Kamehameha Schools. Hawii.
    <http://ksdl.ksbe.edu/writingresource/processanalysis.html>

Writing A Process Essay. LEO: Literacy Education Online. St. Cloud State University.
    <http://leo.stcloudstate.edu/acadwrite/process.html>

The Process Essay. Capital Community College.
    <http://grammar.ccc.commnet.edu/grammar/composition/process.htm>

Process Analysis. Tidewater Community College.
    <http://www.tcc.edu/students/resources/writcent/HANDOUTS/writing/process.htm>

EXERCISES

Process I Exercise

Below are several scrambled steps listing a series of events that makes up a process sequence. Unscramble these items and arrange them in chronological order. Then outline the process, indicating how you would group the events and what you would call each group. Make sure each level is parallel.

_____ 1. Pour a cup of coffee.

_____ 2. Re-wet hair and try again.

_____ 3. Put on shirt and tie after brushing lint off pants.

_____ 4. Dry off

_____ 5. Turn on kitchen light while rubbing knot on forehead

_____ 6. Start car

_____ 7. Brush teeth after changing shirts

_____ 8. Arrive at class 10 minutes late

_____ 9. Find key in sofa

_____ 10. Dodge vicious squirrel on the way to the car

_____ 11. Scald yourself in the shower—you forgot to check temperature

_____ 12. Spill coffee on shirt while putting lint brush away

_____ 13. Hit "snooze" on clock again

_____ 14. Stumble over tub edge trying to get out of shower

_____ 15. Get stuck in traffic on the freeway

_____ 16. Burn tongue with hot coffee

_____ 17. Put pants on after putting on socks

_____ 18. Finish showering

_____ 19. Drag yourself out of bed

_____ 20. Turn off lights after finding keys in sofa

_____ 21. Change tie before leaving for school

_____ 22. Adjust the shower's water temperature

_____ 23. Put socks on after hair is dried the second time

_____ 24. Stumble back into the kitchen again with hair still dripping wet

_____ 25. Fix coffee

_____ 26. Search frantically for the keys

_____ 27. Drive 75 mph to make up for lost time changing clothes

_____ 28. Change shirt

_____ 29. Having selected your wardrobe, time to dry hair

_____ 30. Shower after coffee begins to brew

_____ 31. Lock house

_____ 32. Drip toothpaste on tie

_____ 33. Hit snooze on alarm clock

_____ 34. With tongue still burning from coffee, pick out clothes for the day

_____ 35. Bump into wall as you move toward the kitchen

_____ 36. Run over neighbor's cat but no time to stop now

_____ 37. Class canceled because professor's favorite cat was run over in the neighbor's driveway

_____ 38. Back out of driveway

Process II Exercise

Assume you have a big, mid-semester exam in history. What are the steps in studying for the test? List the steps and then group them into logical categories. Finally, outline the process based on these steps and supply a thesis. Include your transitional devices to show the chronology of your process.

Thesis:_____

_____

I. _____

_____

_____

II. _____

_____

_____

III. _____

_____

_____

IV. _____

_____

_____

7 Illustration *and* Example

One of the most commonly used patterns of expository writing is the development of a thesis, idea, or statement by means of illustration/example or exemplification. If, for example, you wish to tell your audience that, in your opinion, Marvin is not the best choice for the position of Chief Cashier at Citibank, you might proceed to illustrate your opinion with examples of Marvin's behavior. You might provide three examples to illustrate your assertion: (1) Marvin is a chain smoker and lights his cigarettes with $10 bills. (2) Although his salary is now only $100 a week and his parents live in a one-room apartment, Marvin drives a new Lexus and goes on vacations in Bora Bora. (3) Two months ago Marvin returned after another kind of vacation where he was serving 10 to 20 years for embezzling two hundred thousand dollars from the Second Interstate Bank. Each of these examples serves to show your reader why you do not think highly of Marvin as a bank employee. You have made a statement (Don't make Marv Chief Cashier) and illustrated your statement with three effective examples of his behavior that should disqualify him from the job. In the exemplification essay, you make a statement and then provide examples to clarify your statement for the audience. The examples should be clear, concrete, appropriate, interesting, and supportive of the thesis statement.

Strategy

Effective examples have a number of common characteristics: they are clear, concrete, appropriate, vivid, interesting, and supportive of your thesis statement.

Good Examples are Clear.

Since the purpose of using examples is to make your general idea clearer to your audience, it should be obvious that the examples must be carefully chosen for their clarity. How clear the example is will depend to some extent on who the readers of the essay are likely to be. If you want to illustrate the economic principle of Supply and Demand, for instance, you would choose different examples for a professor of business administration than you would for a 9th-grade history textbook. The professor will understand references to Gross Domestic Product, and a good example for her might be a fairly complicated graph showing annual consumption of fuel oil per capita. The 9th-grader, however, would probably not find these examples helpful because they would not be clear to him. He would probably benefit more from an illustration based on a sporting goods store and the different price of baseball caps at various time of the year. When you show him that ball caps cost more in January than in July because there were fewer caps available in January, he will begin to see what you mean by "Supply and Demand." Whenever you choose an example, therefore, you should be sure that it will be clear to your intended audience and that it will make your general statement or thesis clearer to them.

Good Examples are Concrete.

This characteristic is closely allied to clarity since most examples are clearer when they are most concrete. Because of the way most of us think, readers are attracted to and benefit most from particular, specific, detailed examples. In the example already suggested—the illustration of Supply and Demand by a reference to the price of baseball caps in January—the example will be more effective if you specify "baseball cap" than if you use a more abstract term like "wearing apparel." By referring to specific months, like January and July, to explain why production is lowest, too, will probably be more effective than talking about felicitous and infelicitous manufacturing periods. To illustrate your point, you might even decide to write a short narrative in which Coach Neander complains in a rage to Mr. Strapp, the manager of the sporting goods store (frightening him and causing him to knock down an 8-foot replica of a Dallas Cowboy linebacker display he was putting up), that the caps the coach wants for this team cost $20. The idea is to make the example specific, particular, and concrete because then the thesis will be easier for your audience to understand.

Good Examples are Appropriate.

In order to be effective, to do a good job of illustrating your point, an example should be appropriate; it should be suitable to the idea it illustrates (valid, reasonable) and also to the intended audience (appropriate for their experience, background, and knowledge of the subject). If you wanted to choose an appropriate example of how advertising can sway the consumer and force him to buy something he does not really want or need, you probably would not use the Ford Motor Company's greatest flop, the Edsel, as your example. Such an example would be neither valid nor reasonable since it suggests the opposite of what you want to demonstrate. The Edsel was heavily advertised, but it looked so awful that people refused to buy it. By the same token, you do not want to choose an example that is so outlandish or exaggerated that it fails to convince your readers because it is not representative. Such an example to demonstrate how advertising can influence the consumer might be "subliminal" advertising. Some years ago there were allegations that advertising messages like "Buy a Coke" were inserted on single frames of motion pictures. The message would flash on the screen for only a fraction of a second, and the movie patrons would not even be aware they had seen it. They supposedly got thirsty, and Coke sales in the lobby went up. Now this example might illustrate the power of advertising, and it can be made clear and concrete enough, but it probably is not a good example because it is not appropriate. It is too exceptional and, therefore, unlikely to convince your audience. The charges were never proven, few theaters would have been involved anyway, and it is unlikely that your audience would feel such tactics applicable to them. The example, therefore, is not appropriate for your thesis. A more appropriate example could be the number of poor people who can barely afford to feed their families, but who buy the so-called "miracle drugs" advertised on television and in the newspapers. The drugs are often worthless, but clever advertising succeeds in selling them anyway.

Good Examples are Vivid and Interesting.

No example is very useful if the reader does not read it because it is boring. Some of the characteristics already discussed are relevant to interesting examples since an interesting example will probably be clear, appropriate, and (especially) concrete. While some examples are vivid and interesting because of the material presented, almost all examples will gain by presentation in very specific and descriptive terms.

If for some reason you had to write an essay about "The Best Teacher I have Known," you would write a more effective and interesting essay if, instead of talking about the "vast knowledge" and "truly wonderful personality" of the teacher, you illustrated your essay with a vividly described example of the time the teacher taught you about propulsion and Newton's laws of motion by having the class build and launch a 29" rocket. If you want to write a propaganda leaflet about the awful food in your school cafeteria, don't talk vaguely about inedible food and slime in the ice machine. Instead, describe in sickening detail the barbecued cockroach nestled in your friend's cheeseburger or the ability of the coffee to etch glass and dissolve your spoon in 18 seconds. Make your reader participate in the essay to get your point across more quickly and thoroughly than you could with any amount of general verbiage about the teacher's "immense contribution to learning" or the cafeteria's wretched cuisine. Vivid examples can make an essay interesting, exciting, and effective. Dull, generalized examples will put your reader to sleep faster than ether, a rubber hammer, or an interview with Britney Spears.

Organization

The purpose of developing an essay or a paragraph through illustration and example is to make clear the thesis, idea, or subject that you are trying to get across to your readers. You give your audience an illustration in order to explain a more general statement. The examples are samples of the general thesis, giving your readers more specific and concrete illustrations of the idea. The example thus acts as a kind of bridge from you to the readers, making the idea or subject clearer. Suppose you want to convey to your history professor your idea that the bombings of Afghanistan and war in Iraq did a great deal to heighten the American spirit. This is a general, broad idea, but your audience would like (1) to have it made clearer and more specific for them and easier to understand, and (2) they might like you to give some evidence for your assertion or at least offer them some reasons to believe that what you say about the incidents and America is true. You can give them both of these things by providing them with good examples.

You could, for instance, include in your essay either a single extended example or several examples that will show that what you say is true. In order to demonstrate that the events did enliven the American spirit, you might choose the following examples:

1. Historical documents of public polls indicate that over 70% of the Americans surveyed felt that the bombings in Afghanistan and the war in Iraq were justifiable.

2. Americans generally rallied in support of a military retaliation for the September 11 attacks on New York City and Washington D.C. (flag sales, yellow ribbons, fundraisers for victims' families).

3. The threat of "weapons of mass destruction" unified the American spirit and a desire to eliminate forces that put national security in peril (military reserve forces called up, billions of dollars appropriated for the war effort, a new cabinet post created).

Your method is thus to illustrate your general statement (that the wars solidified the American spirit) with three examples that make clear to the audience precisely what you mean. You could also have chosen only one of the examples and presented an extended discussion of even greater detail to illustrate your point. Whether an essay is formally called exemplification or not, every composition needs concrete, detailed examples. In either case the examples clarify your basic point.

These characteristics obviously apply to essays that use illustration and examples as the structural principle, but it is important to note that we use examples in all of our rhetorical patterns, in every kind of expository and persuasive writing. Examine almost any good piece of writing, and you will find examples that are vivid, concrete, clear, interesting, and appropriate. Essays developed by definition, classification, comparison and contrast, process analysis, causal analysis, argumentation, and critical analysis depend on examples to help get their ideas across to their audience. The difference is that an essay developed by illustration uses examples as the structural principle on which it is organized. Review the general principles of composition and the checklist discussed in Chapter Two of this text. The general method of development in that chapter is based on the structure of illustration/example.

◆

CHECKLIST FOR ILLUSTRATION / EXAMPLE ESSAY

1. Does your thesis have a narrowed subject and restricted focus?
2. Did you use three or four examples, or did you use a simple extended example?
3. Are your primary examples adequately developed?
4. Did you provide appropriate transition between your paragraphs?
5. Did you provide a sufficient number of specific details to support your general observations?
6. Did you provide an effective conclusion?
7. Did you include an interesting title for the essay?
8. Did you edit your paper carefully, checking for major grammatical and spelling errors?

In the following student essay written by Allison K. Hinson, notice the organization of the paragraphs and their relationship to the thesis statement. Also important are the specific examples used to discuss each of the divisions.

HORROR NOVELS AS THERAPY

Allison Hinson

We humans have a coping mechanism for dealing with the world's problems. Instead of going to a therapist we go to a movie or open a book. In the fifties, to help America accept the fear caused by the atom bomb, Hollywood gave us *Them!* and a series of "big bug" movies. To escape the social ills of today, we open a horror novel. Horror is defined as a feeling of extreme fear or dislike, a disgust that makes one shudder. However, people pay for the pleasure of being horrified. In fiction, the horror genre can be recognized by Gothic settings, psychological conflicts, and supernatural events.

Gothic horror draws us into a gloomy setting with the beauty of its prose. One of the best examples is Shirley Jackson's *The Haunting of Hill House:* "[W]alls continued upright, bricks met neatly, floors were firm, and doors were sensibly shut; silence lay steady against the wood and stone of Hill House, and whatever walked there, walked alone." With this beautifully paced opening, Ms. Jackson sets the tone for her frightening tale. In Edgar Allan Poe's "The Cask of Amontillado," we see the cobwebs and feel the nitre seep into our bones as we follow our narrator on his dark journey: "'The nitre!' I said; 'see, it increases. It hangs like moss upon the vaults. . . . The drops of moisture trickle among the bones.'" Similarly, we know that no good will come from Dracula's castle as Bram Stoker weaves his tale around us.

While Gothic settings can set the mood, psychological horror creates terror in the actual plot. Psychological horror disturbs reality, changing the way we think and act. Horror novels that are based on psychological conflicts create a feeling of terror in the reader because they are plausible. It is conceivable to experience the terror that the young mother and child feel in Stephen King's *Cujo* when they are trapped by the rabid dog. In Anthony Burgess' *A Clockwork Orange* the real horror is not that Alex and his "droogs" are on a rampage in England, but rather that the state forces mind control on him. The psychological conflict in V.C. Andrews' *Flowers in the Attic* is a struggle for power as a mother is slowly brainwashed into giving up her children. Likewise, Robert Louis Stevenson's *Dr. Jekyll and Mr. Hyde* creates horror by bringing attention to the destructive evil inside us all, symbolized by the werewolf. We all possess to some degree the split personalities between what we are and what we know. Thus, it is our identification with these psychological conflicts that make these novels horrifying.

Supernatural horror, on the other hand, does the opposite of psychological horror; it brings us outside the known laws of nature. Mary Shelley's *Frankenstein* shows us men reaching beyond set boundaries and finding only pain. Certainly the monster was furious at being brought to life and then denied companionship, and the doctor's irresponsibility brought disaster. In Ira Levin's *Rosemary's Baby* the terror is in the powerlessness Rosemary feels against the supernatural Satanic forces at work within her body. In Stephen King's *Tommyknockers* we find alien ghosts hoping to take over the world by gaining a foothold in a small town in Maine. This story gives us Pandora's box and allows us to open it, spilling forth the horrors that we knew were inside. Supernatural horror scares us because we feel so helpless before such powerful and mysterious forces.

These three components of horror fiction provide the basis of what makes horror fiction so entertaining and cathartic. The human mind can handle only so much horror in daily life. It is better to release this horror by opening a good book than to succumb to it by opening a vein.

Brent Staples, Ph.D. in Psychology from the University of Chicago, began his career in journalism and presently serves on the editorial board of the *New York Times*. His interest in psychology led him to be a keen observer of human behavior. These observations were recorded in his journal describing neighborhoods and people in Chicago. The following selection depicts the author's response to racism and stereotyping, providing a number of examples to illustrate his point.

JUST WALK ON BY:

A Black Man Ponders His Power To Alter Public Space

Brent Staples

My first victim was a woman—white, well dressed, probably in her early twenties. I came upon her late one evening on a deserted street in Hyde Park, a relatively affluent neighborhood in an otherwise mean, impoverished section of Chicago. As I swung onto the avenue behind her, there seemed to be a discreet, uninflammatory distance between us. Not so. She cast back a worried glance. To her, the youngish black man—a broad six feet two inches with a beard and billowing hair, both hands shoved into the pockets of a bulky military jacket—seemed menacingly close. After a few more quick glimpses, she picked up her pace and was soon running in earnest. Within seconds she disappeared into a cross street.

That was more than a decade ago. I was twenty-two years old, a graduate student newly arrived at the University of Chicago. It was in the echo of that terrified woman's footfalls that I first began to know the unwieldy inheritance I'd come into—the ability to alter public space in ugly ways. It was clear that she thought herself the quarry of a mugger, a rapist, or worse. Suffering a bout of insomnia, however, I was stalking sleep, not defenseless wayfarers. As a softy who is scarcely able to take a knife to a raw chicken—let alone hold it to a person's throat, I was surprised, embarrassed, and dismayed all at once. Her flight made me feel like an accomplice in tyranny. It also made it clear that I was indistinguishable from the muggers who occasionally seeped into the area from the surrounding ghetto. That first encounter, and those that followed, signified that a vast, unnerving gulf lay between nighttime pedestrians—particularly women—and me. And I soon gathered that being perceived as dangerous is a hazard in itself. I only needed to turn a corner into a dicey situation, or crowd some frightened, armed person in a foyer somewhere, or make an errant move after being pulled over by a policeman. Where fear and weapons meet—and they often do in urban America—there is always the possibility of death.

In that first year, my first away from my hometown, I was to become thoroughly familiar with the language of fear. At dark, shadowy intersections in Chicago, I could cross in front of a car stopped at a traffic light and elicit the *thunk, thunk, thunk, thunk* of the driver—black, white, male, or female—hammering down the door locks. On less traveled streets after dark, I grew accustomed to but never comfortable with people who crossed to the other side of the street rather than pass me. Then there were the standard unpleasantries with police, doormen, bouncers, cabdrivers, and others whose business is to screen out troublesome individuals before there is any nastiness.

I moved to New York nearly two years ago, and I have remained an avid night walker. In central Manhattan, the near-constant crowd cover minimizes tense one-on-one street encounters.

Elsewhere—visiting friends in SoHo, where sidewalks are narrow and tightly spaced buildings shut out the sky—things can get very taut indeed.

Black men have a firm place in New York mugging literature. Norman Podhoretz, in his famed (or infamous) 1963 essay, "My Negro Problem—And Ours," recalls growing up in terror of black males; they "were tougher than we were, more ruthless," he writes—and as an adult on the Upper West Side of Manhattan, he continues, he cannot constrain his nervousness when he meets black men on certain streets. Similarly, a decade later, the essayist and novelist Edward Hoagland extols a New York where once "Negro bitterness bore down mainly on other Negroes." Where some see mere panhandlers, Hoagland sees "a mugger who is clearly screwing up his nerve to do more than just ask for money." But Hoagland has "the New Yorker's quick-hunch posture for broken-field maneuvering," and the bad guy swerves away.

I often witness that "hunch posture" from women after dark on the barrenlike streets of Brooklyn where I live. They seem to set their faces on neutral and, with their purse straps strung across their chests bandolier style, they forge ahead as though bracing themselves against being tackled. I understand, of course, that the danger they perceive is not a hallucination. Women are particularly vulnerable to street violence, and young black males are drastically overrepresented among the perpetrators of that violence. Yet these truths are no solace against the kind of alienation that comes of being ever the suspect, against being set apart, a fearsome entity with whom pedestrians avoid making eye contact.

It is not altogether clear to me how I reached the ripe old age of twenty-two without being conscious of the lethality nighttime pedestrians attributed to me. Perhaps it was because in Chester, Pennsylvania, the small, angry industrial town where I came of age in the 1960s, I was scarcely noticeable against a backdrop of gang warfare, street knifings, and murders. I grew up one of the good boys, had perhaps a half-dozen fistfights. In retrospect, my shyness of combat has clear sources.

Many things go into the making of a young thug. One of those things is the consummation of the male romance with the power to intimidate. An infant discovers that random flailings send the baby bottle flying out of the crib and crashing to the floor. Delighted, the joyful babe repeats those motions again and again, seeking to duplicate the feat. Just so, I recall the points at which some of my boyhood friends were finally seduced by the perception of themselves as tough guys. When a mark cowered and surrendered his money without resistance, myth and reality merged—and paid off. It is, after all, only manly to embrace the power to frighten and intimidate. We, as men, are not supposed to give an inch of our lane on the highway; we are to seize the fighter's edge in work and in play and even in love; we are to be valiant in the face of hostile forces.

Unfortunately, poor and powerless young men seem to take all this nonsense literally. As a boy, I saw countless tough guys locked away; I have since buried several, too. They were babies, really—a teenage cousin, a brother of twenty-two, a childhood friend in his midtwenties—all gone down in episodes of bravado played out in the streets. I came to doubt the virtues of intimidation early on. I chose, perhaps even unconsciously, to remain a shadow—timid, but a survivor. The fearsomeness mistakenly attributed to me in public places often has a perilous flavor.

The most frightening of these confusions occurred in the late 1970s and early 1980s when I worked as a journalist in Chicago. One day, rushing into the office of a magazine I was writing for with a deadline story in hand, I was mistaken for a burglar. The office manager called security and, with an ad hoc posse, pursued me through the labyrinthine halls, nearly to my editor's door. I had no way of proving who I was. I could only move briskly toward the company of someone who knew me.

Another time I was on assignment for a local paper and killing time before an interview. I entered a jewelry store on the city's affluent Near North Side. The proprietor excused herself and returned with an enormous red Doberman pinscher straining at the end of a leash. She stood, the dog extended toward me, silent to my questions, her eyes bulging nearly out of her head. I took a cursory look around, nodded, and bade her good night. Relatively speaking, however, I never fared as badly as another black male journalist. He went to nearby Waukegan, Illinois, a couple of summers ago to work on a story about a murderer who was born there. Mistaking the reporter for the killer, police hauled him from his car at gunpoint and but for his press credentials would probably have tried to book him. Such episodes are not uncommon. Black men trade tales like this all the time.

In "My Negro Problem—And Ours," Podhoretz writes that the hatred he feels for blacks makes itself known to him through a variety of avenues—one being his discomfort with that "special brand of paranoid touchiness" to which he says blacks are prone. No doubt he is speaking here of black men. In time, I learned to smother the rage I felt at so often being taken for a criminal. Not to do so would surely have led to madness—via that special "paranoid touchiness" that so annoyed Podhoretz at the time he wrote the essay.

I began to take precautions to make myself less threatening. I move about with care, particularly late in the evening. I give a wide berth to nervous people on subway platforms during the wee hours, particularly when I have exchanged business clothes for jeans. If I happen to be entering a building behind some people who appear skittish, I may walk by, letting them clear the lobby before I return, so as not to seem to be following them. I have been calm and extremely congenial on those rare occasions when I've been pulled over by the police.

And on late-evening constitutionals along streets less traveled by, I employ what has proved to be an excellent tension-reducing measure: I whistle melodies from Beethoven and Vivaldi and the more popular classical composers. Even steely New Yorkers hunching toward nighttime destinations seem to relax, and occasionally they even join in the tune. Virtually everybody seems to sense that a mugger wouldn't be warbling bright, sunny selections from Vivaldi's *Four Seasons*. It is my equivalent of the cowbell that hikers wear when they know they are in bear country.

ON THE NET

Using Examples. Capital Community College.
<http://grammar.ccc.commnet.edu/grammar/composition/examples.htm>

A Brief Guide to Writing Example Essays. Kimberly Davis. RSCC Online Writing Lab. <
http://www.rscc.cc.tn.us/owl&writingcenter/OWL/GuidetoExamples.html>

8 **Definition**

We are all curious beings. We begin asking questions in early childhood, and we develop this inquisitive nature throughout our lives. Our curiosity leads us to seek meanings constantly in order to learn or to clarify our understanding. In addition, we are often asked to explain our own ideas or to clarify, through more specific language, something we have said, whether we are having a friendly discussion among friends or responding orally or in writing to an instructor's question. One of the methods of making ourselves more precise is through definition. When someone asks, "What do you mean by that?" your answer may be a constructed definition, relating precisely what the specific idea or term means. In putting together that definition, we often have to "translate" what we mean so our audience will understand our meaning better; we literally put our thoughts into other words in order to convey our message in an understandable language. When a definition is precise enough, it enables the audience to distinguish the particular term being defined from other, similar terms with which it could be confused. The rhetorical pattern called definition is a convenient method of clarifying or analyzing a word or concept while you examine the term for a broader understanding.

There are at least three types of definitions: the informal definition, the formal definition, and the extended definition. Although the first two require little more than a word or perhaps a sentence, the third method of definition may run into a paragraph or even several pages. Definition can be used as a method to introduce your essay, to clarify your terms within other methods of expository writing, or as a means to an end in itself.

Strategy

1. **Informal definition (synonyms)** —This definition is usually associated with the speaker's or writer's own explanation of the word with his particular purpose in mind. This is the connotative meaning of the word being defined. It defines the term by offering a synonym, a word that has a meaning similar to that of another word in the same language. The use of a synonym lets the writer clarify his expression by providing a word or term that is more familiar to the audience. For example, if you were asked what you meant by the word "mooncalf," you could simply respond with a synonym like "idiot" or "cretin."

Remember that a definition requires a common ground between the writer and his audience. This common ground implies that the definition is for a specific person or persons involved in the exchange of ideas. Consider the following conversation between a father and his 16-year old son:

> SON: "I want a new Supercharged Model X1100 convertible, Dad. It's so bad!"
>
> DAD: "You mean you don't like it then?"
>
> SON: "No, dude. I mean it's hot!
>
> DAD: "Then I'm really confused, son."

It is no wonder that dad is confused. There is no common ground of understanding here between him and his son. For the son's meaning to be understood, his audience, Dad in this case, must know that "bad" means "awesome." Some terms, however, require more than just a synonym. The term "sexual harassment" could be defined as "office abuse." Because this synonymous term does not quite reflect a true parallel meaning, you can see why "sexual harassment" might require further explanation through a formal definition or an extended definition.

2. **Formal definition**—This type of definition is that which is most likely to be found in dictionaries and other reference sources. It provides the denotative meaning of the word being defined and is composed of two distinct parts. You must first classify the term to be defined and then distinguish it from other similar terms in the same classification. Note the three steps in the following examples:

Term	Classification	Distinguishing Characteristics
A mooncalf	is a person	who is congenitally foolish or mentally defective.
A wife	is a woman	who is married to a man.

Note that the above two terms—mooncalf and wife—are placed into a broader category or class, limiting the terms to a kind of person or woman, respectively. Then we add the characteristics that distinguish that person or woman from all the other people or women. Not all definitions, however, are this simple. Some are more complex and require even more specific descriptions of the distinguishing traits. Consider the following:

> Existentialism *is a philosophy that focuses on the uniqueness and isolation of individual experiences in an indifferent universe, regards human existence as unexplainable, and emphasizes man's freedom of choice and responsibility for the consequences of his actions.*

> Sexual harassment *is a human social interaction whereby a person violates federal law by compelling another person to submit or to feel obligated to submit to sexual pressure.*

3. **Extended definition**—You will most likely want to use the extended definition method when your definition is as complex as those for existentialism or sexual harassment. This method of definition is what your instructor will most likely expect from you in analyzing some term, phrase, or concept in an essay of several hundred words. Such an examination involves writing an essay on this concept, delving more deeply into its meaning, and citing examples that illustrate the term and the difficulties in defining it. Definition, however, is not just an academic exercise. In the matter of sexual harassment, for instance, much work has gone into arriving at an explicit legal definition, for company policy and civil rights cases before the courts all hinge on how the term is defined.

Organization

Extended definitions may include one or several methods of development: synonyms, antonyms, formal definitions, narration and description, illustration, comparison or contrast, classification, or causal analysis. Regardless of which method of development you use to define your term or phrase, you will probably want to use the formal definition for your thesis statement and then develop your essay according to the requirements of that particular rhetorical method. You may wish to define what your term means by negation, that is, by telling your audience what your term does not mean. Dr. Samuel Johnson once defined darkness as the "want of light." If you wish to define the term wife, you may choose to tell your audience that a wife is not a nanny, a maid, or a mistress. While negation is effective in explaining what a term does not mean, it must be accompanied by additional methods of definition. Negation can only help to clarify other statements about what your term does mean.

Regardless of which method you use to write your definition, you should realize in the process that definition is a flexible method of expository writing. It can accommodate you and persuade your audience through almost any format you choose. It helps us to understand the things we see and sometimes the things we do not see.

◆

CHECKLIST FOR DEFINITION ESSAY

1. Is your audience clearly determined and is your purpose clearly stated?
2. Is the method of development you used the best means for achieving your audience and purpose?
3. Is your organization logical and suitable for your purpose?
4. Did you avoid repeating in your predicate or in your discussion the term you are defining, thus avoiding circularity? For instance, you should not define sexual harassment as "harassment of a sexual nature."

5. Does your definition avoid vagueness and generalities? Are you precise and clear?
6. Did you edit your paper carefully, checking for major grammatical and spelling errors?

In the following student essay, the author defines "wisdom" by suggesting that the idea is much more than just the accumulation of knowledge.

WISDOM

Jennifer Murray

If one asks the majority of people what the word *wisdom* means, most will answer vaguely that it is the knowledge gained during a lifetime. However, wisdom is much more than just knowledge gained; it signifies the accumulation of knowledge, the application of learning, and the personification of God's will in the creation of the universe (according to the *American Heritage Dictionary*, 6th ed.).

The abstract nature of the word *wisdom* allows for broad interpretation of its context. To limit the vagueness of the definition, many interpret wisdom as the accumulation of knowledge. In Greek mythology, the goddess Athena was known for her wisdom. Additionally, the personification of animals as possessing wisdom also heavily influenced Greek lore. Owls, for example, are synonymous with wisdom; likewise, foxes, with their cunning nature and ability to outsmart their prey, are considered insightful animals. Age plays a prominent part in the accumulation of learning. In many societies the elderly receive top status as preservers of both culture and knowledge, making them wise and respected members of the community. On a different level, teeth are described as being "wise"; however, these teeth actually do not differ from the rest of the secondary molars except for their tardiness.

Just as the accumulation of knowledge is a part of wisdom, so is the application of learning. The ancient Greeks believed that *logos*, or reason and thought, led to *sophia*, or wisdom. These early lovers of wisdom, or philosophers, sought knowledge and attempted to apply it to solving the puzzles of the universe. Further, philosophers such as Aristotle believed that wisdom was necessary to make judgments which coincide with one's understanding of life. This view, also known as "Philosophical Wisdom," is thought to be one of the highest attainable virtues. The Stoics, Greek and Roman philosophers, also had their own ideas about wisdom. To them, not only is wisdom a way of attaining human excellence, it also serves as a way to act according to one's personal ideals. Attaining wisdom places the philosopher in an enlightened Nirvana-like state; however, it occasionally creates conflict for the individual having to deal with a dog-eat-dog existence. In order to release the enlightened man's tortured mind, Stoics, therefore, believed suicide was permissible to relieve the pain of existence. The way to true happiness, Stoics believed, was to want what one gets rather than to try to get what one wants.

Finally, wisdom can also explain God's will in the creation of the universe. The idea of a God who created the heavens and the earth invokes images of a wise and powerful being. The term "God-like" creates the idea of a wise person who has attained supreme knowledge. Also, in Roman Catholic and orthodox versions of the Old Testament, the Hebrew King Solomon urges his people to love righteousness and to seek wisdom. Christians may also remember the three wise men from the Orient who follow the North Star to Bethlehem in search of the baby Jesus. Wisdom, long regarded as one of the highest virtues, allows one to understand God as the ultimate holder of wisdom and the one who bestows wisdom upon the person who seeks Him.

The many meanings of the word wisdom should not be ignored. Whether the accumulation of knowledge, the intellectual application of that knowledge, or an explanation of God's creation of the universe, wisdom indicates a person's struggle to attain mankind's highest goal.

In the following essay, Michael Shermer approaches his definition of "skepticism" from several angles—historically, scientifically, and philosophically.

SKEPTICISM AS A VIRTUE:
An Inquiry Into the Original Meaning of the Word 'Skeptic'

Michael Shermer

Poets often express deep insights into human nature with far less verbiage than scientists. Alexander Pope's *Essay on Man*, for example, is filled with pithy observations on the dualistic tensions of the human condition:

> Placed on this isthmus of a middle state,
> A Being darkly wise, and rudely great:
> With too much knowledge for the Sceptic side,
> With too much weakness for the Stoic's pride,
> He hangs between; in doubt to act, or rest,
> In doubt to deem himself a God, or Beast,
> In doubt his mind or body to prefer;
> Born but to die, and reasoning but to err.

Pope has packed a lot into this refrain, but the final clause is an important challenge to science: Is all our reasoning for naught, to end only in error? Such fear haunts us in our quest for understanding, and it is precisely why skepticism is a virtue. We must always be on guard against errors in our reasoning. Eternal vigilance is the watchword not just of freedom but of thought. That is the very nature of skepticism.

To my considerable chagrin, it was five years into the editing and publishing of *Skeptic* magazine before I realized I had never bothered to define the word or even examined how others had used it. Then Stephen Jay Gould, in the foreword to my book *Why People Believe Weird Things*, mentioned that it comes from the Greek *skeptikos*, for "thoughtful." Etymologically, in fact, its Latin derivative is *scepticus*, for "inquiring" or "reflective." Further variations in the ancient Greek include "watchman" or "mark to aim at." Hence, skepticism is thoughtful and reflective inquiry. To be skeptical is to aim toward a goal of critical thinking. Skeptics are the watchmen of reasoning errors, the Ralph Naders of bad ideas.

This is a far cry from modern misconceptions of the word as meaning "cynical" or "nihilistic," although a consideration of the word's history gives some insight into why its original definition has shifted. The *Oxford English Dictionary* offers this as its first definition of "sceptic": "one who, like Pyrrho and his followers in Greek antiquity, doubts the possibility of real knowledge of any kind; one who holds that there are no adequate grounds for certainty as to the truth of any proposition whatever." This may be true in philosophy, but not in science. There are more than adequate grounds for the probability of the truth of propositions—if we substitute "probability" for "certainty," because there are no incontrovertible facts in science if fact is a belief held with 100 percent certitude.

Superstring theory may be uncertain, but heliocentrism is not. Whether the history of life is best described by gradualism or punctuated equilibrium may still be in dispute, but the fact that life has evolved is not. The difference is one of probabilities, and this is reflected in a second usage of "sceptic": "one who doubts the validity of what claims to be knowledge in some particular department of inquiry." Okay, so we don't doubt everything, just some things—particularly those lacking in evidence and logic. Unfortunately, it is also true that some skeptics fall into a third usage of the word: "one who is habitually inclined rather to doubt than to believe any assertion or apparent fact that comes before him; a person of sceptical temper." Why some people are, by temperament, more skeptical than others is a subject for another essay. But suffice it to say that the reverse is also true—some folks are, by temperament, habitually inclined to believe rather than to doubt any assertion. Neither extreme is healthy.

Perhaps the closest fit to what we equate with a skeptical or scientific attitude is a fourth meaning: "a seeker after truth; an inquirer who has not yet arrived at definite convictions." Skepticism is not "seek and ye shall find"—a classic case of what is called the confirmation bias—but "seek and keep an open mind." What does it mean to have an open mind? It is to find the essential balance between orthodoxy and heresy, between a total commitment to the status quo and the blind pursuit of new ideas.

ON THE NET

The Definition Essay. LEO: Literacy Education Online. St. Cloud State University.
<http://leo.stcloudstate.edu/acadwrite/definition.html>

Developing A Definition. Capital Community College.
<http://grammar.ccc.commnet.edu/GRAMMAR/composition/definition.htm>

Writing Definitions. The OWL at Purdue.
<http://owl.english.purdue.edu/owl/resource/622/01/>

EXERCISE

Provide the missing sections of the following definitions. Remember that each term must be put into its class and then be distinguished from other items of the same class.

1. A bachelor is _____ who _____.

2. A sitcom is _____ that _____.

3. A conspiracy is _____ that _____.

4. Genius is _____ that _____.

5. Graffiti is_____ that _____.

6. Compassion is _____ that _____.

7. A hypothesis is _____ that _____.

Take one of the above definitions and construct THREE topic sentences that would support and develop your thesis. Be precise in your sentences.

Thesis: (your choice from the list above): _____

_____

I._____

_____

II. _____

_____

III. _____

_____

9 Comparison *and* Contrast

Although comparison and contrast are seldom used entirely by themselves (often being combined with other rhetorical patterns in the same essay), you have used them yourself while others have used them to make things clear to you. When you were a child, you might have asked your father what a "giraffe" was. His response might have been something like this: "It is an animal that looks something like a horse, except that it has long legs and a very long neck—much longer than a horse's neck. Its color is much like a leopard's, yellow with black spots, but the giraffe's spots are larger and he has fewer of them than a leopard has. A giraffe has a black tongue, too—very different from cats and dogs and most other animals." Your father answered your question by comparing and contrasting the giraffe's size, legs, neck, color, and tongue with those of other animals. Because the giraffe is an animal, the best things to compare it with are other animals, members of the same classification. It would be possible to compare the giraffe to a Chevrolet (the giraffe is taller, not a machine, and a different color; it lacks bucket seats and a vinyl roof) or to a telephone pole (the giraffe is not as tall, can move around better, and does/does not smell better), but the comparisons and contrasts possible would not be as useful as the animal comparisons are in giving a child an idea of what a giraffe is. In general, then, we usually compare and contrast things in a group or class defined by our interest, things that have important similarities as well as differences.

There are three reasons for developing an essay by comparison and contrast. The first is that we might want to describe or define one item, and we do so by relating it to another item with which our reader is familiar. If you wanted to tell your reader how the Texas Senate operates, you might do it by comparing and contrasting the Texas Senate with the United States Senate. You assume that your reader knows something about the U.S. Senate and that he will be able to make the correct associations with the Texas Senate. Obviously, it is important to choose one item with which your reader is already familiar. Comparing the Texas Senate to England's Parliament will not do much good if your reader has no idea how that Parliament operates.

The second reason for developing an essay by comparison and contrast is to tell your reader something about both of the subjects by discussing them in relation to some general principle. The general principle should be applicable in both and familiar to the reader. So you might compare and contrast the Texas Senate and England's Parliament, about neither of which your reader knows anything, by relating them to principles of democratic government that your reader understands. You might begin by showing that both the Texas Senate and England's Parliament use forms of representative government. The people elect representatives to these legislative bodies, and the elected legislators make laws on behalf of the electorate. Here you have compared the Texas Senate and England's Parliament in relation to representative government. Because our reader understands how representative government works (the people elect representatives to the legislative body), he now knows something about the Texas Senate and England's Parliament.

Finally, you may compare and contrast several things with which the reader is already familiar in order to help him understand some general principles or ideas with which he is not familiar. If you want your reader to understand what government is, you might compare and contrast American democracy, British parliamentary rule, and the emerging Russian system to show what they have in common. If you want your reader to get an idea of what "Social Science" is, you can compare and contrast the academic disciplines of psychology, history, and economics to show what they have in common. In these cases you would be using comparison and contrast to move from your examples with which the reader is already familiar (American democracy, psychology) to a general description of the classes under which your examples belong (government, social science) about which your reader knows very little or nothing.

Strategy

Once you decide to use comparison and contrast, there are two basic ways of organizing your essay. You can present one item fully and then discuss the other, called the block method, or you can present a part of one item, then a part of the other, and so on until both are fully demonstrated, which is called the alternating method.

Block Pattern

The first method, sometimes called the block pattern, is usually most appropriate when the elements of comparison and contrast are rather simple, broad, and obvious. The assumption the writer makes when presenting the whole of one subject and then the whole of the other is that his reader will be able to remember the first subject while reading the comparisons and contrasts of the second. Since a complex or extended comparison/contrast would probably be difficult for the reader to remember, we normally use the first method for simple subjects. Here is a short example of the first method of organization; observe the organization of the essay as you read.

The Scientist and the Humanist

One of the best places for a people watcher to practice his observations is on any college campus. Close examination of the large flocks of students will soon lead the dedicated observer to the conclusion that there are at least two easily identifiable subgroups among the student population. These kinds have been classified as *studens scientiae* (scientists) and *studens humani* (humanists); they are identifiable by their appearance, natural habitats, and conversations.

The two types are easily discernible by their appearance alone. The scientist and the humanist can be recognized by their appearance and grooming habits. The male of the species is characterized by a bow tie (usually polka dotted), and numerous pens and mechanical pencils in a plastic case protruding from his pants pocket. It is extremely unusual, but not impossible, to observe facial hair on the male. Both male and female are generally drab and colorless in appearance, the male tending to white shirts and brown polyester slacks, while the female wears severely tailored beige tweed suits and little or no makeup. She wears her hair tied neatly in a bun and often exhibits yellow nitric acid stains on the fingers of the right hand. In addition, the normal habitat of the scientist is the laboratory or computer center, where he drinks coffee from a beaker and turns dials. When forced to move from these sites by hunger, examination, or fire, scientists travel in small groups at a very rapid pace, as if hurrying to a meeting or from an explosion. If the observer can get close enough to hear their conversation, he will hear repeated utterances of "integer, integer." When excited or animated, the species emits a shrill repeated cry of "valence," interspersed with numerical and alphabetical designations on such recitations as "approximating the irrational zeros of polynomial functions." When away from their laboratory or computer sites, scientists become nervous and irritable, refusing to approach other species.

A very different picture is evident when the humanist is scrutinized. He is much more brightly colored, though usually less neatly groomed. Males tend to blue jeans, black Metallica T-shirts, and tennis shoes. The females are difficult to distinguish from the males of the species, except that long facial hair is more often characteristic of the male while the female may have two or three more pierced earrings in each ear. Hair length for both male and female is uniformly long, and in either case it may hide the face completely or be shaved on one side of the head. The habitat and habits of the humanist, too, present a striking contrast with those of the scientist. The humanist avoids the laboratory and computer sites of the scientist, congregating instead on grassy knolls in the front of the campus or beneath campus trees. Humanists move as little as possible and never in accelerated fashion. Their favorite position is to lie fully extended and apparently asleep in the sun. The observer should recognize approaching humanists fairly easily since they are often dozing beneath earphones, or engaged in desultory conversations on the lawn or in the courtyard. Their normal call when at rest is a plaintive "Kierkegaard, Kierkegaard," with an occasional variation of "Existential Phenomenology." When aroused or excited, though, humanists can be quite dangerous. They collect quickly into large groups; their call changes to a shrill "Save the whales," and their behavior is marked by chanting and the waving of protest signs.

We can see, then, a clear profile of each dominant type and how each differs in several ways. Although there are other species of student life on the campus, the scientists and humanists form two of the most colorful, distinctive, and intriguing subjects for the interested observer. These two types of appearances, natural habitats, and conversations mark these groups as two very distinctive classes of student life.

The author of this essay wanted to acquaint his reader with two types of college students. He illustrated one of these types, which he calls "scientists," with examples of their appearance, habits, and conversations. Then, assuming that the reader will be able to remember the description of the scientists, he compares and contrasts them with another group, which he calls humanists. He describes this group, giving examples of their appearance, habits, and conversations that point up the differences between the scientists and humanists.

Alternating Pattern

In the second basic organizational method, the alternating pattern, the writer structures his essay differently. He discusses one characteristic of the first subject and then a corresponding characteristic of the second subject. He continues alternating the two subjects until the comparison/contrast is complete and both subjects are fully revealed. This pattern is better than the block pattern for long, complex comparison/contrast essays where the subjects are related at a number of points or where the comparisons and contrasts require extensive explanation. The writer decides on the alternating pattern when use of the block pattern would make it too difficult for his reader to remember the details of the first description while reading the second. In the example of the alternating pattern that follows, we will use the same humanist-scientist subject matter as was used in the previous example. You have seen the essay structure according to the block pattern; now read the following portion of an essay using the alternating pattern and notice the structural differences.

The Scientist and the Humanist

One of the best places for a people watcher to practice his observations is on any college campus. Close examination of the large flocks of students will soon lead the dedicated observer to the conclusion that there are at least two easily identifiable subgroups among the student population. These kinds have been classified as *studens scientiae* (scientists) and *studens humani* (humanists), distinctive for their appearance, natural habitats, and conversations.

The two types are easily discernible from their appearance alone. The scientist and the humanist can be recognized by their appearance and grooming habits. The male of the species is characterized by a bow tie (usually polka dotted), numerous pens and mechanical pencils in a plastic folder in his shirt pocket, and a pocket calculator in a leather case protruding from his pants pocket. It is extremely unusual, but not impossible, to observe facial hair on the male. Both male and female are generally drab and colorless in appearance, the male tending to white shirts and brown polyester slacks, while she wears her hair tied neatly in a bun and often exhibits yellow nitric acid stains on the fingers of the right hand. The humanist, by contrast, is much more interestingly attired, though usually less neatly groomed. The males tend to blue jeans, black Metallica T-shirts, and tennis shoes, combat boots, or Birkenstock sandals. The females are difficult to distinguish from the males of the species, except that long facial hair is more often characteristic of the male, while the female exhibits three or more pierced earrings on each ear. Hair length for both male and female is uniformly long, and, in either case, it may hide the face completely or be shaved on one side of the head. The two types are differentiated with little difficulty at forty paces.

The contrast in appearance extends to the normal habits and habitats of the two species as well. etc., etc.

Organization

These two essays have a number of things in common. The first (introductory) paragraphs are the same; it is only when they get midway into the second paragraph (first body paragraph) that the essays begin to vary. Both contrast the humanist and the scientist, and both use a mock-scientific tone, implying that the students are species of animals or birds. The differences between the two are organizational and can be represented in outline form. An outline of the first essay, using the block pattern, looks like this:

Introduction (*with thesis statement*)
Body
I. The Scientist
    A. Appearance
    B. Habits and Habitats
    C. Conversations
II. The Humanist
    A. Appearance
    B. Habits and Habitats
    C. Conversations
Conclusion

The second essay (or portion of it) uses the alternating pattern and looks like this in outline form:

Introduction (*with thesis statement*)
Body
I. Appearance (*Only this paragraph appears in the example above.*)
    A. The Scientist
    B. The Humanist
II. Habits and Habitats
    A. The Scientist
    B. The Humanist
III. Conversations
    A. The Scientist
    B. The Humanist
Conclusion

As is obvious from these two outlines, the first essay treats the scientist first (I, A & B), and then the humanist (II, A & B). The second essay treats both the scientist and the humanist in turn, first according to appearance (I), then according to habits and habitats (II), and then according to conversations of both (III).

While the two organizational patterns so far identified are the basic and usual ones for an essay of comparison and contrast, it is possible to combine the two if the writer feels that would make his essay clearer or better. In this combined pattern the first subject is presented fully, just as in the sample essay illustrating the block pattern. Then in the second part of the essay the reader is referred, point by point, to the first subject. The writer provides a brief summary of the relevant part of the full presentation and then compares and contrasts the relevant part of the second subject to it. Either of the two basic patterns or the combined pattern should be chosen based on the determination of which is most suitable for the subject, the purpose, and the audience.

The block method, remember, is generally most suitable for a fairly simple and straightforward comparison/contrast, while the alternating pattern works better for complex and lengthy subject matter. The combined method, too, is generally used for a more difficult or extended comparison and contrast than the block pattern—one in which it will be useful to be able to refer the reader, point by point, back to the full description in the first section. While the patterns are presented here as expository, they may be used to structure your argument in a persuasive essay, where rather than merely presenting the alternatives informatively, you must make choices. You will take a stand and use comparison and contrast as your major method of development.

◆

Checklist for Comparison/Contrast Essay

Does your essay:

1. Use the appropriate pattern of comparison/contrast for your subject matter, audience, and purpose?
2. Include topic sentences that contain references to both items if you have chosen the alternating pattern?
3. Contain a thesis statement that indicates your purpose (i.e., comparing or contrasting or both), that mentions both items to be discussed, that makes clear the point you intend to show in the essay?
4. Offer the best logical order for the purpose you want to achieve?
5. Avoid commonplace comparisons and contrasts?
6. Did you edit your paper carefully, checking for major grammatical and spelling errors?

Read the following student essay and see how Jona Roy clearly delineates the differences between two very popular local restaurants. Are the bases of comparison apparent?

PAPPADEUX AND JOE'S CRAB SHACK

Jona Roy

From a succulent fresh lobster tail to a mouth-watering red snapper filet, everyone loves some type of seafood. Houstonians are lucky; the Gulf of Mexico lies at their back door. Restaurants specializing in seafood are plentiful here. Many Houstonians consider Pappadeux and Joe's Crab Shack to be the best. Although they both serve wonderful, fresh seafood, the differences in the menu, the service, and the overall atmosphere set them apart from one another.

Pappadeux offers elegant, elaborate dishes on its menu, while the food described on the menu of Joe's Crab Shack is the sort that tastes best when accompanied by an ice-cold beer and a large plate of french fries. For example, my favorite meal at Pappadeux consists of a flaky filet of red snapper blackened in hot Cajun spices and smothered in a rich béarnaise sauce. It is then topped with lightly sautéed crawfish tails and mushrooms. Once this concoction touches the tongue, it simply melts. On the other hand, Joe's Crab Shack is famous for its barbecued crabs. The cook begins by slowly cooking small Dungeoness crabs in a large barbecue pit. Once the crabs have been seared to perfection, the cook tosses them on a large tray, and they are ready for presentation. The waiter then serves these divine crabs with a hammer, a bib, and a roll of paper towels. After pounding on the shell for five minutes, the lucky diner discovers a piece of crabmeat which, like the snapper filet, melts in the mouth.

Distinguishing each restaurant further is the service; although it is impeccable at both Pappadeux and Joe's Crab Shack, the manner in which one is served varies greatly. When dining at the classy Pappadeux, each patron is greeted by an exquisitely dressed staff. The waitstaff is clad in black slacks, white tuxedo shirts, and classic bow ties, while the hostess dons an elegant dress. The staff greets each diner with the traditional "ma'am" and "sir" and treats her or him with the utmost respect and dignity. In contrast, at the relaxed Joe's Crab Shack the entire staff wears t-shirts and shorts or jeans and treats everyone as if he were a life-long friend; greeting patrons with "Hey! How's it going?" is the norm.

The final distinguishing characteristic is each restaurant's atmosphere. The atmosphere at Pappadeux reminds one of a traditional wedding reception while the atmosphere at Joe's Crab Shack takes one back to an end-of-the-summer beach party. An immaculate white table-cloth adorns each table at Pappadeux, and large, leafy, green plants dot the interior of the building. Soft, relaxing, classical music is piped through speakers throughout the restaurant. Diners feel compelled to speak in low, hushed tones, making sure not to disrupt the elegant feel of the restaurant. The atmosphere at Joe's Crab Shack conveys an entirely different ambience; lop-sided paintings and photographs cover the walls from top to bottom, and the music blares from every corner. On weekends, management provides live music, and when one of Houston's hometown favorite teams is playing, the game is on one, if not all, of the many televisions. As a finishing touch to this informal setting, old-fashioned beer buckets are placed on each table for use as trash receptacles.

In their menu, service, and atmosphere, Pappadeux and Joe's Crab Shack could not be more different. The one thing they have in common, other than great service of course, is their amazing, fresh seafood; it is delectable at both.

In the following essay, Deborah Tannen, an English Professor at Georgetown University, demonstrates through her appeals to authority that she has done considerable research on her topic of the differences between men and women. Who is her audience? Women? Men? Both? Consider the voice and tone in the essay.

SEX, LIES, AND CONVERSATION

Deborah Tannen

I was addressing a small gathering in a suburban Virginia living room—a women's group that had invited men to join them. Throughout the evening, one man had been particularly talkative, frequently offering ideas and anecdotes, while his wife sat silently beside him on the couch.

Toward the end of the evening, I commented that women frequently complain that their husbands don't talk to them. This man quickly concurred. He gestured toward his wife and said, "She's the talker in our family." The room burst into laughter; the man looked puzzled and hurt. "It's true," he explained. "When I come home from work I have nothing to say. If she didn't keep the conversation going, we'd spend the whole evening in silence." This episode crystallizes the irony that although American men tend to talk more than women in public situations, they often talk less at home. And this pattern is wreaking havoc with marriage.

The pattern was observed by political scientist Andrew Hacker in the late '70s. Sociologist Catherine Kohler Riessman reports in her new book *Divorce Talk* that most of the women she interviewed—but only a few of the men—gave lack of communication as the reason for their divorces. Given the current divorce rate of nearly 50 percent, that amounts to millions of cases in the United States every year—a virtual epidemic of failed conversation. In my own research, complaints from women about their husbands most often focused not on tangible inequities such as having given up the chance for a career to accompany a husband to his, or doing far more than their share of daily life-support work like cleaning, cooking, social arrangements, and errands. Instead, they focused on communication—"He doesn't listen to me," "He doesn't talk to me." I found, as Hacker observed years before, that most wives want their husbands to be, first and foremost, conversational partners, but few husbands share this expectation of their wives.

In short, the image that best represents the current crisis is the stereotypical cartoon scene of a man sitting at the breakfast table with a newspaper held up in front of his face, while a woman glares at the back of it wanting to talk.

LINGUISTIC BATTLE OF THE SEXES

How can women and men have such different impressions of communication in marriage? Why the widespread imbalance in their interests and expectations?

In the April issue of *American Psychologist*, Stanford University's Eleanor Maccoby reports the results of her own and others' research showing that children's development is most influenced by the social structure of peer interactions. Boys and girls tend to play with children of their own gender, and their sex-separate groups have different organizational structures and interactive norms.

I believe these systematic differences in childhood socialization make talk between women and men like cross-cultural communication, heir to all the attraction and pitfalls of that enticing but difficult enterprise. My research on men's and women's conversations uncovered patterns similar to those described for children's groups. For women, as for girls, intimacy is the fabric of relationships, and talk is the thread from which it is woven. Little girls create and maintain friendships by exchanging secrets; similarly, women regard conversation as the cornerstone of friendship. So a woman expects her husband to be a new and improved version of a best friend. What is important is not the individual subjects that are discussed but the sense of closeness of a life shared that emerges when people tell their thoughts, feelings, and impressions.

Bonds between boys can be as intense as girls', but they are based less on talking, more on doing things together. Since they don't assume talk is the cement that binds a relationship, men don't know what kind of talk women want, and they don't miss it when it isn't there.

Boys' groups are larger, more inclusive, and more hierarchical, so boys must struggle to avoid the subordinate position in the group. This may play a role in women's complaints that men don't listen to them. Some men really don't like to listen, because being the listener makes them feel one-down, like a child listening to adults or an employee to a boss. But often when women tell men, "You aren't listening," and the men protest, "I am," the men are right. The impression of not listening results from misalignments in the mechanics of conversation. The misalignment begins as soon as a man and a woman take physical positions. This became clear when I studied videotapes made by psychologist Bruce Dorval of children and adults talking to their same-sex best friends. I found that at every age, the girls and women faced each other directly, their eyes anchored on each other's faces. At every age, the boys and men sat at angles to each other and looked elsewhere in the room, periodically glancing at each other. They were obviously attuned to each other, often mirroring each other's movements. But the tendency of men to face away can give women the impression they aren't listening even when they are. A young woman in college was frustrated: Whenever she told her boyfriend she wanted to talk to him, he would lie down on the floor, close his eyes, and put his arm over his face. This signaled to her, "He's taking a nap." But he insisted he was listening extra hard. Normally, he looks around the room, so he is easily distracted. Lying down and covering his eyes helped him concentrate on what she was saying.

Analogous to the physical alignment that women and men take in conversation is their topical alignment. The girls in my study tended to talk at length about one topic, but the boys tended to jump from topic to topic. The second-grade girls exchanged stories about people they knew. The second-grade boys teased, told jokes, noticed things in the room, and talked about finding games to play. The sixth-grade girls talked about problems with a mutual friend. The sixth-grade boys talked about 55 different topics, none of which extended over more than a few turns.

LISTENING TO BODY LANGUAGE

Switching topics is another habit that gives women the impression men aren't listening, especially if they switch to a topic about themselves. But the evidence of the 10th-grade boys in my study indicates otherwise. The 10th-grade boys sprawled across their chairs with bodies parallel and eyes straight ahead, rarely looking at each other. They looked as if they were riding in a car, staring out the windshield. But they were talking about their feelings. One boy was upset because a girl had told him he had a drinking problem, and the other was feeling alienated from all his friends.

Now, when a girl told a friend about a problem, the friend responded by asking probing questions and expressing agreement and understanding. But the boys dismissed each other's problems. Todd assured Richard that his drinking was "no big problem" because "sometimes you're funny when you're off your butt." And when Todd said he felt left out, Richard responded,

"Why should you? You know more people than me." Women perceive such responses as belittling and unsupportive. But the boys seemed satisfied with them. Whereas women reassure each other by implying, "You shouldn't feel bad because I've had similar experiences," men do so by implying, "You shouldn't feel bad because your problems aren't so bad."

There are even simpler reasons for women's impression that men don't listen. Linguist Lynette Hirschman found that women make more listener-noise, such as "mhm," "uhuh," and "yeah," to show "I'm with you." Men, she found, more often give silent attention. Women who expect a stream of listener-noise interpret silent attention as no attention at all.

Women's conversational habits are as frustrating to men as men's are to women. Men who expect silent attention interpret a stream of listener-noise as overreaction or impatience. Also, when women talk to each other in a close, comfortable setting, they often overlap, finish each other's sentences, and anticipate what the other is about to say. This practice, which I call "participatory listenership," is often perceived by men as interruption, intrusion, and lack of attention.

A parallel difference caused a man to complain about his wife, "She just wants to talk about her own point of view. If I show her another view, she gets mad at me." When most women talk to each other, they assume a conversationalist's job is to express agreement and support. But many men see their conversational duty as pointing out the other side of an argument. This is heard as disloyalty by women, and refusal to offer the requisite support. It is not that women don't want to see other points of view, but that they prefer them phrased as suggestions and inquiries rather than as direct challenges.

In his book *Fighting for Life*, Walter Ong points out that men use "agonistic," or warlike, oppositional formats to do almost anything; thus discussion becomes debate, and conversation a competitive sport. In contrast, women see conversation as a ritual means of establishing rapport. If Jane tells a problem and June says she has a similar one, they walk away feeling closer to each other. But this attempt at establishing rapport can backfire when used with men. Men take too literally women's ritual "troubles talk," just as women mistake men's ritual challenges for real attack.

THE SOUNDS OF SILENCE

These differences begin to clarify why women and men have such different expectations about communication in marriage. For women, talk creates intimacy. Marriage is an orgy of closeness: you can tell your feelings and thoughts, and still be loved. Their greatest fear is being pushed away. But men live in a hierarchical world, where talk maintains independence and status. They are on guard to protect themselves from being put down and pushed around.

This explains the paradox of the talkative man who said of his silent wife, "She's the talker." In the public setting of a guest lecture, he felt challenged to show his intelligence and display his understanding of the lecture. But at home, where he has nothing to prove and no one to defend against, he is free to remain silent. For his wife, being home means she is free from the worry that something she says might offend someone, or spark disagreement, or appear to be showing off; at home she is free to talk.

The communication problems that endanger marriage can't be fixed by mechanical engineering. They require a new conceptual framework about the role of talk in human relationships. Many of the psychological explanations that have become second nature may not be helpful, because they tend to blame either women (for not being assertive enough) or men (for not being in touch with their feelings). A sociolinguistic approach by which male–female conversation is seen as cross-cultural communication allows us to understand the problem and forge solutions without blaming either party.

Once the problem is understood, improvement comes naturally, as it did to the young woman and her boyfriend who seemed to go to sleep when she wanted to talk. Previously, she had accused him of not listening, and he had refused to change his behavior, since that would be admitting fault. But then she learned about and explained to him the differences in women's and men's habitual ways of aligning themselves in conversation. The next time she told him she wanted to talk, he began, as usual, by lying down and covering his eyes. When the familiar negative reaction bubbled up, she reassured herself that he really was listening. But then he sat up and looked at her. Thrilled, she asked why. He said, "You like me to look at you when we talk, so I'll try to do it." Once he saw their differences as cross-cultural rather than right and wrong, he independently altered his behavior.

Women who feel abandoned and deprived when their husbands won't listen to or report daily news may be happy to discover their husbands trying to adapt once they understand the place of small talk in women's relationships. But if their husbands don't adapt, the women may still be comforted that, for men, this is not a failure of intimacy. Accepting the difference, the wives may look to their friends or family for that kind of talk. And husbands who can't provide it shouldn't feel their wives have made unreasonable demands. Some couples will still decide to divorce, but at least their decisions will be based on realistic expectations.

In these times of resurgent ethnic conflicts, the world desperately needs cross-cultural understanding. Like charity, successful cross-cultural communication should begin at home.

ON THE NET

Comparison/Contrast Essays. LEO: Literacy Education Online. St. Cloud State University.
<http://leo.stcloudstate.edu/acadwrite/comparcontrast.html>

Writing the Comparison and Contrast Essay. Daniel Keys. Department of English. College of DuPage.
<http://papyr.com/hypertextbooks/comp1/compare.htm>

Comparison and Contrast Guide. Read. Write. Think. org. NCTE.
<http://www.readwritethink.org/materials/compcontrast/>

Comparing and Contrasting. University of North Carolina at Chapel Hill.
<http://www.unc.edu/depts/wcweb/handouts/comparison_contrast.html>

EXERCISES

I. Several pairs of items are listed below. Some of the items can be compared, some contrasted. Follow the suggestions of each and list under the items those bases of comparison you would use in an essay. For example, if you are asked to compare two military leaders of the American Civil War, you might select their origins, educational backgrounds, personalities, and military experiences. You would simply list these four bases of comparisons under the items.

1. Compare a computer repairman and a medical surgeon.

Bases of comparison:

a. _____ b. _____

c. _____ d. _____

2. Compare a loving relationship with a roller coaster.

Bases of comparison:

a. _____ b. _____

c. _____ d. _____

3. Compare a rock concert with a religious service.

Bases of comparison:

a. _____ b. _____

c. _____ d. _____

4. Contrast high school students and college students.

Bases of comparison:

a. _____ b. _____

c. _____ d. _____

II. Now write an appropriate thesis statement for each of the exercises listed above. Make certain that each thesis reflects your purpose and that each has a definite focus. The focus should contain each of the bases of comparison.

1. _____

_____

10 Classification *and* Division

Classification and division are forms of analysis used often by most of us even if we do not know the name of the techniques. Although they are methods of expository writing, classification and division are also ways of looking at the world around us and of thinking about things. Like illustration and comparison and contrast, classification is a process that involves bringing order out of experience. Like these other methods of expository writing, classification and division are concerned with the general (class) and the relationship to its parts.

Almost all parts fall into a class of some kind, sharing certain characteristics that allow these parts to be classified with a certain group. Thus, a class is determined by a network of significant characteristics shared by all members of the category. If you see a heavy-set man about 25 years old walking down the street, you will probably pass by him without thinking about him much. Put him into a blue uniform and give him a badge and a gun, and you will both notice him and make judgments about him (he is a police officer, or he is a fascist pig cop). If the man is not dressed in a uniform but is carrying a baby, you think of him as a father and assume that the woman with him is his wife and the mother of the child. In each of these cases you are classifying the man; you are putting him into a category and seeing him as a part of a whole (class). He is a policeman, father or husband. We are always classifying that which we experience in the world around us even when we have not the slightest intention of writing an essay of classification.

In the same way, *division* is a way of thinking about and reacting to our world. We know that things have parts, and we talk about things in terms of those parts. In fact, we often define terms by identifying the parts that make up those terms. A sailboat can be divided into hull, mast, and sails. Social Science is made up of history, economics, sociology, geography, and psychology. The government of the United States has three main branches: the executive, legislative, and judicial.

CLASSIFICATION

Strategy

The need for care in setting up classifications can be demonstrated by examples of the two kinds of classification used in analysis. The kinds are called simple and complex classifications.

Simple classification

This form of classification usually involves grouping your subject into two categories. For example, if your purpose is to investigate your experiences with good male teachers, a simple classification merely involves separating the subject "teachers" into good teachers and those who were not considered good (level one of classification). Step two would be to take the good teachers classification and organize it again (level two) into two classes—male and female. If your purpose is to determine how many good male teachers you have had in your academic experience, you pursue only the male classification and abandon the female portion. We call this a simple classification because at each stage or level the analysis primarily consists simply of two opposites to establish two sub-groups.

Complex classification

You most likely will decide to select the complex classification for your composition assignments because this method demands that you delve more deeply into the multiple categories / levels required by your instructor. For instance, if you are expected to consider the full range of your experience with weight lifters in health clubs, you would choose the complex classification method, beginning with level one. You could, therefore, classify the types of weight lifters one most likely would encounter in health clubs—the annoying socializers, the serious competitive athletes, and the predatory lifters. Next, if you have chosen the annoying socializers as your focus, you would further classify that group (level two)—the "show off," the "know-it-all," and the "wanderer." Although this level does not exhaust the types of weight lifters you have experienced, it does include those specific types you wish to discuss in your present analysis (focus). Notice that your analysis in a complex classification is of a much narrower, deeper, more interesting, imaginative, and complex nature than a simple classification.

Organization

When writing a classification essay, make sure you adhere to the following:

1. You must set up a clear basis for the classification, and you must follow the classification through logically and thoroughly. This means you must be careful to classify your subject distinctly at each level of the analysis. To say that there are three types of bad teachers—the boring, the incomprehensible, and those who drive pickup trucks—is using an indistinct method of classification. Then make certain you discuss each category in relation to those elements that link the category to the other categories of the same class, in this case, their methods of instruction. This basis of comparison is used similarly in your comparison and contrast; it is essential in classification as well to make your purpose clear to your audience in examining your categories by classifying them.

2. You should develop your analysis by classification as completely as is necessary for your purpose. Your purpose determines how complete and extensive the classification will be. Your analysis will always be based on some specific interest in the subject being analyzed, and that specific interest must be clearly stated to your reader in the thesis.

The following diagram illustrates the process of complex classification:

FIGURE III-A

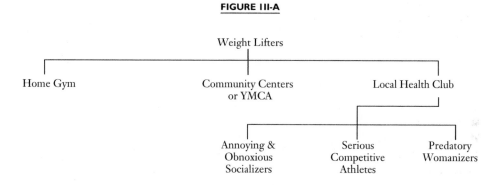

You should develop your classification as completely as is necessary for your purpose in the analysis. Your thesis and your discussion, then, will include only those types with whom you are personally familiar although there exist other categories of weight lifters. Just make certain that your reader understands that your classification is limited by your focus / purpose.

◆ CHECKLIST FOR CLASSIFICATION ESSAY

Be sure that:

1. Your purpose for classification is clear to your audience and is included in your thesis statement.
2. The classification is applied to a plural subject (like different types of pumpers at a gas station, for instance, or teachers), and that the focus is on types, categories, or kinds.
3. The basis of the classification is consistent with your purpose and audience.
4. The classification is complete; all pertinent categories to your specific interest are included.
5. The categories are arranged in logical or emphatic order.
6. The categories do not overlap. If an individual member of one category can also be put into another category (i.e., an incomprehensible teacher who

drives a pickup truck) then your categories need rethinking. They must be mutually exclusive and parallel.

7. Did you edit your paper carefully, checking for major grammatical and spelling errors?

As you read the following essay, note how student Roberto Loucel sets up and sticks to a clear basis for his classification—the typical types of weight lifters one might observe in a health club, especially the annoying, obnoxious types.

WEIGHT LIFTERS

Roberto Loucel

Entertainment has been an established part of the American culture almost since its founding. The types of entertainment that most Americans enjoy in today's world are going to the movies, going out to eat, and exercising. Different forms of exercise vary from running and playing sports to weight lifting. Those who enjoy weight lifting can choose to do so in the privacy of their home, in a community center like the YMCA, or in a health club. At a health club one can expect to find a wide variety of male club members. These categories include the obnoxious socializers, the serious competitive athletes, and the predatory womanizers. Those who contribute most to the downside of working out at a local health club are the obnoxious, annoying members. Three types of these annoying, obnoxious people found at the weight room are the show-off, the know-it-all, and the wanderer; they easily can be identified by their physical appearance, their social behavior, and their attitude.

The first type, the show-off, is known by his flashy appearance, his misanthropic social skills, and his arrogant attitude. The show-off is a single male in his twenties who drives a European luxury car; he always comes to the gym wearing a tank top to display his deep tan and a pair of black and green spandex shorts. He is heavily built and all his muscles are well defined. But he is a man with poor social skills; he seldom talks to another soul and always works out by himself. He frequently ignores the greetings and good-byes of the health club employees; when he does answer a friendly "Hey, what's up?" or a "See you later," he does so in a deep, blunt, morbid tone of voice. He also likes to emphasize how strong and masculine he is by working out at the very front and center of the weight room, where everyone can see him. He refuses requests for help from others like a cheerleader refusing to go on a date with a pimply, nerdy classmate. Most people who work out at health clubs would be glad to be free of the show-off.

The second type is the know-it-all; he is identified by his commonplace appearance, moderately developed social skills, and commanding attitude. He is strong and well built, but not to the extent of the show-off. He is a married man in his mid thirties to early forties who wears athletic shorts and a gray, short-sleeve T-shirt with the name of the health club printed on the front. He is not aloof like the show-off; he engages in conversations with his friends and makes small talk with strangers at the gym. Unlike the show-off, he tends to work out with groups of two or three and is not reluctant to ask for the help of others. He can be quite unpleasant because he verbally reprimands others for not doing an exercise in the correct form; he never misses a chance to remind everyone that he is an expert at weight lifting and finds joy and fulfillment in showing others the proper ways to lift weights. Working out in the presence of a know-it-all is a very frustrating experience for most people.

The third type is the wanderer; he is a family man in his late forties who finds coming to a health club a way to escape from his life at home. He wears a white headband, a pair of casual shorts, a white, cotton T-shirt one size too large, and a pair of old sneakers. This guy's strong point is his social skills because he is addicted to socializing. He talks to anyone—the gym employees, the lady on the treadmill, the guy doing squats—because he can't live without hearing himself talk for more than a minute. As one would imagine, he has no work-out routine; therefore, he is overweight and out of shape. His attitude can best be described as free loading because he relies on the help of other people when he is working out. When he asks the guy doing the leg press to spot him on the bench press, he puts in as little effort as possible and makes the spotter do most of the lifting. The wanderer is by far the most dangerous to a regular client's routine because he constantly interrupts it by talking or by asking for help.

In conclusion, the three types of people whom one needs to watch out for are the show-off, the know-it-all, and the wanderer. The show-off breaks one's concentration like a dry twig, the know-it-all lets all the air out of one's confidence, and the wanderer interrupts one's will to work out like a constantly ringing cell phone. One should avoid excessive exposure to any of these three at all costs; otherwise, the routine that one has put so much effort into to perfect, and the body one has worked so arduously to sculpt, will be a distant memory.

Student Steven Warman describes in the following essay how he classified certain types of individuals whom he met in a recovery group. Reconstruct the levels of his classification. Are they consistent? Parallel? Exclusive? Is there any overlapping of subgroups?

THE RECOVERING DYSFUNCTIONALS

Steven W. Warman

Art Linkletter, a once famous television personality, coined the phrase "Kids say the darnedest things!" I have found this also to be true of friends. We all have friends, from mere acquaintances to intimate relationships, with social friends being somewhere in the middle of the span.

We meet them at work, church, and, sometimes, at meetings of various types of recovery groups. To protect the innocent (and the not so innocent), I'll refrain from naming the recovery group I attended as well as any individuals involved; let's just call these individuals recovering dysfunctionals. I had the pleasant misfortune of making friends with three very different types of people whom I'll call the dominators, the dependers, and the equalizers.

The dominators are those "know-it-all" types that have to be the center of attention in nearly every situation. They seem to have knowledge covering every subject known to mankind, but especially that of recovering dysfunctionals. They proudly display their knowledge in each and every meeting by speaking with self-appointed authority about the topic under discussion. Being courteous, they wait to be the last person to share in a meeting (or until the internal pressure is about to cause spontaneous combustion) before gracing the group with their vast wisdom. They then go through a series of "one-upmanship" comments about previous speakers to prove how much more knowledge they have than their peers. In or out of the meetings they are always ready to tell others the right way (their way) to manage their lives. One friend, I'll call her Lynda, constantly seeks to tell others how she has found the answers. She'll pry her way into a conversation, probing a person to reveal a personal dilemma, all in the name of helping a fellow human being. Then Lynda will fill the next 15 minutes with a non-stop harangue on what to do to fix the problem. Another example of this type is Fred. He always tells others how "he thought that he knew he knew." Of course, that was before he really knew anything, but now he knows. Dominators also seek to be the center of attention. They accomplish this feat by quite literally dominating conversations. One way they do this is by speaking as frequently and as long as present company will permit. Frequently, they speak and act outside the "norm." That is, the normal speech volume for them is usually twice as loud as most people. They will also act with an over-exuberant amount of compassion for their point, as they speak down from their Olympian heights.

The next group, the dependers, are on the other end of the spectrum. They are always seeking help but seem to share a similar need with the dominators—to be at the center of attention. Their grand purpose in life appears to be draining the life out of others. Easily recognizable, they speak with a chronic neediness and will beg for help from nearly anyone. Seldom will they try to seek answers for their problems in any manner other than to act on what others tell them to do. Being considerate of others is not usually part of their character. If they need to call at 3 a.m. to cry out their blues to a sleepy sponsor, that is perfectly acceptable to dependers. Or if they need to spill their guts for two hours over coffee, that's all right, too. Dependers have a dire need for attention, but they display it with a whine that any three-year-old wouldn't be caught using. They operate on the opposite extreme from dominators, usually as emotional wrecks. They are easy to spot because of their tear-soaked faces and tissues. Speech for them is usually interrupted by gasps for breath between their broken sentences. What causes further amazement is their repeated tales of woe. These can be told ten different times in a day and never lose an ounce of intensity. Ninety percent of these tales are about broken relationships. If these dependers are lucky, someone from the next group of friends will be there for them.

Somewhere in the middle between the dominators and the dependers are the equalizers, those who are knowledgeable yet open-minded, and helpful rather than self-seeking. First are the "knowledgeable yet open-minded." These equalizers have a firm grasp of the entire program for recovering dysfunctionals. They have gained this knowledge through diligent study of the program's text. In addition, they have practical knowledge from working through all the various stages of recovery. Although knowledgeable, they maintain a significant degree of humility. They don't pretend to offer advice they are not qualified to give, such as a psychologist or marriage counselor might give. They also know there is always more to learn, never claiming to have reached any saintly status. Second, unlike the other two groups, equalizers tend to be more helpful than self-seeking. They accomplish this by being attentive listeners. They will read between the lines to see what a person may not be saying. Visually they will watch to see if another person's body language matches his verbal message. Finally, they have a sincere desire to help others. Their point of view is never more important than the person they are helping; what motivates equalizers is the satisfaction they gain from giving freely of themselves.

In conclusion, recovering dysfunctionals share a common behavioral problem in their pasts. However, the first, the dominators, are loud, pompous, know-it-all types. The second, the dependers, are the over-dependent whiners who live off other people's advice. Finally, the equalizers are the stable and compassionate glue that holds the whole group together. Although these types can be found in recovery groups, they can also be found among friends in general. We all probably have friends like these somewhere; wouldn't life be boring without them?

THE WAYS WE LIE

Stephanie Ericsson

The bank called today and I told them my deposit was in the mail, even though I hadn't written a check yet. It'd been a rough day. The baby I'm pregnant with decided to do aerobics on my lungs for two hours, our three-year-old daughter painted the living-room couch with lipstick, the IPS put me on hold for an hour, and I was late to a business meeting because I was tired.

I told my client the traffic had been bad. When my partner came home his haggard face told me his day hadn't gone any better than mine, so when he asked, "How was your day?" I said, "Oh, fine," knowing that one more straw might break his back. A friend called and wanted to take me to lunch. I said I was busy. Four lies in the course of a day, none of which I felt the least bit guilty about.

We lie. We all do. We exaggerate, we minimize, we avoid confrontation, we spare people's feelings, we conveniently forget, we keep secrets, we justify lying to the big-guy institutions.

Like most people, I indulge in small falsehoods and still think of myself as an honest person. Sure I lie, but it doesn't hurt anything. Or does it?

I once tried going a whole week without telling a lie and it was paralyzing. I discovered that telling the truth all the time is nearly impossible. It means living with some serious consequences: The bank charges me $60 in overdraft fees, my partner keels over when I tell him about my travails, my client fires me for telling her I didn't feel like being on time, and my friend takes it personally when I say I'm not hungry. There must be some merit to lying.

But if I justify lying, what makes me any different from slick politicians or the corporate robbers who raided the S&L industry? Saying it's okay to lie one way and not another is hedging. I cannot seem to escape the voice deep inside me that tells me: When someone lies, someone loses.

What far-reaching consequences will I, or others, pay as a result of my lie? Will someone's trust be destroyed? Will someone else pay my penance because I ducked out? We must consider the meaning of our actions. Deception, lies, capital crimes, and misdemeanors all carry meanings. Webster's definition of lie is specific:

1: a false statement or action especially made with the intent to deceive;

2: anything that gives or is meant to give a false impression.

A definition like this implies that there are many, many ways to tell a lie. Here are just a few.

THE WHITE LIE

A man who won't lie to a woman has very little consideration for her feelings.

——BERGEN EVANS

The white lie assumes that the truth will cause more damage than a simple, harmless untruth. Telling a friend he looks great when he looks like hell can be based on a decision that the friend needs a compliment more than a frank opinion. But, in effect, it is the liar deciding what is best for the lied to. Ultimately, it is a vote of no confidence. It is an act of subtle arrogance for anyone to decide what is best for someone else.

Yet not all circumstances are quite so cut-and-dried. Take, for instance, the sergeant in Vietnam who knew one of his men was killed in action but listed him as missing so that the man's family would receive indefinite compensation instead of the lump-sum pittance the military gives widows and children. His intent was honorable. Yet for twenty years this family kept their hopes alive, unable to move on to a new life.

FAÇADES

Et tu, Brute?

— CAESAR

We all put up facades to one degree or another. When I put on a suit to go to see a client, I feel as though I am putting on another face, obeying the expectation that serious businesspeople wear suits rather than sweatpants. But I'm a writer. Normally, I get up, get the kid off to school, and sit at my computer in my pajamas until four in the afternoon. When I answer the phone the caller thinks I'm wearing a suit (though the UPS man knows better).

But facades can be destructive because they are used to seduce others into an illusion. For instance, I recently realized that a former friend was a liar. He presented himself with all the right looks and the right words and offered lots of new consciousness theories, fabulous books to read, and fascinating insights. Then I did some business with him, and the time came for him to pay me. He turned out to be all talk and no walk. I heard a plethora of reasonable excuses, including in-depth descriptions of the big break around the corner. In six months of work, I saw less than a hundred bucks. When I confronted him, he raised both eyebrows and tried to convince me that I'd heard him wrong, that he'd made no commitment to me. A simple investigation into his past revealed a crowded graveyard of disenchanted former friends.

IGNORING THE PLAIN FACTS

Well, you must understand that Father Porter is only human.
——A MASSACHUSETTS PRIEST

In the '60s, the Catholic Church in Massachusetts began hearing complaints that Father James Porter was sexually molesting children. Rather than relieving him of his duties, the ecclesiastical authorities simply moved him from one parish to another between 1960 and 1967, actually providing him with a fresh supply of unsuspecting families and innocent children to abuse. After treatment in 1967 for pedophilia, he went back to work, this time in Minnesota. The new diocese was aware of Father Porter's obsession with children, but they needed priests and recklessly believed treatment had cured him. More children were abused until he was relieved of his duties a year later. By his own admission, Porter may have abused as many as a hundred children.

Ignoring the facts may not in and of itself be a form of lying, but consider the context of this situation. If a lie is a false action done with the intent to deceive, then the Catholic Church's conscious covering for Porter created irreparable consequences. The church became a co-perpetrator with Porter.

DEFLECTING

When you have no basis for an argument, abuse the plaintiff.
— CICERO

I've discovered that I can keep anyone from seeing the true me by being selectively blatant. I set a precedent of being up-front about intimate issues, but I never bring up the things I truly want to hide; I just let people assume I'm revealing everything. It's an effective way of hiding.

Any good liar knows that the way to perpetuate an untruth is to deflect attention from it. When Clarence Thomas exploded with accusations that the Senate hearings were a "high-tech lynching," he simply switched the focus from a highly charged subject to a radioactive subject. Rather than defending himself, he took the offensive and accused the country of racism. It was a brilliant maneuver. Racism is now politically incorrect in official circles—unlike sexual harassment, which still rewards those who can get away with it.

Some of the most skillful deflectors are passive-aggressive people who, when accused of inappropriate behavior, refuse to respond to the accusations. This you-don't-exist stance infuriates the accuser, who, understandably, screams something obscene out of frustration. The trap is sprung and the act of deflection successful, because now the passive-aggressive person can indignantly say, "Who can talk to someone as unreasonable as you?" The real issue is forgotten and the sins of the original victim become the focus. Feeling guilty of name-calling, the victim is fully tamed and crawls into a hole, ashamed. I have watched this fighting technique work thousands of times in disputes between men and women, and what I've learned is that the real culprit is not necessarily the one who swears the loudest.

OMISSION

The cruelest lies are often told in silence.

— R. L. STEVENSON

Omission involves telling most of the truth minus one or two key facts whose absence changes the story completely. You break a pair of glasses that are guaranteed under normal use and get a new pair, without mentioning that the first pair broke during a rowdy game of basketball. Who hasn't tried something like that? But what about omission of information that could make a difference in how a person lives his or her life?

For instance, one day I found out that rabbinical legends tell of another woman in the Garden of Eden before Eve. I was stunned. The omission of the Sumerian goddess Lilith from Genesis—as well as her demonization by ancient misogynists as an embodiment of female evil—felt like spiritual robbery. I felt like I'd just found out my mother was really my step-mother. To take seriously the tradition that Adam was created out of the same mud as his equal counterpart, Lilith, redefines all of Judeo-Christian history.

Some renegade Catholic feminists introduced me to a view of Lilith that had been suppressed during the many centuries when this strong goddess was seen only as a spirit of evil. Lilith was a proud goddess who defied Adam's need to control her, attempted negotiations, and when this failed, said adios and left the Garden of Eden.

This omission of Lilith from the Bible was a patriarchal strategy to keep women weak. Omitting the strong-woman archetype of Lilith from Western religions and starting the story with Eve the Rib has helped keep Christian and Jewish women believing they were the lesser sex for thousands of years.

STEREOTYPES AND CLICHÉS

Where opinion does not exist, the status quo becomes stereotyped
and all originality is discouraged.

— BERTRAND RUSSELL

Stereotypes and clichés serve a purpose as a form of shorthand. Our need for vast amounts of information in nanoseconds has made the stereotype vital to modern communication. Unfortunately, it often shuts down original thinking, giving those hungry for the truth a candy bar of misinformation instead of a balanced meal. The stereotype explains a situation with just enough truth to seem unquestionable.

All the "isms"—racism, sexism, ageism, et al.—are founded on and fueled by the stereotype and the cliché, which are lies of exaggeration, omission, and ignorance. They are always dangerous. They take a single tree and make it a landscape. They destroy curiosity. They close minds and separate people. The single mother on welfare is assumed to be cheating. Any black male could tell you how much of his identity is obliterated daily by stereotypes. Fat people, ugly people, beautiful people, old people, large-breasted women, short men, the mentally ill, and the homeless all could tell you how much more they are like us than we want to think. I once admitted to a group of people that I had a mouth like a truck driver. Much to my surprise, a man stood up and said, "I'm a truck driver, and I never cuss." Needless to say, I was humbled.

GROUP THINK

Who is more foolish, the child afraid of the dark, or the man afraid of the light?

— MAURICE FREEHILL

Irving Janis, in *Victims of GroupThink*, defines this sort of lie as a psychological phenomenon within decision-making groups in which loyalty to the group has become more important than any other value, with the result that dissent and the appraisal of alternatives are suppressed. If you've ever worked on a committee or in a corporation, you've encountered groupthink. It requires a combination of other forms of lying—ignoring facts, selective memory, omission, and denial, to name a few.

The textbook example of groupthink came on December 7, 1941. From as early as the fall of 1941, the warnings came in, one after another, that Japan was preparing for a massive military operation. The Navy command in Hawaii assumed Pearl Harbor was invulnerable—the Japanese weren't stupid enough to attack the United States' most important base. On the other hand, racist stereotypes said the Japanese weren't smart enough to invent a torpedo effective in less than 60 feet of water (the fleet was docked in 30 feet); after all, U.S. technology hadn't been able to do it.

On Friday, December 5, normal weekend leave was granted to all the 25 commanders at Pearl Harbor, even though the Japanese consulate in Hawaii was busy burning papers. Within the tight, good-ole-boy cohesiveness of the U.S. command in Hawaii, the myth of invulnerability stayed well entrenched. No one in the group considered the alternatives. The rest is history.

OUT-AND-OUT LIES

The only form of lying that is beyond reproach is lying for its own sake.

— OSCAR WILDE

Of all the ways to lie, I like this one the best, probably because I get tired of trying to figure out the real meanings behind things. At least I can trust the bald-faced lie. I once asked my five-year-old nephew "Who broke the fence?" (I had seen him do it.) He answered, "The murderers." Who could argue?

At least when this sort of lie is told it can be easily confronted. As the person who is lied to, I know where I stand. The bald-faced lie doesn't toy with my perceptions—it argues with them. It doesn't try to refashion reality, it tries to refute it. Read my lips. ... No sleight of hand. No guessing. If this were the only form of lying, there would be no such thing as floating anxiety or the adult-children of alcoholics movement.

DISMISSAL

Pay no attention to that man behind the curtain! I am the Great Oz!

—— THE WIZARD OF OZ

Dismissal is perhaps the slipperiest of all lies. Dismissing feelings, perceptions, or even the raw facts of a situation ranks as a kind of lie that can do as much damage to a person as any other kind of lie.

The roots of many mental disorders can be traced back to the dismissal of reality. Imagine that a person is told from the time she is a tot that her perceptions are inaccurate. "Mommy, I'm scared." "No, you're not, darling." "I don't like that man next door, he makes me feel icky." "Johnny, that's a terrible thing to say, of course you like him. You go over there right now and be nice to him."

I've often mused over the idea that madness is actually a sane reaction to an insane world. Psychologist R. D. Laing supports this hypothesis in *Sanity, Madness & the Family*, an account of his investigations into families of schizophrenics. The common thread that ran through all of the families he studied was a deliberate, staunch dismissal of the patient's perceptions from a very early age. Each of the patients started out with an accurate grasp of reality, which, through meticulous and methodical dismissal, was demolished until the only reality the patient could trust was catatonia.

Dismissal runs the gamut. Mild dismissal can be quite handy forgiving the foibles of others in our day-to-day lives. Toddlers who have just learned to manipulate their parents' attention sometimes are dismissed out of necessity. Absolute attention from the parents would require so much energy that no one would get to eat dinner. But we must be careful and attentive about how far we take our "necessary" dismissals. Dismissal is a dangerous tool because it's nothing less than a lie.

DELUSION

We lie loudest when we lie to ourselves.

—— ERIC HOFFER

I could write the book on this one. Delusion, a cousin of dismissal, is the tendency to see excuses as facts. It's a powerful lying tool because it filters out information that contradicts what we want to believe. Alcoholics who believe that the problems in their lives are legitimate reasons for drinking rather than results of the drinking offer the classic example of deluded thinking. Delusion uses the mind's ability to see things in myriad ways to support what it wants to be the truth.

But delusion is also a survival mechanism we all use. If we were to fully contemplate the consequences of our stockpiles of nuclear weapons or global warming, we could hardly function on a day-to-day level. We don't want to incorporate that much reality into our lives because to do so would be paralyzing.

Delusion acts as an adhesive to keep the status quo intact. It shamelessly employs dismissal, omission, and amnesia, among other sorts of lies. Its most cunning defense is that it cannot see itself.

The liar's punishment... is that he cannot believe anyone else.

—— GEORGE BERNARD SHAW

These are only a few of the ways we lie. Or are lied to. As I said earlier, it's not easy to entirely eliminate lies from our lives. No matter how pious we may try to be, we will still embellish, hedge, and omit to lubricate the daily machinery of living. But there is a world of difference between telling functional lies and living a lie. Martin Buber once said, "The lie is the spirit committing treason against itself." Our acceptance of lies becomes a cultural cancer that eventually shrouds and reorders reality until moral garbage becomes as invisible to us as water is to a fish.

How much do we tolerate before we become sick and tired of being sick and tired? When will we stand up and declare our right to trust? When do we stop accepting that the real truth is in the fine print? Whose lips do we read this year when we vote for president? When will we stop being so reticent about making judgments? When do we stop turning over our personal power and responsibility to liars?

Maybe if I don't tell the bank the check's in the mail I'll be less tolerant of the lies told me every day. A country song I once heard said it all for me: "You've got to stand for something or you'll fall for anything."

DIVISION

Having studied one part of the process of analysis, classification, let us now look at its partner, division. *Division* is a way of analyzing a subject, too. But instead of sorting the subject matter into categories as we do in classification, we divide a single subject into its component parts. When we say that *Hamlet* has five acts or that a certain book has fifteen chapters, we are dividing *Hamlet* and the book into parts. When a sports-car lover talks of the engine, transmission, and body of a new Ferrari, he is talking about parts of the whole.

Strategy

The same rules that apply to a successful analysis by classification apply to division as well. First, a clear basis for the division must be established. If we divide water into its chemical elements, we divide it into hydrogen and oxygen. We do not say that water is composed of hydrogen, oxygen, and the ability to freeze at 0 degrees Celsius; since we are only interested in the chemical makeup of water, this third attribute is irrelevant to our division. Every division, just like every classification, is made on the basis of some particular interest in the subject, and the division must confine itself to the parts of the subject that relate to that interest.

Also, as in classification, you must continue your analysis by division logically and completely until it is finished. (You cannot discuss only four acts of *Hamlet*, for example.) If you plan to divide a subject only into its main parts or focus on particular parts, you must make this limitation clear to your audience. This focus should appear in your introductory paragraph, preferably in your thesis statement. Otherwise, your readers have the right to expect a complete division. If you tell them that you are going to discuss the organization of the police force and talk only about the Narcotics Squad and the Police Laboratory, they will wonder what happened to the Vice Squad, the Traffic Bureau, and the Homicide Division. If you want to discuss only two of the parts of the police force, then you must say something like "The control and suppression of narcotics traffic are the responsibility of two allied parts of the police force, the Narcotics Squad and the Police Laboratory, whose operation and organization are important parts of one aspect of the police force." Here you have made clear to your audience your intention to discuss only two of the parts that make up the police force, and your audience will not expect to read about the Homicide Division or the Vice Squad.

Organization

The following skeletal outline is an example of division. As you read it, notice what the subject is that is being divided, into what parts it is being divided, and how the division is structured.

Hamiltonian America

Thesis: Unlike Jefferson's democratic governmental theories, Hamilton's picture of the future of America was based on three main ideas—centralized government, aristocratic rule, and progress through industrialization.

    I. Hamilton believed in a strong, centralized government, not in the decentralized regionally-oriented government of Jefferson.

    II. While Jefferson believed in the common man's right to democratic process, Hamilton felt that the aristocratic, well-educated minority was better equipped to govern.

    III. Finally, Hamilton based the two preceding principles on his vision of America as a strong industrial country with an emphasis on progress and technology.

The subject of analysis is Alexander Hamilton's political theory. This rather scant outline divides his philosophy into three main ideas or parts. Hamilton had other ideas (he believed, for example, in a pro-British foreign policy), but the writer is specifically interested only in "three main ideas," which he tells his readers in his thesis statement. Not only does the writer's thesis state the specific ideas to be discussed in the division process, it also provides a clear notion of what specific point the writer wishes to make about those three parts, that they differed from Jefferson's ideas.

It is worth noting, too, that the intended essay will not be developed by division alone. Although the writer's chief subject is Alexander Hamilton's political philosophy, he finds it impossible to discuss Hamilton's ideas without reference to Hamilton's great opponent, Thomas Jefferson. The essay, then, also employs comparison and contrast; the writer should observe the guidelines for comparison and contrast by following the rule of consistency in comparison throughout the essay. However, division remains the writer's main method of organization and development. It is not unusual to find several different modes of expository prose being used in a single essay.

◆

CHECKLIST FOR DIVISION ESSAY

Be sure that the division:

1. Is applied to a singular subject. Only one thing at a time can be divided.
2. Is consistent with your purpose.
3. Is complete in fulfilling your purpose.
4. Is clearly stated in your thesis statement and that your point is appropriate for your audience.

5. Uses logical subdivisions to make the point and arranges them in a logical or emphatic order.
6. Did you edit your paper carefully, checking for major grammatical and spelling errors?

ON THE NET

Classification Writing. Virtual Classroom: Mt. San Antonio College.
   <http://vclass.mtsac.edu/vesl1wc/classificationhandout.htm>

Classification. University of Bremen.
   <http://www-user.uni-bremen.de/~jsuther/classification.html>

Classification and Analysis. Capital Community College.
   <http://grammar.ccc.commnet.edu/grammar/composition/classification.htm>

EXERCISE

Circle the item in each group below that violates the unity of classification and briefly explain your choice.

Topic: Friends
Classes:
intimate friends
social friends
weird friends
work friends

Topic: Movies
Classes:
adventure
romantic
blockbusters
horror
suspense

Topic: Schools
Classes:
elementary
private
secondary
college
technical

Topic: Computer
Division:
monitor
mouse
hard drive
keyboard
lap top

Topic: Students
Classes:
metal heads
preppies
kickers
jocks
lazy

Topic: Trees
Classes:
exotic
maple
oak
pine
birch

Topic: Branches of U.S. government
Division:
legislative
judicial
cabinet
executive

Topic: Stores in a shopping mall
Classes:
department stores
shoe stores
bookstores
The Gap

11 Cause and Effect

Any time we respond to the question "Why?" we are concerned with the causes of an event.

Q. Why did you wreck your new car?

A. I was busy selecting a CD to play and was not paying attention to the changing signal light.

Q. Why did you perform so poorly on the biology final exam?

A. I spent all the previous night bailing water out of my bedroom after our subdivision flooded from the heavy rains.

We look for causes when we want to know why something happened. Similarly, when we want to know what happened as a result of the cause or causes, we attempt to determine the effects. When we respond to the questions "What happened then?" or "What would happen if. . . ?" we engage in discovering the effect.

Q. What happened because you performed so poorly on the biology final exam?

A. I was placed on scholastic probation for a semester.

Q. What will happen if you cannot raise your GPA sufficiently next semester?

A. I will be forced to drop out of school and to get a job.

We are constantly being required to use causal analysis in our attempt to understand events around us.

Strategy

Causal analysis may be simple or complex. Sometimes a causal analysis simply involves determining the cause or the effect of, say, why your car would not start.

However, a more complex analysis might be required when the cause and effect arrangement involves a causal chain. The process requires that the writer begin with either a cause or an effect and then work backward or forward to determine related causes and effects. For example, consider the following scenario. Mr. Strump failed to pay his income tax this year, and the investigating Internal Revenue Service agent discovers that Mr. Strump died on January 1 and thus had no income for the year.

Here is an example of a simple causal analysis. The effect (Mr. Strump's not paying taxes) can be traced to a specific cause (he died on January 1). A more thorough analysis may be required, however, and thorough analyses can be quite complicated. The IRS agent will probably be satisfied with the reason Mr. Strump paid no income taxes. He dies, he has no income, he pays no tax: case closed. But suppose the agent mentions Mr. Strump's death to Detective Sergeant Wexley of the police department. The sergeant might want to undertake a more thorough analysis. Here, Mr. Strump's death becomes the "effect" in question, and the sergeant goes looking for the causes of that death.

He discovers that Mr. Strump's corpse contains enough potassium cyanide to kill an elephant, much less a 92 year-old millionaire. He also finds that Miss Goldie May Goodbody, Mr. Strump's faithful 22-year old secretary and ex-Miss International Seafood, has inherited Mr. Strump's six million dollar fortune and now lives in a penthouse in Miami Beach. Mr. Strump had his fatal "heart attack" after drinking the special tea Miss Goodbody always brought him at his bedtime. The teacup was washed, but Sergeant Wexley discovers a bottle of potassium cyanide crystals with Miss Goodbody's fingerprints on it and a note from the old gentleman telling her that he is changing his will. Instead of leaving everything to her, Mr. Strump was planning to endow a foundation for the study of the mating habits of the bubble-eyed goldfish, and he had an appointment with his lawyer for the morning after he died. Sergeant Wexley reconstructs the cause-effect sequence like this: (1) Miss Goodbody is such a good secretary that old Mr. Strump makes a will leaving her $6,000,000. (2) Mr. Strump develops a mania for bubble-eyed goldfish and tells Miss Goodbody that the fish, not she, will get the fortune once he talks to his lawyer. (3) Miss Goodbody feeds the old boy a cup of cyanide tea to help him sleep. (4) Mr. Strump has his "heart attack," and Miss Goodbody has six million dollars. As a matter of fact, we could follow the sequence further since Sergeant Wexley retired abruptly from the police department and married the lovely Miss Goodbody. They moved to their Kentucky estate where the ex-sergeant raises quarter horses. The fingerprints, cyanide, and note strangely disappeared.

Anyway, before retiring from the force, the sergeant unearthed a cause-effect relationship leading up to Mr. Strump's death. He went further than the IRS agent, who was only concerned with nonpayment of taxes. It would be possible to carry the analysis further than the sergeant did to discover not only the immediate causes of the death but also the ultimate or remote causes—the basic, underlying factors that explain the more obvious ones. Why, for example, did Mr. Strump turn from the attractions of Miss Goodbody (blond, 5'9" tall, 39-24-37) to those of the bubble-eyed goldfish (also blond, 3" long, 1-2-1)? What reasons did Miss Goodbody have for changing from a beauty queen to a secretary, and why did she want to work for Mr. Strump? (The six million dollars may have had something to do with it.) The point to be made here is that the writer must decide how far to take any causal analysis, and the writer will make the decision to suit the purpose of the analysis to the audience for whom it is intended. The IRS agent was interested only in the non-payment of taxes, and the purpose of his analysis was accomplished when he found out that Mr. Strump was dead. He did not need to continue the analysis. If Sergeant Wexley had been doing his analysis for publication in a psychological journal, he would have had to discover the underlying psychological reasons for Mr. Strump's sudden love of goldfish and Miss Goodbody's deep love of six million dollars. Because he was analyzing the events for a police report, however, he needed only to go as far as a determination of guilt for Mr. Strump's death. As you can see from the example above, causality involves two questions.

1. What caused the effect to occur?

2. Under certain conditions, what will be the resulting effect or effects?

The first question involves tracing backward the relationship between cause and effect; the second question involves tracing the relationship forward from cause to effect.

CAUSES

The rules of causation are twofold. (1) Without event A, effect B will not occur, and (2) whenever event A occurs, B will later occur. Several types of causes exist, and the writer must be able to distinguish them in order to sort out the essential events that result in causation. Three types of causes include the following:

1. **necessary cause**—this cause must be present for an effect to occur; without it the effect cannot happen. For example, in order to have light in your kitchen at home, you must turn on the light switch. The switch mechanism is a necessary cause, but it will not provide light by itself. Electricity must also be present. Event A (switch), in other words, must be present for B (light) to occur.

2. **contributing cause**—this cause may determine a particular effect but cannot singly determine it. For instance, you may make a good grade on an exam if you study your class notes thoroughly; however, other factors come into play as well, such as the quality of your notes, regular attendance in class, and your ability to remember what you reviewed in your notes. Event A (study) may be present for event B (good grade) to occur, but event A does not automatically result in event B. Other factors may also have contributed to your good grade.

3. **sufficient cause**—this cause can determine a particular effect by itself, but the effect does not always follow as a result of the cause. For example, a student may fail a course because of poor attendance, but this cause alone does not always lead to failure. A grade average below 60 must be present as well. Event A (poor attendance) can be present for event B (failure), but A does not automatically result in event B.

Causal analysis, then, is concerned with the reasons that things happen. Because of this concern, it is one of the basic techniques of reasoning. When a writer decides to write an essay based on causal analysis, it is very important that he be convincing, for he is discussing something more complex than a light switch. The writer's aim is to demonstrate for the reader why event B (effect) occurred. Why, for example, does high cholesterol cause heart disease? Why did my daughter fail her college courses? In order to do the job convincingly, the writer must make the reader appreciate the logic and thoroughness of the essay. The writer is actually engaged in an intellectual process, and because he is usually appealing to the reader's mind, he must be sure that his analysis is rationally satisfying.

Causal Chain

The causal chain works like a series of dominoes aligned in a row. If you knock the first over, the second and the third dominoes will fall in succession, and so on until they have all tumbled. In a causal chain, the remote cause is like the fall of the first domino in the chain, which causes an effect (fall of second domino). This effect becomes the cause of the next effect (fall of third domino). This sequence continues until the immediate cause (the third domino) results in the final event (effect) of the chain process. The causal chain process looks like the following figure:

FIGURE III-B

There are several ways to structure a causal analysis. Ordinarily, either the writer will work logically from the most immediate cause back toward the most basic or remote cause, or he will start with the basic/remote and work forward to the immediate cause. An example of the immediate to remote sequence would be an analysis of the reasons for today's high cost of living. The writer might begin with high and rising prices for meat and clothing, suggest inflation as the reason for the price trend, point out high demand and limited supplies as the reason for inflation, discuss the basic economic law of supply and demand as responsible for the situation, and finally blame the whole thing on our capitalistic, money-oriented society. This analysis would have moved from the immediate level (the high price of food and clothing items), through an intermediate level (inflation and the supply and demand principles), to a very basic cause (the economic structure of the country). An example of the second pattern (basic/remote to immediate) would be an analysis of the reasons for American involvement in Vietnam, which begins with a discussion of the American spirit as dominated by a Protestant ethic of aggressive morality (remote cause). The author might assert that this morality makes Americans want to assert their own ideas of justice and ethical behavior on the world (intermediate cause) and finally suggest that our desire to impose "righteousness" on others (immediate cause) was the reason we became involved in Southeast Asia. Here the analysis has moved from the author's basic premise (the American spirit of aggressive morality) to the effect of that premise (U.S. involvement in Vietnam). When putting together a causal chain analysis, you must remember to observe some very important guidelines. First, because your analysis depends on demonstrating a causal chain, you must make clear to your reader how each cause is directly linked to the other causes included in your essay. For example, after you have discussed one of the causes in the first body paragraph, make certain that you show the connection of your second cause with the one already discussed, whether the second cause is the effect of the first or the cause of the first cause discussed, depending upon whether you began your analysis with the remote or the immediate cause. The same rule applies to the next paragraph. **This causal link must be clearly shown in the topic sentence of each paragraph.** Otherwise, the chain process will not be apparent to your audience. Study the two following outlines and note how the structure of each differs slightly. The first outline contains several causes that are not linked together but are combined to create a single effect.

I.   Introduction/thesis—Thesis identifies single effect (subject)
     and multiple causes (focus).
Body
II.   Cause #1
III. Cause #2
IV.   Cause #3
V.   Conclusion (restates effect and three causes)

An outline indicating a causal chain analysis looks similar to the one above, but some distinctions should be noted. Consider the following example.

I.   Introduction/thesis—Thesis identifies single effect (subject)
     and multiple causes connected by a causal chain (focus)
Body
II.   Cause #1 remote/basic cause
III. Cause #2 intermediate cause (effect of cause #1)
IV.   Cause #3 immediate cause (effect of cause #2)
V.   Conclusion

EFFECTS

Sometimes a single cause may have multiple effects. For example, what would be the effects on a student who failed a college course? His failure may lead to low self esteem (effect 1), he may have to forfeit his financial aid (effect #2), and his parents may refuse to pay for any further education (effect #3). Note that these three effects are independent of one another; in other words, one effect does not lead to another. Determining the effects of an event means we are predicting into the future what we assume will happen based on the evidence we have at the present time. We use this method of analysis every day. Before we commit ourselves to a particular act or opt for a specific choice, we often consider the consequences of such an act or choice. In this case, we are speculating about the future results of our decision today. Economic trends and weather predictions are determined by people who are informed enough about certain historical conditions to make educated prognostications regarding the future. You know what the potential effects would be if you failed to succeed in college. Causal analysis is the process that sets this same process into a coherent, logical structure. Just like the essay outline shown above that lists the causes for a single effect, the outline traces the multiple effects of a single cause and arranges them in a similar fashion.

FIGURE III-C

Event ⟶ **Effect 1** ⟶ **Effect 2** ⟶ **Effect 3**
            (immediate)   (intermediate)   (remote)

The thesis statement will contain the cause (subject of thesis) and the effects (focus of thesis), listing the effects in the order that you will discuss them in the subsequent paragraphs, moving downward either to the most important effect (if there is no causal chain of effects) or to the remote/basic effect or the immediate effect (in a causal chain process), depending on your purpose in the essay. If you wish to write an essay that discusses the effects in some preferential/emphatic order, the outline will have the following format:

I. Introduction/thesis—Identifies single event (subject) and
    multiple effects (focus)
Body
II. Effect #1 least important
III. Effect #2 more important
IV. Effect #3 most important
V.   Conclusion

The same general outline will serve as the format for an essay that discusses the causal chain resulting in the multiple effects of a single event/cause. The major difference here will be the arrangement of effects usually from immediate effect to remote or remote to immediate effect. Consider the following example.

I. Introduction/thesis—single cause/event (subject of thesis) and
    multiple effects (focus of thesis) listed by a time sequence (chain)
Body

II. Effect #1immediate effect (cause of effect #2)
III. Effect #2intermediate effect (result of effect #1)
IV. Effect #3remote effect (result of effect #2)
V.   Conclusion

Should you be required to write a causal analysis that examines both causes and effects, the process is a bit more complex but is consistent with the outlines described above. Whether you choose to write a causal chain or simply an essay showing multiple causes and effects, you must be consistent in considering your method. For instance, if you use the causal chain in tracing the causes, make certain that you use the causal chain also in examining the multiple effects. For a sample outline of the causal chain of both causes and effects of failing a course, consider the following outline.

I. Introduction/thesis —Effect #1 (subject of thesis—the failure of the course) and the causes and effects of failure (focus of thesis statement) in a logical order.

Body

II.   Cause #1
III.   Cause #2
IV.   Cause #3
V.   Effect #1
VI.   Effect #2
VII.   Effect #3
VIII. Conclusion

(One option might be to include all three effects into a single paragraph. Consult your instructor for perferred format.)

Organization

A simple analysis that examines some of the causes for the deaths of 1500 passengers aboard the *Titanic* might look like the following:

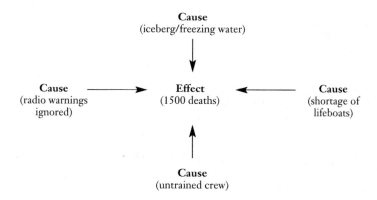

Although there is an endless number of reasons why so many passengers died, your consideration of the causes might be limited to accommodate your purpose / focus. Notice that each cause leading to the effect in the above diagram is independent of the other causes. How would you classify some of these causes? Necessary, contributing, sufficient? What other causes might be examined to determine why this ship and her crew were ill fated?

There are several potential hazards the writer of a causal analysis must be aware of if he wishes his essay to be convincing. (1) One is the *post hoc ergo propter hoc* fallacy. The Latin words mean "after this; therefore, because of this" and suggest that because one event follows another event, the first necessarily is the cause of the second. An extreme example might be to say that, as you were driving to class one day, a black cat crossed in front of your car and soon afterwards you were involved in a collision. You then conclude that black cats are omens of bad luck. This is an example of the *post hoc* fallacy and is obviously silly, but the writer must beware of asserting that just because something happened first (failure of the final exam) it caused something else (failure of the course) to happen. (2) Another hazard can be avoided if the writer makes sure that his analysis considers all the relevant causes and factors leading up to a certain effect. It may be true that the student's failing the final exam was a cause of his failure of the course, but other causes (poor attendance, poor daily quiz average, sleeping through lectures, assignments usually submitted late if at all, never purchasing the textbook, having a serious attitude problem, to name a few) may also have to be considered. (3) In order to be convincing, the writer should also offer evidence for his assertions. Simply saying that something was caused by something else is not enough. Because the writer wants his reader's intellectual assent, he must accompany his assertions with proof. If, for example, the writer says that the student's social life was responsible for his failure, then he must give evidence of how it was responsible: that it kept him from studying and that it was more important to him than his academic responsibilities. This third hazard can be avoided if the writer is objective, reasonable, and honest. If it becomes evident to the audience that the writer is condemning the failing student because of his hedonistic, immoral social behavior, and because of his love of heavy metal music and companions with fried brains, then the reader will not be convinced of the validity of the essay's analysis.

◆ CHECKLIST FOR CAUSE AND EFFECT ESSAY

As you prepare to write your causal analysis, keep the following in mind:

1. Focus on your purpose. A causal analysis can be primary or supplementary. Its purpose can be to inform, to speculate on possibilities, and/or to persuade. Regardless of the essay's primary purpose, your purpose is, of course, to persuade your audience of the legitimacy of your analysis.

2. Think logically. Indicate the complexity of the situation and look beyond the obvious and superficial. Recognize reasonable probability and do not over-state. Neither should you settle for simplistic explanations. Determine and differentiate between immediate and remote causes or effects and provide facts, statistics, details, and/or a personal narrative to explain and exemplify your reasoning.

3. Write a thesis statement that focuses on your purpose and your approach. Indicate whether you intend to talk about causes, effects, or both to show your order and development. Make your point clear and remember who your audi-ence is.

4. Choose an organizational plan. Some causal analyses are organized chrono-logically: causes and effects are presented in the order in which they happen, but a strict time sequence can be a problem if the primary causes are buried in the middle of the essay. Your causal analysis should be arranged emphatically with the most significant cause or effect reserved for last.

5. Use effective language that hints at the complexity of cause and effect rela-tionships. While you should qualify what you say, you should be careful not to undercut your own thinking.

6. Did you edit your paper carefully, checking for major grammatical and spelling errors?

The following student essay focuses on three reasons why some alcoholics turn to sobriety. The writer does not use a causal chain method of development, allowing each cause to serve independently of the other two causes. Is her discussion supported by sufficient illustrations and specific details or could the paragraphs be developed more?

GETTING SOBER

Krystal Holifield

To recognize that they have drinking problems, alcoholics have to be completely miserable and willing to change. When they get to this point, it is called their "bottom." There are "high bottom" and "low bottom" drunks, but it doesn't matter as long as they get sober. There are many different reasons why an alcoholic decides to get sober, but in my own case, I lost my self-esteem, I couldn't control my drinking, and my life became unmanageable.

The first thing that made me think about getting sober was that I lost my self-esteem. I always used to cut myself down in front of people and never knew how to accept compliments—sure signs of low self-esteem. The biggest symptom I had of low self-esteem was that I wasn't comfortable in my own skin or around people unless I was drunk because the only way I could stand myself was when I drank. I also never cared about my appearance, so I wouldn't wear make-up, fix my hair, or bathe regularly. Still, low self-esteem was something I would never have guessed I had—that is, until I thought about killing myself. Then I knew something might be wrong.

The second reason that made me want to get sober was the realization that I couldn't control my drinking. It had become a mental and physical obsession. Since my first drink at the age of twelve I couldn't go a day without a drink, and I could never have just one. By the age of seventeen I was used to drinking a case and a half of beer a day, and for the next two years I lived in a drunken fog. I could not go to school, work, or anywhere else outside my front door without a drink or the promise of one. I finally realized something had to be done when I couldn't get a drink one day and swallowing my own saliva made me violently ill. I was forced to drink NyQuil to keep from throwing up since it was the only alcohol in the house.

But the main reason I got sober was that my life became unmanageable. The first thing that made me notice I was out of control was getting kicked out of high school two weeks before graduation. During and after high school I also totaled three cars while driving drunk. In college things didn't get any better. I had a boyfriend who robbed houses, as well as me, so cops came to my house looking for him. Finally I realized that something had to change when I started waking up in places I didn't recognize or know how I got there.

Getting sober is usually the last thing an alcoholic wants to do. Practicing alcoholics usually have low self-esteem, can't control their drinking, and have unmanageable lives, but sobriety always helps remedy these problems. I have been sober for two-and-a-half years, and I cannot imagine going back to the way I lived before.

Another student decided that her causal analysis would best be served by employing the causal chain method in discussing why so many marriages end up in divorce. Follow her chain from remote to immediate stages of causation.

RINGS TO RUIN

Debbie Born

According to recent statistics, there are more divorces now than ever before. At the rate things are going, the divorce rate may soon surpass the marriage rate. There are many reasons for such a high divorce rate, but one of the main ones is that people do not realize what they are getting themselves into when they marry. Couples do not realize that marriage is a job that must be worked at continuously in order for it to go well. Because many couples marry for the wrong reasons, a breakdown in communication results, which leads to a couple's growing apart. This process, all too often, ends in divorce.

People marry the wrong people for the wrong reasons. Of course, they seem to be the right people and the right reasons at the time the decision is made, but the trouble really begins here. For example, many couples are too young when they marry. They meet in high school or college, "fall in love," which is really just lust, and know that they have found the person they are going to marry. Further, many young girls think that they are ready to marry, but many times they simply want to get out of their parents' house. The situation may involve abuse in some form or another, or the girl simply may not be getting along with her folks and sees marriage as a way out. She believes that if she can just make a home of her own everything will be fine. She looks on the young man as her salvation, and he begins to see himself in that role. In addition, she could also be pregnant. This situation always makes things worse for the young couple. The coming baby takes many choices away from the pair and adds many responsibilities that they are just not prepared to take on. There are financial burdens to be dealt with, such as hospital and doctor bills, as well as the burdens of trying to be parents when they themselves are little more than children. The frustration and the stress of all these burdens can be devastating to everyone concerned, which makes the situation all the more tragic.

When people get married for the wrong reasons, they usually find that they have trouble talking to one another once the first bloom of passion starts to fade and they get down to the business of every day living. The problems usually are not as simple as whether or not he squeezes the toothpaste from the middle or the bottom, or if she prefers movies to basketball. Those kinds of problems can be fixed or compromised. They do not have to get in the way of the relationship unless the parties involved allow them to. The real problems are basic to any relationship. Each spouse has to know what kind of person he or she is and what he or she believes in and wants out of life. The spouse must then be able to communicate those beliefs to the other person. If this cannot be done, then everything is lost. When marriage partners stop talking and listening to one another, then arguments start. The arguments are usually over little things and stem from the frustration of not being able to communicate. The individuals then begin to feel isolated because they do not know what is expected of them or which way to turn. What they do is turn away from each other. They may not like what they are seeing in their marriage, but they don't have a clue as to how to fix it because they don't know how to talk and listen to one another. Walls have now been erected between them.

At this point the two people involved begin to look at different things and different people to try and find satisfaction and fulfillment in their lives. They take a new job or spend longer hours at the one they already have. Staying at work is a good excuse to stay away from home and all the problems there. They may not even recognize or acknowledge this excuse to get away from their marriage. Another path that may be taken is the development of new interests or hobbies, which usually follows with the development of new friends. Most of the time the individual looks for interests and hobbies that do not include the spouse. This decision may or may not be made on a conscious level. Sometimes the futility of the situation takes over, and the only thing on a person's mind is getting out and away from the spouse. This way of thinking only leads to disaster. The two people either stay together and wind up being miserable, or they separate and divorce. Either way there is unhappiness for everyone involved.

Divorce has touched us all either directly or indirectly. There are normally no winners involved; everyone loses something. Things could begin to get a little better, however, if prospective couples would take some time to get to know each other better. When couples learn to communicate with one another and work to keep those lines open, there is growth together, not apart. This process does take a lot of work, but the rewards can be life-sustaining.

In the following excerpt from Chapter Three of *Guns, Germs, and Steel: The Fates of Human Societies* (1997), Jared Diamond traces the causes that enabled a small band of Spanish Conquistadores, "62 soldiers mounted on horses, along with 106 foot soldiers," to capture the great Inca Emperor Atahuallpa, who had an army of "about 80,000." This discussion follows his dramatic retelling of the event, which occurred on November 16, 1532, and sets up his wider discussion of the geographic conditions that allowed Europeans, beginning in the late fifteenth century, to conquer the American continent.

COLLISION AT CAJAMARCA

Jared Diamond

Let us now trace the chain of causation in this extraordinary confrontation, beginning with the immediate events. When Pizarro and Atahuallpa met at Cajamarca, why did Pizarro capture Atahuallpa and kill so many of his followers, instead of Atahuallpa's vastly more numerous forces capturing and killing Pizarro? After all, Pizarro had only 62 soldiers mounted on horses, along with 106 foot soldiers, while Atahuallpa commanded an army of about 80,000. As for the antecedents of those events, how did Atahuallpa come to be at Cajamarca at all? How did Pizarro come to be there to capture him, instead of Atahuallpa's coming to Spain to capture King Charles I? Why did Atahuallpa walk into what seems to us, with the gift of hindsight, to have been such a transparent trap? Did the factors acting in the encounter of Atahuallpa and Pizarro also play a broader role in encounters between Old World and New World peoples and between other peoples?

Why did Pizarro capture Atahuallpa? Pizarro's military advantages lay in the Spaniards' steel swords and other weapons, steel armor, guns, and horses. To those weapons, Atahuallpa's troops, without animals on which to ride into battle, could oppose only stone, bronze, or wooden clubs, maces, and hand axes, plus slingshots and quilted armor. Such imbalances of equipment were decisive in innumerable other confrontations of Europeans with Native Americans and other peoples.

The sole Native Americans able to resist European conquest for many centuries were those tribes that reduced the military disparity by acquiring and mastering both horses and guns. To the average white American, the word "Indian" conjures up an image of a mounted Plains Indian brandishing a rifle, like the Sioux warriors who annihilated General George Custer's U.S. Army battalion at the famous battle of the Little Big Horn in 1876. We easily forget that horses and rifles were originally unknown to Native Americans. They were brought by Europeans and proceeded to transform the societies of Indian tribes that acquired them. Thanks to their mastery of horses and rifles, the Plains Indians of North America, the Araucanian Indians of southern Chile, and the Pampas Indians of Argentina fought off invading whites longer than did any other Native Americans, succumbing only to massive army operations by white governments in the 1870s and 1880s.

Today, it is hard for us to grasp the enormous numerical odds against which the Spaniards' military equipment prevailed. At the battle of Cajamarca recounted above, 168 Spaniards crushed a Native American army 500 times more numerous, killing thousands of natives while not losing a single Spaniard. Time and again, accounts of Pizarro's subsequent battles with the Incas, Cortés' conquest of the Aztecs, and other early European campaigns against Native Americans describe encounters in which a few dozen European horsemen routed thousands of Indians with great slaughter. During Pizarro's march from Cajamarca to the Inca capital of Cuzco after Atahuallpa's death, there were four such battles: at Jauja, Vilcashuaman, Vilcaconga, and Cuzco. Those four battles involved a mere 80, 30, 110, and 40 Spanish horsemen, respectively, in each case ranged against thousands or tens of thousands of Indians.

These Spanish victories cannot be written off as due merely to the help of Native American allies, to the psychological novelty of Spanish weapons and horses, or (as is often claimed) to the Incas' mistaking Spaniards for their returning god Viracocha. The initial successes of both Pizarro and Cortés did attract native allies. However, many of them would not have become allies if they had not already been persuaded, by earlier devastating successes of unassisted Spaniards, that resistance was futile and that they should side with the likely winners. The novelty of horses, steel weapons, and guns undoubtedly paralyzed the Incas at Cajamarca, but the battles after Cajamarca were fought against determined resistance by Inca armies that had already seen Spanish weapons and horses. Within half a dozen years of the initial conquest, Incas mounted two desperate, large-scale, well-prepared rebellions against the Spaniards. All those efforts failed because of the Spaniards' far superior armament.

By the 1700s, guns had replaced swords as the main weapon favoring European invaders over Native Americans and other native peoples. For example, in 1808 a British sailor named Charlie Savage equipped with muskets and excellent aim arrived in the Fiji Islands. The aptly named Savage proceeded single-handedly to upset Fiji's balance of power. Among his many exploits, he paddled his canoe up a river to the Fijian village of Kasavu, halted less than a pistol shot's length from the village fence, and fired away at the undefended inhabitants. His victims were so numerous that surviving villagers piled up the bodies to take shelter behind them, and the stream beside the village was red with blood. Such examples of the power of guns against native peoples lacking guns could be multiplied indefinitely.

In the Spanish conquest of the Incas, guns played only a minor role. The guns of those times (so-called harquebuses) were difficult to load and fire, and Pizarro had only a dozen of them.

They did produce a big psychological effect on those occasions when they managed to fire. Far more important were the Spaniards' steel swords, lances, and daggers, strong sharp weapons that slaughtered thinly armored Indians. In contrast, Indian blunt clubs, while capable of battering and wounding Spaniards and their horses, rarely succeeded in killing them. The Spaniards' steel or chain mail armor and, above all, their steel helmets usually provided an effective defense against club blows, while the Indians' quilted armor offered no protection against steel weapons.

The tremendous advantage that the Spaniards gained from their horses leaps out of the eyewitness accounts. Horsemen could easily outride Indian sentries before the sentries had time to warn Indian troops behind them, and could ride down and kill Indians on foot. The shock of a horse's charge, its maneuverability, the speed of attack that it permitted, and the raised and protected fighting platform that it provided left foot soldiers nearly helpless in the open. Nor was the effect of horses due only to the terror that they inspired in soldiers fighting against them for the first time. By the time of the great Inca rebellion of 1536, the Incas had learned how best to defend themselves against cavalry, by ambushing and annihilating Spanish horsemen in narrow passes. But the Incas, like all other foot soldiers, were never able to defeat cavalry in the open. When Quizo Yupanqui, the best general of the Inca emperor Manco, who succeeded Atahuallpa, besieged the Spaniards in Lima in 1536 and tried to storm the city, two squadrons of Spanish cavalry charged a much larger Indian force on flat ground, killed Quizo and all of his commanders in the first charge, and routed his army. A similar cavalry charge of 26 horsemen routed the best troops of Emperor Manco himself, as he was besieging the Spaniards in Cuzco.

The transformation of warfare by horses began with their domestication around 4000 B.C., in the steppes north of the Black Sea. Horses permitted people possessing them to cover far greater distances than was possible on foot, to attack by surprise, and to flee before a superior defending force could be gathered. Their role at Cajamarca thus exemplifies a military weapon that remained potent for 6,000 years, until the early 20th century, and that was eventually applied on all the continents. Not until the First World War did the military dominance of cavalry finally end. When we consider the advantages that Spaniards derived from horses, steel weapons, and armor against foot soldiers without metal, it should no longer surprise us that Spaniards consistently won battles against enormous odds.

How did Atahuallpa come to be at Cajamarca? Atahuallpa and his army came to be at Cajamarca because they had just won decisive battles in a civil war that left the Incas divided and vulnerable. Pizarro quickly appreciated those divisions and exploited them. The reason for the civil war was that an epidemic of smallpox, spreading overland among South American Indians after its arrival with Spanish settlers in Panama and Colombia, had killed the Inca emperor Huayna Capac and most of his court around 1526, and then immediately killed his designated heir, Ninan Cuyuchi. Those deaths precipitated a contest for the throne between Atahuallpa and his half brother Huascar. If it had not been for the epidemic, the Spaniards would have faced a united empire.

Atahuallpa's presence at Cajamarca thus highlights one of the key factors in world history: diseases transmitted to peoples lacking immunity by invading peoples with considerable immunity. Smallpox, measles, influenza, typhus, bubonic plague, and other infectious diseases endemic in Europe played a decisive role in European conquests, by decimating many peoples on other continents. For example, a smallpox epidemic devastated the Aztecs after the failure of the first Spanish attack in 1520 and killed Cuitláhuac, the Aztec emperor who briefly succeeded Montezuma. Throughout the Americas, diseases introduced with Europeans spread from tribe to tribe far in advance of the Europeans themselves, killing an estimated 95 percent of the pre-Columbian Native American population. The most populous and highly organized native societies of North America, the Mississippian chiefdoms, disappeared in that way between 1492 and the late 1600s, even before Europeans themselves made their first settlement on the Mississippi River. A smallpox epidemic in 1713 was the biggest single step in the destruction of South Africa's native San people by European settlers. Soon after the British settlement of Sydney in 1788, the first of the epidemics that decimated Aboriginal Australians began. A well-documented example from Pacific islands is the epidemic that swept over Fiji in 1806, brought by a few European sailors who struggled ashore from the wreck of the ship Argo. Similar epidemics marked the histories of Tonga, Hawaii, and other Pacific islands.

I do not mean to imply, however, that the role of disease in history was confined to paving the way for European expansion. Malaria, yellow fever, and other diseases of tropical Africa, India, Southeast Asia, and New Guinea furnished the most important obstacle to European colonization of those tropical areas.

How did Pizarro come to be at Cajamarca? Why didn't Atahuallpa instead try to conquer Spain? Pizarro came to Cajamarca by means of European maritime technology, which built the ships that took him across the Atlantic from Spain to Panama, and then in the Pacific from Panama to Peru. Lacking such technology, Atahuallpa did not expand overseas out of South America.

In addition to the ships themselves, Pizarro's presence depended on the centralized political organization that enabled Spain to finance, build, staff, and equip the ships. The Inca Empire also had a centralized political organization, but that actually worked to its disadvantage, because Pizarro seized the Inca chain of command intact by capturing Atahuallpa. Since the Inca bureaucracy was so strongly identified with its godlike absolute monarch, it disintegrated after Atahuallpa's death. Maritime technology coupled with political organization was similarly essential for European expansions to other continents, as well as for expansions of many other peoples.

A related factor bringing Spaniards to Peru was the existence of writing. Spain possessed it, while the Inca Empire did not. Information could be spread far more widely, more accurately, and in more detail by writing than it could be transmitted by mouth. That information, coming back to Spain from Columbus's voyages and from Cortés' conquest of Mexico, sent Spaniards pouring into the New World. Letters and pamphlets supplied both the motivation and the necessary detailed sailing directions. The first published report of Pizarro's exploits, by his companion Captain Cristóbal de Mena, was printed in Seville in April 1534, a mere nine months after Atahuallpa's execution. It became a best-seller, was rapidly translated into other European languages, and sent a further stream of Spanish colonists to tighten Pizarro's grip on Peru.

Why did Atahuallpa walk into the trap? In hindsight, we find it astonishing that Atahuallpa marched into Pizarro's obvious trap at Cajamarca. The Spaniards who captured him were equally surprised at their success. The consequences of literacy are prominent in the ultimate explanation.

The immediate explanation is that Atahuallpa had very little information about the Spaniards, their military power, and their intent. He derived that scant information by word of mouth, mainly from an envoy who had visited Pizarro's force for two days while it was en route inland from the coast. That envoy saw the Spaniards at their most disorganized, told Atahuallpa that they were not fighting men, and that he could tie them all up if given 200 Indians. Understandably, it never occurred to Atahuallpa that the Spaniards were formidable and would attack him without provocation.

In the New World the ability to write was confined to small elites among some peoples of modern Mexico and neighboring areas far to the north of the Inca Empire. Although the Spanish conquest of Panama, a mere 600 miles from the Incas' northern boundary, began already in 1510, no knowledge even of the Spaniards' existence appears to have reached the Incas until Pizarro's first landing on the Peruvian coast in 1527. Atahuallpa remained entirely ignorant about Spain's conquests of Central America's most powerful and populous Indian societies.

As surprising to us today as Atahuallpa's behavior leading to his capture is his behavior thereafter. He offered his famous ransom in the naive belief that, once paid off, the Spaniards would release him and depart. He had no way of understanding that Pizarro's men formed the spearhead of a force bent on permanent conquest, rather than an isolated raid.

Atahuallpa was not alone in these fatal miscalculations. Even after Atahuallpa had been captured, Francisco Pizarro's brother Hernando Pizarro deceived Atahuallpa's leading general, Chalcuchima, commanding a large army, into delivering himself to the Spaniards. Chalcuchima's miscalculation marked a turning point in the collapse of Inca resistance, a moment almost as significant as the capture of Atahuallpa himself. The Aztec emperor Montezuma miscalculated even more grossly when he took Cortes for a returning god and admitted him and his tiny army into the Aztec capital of Tenochtitlan. The result was that Cortés captured Montezuma, then went on to conquer Tenochtitlán and the Aztec Empire.

On a mundane level, the miscalculations by Atahuallpa, Chalcuchima, Montezuma, and countless other Native American leaders deceived by Europeans were due to the fact that no living inhabitants of the New World had been to the Old World, so of course they could have had no specific information about the Spaniards. Even so, we find it hard to avoid the conclusion that Atahuallpa "should" have been more suspicious, if only his society had experienced a broader range of human behavior. Pizarro too arrived at Cajamarca with no information about the Incas other than what he had learned by interrogating the Inca subjects he encountered in1527 and 1531. However, while Pizarro himself happened to be illiterate, he belonged to a literate tradition. From books, the Spaniards knew of many contemporary civilizations remote from Europe, and about several thousand years of European history. Pizarro explicitly modeled his ambush of Atahuallpa on the successful strategy of Cortés.

In short, literacy made the Spaniards heirs to a huge body of knowledge about human behavior and history. By contrast, not only did Atahuallpa have no conception of the Spaniards themselves, and no personal experience of any other invaders from overseas, but he also had not even heard (or read) of similar threats to anyone else, anywhere else, anytime previously in history. That gulf of experience encouraged Pizarro to set his trap and Atahuallpa to walk into it.

Thus Pizarro's capture of Atahuallpa illustrates the set of proximate factors that resulted in Europeans' colonizing the New World instead of Native Americans' colonizing Europe. Immediate reasons for Pizarro's success included military technology based on guns, steel weapons, and horses; infectious diseases endemic in Eurasia; European maritime technology; the centralized political organization of European states; and writing. The title of this book will serve as shorthand for those proximate factors, which also enabled modern Europeans to conquer peoples of other continents. Long before anyone began manufacturing guns and steel, others of those same factors had led to the expansions of some non-European peoples, as we shall see in later chapters.

But we are still left with the fundamental question why all those immediate advantages came to lie more with Europe than with the New World. Why weren't the Incas the ones to invent guns and steel swords, to be mounted on animals as fearsome as horses, to bear diseases to which Europeans lacked resistance, to develop oceangoing ships and advanced political organization, and to be able to draw on the experience of thousands of years of written history? Those are no longer the questions of proximate causation that this chapter has been discussing, but questions of ultimate causation that will take up the next two parts of this book.

ON THE NET

Cause and Effect. Capital Community College.
<http://grammar.ccc.commnet.edu/grammar/composition/cause_effect.htm>

Cause and Effect Paragraphs. Technology Studies in Education.
<http://lrs.ed.uiuc.edu/students/fwalters/cause.html>

A Brief Guide to Writing Cause and Effect Essays. Roane State Community College.
<http://www.roanestate.edu/owl&writingcenter/OWL/Cause.html>

"Cold Comfort": Sample Cause and Effect Essay. Capital Community College.
<http://grammar.ccc.commnet.edu/GRAMMAR/composition/cause/cause_frames.htm>

EXERCISES

Exercise I

Think of something (good or bad) that happened to you recently and trace the causal chain that resulted in this event.

What happened recently:_____

_____

(effect)

_____

⇑ (caused)

_____

⇑ (immediate cause)

_____

⇑ (caused)

_____

⇑ (caused)

_____

⇑ (caused)

_____

⇑ (caused)

_____

⇑ (caused)

_____

⇑ (caused)

_____

⇑ (caused)
(remote cause) _____

Exercise II

Diagram the multiple causes that led to your being a student at this particular school. For one of the multiple causes construct a causal chain.

Cause 1: _____

Cause 2: _____

Cause 3: _____

(Effect) Why I am attending this particular school

Cause 4: _____ (immediate)

_____ (intermediate)

_____ (remote)

12 Constructing an Argument

We are all expected on occasion to explain our ideas. When we engage in such an explanation, we call upon evidence to convince our listener or reader that our ideas are true and correct and, therefore, worthy of attention. Sometimes we are expected to present and defend our ideas in writing. For example, in your academic career and in the workplace you will be called upon to analyze situations and texts and to argue for or against certain ideas or opinions. From small businesses to large corporations, employees who can articulate their views logically have an advantage in being considered for advancement. As a student, a citizen, a parent, an employee, or a consumer, you will have many opportunities to express your ideas. Being familiar with argumentative skills will improve your chances of being convincing and persuasive. But, more importantly, you will be able to use these same skills in distinguishing between truth and falsehood in the world around you. Being familiar with the tools of argument, you will be able to determine the correctness of claims made by political figures, employers, salespeople, advertisers, and friends. You can then not only determine the validity of others' arguments, but also formulate your own strategy of reasoned argument to counter the beliefs with which you disagree.

The word *argument* itself usually suggests a negative activity. We think of an argument as a synonym for a quarrel or disagreement: we argue with parents, spouses, and friends. This use of the term, however, differs from its original and still primary meaning, which is associated with reason and objectivity. An *argument* is defined as the process of demonstrating, through reason, the likelihood or necessity of a given proposition. The purpose of an argument is to persuade. It is the process of influencing others, through reasoning, to respond as we wish them to respond. If everyone always agreed on everything, there would be no need for argument. But we know that disagreements do exist at all levels of life. The fact that some of our disagreements are ancient ones suggests the difficulty people have in reaching agreement. For example, consider the controversial topics of abortion, censorship, and capital punishment. These controversies will never approach resolution until the truth is discovered and there is agreement as to that truth. Yet truth can never be discovered until there is a free and open encounter between opposing views. This very encounter is at the heart of argumentative discourse; therefore, disagreements must be addressed reasonably, objectively, and thoroughly if we are ever to attain the truth. Once we have demonstrated the truth of an argument, however, we must then persuade others of the correctness of that truth. This attempt at persuasion is a complicated undertaking. To gain our reader's assent to our proposition, we must organize our supporting evidence in a format that will present our ideas most effectively. Thus, since rhetoric is the art of using language persuasively, we employ rhetoric every time we try to convince others of the truth of our convictions.

Strategy

To construct a persuasive argument, you must first determine what your purpose is. Do you intend to persuade by offering a defense or an attack? Since you will be expected to argue your views in an attempt to persuade your reader to see the issues as you do, and, possibly, to act upon the views or recommendations you have prescribed, you must understand and be able to use effectively the rhetorical elements involved in writing persuasive arguments. In addition, you will be expected to identify your specific audience for your essay. The audience determines the approach you take to your argument. Next, with your purpose and audience in mind, you must take a stand on your topic, state a claim that reflects that stand, and finally provide evidence to support that claim.

Audience

You must first have a clear understanding of your audience. Your audience will shape a great deal of what you say and how you say it and will guide you in determining your particular approach to your topic. First, your language must be appropriate for your readers. It would be unwise to address a group of middle-school readers with complex language and reasoning, just as it would be imprudent to address a group of experts on your topic in a manner that assumes no knowledge on their part. You must always be both clear and respectful of your audience. In addition, knowing your audience allows you to make certain assumptions in order to select the appropriate and most convincing points to be discussed. It also gives you the ability to anticipate what objections to your ideas your audience will have. Generally, you should assume that your audience is intelligent, informed about your topic, and not only opposes your position but resists it. By anticipating your audience's opposition, your stand on a given topic will be stronger and more convincing.

While argument begins in conflict, it should, ideally, end in resolution. However, since your topic is controversial, both sides believe they are right, and your opponent will probably have at least one sound argument on his side. Yet even if your reader remains unconvinced that you are right and he is wrong, you can present such a clear and coherent argument that he must admit, at least, the credibility of your position.

Definition of Terms

Many arguments fail because the writer does not define the terms on which his essay is based. Therefore, make certain you clearly define the terms you discuss. State, for example, what you mean by "affirmative action," "sexual harassment," "censorship," "pornography," "aesthetic value," or "redeeming quality." You must define any term your audience, for one reason or another, might misunderstand. Consult a dictionary or construct your own definition based on your understanding of the term and on the manner in which you discuss the term in your argument. You might review the section on Definition in **Chapter Eight** to familiarize yourself with the methods of defining a term.

THE APPEAL TO REASON

The rational appeal is one of three methods of persuasion identified by Aristotle and since discussed, expanded, and analyzed by philosophers, rhetoricians, and scientists. The other two, the emotional appeal and the ethical appeal, are discussed at length in **Chapter Three.** The rational appeal is used to convince an audience that the writer's claims are true. To construct an argument using the rational appeal, the writer will employ either **induction** or **deduction,** both forms of logic.

Terms

In order to employ the rational appeal effectively, the writer must first understand some basic concepts and terms:

Logic. Logic is a method of distinguishing between correct and incorrect reasoning. Since reasoning is represented in arguments, logic is a method for evaluating arguments.

Argument. An argument is an organized discussion of an idea or an issue. It can proceed from a premise or several premises to a conclusion, or it can start with a claim and then give evidence to support that claim. An argument is meant to persuade its readers or listeners that the belief or position held by the arguer is true and valid.

Claim. A claim is a statement that affirms or denies the truth of something. It can be as concrete and as easily verified as the statement *Houston is the largest city in Texas,* or as abstract and difficult to prove as the statement *The soul is immortal.* Claims are like thesis statements of essays.

Truth. While *Truth* is hard to define, the following will provide a working definition: Truth is the state of affairs in which a claim corresponds to reality or expresses a tautology (truth by definition). Correspondence with reality can only be determined empirically, that is through observation and experience. For example, the statement that the sun is approximately 93,000,000 miles from earth can be verified by experiment. Truth by definition is a matter of how speakers of a language have agreed (often implicitly) upon meanings of words. For example, the statement that bachelors are unmarried men is true because "unmarried men" and "bachelors" mean the same thing in English.

Arguments are composed of two types of claims:

Premises. A premise is a claim stated by the arguer as evidence for the belief that he or she is trying to prove. Either the premise will be readily accepted by the audience as being true, or it will be necessary to devise further arguments to show that the premises of the main argument are true. (This usually involves the minor premises.)

Conclusion. The conclusion is the claim expressing the belief that the arguer is trying to persuade the hearer or reader to accept. In a sound argument the conclusion follows logically from the premises.

A sound or cogent argument not only provides evidence that its claims are **true,** it also makes sure that its conclusions are **validly** drawn from its premises.

Validity. The process by which arguments are determined to be correct. An argument is valid if its conclusion is properly drawn from its premises, that is, if the rules of logic have been followed in proceeding from premise to conclusion.

Deductive Reasoning

Deduction. Deduction is a strict form of argument aiming for the strongest possible connection between premises and conclusion. The writer using deductive reasoning aims to set forth evidence so that if the premises are true, the conclusion necessarily follows as true. Alternatively, the writer tries to make it impossible for the premises to be true and the conclusion false. For example, if

$$A \rightarrow B$$
$$C \rightarrow A$$
$$C = B$$

The above example is a *syllogism*, which is a form of deductive argument. There are several types of syllogisms, but the one most commonly known and used is the categorical syllogism.

Categorical Syllogism. The categorical syllogism is composed of two premises and a conclusion, as in the following example:

Parts

Major Premise	All men are mortal.
Minor Premise	Socrates is a man.
Conclusion	Socrates is mortal.

Terms

Major term	The predicate of the conclusion (mortal)
Minor term	The subject of the conclusion (Socrates)
Middle term	The term common to both premises but not included in the conclusion (man/men)

◆

CHECKLIST FOR CATEGORICAL SYLLOGISMS

1. The middle term (Man) must be *distributed* at least once. That is, we must say something about all or no members of the class to which the middle term belongs.
2. There must be only three terms.
3. If a term is distributed in the conclusion, it must be distributed in the premises.
4. If both premises are affirmative, the conclusion must be affirmative.
5. If one premise is negative, the conclusion must be negative.
6. If both premises are negative, no valid conclusion is possible.

Enthymemes. An enthymeme is a syllogism with one of its premises omitted (usually the major premise). In order to test the validity of the syllogistic argument, we must supply the omitted premise.

> Example 1.   He couldn't have stolen that money; he is a church deacon.
> Suppressed Premise: Church deacons do not steal.

> Example 2.   They must be rich because they spend every summer in Europe.
> Suppressed Premise: People who spend their summers in Europe are rich.

> Example 3.   You can't deny a criminal his natural rights; after all, he is a human being.
> Suppressed Premise: Humans cannot be denied their natural rights.

A danger in using an enthymeme is that your readers may not recognize it as an enthymeme and, therefore, fail to realize the full import of your argument. The advantage, however, is that if the enthymeme is recognized it creates greater reader involvement in the argument and the essay as a whole.

While your thesis can be a statement that contains the whole syllogism, it can be shortened to include only an enthymeme. If you choose to use the enthymeme as your thesis, as in the examples above, you must still discuss the omitted premise in the body of the essay. Sometimes you may not want to use the syllogism or enthymeme as your thesis. Even though you employ deductive argument and it is based on a syllogism, you may have a thesis statement independent of the syllogism. For example, suppose that your discussion is organized around a syllogism that shows the validity of an argument indicating the benefits of America's space program. Your reason for using the syllogism is to suggest that Congress should increase NASA's long term appropriations. Your purpose, therefore, is to advocate more money for the program while the syllogism itself argues, deductively, that the United States benefits from such a program. Your thesis statement might look something like the following: "Because the United States benefits from the space program, Congress should increase NASA's appropriations."

A good deductive argument is a **sound argument,** that is one whose premises are all true and whose form is valid. The reader must be satisfied with both before he can give assent to the conclusion. The fact that an argument is valid does not make it automatically acceptable because the premises may be false. For example:

Major Premise	All college students must take American history.
Minor Premise	You are a college student.
Conclusion	You must take American history.

This argument/syllogism is valid in the sense that if the premises are true, the conclusion necessarily follows; remember that validity is about the connection between the premises and the conclusion. The problem here, however, is that the major premise is untrue. (American history is only a Texas state requirement for a college degree.) This argument, then, would be classified as valid but not true.

When you are evaluating a deductive argument, ask yourself two questions:

1. Is it valid? Is the connection between the premises and the conclusion logical?

2. Are the premises true?

If your answer to both questions is "yes," the argument is **sound.** If your answer to either question is "no," you have a basis for rejecting the argument. The fact that the argument is unsound, however, does not mean that the conclusion is false; it simply means that the logic of this particular attempt to prove the conclusion has failed.

Inductive Reasoning

Induction is a less strict form of argument than deduction. The writer of an inductive essay aims to set forth evidence so that if the premises are true, the conclusion

probably follows as true. Yet it is possible for the premises to be true and the conclusion false. Induction is often used in science, history, and everyday life when one cannot obtain enough evidence to make the conclusion absolutely certain. An inductive argument is **strong** when the writer has succeeded in arranging the premises so that, if they are true, the conclusion follows. Here are some examples of strong inductive arguments listed by type:

1. **Generalization.**

   Mockingbird #1 was observed to eat worms.

   Mockingbird #2 was observed to eat worms.

   Mockingbird #99 was observed to eat worms.

   Conclusion: All mockingbirds eat worms.

2. **Prediction.**

   In the past, an increase in stock prices has been followed shortly by a decrease in bond prices.

   Stock prices increased last week.

   Conclusion: Bond prices will decrease this week.

3. **Analogy.**

   The car I am now driving weighs 3500 pounds, has a fuel-injected V-8, has wind resistance coefficient of .29, and gets 30 mpg on the highway.

   The car I am about to buy has the same characteristics.

   Conclusion: The car I am about to buy will get 30 mpg on the highway.

4. **Causal Inference.**

   The old bridge that was here yesterday is not here today. It was inspected last month and was found to be dangerously weak. We have had torrential rains for the past week, and the creek has risen up to a level above the roadway on the bridge.

   Conclusion: The old bridge was probably swept away by the floodwaters in the creek.

In addition, a **cogent** inductive argument is one that is strong and whose premises are all true. When you are evaluating an inductive argument, ask yourself two questions:

1. Is it strong? Is the connection between the premises and the conclusion logical?

2. Are the premises true?

If your answer to both questions is "yes," the argument is **cogent.** If the answer to either question is "no," you have a basis for rejecting the argument. Once again, finding that an argument is not cogent does not mean that the conclusion is false; it merely means that this particular attempt to prove the conclusion has failed.

Evidence

The most difficult task for the writer using inductive reasoning is to know whether he or she has sufficient evidence from which to draw a conclusion. All the writer can do is establish as high a degree of probability as possible. Once the writer is certain that the evidence provided for the inductive argument is sufficient, random (there are a variety of examples), accurate, and relevant, the writer must make what is known as the **"inductive leap,"** a conclusion he or she reaches based on the evidence discussed. Unless the evidence meets these criteria, the argument will not be convincing, and the writer will appear to have made a hasty generalization.

If in developing evidence for an inductive argument you discover an **exception** to your proposition, **you should include it, too, in your discussion.** A couple of reasons suggest this course of action. First, the inclusion of the single exception (negative evidence) can work to your advantage psychologically and ethically since, by including the exception with your evidence, you suggest to your reader that you are trustworthy in reporting such potentially damaging evidence. Second, you can take the opportunity to mitigate the force of the exception.

Kinds of Evidence

Facts. According to the National Academy of Sciences, a fact is "an observation that has been repeatedly confirmed and for all practical purposes is accepted as 'true.'" However, what constitutes a "fact" may be open to discussion. Be sure to distinguish between **fact, opinion, and judgment.** An opinion is an unsupported statement of belief, while a judgment is a conclusion that sums up a large number of previous observations.

Examples. Examples are used to support generalizations. They give specific instances to illustrate the material from which inductive generalizations are derived. Examples should be **relevant** and **appropriate;** that is, they should directly bear on the issue being discussed, and they should be suitable and fitting, not extreme or unusual.

Authorities. Authorities are experts in various fields. Their work or statements are used as evidence to support claims. An authority may be an expert by virtue of his knowledge, skill, experience, training, or education.

Statistics. Numerical data in the form of tables, graphs, or charts are used to support claims. Since contradictory conclusions can be drawn from the same data, especial care must be taken in evaluating statistics. Good statistical data are usually presented visually (as a chart or table) as well as numerically; they should also be accompanied by an analysis, and the sources of the data should be clearly stated.

Public Records. Information drawn from public records, such as the Bureau of the Census, state agencies, or historical archives is frequently used as evidence.

Interviews. Personal interviews with people with experience can also be used as evidence, either as examples or as expert testimony.

Personal Experience. If one has relevant personal experience, it can also be used as evidence as example or testimony.

Sources

Since a crucial element of persuasive argumentation is the evidence you use to support your assertions, you must pay particular attention to the sources of that evidence. Sources include reports in the media, statistics, testimonials, research, and authority. More weight is generally attributed to primary sources than to secondary sources. **Primary sources** include such things as original documents and eyewitness accounts. **Secondary sources** are those materials that are based on primary sources. For example, in a political science class you might be asked to write a paper on the freedom of religion in this country. One of your primary sources might be the Constitution itself; your secondary sources might include analyses and interpretations of what the Constitution means by historians, scholars, and legal experts.

Secondary sources should be assessed in relation to whatever primary evidence is accessible. You will find that among secondary sources there is usually disagreement, which makes your task of **evaluating** them more difficult. Sources should be **reliable, current, appropriate, unbiased, and authoritative.** For example, check the date of the published source, see if there is any material on the author (Is she a university professor? Has he published other articles on this topic?), and find out who published the material (Is it a university press, a political organization, a state government?). The more secondary sources you are able to accumulate, the better your chances are at arriving at some general assumptions regarding the validity of the sources you actually use.

Informal Fallacies

A fallacy is a particular kind of defect in an argument caused by unsound or incomplete reasoning. It weakens an argument and makes it vulnerable to attack. However, sometimes writers consciously use such unsound reasoning to bolster their own side of an argument or to deflect criticism away from a weak argument. There are two kinds of fallacies: Formal fallacies result from not following the rules of formal logic, such as not distributing the middle term in a categorical syllogism. Informal fallacies result from the ambiguity inherent in language, such as when a word is used in two different senses in the same argument, called equivocation. Of the two, the informal fallacies are more regularly employed in every day argument. After all, normal arguments between people are conducted through language, not mathematical symbols. Therefore, not only should you be familiar with informal fallacies so you can avoid them in your own argumentative essays, you *should* also be able to identify your opponent's defective arguments, allowing you to refute his claims more easily. The following list includes some of the most common informal fallacies:

Hasty Generalization. An argument that draws a conclusion based on insufficient or inappropriate samplings: "My Oldsmobile is a real lemon; therefore, General Motors manufactures inferior automobiles." "Students at Hudson University are rude. Last night the guys in the room next to mine played their stereo at full blast until two in the morning, and as I was on my way to class this morning a bicyclist almost ran me down."

Begging the Question. An argument based on an assumption that has not been proven: "The immoral experimentation on animals for research must be abolished" ; "My narrow-minded English instructor seems to have forgotten how difficult it is to be a student."

Circular Reasoning. An argument that goes in a circle, where one proves the premise by the conclusion and the conclusion by the premise: "The governor would never lie to the public because he is an honest man." "Drugs are harmful because they injure the body." "I believe in God because I believe in the truth of the Bible; I believe in the truth of the Bible because it is the inspired word of God."

Either/or Reasoning. An argument, also called a **false dilemma,** that suggests that only two alternatives exist when more than two actually exist. Valid inferences can be drawn only from alternatives that are exhaustive: "Either he voted Republican or he did not vote Republican" is quite different from "Either he voted Republican or he voted Democratic." People have a tendency to turn difficult issues into simple ones with two sides—black/white, right/ wrong, good/bad. "If you quit college, you will never succeed in anything you do." "We can recognize that athletes who participate in major sports must be given special consideration at Hudson University, or we can let the university sink into athletic oblivion."

Faulty Analogy. An argument based on a comparison of two things that share few or no common and relevant features. An analogy should be carefully examined to be sure that the things being compared are alike in ways essential to the conclusion being drawn. The fact that they are alike in some ways is not enough. "Since he was a good governor, I'm sure he will make a good President." "Bill, you are a superb computer technician. You seem to have a natural talent for analyzing system problems and remedying them. Surely, then, you should be able to analyze the problems in the rough drafts of your papers and turn them into polished essays."

Argumentum ad Hominem.   The Latin phrase means *argument against the man* and names the fallacy of attacking the person rather than his argument. Such an attack may be legitimate when someone presents no argument but his own unsupported testimony. For example, the procedure is frequently used in courts to impeach witnesses who are testifying as experts. If it can be shown that they are not experts or that their testimony cannot be relied on, their trustworthiness as witnesses is seriously challenged. However, if someone presents evidence to support a claim, simply attacking his character is illegitimate. "Mr. Grumpky shouldn't be allowed to serve on the school board; he is a non-Christian." "Of course Senator Sparky voted for the big bailout of Global Mortgage; I hear he's received lots of money from their political action committee."

Argumentum ad Populum.   This "appeal to the people" is used particularly by politicians and advertisers. This fallacy ignores the issue at hand to appeal to the ingroup loyalties and fears of the audience. Appeals to prejudice and self-interest are also part of this appeal. For example, one might argue that people should be against any form of government regulation of business since America was founded on the principle of freedom from oppression.

Appeal to Ignorance.   This argument implies that since no one has proved a particular claim, it must be false; or, since no one has disproved a claim, it must be true. This fallacy usually involves a matter that is either incapable of being proved or has not yet been proved. For example, a frequently heard retort in an argument, say, about the existence of telepathy, is: "Well, you can't prove that it doesn't exist!" This is not a clinching argument, for our ignorance about how to disprove a proposition does not establish its truth or falsehood. Keep in mind that the burden of proof rests with the person making a claim.

Tokenism.   This fallacy occurs when one makes only a token gesture (does very little of what is required), but then shouts or brags about it as loudly as one can. For example, a company might point to a highly placed executive who is female to show how well they treat and promote women when, in fact, she is the only woman in an executive position in the whole company.

The Straw Man Fallacy.   This fallacy occurs when a person misinterprets or distorts an opponent's position to make it easier to attack, or when he attacks weaker opponents while ignoring stronger ones. For example, when opponents of gun control characterize those who are for some limitations on the ownership and use of weapons as radicals who would do away with hunting and Americans' constitutional right to bear arms, they are attacking a straw man.

Bandwagon Fallacy. An argument that claims that something cannot be true (or false) because a majority of people support (or oppose) it. Based on popular opinion, the argument appeals to prejudice and ignores the facts. For example, "It is obvious that any caring parent would not want his / her child attending school where a classmate has HIV."

Slippery Slope. An argument based on an unlikely chain reaction. It consists in objecting to a particular action on the grounds that once an action is taken it will lead inevitably to a similar but less desirable action which, in turn, will lead to an even less desirable action and so on. For example, "If we legalize marijuana, the United States will become a nation of addicts and criminals." "If we allow physician-assisted suicide, it will eventually lead to the wholesale killing of the very ill or permanently disabled."

Selective Sampling. Proof offered that contains part of, but not the whole truth. Since not all the facts are stated, the claim can be true and false (misleading?) at the same time (half-truths). For example, "Three out of five dentists surveyed preferred Brand X toothpaste."

Unreliable Testimony. An argument based on an untrustworthy, biased, or unqualified authority. Fame or celebrity does not qualify one as authoritative or expert. For example, "Several of my well-educated neighbors support the termination of our school's head coach."

False Cause. An argument that confuses a causal relationship (see Chapter 11). For example, one might mistake a contributory cause for a sufficient one, or assume that because one event occurred before a second event, the first caused the second (an example of the **post hoc, ergo propter hoc** fallacy, a Latin phrase meaning *after this; therefore because of this*.) "Since the city council outlawed firearms, the crime rate has risen." "Research shows that successful people have large vocabularies; therefore, one way to become successful is to develop a large vocabulary."

ORGANIZATION

In his *Rhetoric*, Aristotle discusses the five parts of the deliberative discourse (a discussion of what we should or should not do to bring about some future goal), only two of which, **invention** and **disposition,** are relevant to the organization of the written essay.

Invention

Invention is the process or method writers use to discover arguments. Aristotle divided the process into two parts, finding arguments and devising arguments from scratch.

Non-Artistic Proofs. What Aristotle called non-artistic proofs are arguments that have already been formulated by others. We call this process research. Properly conducted research will lead to an abundance of information on, and authoritative discussion of, the topic you are writing about.

Artistic Proofs. Artistic proofs are arguments you develop on your own; that is, they are arguments you devise through your own ability, your own art, without reference to outside sources. They include the Logical Appeal, The Emotional Appeal, and The Ethical Appeal. See **Chapter Three** for a complete discussion of the latter two.

Topics. Topics are proofs grouped under common headings. Under **common topics** Aristotle discusses such topics as definition, comparison-contrast, causal analysis, and the proper use of testimony or authority. See **Chapter Four,** and **Chapters Six through Eleven** for detailed discussions of these methods of exposition. Under **special topics** for a deliberative discourse, Aristotle points out that an argument can attempt to persuade the reader that a particular solution to a problem is a Common Good, that it is moral, just, or right. If a writer can do that, readers will more easily offer their assent. In making this kind of an appeal, a writer may refer to our religious beliefs (adultery may be condemned because it is forbidden in the Bible), to our sense of fair play (we may be told that eliminating the capital gains tax will unfairly benefit the very rich who already pay few taxes), to our belief in law (we may be told that we should not smoke marijuana because it is illegal), to our sense of loyalty to an ideal (it may be argued that political action committees should be severely curtailed because they are inherently undemocratic), or to our empathy for fellow humans (all people deserve to have food and shelter).

The power of this appeal comes from its assumption of moral authority. If a writer's audience is composed of strong believers in some holy text, for instance the Bible or the Koran, the writer can use scripture as a source of authority. However, someone who does not accept the moral force of a holy text will hardly be convinced by references to it. The same is true of other groups. Some of the most intractable of contemporary conflicts derive from the fact that different groups have different moral bases for their beliefs. Again, to echo Aristotle, in making this kind of plea, writers appeal to what their audience considers to be good or right over and above what they consider useful or in their own interest. For example, Jane Goodall, in "Some Thoughts on the Exploitation of Non-Human Animals," makes an essentially ethical appeal when she states that "all except the most primitive of non-human animals experience pain, and [. . .] 'higher' animals have emotions similar to the human emotions that we label pleasure or sadness, fear or despair." She implies that, since animals have feelings just as we do, it is no more right for us to subject them to suffering than it would be for us to subject other humans to suffering. Rhetorically, she asks: "How can we, the citizens of civilized, western countries, tolerate laboratories which—from the point of view of animal inmates—are not unlike concentration camps?" Her point is that no matter what benefits we receive, it is simply wrong to experiment on animals.

Finally, one can attempt to persuade readers that a particular solution to a problem will benefit them in some way. Not only will quitting smoking promote one's health, for example, since health is a Common Good, it will also save one money.

Disposition

Disposition is the way one disposes, or organizes, one's argument. According to Aristotle, there are six parts, or sections, to an argument:

Introduction. In your introduction you need to supply an attention-getting opener to your topic and then a statement of your claim (the stand you intend to take).

Narration. The narration is a discussion of the background of the issue under consideration. Readers, for example, may not know that there is a problem to be solved. The amount of background material you provide depends upon the knowledge of your audience and the complexity of the issue you are dealing with.

Division. In the division you list the arguments you will advance in support of your proposition/claim.

Confirmation. The confirmation is the longest and most important part of your argument. Here you give the evidence to support your proposition/claim arranged in the order you have listed in the division.

Refutation. The refutation is a discussion and rebuttal of your opponents' counter arguments. See below.

Conclusion. In your conclusion make a strong appeal for acceptance of your argument.

Refutation

In a face-to-face argument, we have the advantage of responding directly to an opponent. In writing, however, we lack this advantage. Therefore, we must depend on refutation when we argue our ideas in writing. In your **refutation** section, you anticipate your opponent's arguments and prove they are, to some degree, wrong, invalid, or fallacious. Methods of refutation include pointing out an opponent's faulty premise, an error in deductive logic, a deficient definition, a logical fallacy, any inappropriate or inaccurate evidence, insufficient evidence, or a questionable authority, to name a few. For the most part, refutation involves undermining an opponent's argument. You might deny that he has proved his claim. You might refute the truth of his premises or object to the inferences drawn from the premises. You might say, "I admit the truth of your conclusion, but I challenge its appropriateness in this particular instance because [. . .] ." Let good judgment and common sense rule. Consider your audience and their emotional biases, the occasion, the subject, and your own personality to help you determine the best course of action regarding refutation.

Some instructors prefer that you refute the opposition before beginning your confirmation. There is reasonable cause for such placement, especially if your opponents' views are shared strongly by your audience. However, if your opponent's arguments are weak, you can afford to delay refutation until the end of your own argument, using your discussion to build a case against your opponent's views. If your audience is hostile to your views, it might work to your advantage, psychologically, to delay your refutation until the end of your argument, to keep the direct attack of your opposition out of sight as long as possible. You need not remind your audience at the outset of your opposition, thus closing their ears to the remainder of what you have to say. By placing the refutation at the end, you may dispose your audience momentarily to hear what you have to say without compounding their hostility. Finally, you can also incorporate refutation wherever it is needed in each paragraph, rather than placing it in a separate section.

Outline for an Essay Based on Deductive Argument

I.   Introduction
  A. Lead-in to your topic
    1. Startling statistic and/or
    2. Interesting example
  B. Statement of the conclusion of your syllogism; the proposition or claim you are going to defend
II. Narration
  A. Background information to clarify your topic and illustrate the problem for which you are proposing a solution. You might need to include here definitions of terms relevant to your argument.
  B. Statement of the major premise and the minor premise that lead to your conclusion. (**Note:** *One option to this method is to combine paragraphs I and II into a single paragraph. Consult with your instructor.*)
III. Statement of major premise as topic sentence
  A. Evidence #1 supporting the truth of your major premise.
    1. Examples
    2. Statistics
    3. Authority
  B. Evidence #2 supporting the truth of your major premise
    1. Examples
    2. Statistics
    3. Authority
IV. Statement of minor premise as topic sentence
  A. Evidence #1 supporting the truth of your minor premise

        1. Examples
        2. Statistics
        3. Authority
    B. Evidence #2 supporting the truth of your minor premise
        1. Examples
        2. Statistics
        3. Authority

V. Restatement of conclusion of syllogism as topic sentence
    A. Evidence #1 supporting the benefits to your audience of accepting your conclusion.
    B. Evidence #2 supporting the benefits of your audience of accepting your conclusion.

VI. Refutation (optional—see discussion of refutation above)
    A. Statement of counter argument (alternative conclusion) #1
        1. Evidence #1 to refute or mitigate the force of A
        2. Evidence #2 to refute or mitigate the force of A
    B. Statement of counter argument (alternative conclusion) #2
        1. Evidence #1 to refute or mitigate the force of B
        2. Evidence #2 to refute or mitigate the force of B

VII. Conclusion A strong appeal for acceptance of your conclusion and/or a call to action.

While this format is the standard method of organizing a deductive essay, it offers options to the student in the construction of the introductory paragraph (you may wish to combine paragraphs I and II in the above outline), and you may prefer to insert your refutation into each of the body paragraphs rather than have a separate section for refutation at the end of the essay. Consult your instructor for guidelines and preferences.

Outline for an Essay Based on Inductive Argument

I.   Introduction
    A. Lead-in to your topic
        1. Startling statistic and/or
        2. Interesting example
    B. Statement of the generalization you have reached through your research; the proposition or claim you are going to defend in your argument.

II. Narration
    A. Statement of background information to clarify your topic and to illustrate the problem you are dealing with. You might need to include here definitions of terms relevant to your argument.
    B Statement listing in one sentence at least three major pieces of evidence (x, y, and z) that support your generalization or claim.

III. First major piece of supporting evidence as topic sentence.
    A. Subtopic #1 supporting X
        1. Examples
        2 Statistics
        3. Authority
    B. Subtopic #2 supporting X
        1. Examples
        2. Statistics
        3. Authority
IV. Second major piece of supporting evidence as topic sentence.
    A. Subtopic #1 supporting Y
        1. Examples
        2. Statistics
        3. Authority
    B. Subtopic #2 supporting Y
        1. Examples
        2. Statistics
        3. Authority
V. Third major piece of supporting evidence as topic sentence.
    A. Subtopic #1 supporting Z
        1. Examples
        2. Statistics
        3. Authority
    B. Subtopic #2 supporting Z
        1. Examples
        2. Statistics
        3. Authority
VI. Refutation (optional —see discussion of refutation above)
    A. Statement of counter argument (alternative conclusion) #1
        1. Evidence #1 to refute or mitigate the force of A
        2. Evidence #2 to refute or mitigate the force of A
    B. Statement of counter argument (alternative conclusion) #2
        1. Evidence #1 to refute or mitigate the force of B
        2. Evidence #2 to refute or mitigate the force of B
VII. Conclusion A strong appeal for acceptance of your generalization and/or a call
    to action.

While this format is the standard method of organizing an inductive essay, it offers options to the student in the construction of the introductory paragraph (you may wish to combine paragraphs I and II in the above outline), and you may prefer to insert your refutation into each of the body paragraphs rather than have a separate section for refutation at the end of the essay. Consult your instructor for guidelines and preferences.

◆

CHECKLIST FOR ARGUMENT ESSAY

1. Have you identified your audience and adopted the appropriate voice for your audience?
2. Are your premises true? Will your implied premises be clear to your reader?
3. Did you check your premises and reasoning to make sure your argument is sound, true, and valid?
4. Did you make certain that your enthymeme's missing portion does not alter the argument?
5. Is your argument free of logical fallacies?
6. Is your representation of the facts for your argument honest and accurate?
7. Does your proposition or thesis statement say what you want it to say, and does it clearly indicate your purpose?
8. Is your argument supported with adequate and convincing examples?
9. Have you indicated your order or pattern of development, either by listing reasons (inductive) or premises (deductive)?
10. Have you accounted for the arguments of the opposition and refuted them— early in the essay, throughout your discussion, or before your conclusion?
11. Are your transitions clear and logical?
12. Does your conclusion make a significant contribution to your audience's understanding of your purpose?
13. Did you edit your paper carefully, checking for major grammatical and spelling errors?

STUDENT EXAMPLES

In the following student essay, Heather Dunnuck uses **deduction** to argue in favor of animal rights. Does she have sufficient evidence to support her claim? Is the argument convincing? Is she more or less convincing than Jane Goodall in her essay, "Some Thoughts on the Exploitation of Non-Human Animals"? (See **Further Readings**). For a counter argument, read Carl Cohen's essay, "The Case for the Use of Animals in Biomedical Research," also in **Further Readings**.

SAVE THE ANIMALS: STOP ANIMAL TESTING

Heather Dunnuck

Using animals in research and to test the safety of products has been a topic of heated debate for decades. According to data collected by F. Barbara Orlans for her book *In the Name of Science: Issues in Responsible Animal Experimentation*, sixty percent of all animals used in testing are used in biomedical research and product-safety testing (62). People have different feelings for animals; many look upon animals as companions while others view animals as a means for advancing medical techniques or furthering experimental research. However individuals perceive animals, the fact remains that animals are being exploited by research facilities and cosmetics companies all across the country and all around the world. Although humans often benefit from successful animal research, the pain, the suffering, and the deaths of animals are not worth the possible human benefits. Therefore, animals should not be used in research or to test the safety of products.

First, animals' rights are violated when they are used in research. Tom Regan, a philosophy professor at North Carolina State University, states: "Animals have a basic moral right to respectful treatment. . . . This inherent value is not respected when animals are reduced to being mere tools in a scientific experiment" (qtd. in Orlans 26). Animals and people are alike in many ways; they both feel, think, behave, and experience pain. Thus, animals should be treated with the same respect as humans. Yet animals' rights are violated when they are used in research because they are not given a choice. Animals are subjected to tests that are often painful or cause permanent damage or death, and they are never given the option of not participating in the experiment. Regan further says, for example, that "animal [experimentation] is morally wrong no matter how much humans may benefit because the animal's basic right has been ignored. Risks are not morally transferable to those who do not choose to take them" (qtd. in Orlans 26). Animals do not willingly sacrifice themselves for the advancement of human welfare and new technology. Their decisions are made for them because they cannot vocalize their own preferences and choices. When humans decide the fate of animals in research environments, the animals' rights are taken away without any thought of their well-being or the quality of their lives. Therefore, animal experimentation should be stopped because it infringes on the rights of animals.

Next, the pain and suffering to which experimental animals are subjected is not worth any possible benefits to humans. "The American Veterinary Medical Association defines animal pain as an unpleasant sensory and emotional experience perceived as arising from a specific region of the body and associated with actual or potential tissue damage" (Orlans 129). Animals feel pain in many of the same ways that humans do; in fact, their reactions to pain are virtually identical (both humans and animals scream, for example). When animals are used for product toxicity testing or laboratory research, they are subjected to painful and frequently deadly experiments.

Two of the most commonly used toxicity tests are the Draize test and the LD50 test, both of which are infamous for the intense pain and suffering they inflict upon experimental animals. In the Draize test the substance or product being tested is placed in the eyes of an animal (generally a rabbit is used for this test); then the animal is monitored for damage to the cornea and other tissues in and near the eye. This test is intensely painful for the animal, and blindness, scarring, and death are generally the end results. The Draize test has been criticized for being unreliable and a needless waste of animal life. The LD50 test is used to test the dosage of a substance that is necessary to cause death in fifty percent of the animal subjects within a certain amount of time. To perform this test, the researchers hook the animals up to tubes that pump huge amounts of the test product into their stomachs until they die. This test is extremely painful to the animals because death can take days or even weeks. According to Orlans, the animals suffer from "vomiting, diarrhea, paralysis, convulsion, and internal bleeding. Since death is the required endpoint, dying animals are not put out of their misery by euthanasia" (154). In his article, "Time to Reform Toxic Tests," Michael Balls, a professor of medical cell biology at the University of Nottingham and chairman of the trustees of FRAME (the Fund for the Replacement of Animals in Medical Experiments), states that the LD50 test is "scientifically unjustifiable. The precision it purports to provide is an illusion because of uncontrollable biological variables" (31). The use of the Draize test and the LD50 test to examine product toxicity has decreased over the past few years, but these tests have not been eliminated completely. Thus, because animals are subjected to agonizing pain, suffering, and death when they are used in laboratory and cosmetics' testing, animal research must be stopped to prevent more waste of animal life.

Finally, the testing of products on animals is completely unnecessary because viable alternatives are available. Many cosmetic companies, for example, have sought better ways to test their products without the use of animal subjects. In *Against Animal Testing*, a pamphlet published by The Body Shop, a well-known cosmetics and bath-product company based in London, the development of products that "use natural ingredients, like bananas and Basil nut oil, as well as others with a long history of safe human usage" is advocated instead of testing on animals (3). Furthermore, the Draize test has become practically obsolete because of the development of a synthetic cellular tissue that closely resembles human skin. Researchers can test the potential damage that a product can do to the epidermis by using this artificial "skin" instead of testing on animals. Another alternative to this test is a product called Eyetex. This synthetic material turns opaque when a product damages it, closely resembling the way that a real eye reacts to harmful substances. Computers have also been used to simulate and estimate the potential damage that a product or chemical can cause, and human tissues and cells have been used to examine the effects of harmful substances. In another method, *in vitro* testing, cellular tests are done inside a test tube. All of these tests have been proven to be useful and reliable alternatives to testing products on live animals. Therefore, because effective means of product toxicity testing are available without the use of live animal specimens, testing potentially deadly substances on animals is unnecessary.

However, many people believe that animal testing is justified because the animals are sacrificed to make products safer for human use and consumption. The problem with this reasoning is that the animals' safety, well-being, and quality of life are generally not a consideration. Experimental animals are virtually tortured to death, and all of these tests are done in the interest of human welfare, without any thought to how the animals are treated. Others respond that animals themselves benefit from animal research. Yet in an article entitled "Is Your Experiment Really Necessary?" Sheila Silcock, a research consultant for the RSPCA, states: "Animals may themselves be the beneficiaries of animal experiments. But the value we place on the quality of their lives is determined by their perceived value to humans" (34). Making humans' lives better should not be justification for torturing and exploiting animals. The value that humans place on their own lives should be extended to the lives of animals as well.

Still other people think that animal testing is acceptable because animals are lower species than humans and therefore have no rights. These individuals feel that animals have no rights because they lack the capacity to understand or to knowingly exercise these rights. However, animal experimentation in medical research and cosmetics testing cannot be justified on the basis that animals are lower on the evolutionary chart than humans since animals resemble humans in so many ways. Many animals, especially the higher mammalian species, possess internal systems and organs that are identical to the structures and functions of human internal organs. Also, animals have feelings, thoughts, and needs, that are similar to human functions and capacities, and these similarities should be respected, not exploited, because of the selfishness of humans. Tom Regan asserts that "animals are subjects of a life just as human beings are, and a subject of a life has inherent value. They are . . . ends in themselves" (qtd. in Orlans 26). Therefore, animals' lives should be respected because they have an inherent right to be treated with dignity. The harm that is committed against animals should not be minimized because they are not considered to be "human."

In conclusion, animal testing should be eliminated because it violates animals' rights, it causes pain and suffering to the experimental animals, and other means of testing product toxicity are available. Humans cannot justify making life better for themselves by randomly torturing and executing thousands of animals per year to perform laboratory experiments or to test products. Animals should be treated with respect and dignity, and this right to decent treatment is not upheld when animals are exploited for human gain. After all, humans are animals, too.

Works Cited

Against Animal Testing. The Body Shop, 1993.

Balls, Michael. "Time to Reform Toxic Tests." *New Scientist* 134 (1992):31-33.

Orlans, F. Barbara. *In the Name of Science: Issues in Responsible Animal Experimentation.* New York: Oxford UP, 1993.

Silcock, Sheila. "Is Your Experiment Really Necessary?" *New Scientist* 134 (1992): 32-34.

In this next student essay, Esther DeLa Torre employs **inductive reasoning** to speak in favor of euthanasia. Who is her audience? What kinds evidence does she use to support her claim? Is the argument convincing?

THE RIGHT TO ASSISTED SUICIDE

Esther B. De La Torre

Imagine a seventy-year-old woman in extreme pain. She is dying from lymphatic cancer. Her doctors have given her only six months to live. She asks for more pain medication, but her doctor's are prohibited from giving her more. She hangs on in agony. Meanwhile her son and daughter-in-law are accumulating medical debt that threatens to bankrupt them. Finally, the woman asks her doctor to help her die—to allow her to die and escape the unbearable pain and save here child and grandchildren from financial ruin. The doctor is sympathetic, but he can do nothing. The woman lives in Texas, not in Oregon or Washington, where she would be allowed to die with dignity. No, in Texas she does not have a choice; she must suffer to the bitter end no matter how much it hurts and no matter how much it costs. Is this compassion? No. It is cruelty. Terminally-ill patients should have the right to die with dignity; they should be given the right to doctor-assisted suicide.

The right to assisted suicide is a significant topic that concerns people all over the United States. The debates go back and forth about whether a dying patient has the right to die with the assistance of a physician. Some are against it because of religious and moral reasons. Others are for it because of their compassion and respect for the dying. As Richard Worsnop points out: "Opinion polls indicate that Americans are closely divided over laws allowing terminally ill patients to end their lives with a physician's help." Physicians are also divided on the issue. They differ where they draw the line that separates relief from dying—and killing. For many the main concern with assisted suicide lies with the competence of the terminally-ill. Yet many terminally-ill patients who are in the final stages of their lives have requested doctors to aid them in exercising active euthanasia. It is sad to realize that these people are in great agony and that to them the only hope of bringing that agony to a halt is through euthanasia, assisted suicide. When people see the word *euthanasia*, they see the meaning of the word in two different lights. Euthanasia for some carries a negative connotation; it is the same as murder. For others, however, euthanasia is the act of putting someone to death painlessly, or allowing a person suffering from an incurable and painful disease or condition to die by withholding extreme medical measures.

The debate over euthanasia has been going on for a long time, according to Worsnop, who says that "the first bill to legalize voluntary euthanasia in the United States was introduced in the Ohio Legislature in 1906." The issue of dying with dignity became prominent, however, with the activities of the notorious Dr. Kevorkian, the one some call Dr. Death. Dr. Kevorkian, an advocate of assisted suicide, claimed to have assisted in helping 130 patients to end their lives with his "suicide machine" before he was convicted of second-degree murder by a Michigan court in 1999. Dr. Kevorkian was released on parole for good behavior in 2007 and HBO is reported to be developing a film about him. Yet only in the past twelve years has the issue of assisted suicide become a national concern. In 1997 the people of Oregon "enacted the Death with Dignity Act ... which allows terminally-ill Oregonians to end their lives through the voluntary self-administration of lethal medications, expressly prescribed by a physician for that purpose" ("FAQs"). Since that time, according to Robert Steinbrook, physicians have written " a total of 541 prescriptions for lethal doses of medication ... and 341 people died as a result of taking the medications" (2513). And just recently, in November of 2008, "residents of the state of Washington voted 58% to 42% to allow physician-assisted suicide" (2513). According to *USA Today*, "Dr. Robert Thompson, an internist and cardiologist at Swedish Medical Center in Seattle who voted for the [Washington State] measure, said that in his 32 years of practice he has treated patients who would have benefited from this law" ("Washington State"). Therefore, after studying both sides of the issue, a compassionate individual must conclude that competent, terminally-ill patients should be given the right to assisted suicide in order to end their suffering, reduce the damaging financial effects of hospital care on their families, and preserve the individual right of people to determine their own fate.

Medical technology today has achieved remarkable feats in prolonging the lives of human beings. Respirators can support a patient's failing lungs and medicines can sustain that patient's physiological processes. For those patients who have a realistic chance of surviving an illness or accident, medical technology is science's greatest gift to mankind. For the terminally ill, however, it is just a means of prolonging suffering. Medicine is supposed to alleviate the suffering that a patient undergoes. Yet the only thing that medical technology does for a dying patient is give that patient more pain and agony day after day. Some terminal patients in the past have gone to their doctors and asked for a final medication that would take all the pain away—lethal drugs. For example, as Ronald Dworkin recounts, Lillian Boyes, an English woman who was suffering from a severe case of rheumatoid arthritis, begged her doctor to assist her to die because she could no longer stand the pain (184). Another example is Dr. Ali Khalili, Dr. Jack Kevorkian's twentieth patient. According to Kevorkian's attorney, "[Dr. Khalili] was a pain specialist; he could get any kind of pain medication, but he came to Dr. Kevorkian. There are times when pain medication does not suffice"(qtd. in Cotton 363). And then there is the case of Robert Latimer, a Canadian father who killed his daughter in 1993 to release her from a life of pain. According to Charlie Gillis, writing in *McClean's*, "Latimer ... believed he was practicing mercy" (20). He told the court that

> death was the only means of relief for a child unable to enjoy the world around her and facing a life of unbearable pain. Twisted by her condition into physical contortions, unable to eat without a tube inserted into her esophagus, unable to absorb most painkillers, she had become a heart-wrenching spectacle. She was scheduled at the time for a bone-removal operation to relieve the agony of a permanently dislocated hip. Yet, as Latimer pointed out, at least one doctor predicted Tracy would continue to suffer as long as she lived. After 12 agonizing years, he decided that she had lived enough. (20)

Terminally ill patients should have the right to assisted suicide because it is the best means for them to end the pain caused by an illness which no drug can cure. A competent terminal patient must have the option of assisted suicide because it is in the best interest of that person.

Further, a dying person's physical suffering can be unbearable to that person's immediate family. Medical technology has failed to save a loved-one. But, successful or not, medicine has a high price attached to it. The cost is sometimes too much for the terminally ill's family. A competent dying person has some knowledge of this, and with every day that he or she is kept alive, the hospital costs skyrocket. For example, as Shannon Brownlee reported in a 2005 *Los Angeles Times* article, "the average [terminally-ill] patient" at Garfield Medical Center in Monterey Park, California, "spent 23 days in the hospital … and cost Medicare $106, 254" (B19). If a terminally-ill patient were younger, and not able to afford medical insurance, such costs would soon bankrupt her family. And there are millions of people in the United States who cannot afford health insurance. Based on U. S. Census Bureau data, the National Coalition on Health Care reports that "nearly 46 million Americans, or 18 percent of the population under the age of 65, were without health insurance in 2007, the latest government data available" ("Health"). Human life is expensive, and there are only a few affluent terminal patients who can afford to prolong what life is left in them. As for the not-so-affluent patients, the cost of their lives is left to their families. Of course, most families do not consider the cost while the terminally-ill loved-one is still alive. When that loved-one passes away, however, the family has to struggle with a huge hospital bill and are often subject to financial ruin. Further, most terminal patients want their death to be a peaceful one and with as much consolation as possible. As Ronald Dworkin, author of *Life's Dominion*, says, "many people … want to save their relatives the expense of keeping them pointlessly alive …"(193). To leave the family in financial ruin is by no means a form of consolation. Those terminally-ill patients who have accepted their imminent death cannot in most states prevent their families from plunging into financial debt because they do not have the option of halting the medical bills from piling up. If terminal patients were given the option of assisted suicide, they could ease their families' financial burdens as well as their own suffering.

Finally, many terminally-ill patients want the right to assisted suicide because they believe that the right to assisted suicide is an inherent right which does not have to be given to them. It is a liberty which cannot be denied because those who are dying want to use this right to pursue their happiness. For example, Dr. Kevorkian's attorney, Geoffrey N. Fieger, gave voice to the contradiction involved in denying a dying patient the right to assisted suicide, saying that the belief that "a law which does not make anybody do anything, that gives people the right to decide, and prevents the state from prosecuting you for exercising your freedom not to suffer, violates somebody else's constitutional rights is insane" (qtd. in Cotton 364). Terminally ill patients should be allowed to die with dignity. As Dr. Robert Thompson says, "for the sake of compassion, and for a person's own individual rights" assisted suicide "should be an option for them" (qtd. in "Washington"). Choosing the right to assisted suicide would be a final exercise of autonomy for the dying. They will not be seen as people who are waiting to die, but as human beings making one final active choice in their lives.

On the other side of the issue, however, people who are against assisted suicide do not believe that the terminally ill have the right to end their suffering. Many hold, for example, that it is against the Hippocratic Oath for doctors to participate in active euthanasia. Perhaps most of those who hold this argument do not know that, for example, in Canada only a "few medical schools use the Hippocratic Oath" because it is inconsistent with its premises (Barnard 28). The oath makes the physician promise to relieve pain and not to administer deadly medicine. This oath cannot be applied to cancer patients. For treatment, cancer patients are given chemotherapy, a form of radioactive medicine that is poisonous to the body. As a result of chemotherapy, the body suffers incredible pain, hair loss, vomiting, and other extremely unpleasant side effects. Thus, chemotherapy can be considered "deadly medicine" because of its effects on the human body, and this inconsistency is the reason why the Hippocratic Oath cannot be used to deny the right to assisted suicide. Furthermore, to administer numerous drugs to a terminal patient and place him or her on medical equipment does not help anything except the disease itself. Respirators and high dosages of drugs cannot save the terminal patient from the victory of a disease or an illness. Dr. Christaan Barnard, author of *Good Life/Good Death*, quotes his colleague, Dr. Robert Twycross, who said, "To use such measures on the terminally ill, with no expectancy of a return to health, is generally inappropriate and is—therefore—bad medicine by definition" (22).

Other people argue that if the right to assisted suicide is given, the doctor-patient relationship would be damaged. The antithesis of this claim is true. Cheryl Smith, in her article advocating active euthanasia (or assisted suicide), says that "patients who are able to discuss sensitive issues such as this are more likely to trust their physicians" (409). A terminal patient consenting to assisted suicide knows that a doctor's job is to relieve pain, and giving consent to that doctor shows great trust.

Still other opponents of assisted suicide insist that there are potential abuses that can arise from legalizing assisted suicide. They claim that terminal patients might be forced to choose assisted suicide because of their financial situation. This view is to be respected. However, the choice of assisted suicide is in the patient's best interest, and this interest can include the financial situation of a patient's relatives. Competent, terminal patients can easily see the sorrow and grief that their families undergo while they wait for death to take them away. The choice of assisted suicide would allow these terminally-ill patients to end the sorrow and grief of their families as well as their own misery. The choice would also put a halt to the financial worries of these families. It is in the patient's interest that the families that they leave not be subject to financial ruin. This is not a mere "duty to die." It is a caring way for the dying to say, "Yes, I am going to die. It is all right; please do not worry anymore." Further, legalization of assisted suicide will also help to regulate the practice of it. In fact, the laws in Oregon and Washington do just that. According to Steinbrook, "As in Oregon, the Washington initiative requires that an attending physician and a consulting physician independently determine that a patient is qualified to initiate a written request for a prescription for a lethal medication—a determination that includes verification that the person is competent, is acting voluntarily, and has made an informed decision" (2513). So there are, and will be, many legal safeguards to keep abuses from happening.

Finally, there are some who argue that the right to assisted suicide is not a right that can be given to anyone at all. This claim is countered by a judge by the name of Stephen Reinhardt. According to an article in the *Houston Chronicle*, Judge Reinhardt ruled on this issue by saying that "a competent, terminally-ill adult, having lived nearly the full measure of his life, has a strong liberty interest in choosing a dignified and humane death rather than being reduced at the end of his existence to a childlike state of helplessness, diapered, sedated, incompetent" (qtd. in Beck 36). This ruling is the strongest defense for the right to assisted suicide. It is an inherent right. No man or woman should ever suffer because he or she is denied the right. The terminally ill also have rights like normal, healthy citizens do, and they cannot be denied the right not to suffer.

Therefore, the right to assisted suicide must be freely bestowed upon those who are terminally ill. This right would allow them to leave this earth with dignity, save their families from financial ruin, and relieve them of insufferable pain. To give competent, terminally-ill adults this necessary right is to give them the autonomy to close the book on a life well-lived.

Works Cited

Barnard, Christaan. *Good Life/Good Death*. Englewood Cliffs: Prentice, 1980. Print.

Beck, Joan. "Answers to Right-to-Die Questions Hard." *Houston Chronicle* 16 Mar. 1996, late ed.: 36. Print.

Brownlee, Shannon. "Better Final Days: The End of Life Need Not Be Filled with Extreme Medical Costs and Intensive Care." *Los Angeles Times*. Nov. 26, 2005. B19. Web. 14 April 2009.

Cotton, Paul. "Medicine's Position Is Both Pivotal And Precarious In Assisted Suicide Debate." *The Journal of the American Medical Association* 1 Feb. 1995: 363-64. *Proquest*. Web. 25 Mar. 2009.

Dworkin, Ronald. *Life's Dominion*. New York: Knopf, 1993. Print.

"FAQ's About the Death With Dignity Act." *Death With Dignity Act*. Oregon.gov. 22 Sept. 2007. Web. 14 April 2009.

Gillis, Charlie. "Robert Latimer's Angry Crusade: He Served Seven Years in Prison for Killing His Disabled Daughter. Now the Saskatchewan Farmer Is Determined to Clear His Name, And to Prove He Did Nothing Wrong." *McClean's* 17 Mar. 2008. 20-23. *Opposing Viewpoints Resource Center*. Web. 16 Apr. 2009.

"Health Insurance Coverage." *National Coalition on Health Care*. 2009. Web. 14 April 2009.

Smith, Cheryl. "Should Active Euthanasia Be Legalized: Yes." *American Bar Association Journal* April 1993. Rpt. in *CQ Researcher* 5.1 (1995): 409. *CQ Researcher*. Web. 25 Mar. 2009.

Steinbrook, Robert. "Physician-Assisted Death—From Oregon to Washington State." *The New England Journal of Medicine* 359.24 (2008): 2513. ProQuest. Web. 9 April 2009.

"Washington State to Allow Assisted Suicide." *USA Today*. 2 Mar. 2009. Web. 14 April 2009.

Worsnop, Richard L. "Assisted Suicide Controversy: Should Doctors Help the Dying to End Their Lives?" *CQ Researcher* 5.17 (1995): 1-27. Web. 9 April 2009.

Revered by all Americans, the following hallowed statement is an argument. It starts with an introduction, follows with a narration explaining the philosophical basis of a people's right to choose their own government, states a clear claim detailing the English King's attempts to establish "an absolute Tyranny over these States," follows with a long list of examples to prove the claim, continues with a short refutation, and ends with a strong conclusion.

THE DECLARATION OF INDEPENDENCE

Thomas Jefferson and Others

IN CONGRESS, JULY 4, 1776
THE UNANIMOUS DECLARATION OF THE
THIRTEEN UNITED STATES OF AMERICA

When in the Course of human events it becomes necessary for one people to dissolve the political bands which have connected them with another, and to assume among the powers of the earth, the separate and equal station to which the Laws of Nature and of Nature's God entitle them, a decent respect to the opinions of mankind requires that they should declare the causes which impel them to the separation.

We hold these truths to be self-evident, that all men are created equal, that they are endowed by their Creator with certain unalienable Rights, that among these are Life, Liberty and the pursuit of Happiness. That to secure these rights, Governments are instituted among Men, deriving their just powers from the consent of the governed. That whenever any Form of Government becomes destructive of these ends, it is the Right of the People to alter or to abolish it, and to institute new Government, laying its foundation on such principles and organizing its powers in such form, as to them shall seem most likely to effect their Safety and Happiness. Prudence, indeed, will dictate that Governments long established should not be changed for light and transient causes; and accordingly all experience hath shewn that mankind are more disposed to suffer, while evils are sufferable, than to right themselves by abolishing the forms to which they are accustomed. But when a long train of abuses and usurpations, pursuing invariably the same Object evinces a design to reduce them under absolute Despotism, it is their right, it is their duty, to throw off such Government, and to provide new Guards for their future security. Such has been the patient sufferance of these Colonies; and such is now the necessity which constrains them to alter their former Systems of Government. The history of the present King of Great Britain is a history of repeated injuries and usurpations, all having in direct object the establishment of an absolute Tyranny over these States. To prove this, let Facts be submitted to a candid world.

He has refused his Assent to Laws, the most wholesome and necessary for the public good.

He has forbidden his Government to pass laws of immediate and pressing importance, unless suspended in their operation till his Assent should be obtained; and when so suspended, he has utterly neglected to attend to them.

He has refused to pass other Laws for the accommodation of large districts of people, unless those people would relinquish the right of Representation in the Legislature, a right inestimable to them and formidable to tyrants only.

He has called together legislative bodies at places unusual, uncomfortable, and distant from the depository of their Public Records, for the sole purpose of fatiguing them into compliance with his measures.

He has dissolved Representative Houses repeatedly, for opposing with manly firmness his invasions on the rights of the people.

He has refused for a long time, after such dissolutions, to cause others to be elected; whereby the Legislative Powers, incapable of Annihilation, have returned to the People at large for their exercise; the State remaining in the mean time exposed to all the dangers of invasion from without, and convulsions within.

He has endeavored to prevent the population of these States; for that purpose obstructing the Laws for Naturalization of Foreigners; refusing to pass others to encourage their migration hither, and raising the conditions of new Appropriations of Lands.

He has obstructed the Administration of Justice, by refusing his Assent to Laws for establishing Judiciary Powers.

He has made Judges dependent on his Will alone, for the tenure of their offices, and the amount and payment of their salaries.

He has erected a multitude of New Offices, and sent hither swarms of Officers to harass our people, and eat out their substance.

He has kept among us, in times of peace, Standing Armies without the Consent of our legislatures.

He has affected to render the Military independent of and superior to the Civil Power.

He has combined with others to subject us to a jurisdiction foreign to our constitution, and unacknowledged by our laws; giving his Assent to their Acts of pretended Legislation: For quartering large bodies of armed troops among us: For protecting them, by a mock Trial, from punishment for any Murders which they should commit on the Inhabitants of these States: For cutting off our Trade with all parts of the world: For imposing Taxes on us without our Consent: For depriving us in many cases, of the benefits of Trial by Jury; For transporting us beyond Seas to be tried for pretended offenses: for abolishing the free System of English Laws in a neighboring Province, establishing therein an Arbitrary government, and enlarging its Boundaries so as to render it at once an example and fit instrument for introducing the same absolute rule into these Colonies: For taking away our Charters, abolishing our most valuable Laws and altering fundamentally the Forms of our Governments: For suspending our own Legislatures, and declaring themselves invested with power to legislate for us in all cases whatsoever.

He has abdicated Government here, by declaring us out of his Protection and waging War against us.

He has plundered our seas, ravaged our Coasts, burnt our towns, and destroyed the lives of our people.

He is at this time transporting large Armies of foreign Mercenaries to complete the works of death, desolation and tyranny, already begun with circumstances of Cruelty & Perfidy scarcely paralleled in the most barbarous ages, and totally unworthy the Head of a civilized nation.

He has constrained our fellow Citizens taken Captive on the high Seas to bear Arms against their Country, to become the executioners of their friends and Brethren, or to fall themselves by their Hands.

He has excited domestic insurrections amongst us, and has endeavored to bring on the inhabitants of our frontiers, the merciless Indian Savages, whose known rule of warfare, is an undistinguished destruction of all ages, sexes, and conditions.

In every stage of these Oppressions We have Petitioned for Redress in the most humble terms: Our repeated Petitions have been answered only by repeated injury. A Prince, whose character is thus marked by every act which may define a Tyrant, is unfit to be the ruler of a free people.

Nor have We been wanting in attention to our British brethren. We have warned them from time to time of attempts by their legislature to extend an unwarrantable jurisdiction over us. We have reminded them of the circumstances of our emigration and settlement here. We have appealed to their native justice and magnanimity, and we have conjured them by the ties of our common kindred to disavow these usurpations, which would inevitably interrupt our connections and correspondence. They too have been deaf to the voice of justice and of consanguinity. We must, therefore, acquiesce in the necessity, which denounces our Separation, and hold them, as we hold the rest of mankind, Enemies in War, in Peace Friends.

We, THEREFORE, the Representatives of the UNITED STATES OF AMERICA, in General Congress, Assembled, appealing to the Supreme Judge of the world for the rectitude of our intentions, do, in the Name, and by Authority of the good People of these Colonies, solemnly publish and declare, That these United Colonies are, and of Right ought to be FREE AND INDEPENDENT STATES; that they are Absolved from all Allegiance to the British Crown, and that all political connection between them and the State of Great Britain, is and ought to be totally dissolved; and that as Free and Independent States, they have full Power to levy War, conclude Peace, contract Alliances, establish Commerce, and to do all other Acts and Things which Independent States may of right do. And for the support of this Declaration, with a firm reliance on the protection of Divine Providence, we mutually pledge to each other our Lives, our Fortunes, and our sacred Honor.

Camille Paglia is known for her controversial views on current issues, one being "date rape." In the following essay, which was first published in *New York Newsday* in 1991, she challenges those who claim that there is no distinction between rape and date rape; she advocates that women take responsibility for their own actions. Who is her audience? What is her purpose in the essay? Does Paglia offer any refutation? Is her argument inductive or deductive? Is it sound?

IT'S A JUNGLE OUT THERE

Camille Paglia

Rape is an outrage that cannot be tolerated in civilized society. Yet feminism, which has waged a crusade for rape to be taken more seriously, has put young women in danger by hiding the truth about sex from them.

In dramatizing the pervasiveness of rape, feminists have told young women that before they have sex with a man, they must give consent as explicit as a legal contract's. In this way, young women have been convinced that they have been the victims of rape. On elite campuses in the Northeast and on the West Coast, they have held consciousness-raising sessions, petitioned administrations, demanded inquests. At Brown University, outraged, panicky "victims" have scrawled the names of alleged attackers on the walls of women's rest rooms. What marital rape was to the '70s, "date rape" is to the '90s.

The incidence and seriousness of rape do not require this kind of exaggeration. Real acquaintance rape is nothing new. It has been a horrible problem for women for all of recorded history. Once fathers and brothers protected women from rape. Once the penalty for rape was death. I come from a fierce Italian tradition where, not so long ago in the motherland, a rapist would end up knifed, castrated, and hung out to dry.

But the old clans and small rural communities have broken down. In our cities, on our campuses far from home, young women are vulnerable and defenseless. Feminism has not prepared them for this. Feminism keeps saying the sexes are the same. It keeps telling women they can do anything, go anywhere, say anything, wear anything. No, they can't. Women will always be in sexual danger.

One of my male students recently slept overnight with a friend in a passageway of the Great Pyramid in Egypt. He described the moon and sand, the ancient silence and eerie echoes. I will never experience that. I am a woman. I am not stupid enough to believe I could ever be safe there. There is a world of solitary adventure I will never have. Women have always known these somber truths. But feminism, with its pie-in-the-sky fantasies about the perfect world, keeps young women from seeing life as it is.

We must remedy social injustice whenever we can. But there are some things we cannot change. There are sexual differences that are based in biology. Academic feminism is lost in a fog of social constructionism. It believes we are totally the product of our environment. This idea was invented by Rousseau. He was wrong. Emboldened by dumb French language theory, academic feminists repeat the same hollow slogans over and over to each other. Their view of sex is naive and prudish. Leaving sex to the feminists is like letting your dog vacation at the taxidermist's.

The sexes are at war. Men must struggle for identity against the overwhelming power of their mothers. Women have menstruation to tell them they are women. Men must do or risk something to be men. Men become masculine only when other men say they are. Having sex with a woman is one way a boy becomes a man.

College men are at their hormonal peak. They have just left their mothers and are questing for their male identity. In groups, they are dangerous. A woman going to a fraternity party is walking into Testosterone Flats full of prickly cacti and blazing guns. If she goes, she should be armed with resolute alertness. She should arrive with girlfriends and leave with them. A girl who lets herself get dead drunk at a fraternity party is a fool. A girl who goes upstairs alone with a brother at a fraternity party is an idiot. Feminists call this "blaming the victim." I call it common sense.

For a decade, feminists have drilled their disciples to say, "Rape is a crime of violence but not of sex." This sugar-coated Shirley Temple nonsense has exposed young women to disaster.

Misled by feminism they do not expect rape from the nice boys from good homes who sit next to them in class.

Aggression and eroticism are deeply intertwined. Hunt, pursuit, and capture are biologically programmed into male sexuality. Generation after generation, men must be educated, refined, and ethically persuaded away from their tendency toward anarchy and brutishness. Society is not the enemy, as feminism ignorantly claims. Society is woman's protection against rape. Feminism, with its solemn Carry Nation repressiveness, does not see what is for men the eroticism or fun element in rape, especially the wild, infectious delirium of gang rape. Women who do not understand rape cannot defend themselves against it.

The date-rape controversy shows feminism hitting the wall of its own broken promises. The women of my '60s generation were the first respectable girls in history to swear like sailors, get drunk, stay out all night—in short, to act like men. We sought total sexual freedom and equality. But as time passed, we woke up to cold reality. The old double standard protected women. When anything goes, it's women who lose.

Today's young women don't know what they want. They see that feminism has not brought sexual happiness. The theatrics of public rage over date rape are their way of restoring the old sexual rules that were shattered by my generation. Because nothing about the sexes has really changed. The comic film *Where the Boys Are* (1960), the ultimate expression of '50s man-chasing, still speaks directly to our time. It shows smart, lively women skillfully anticipating and fending off the dozens of strategies with which horny men try to get them into bed. The agonizing date-rape subplot and climax are brilliantly done. The victim, Yvette Mimieux, makes mistake after mistake, obvious to the other girls. She allows herself to be lured away from her girlfriends and into isolation with boys whose character and intentions she misreads. *Where the Boys Are* tells the truth. It shows courtship as a dangerous game in which the signals are not verbal but subliminal.

Neither militant feminism, which is obsessed with politically correct language, nor academic feminism, which believes that knowledge and experience are "constituted by" language, can understand pre-verbal or non-verbal communication. Feminism, focusing on sexual politics, cannot see that sex exists in and through the body. Sexual desire and arousal cannot be fully translated into verbal terms. This is why men and women misunderstand each other.

Trying to remake the future, feminism cut itself off from sexual history. It discarded and suppressed the sexual myths of literature, art, and religion. Those myths show us the turbulence, the mysteries and passions of sex. In mythology we see men's sexual anxiety, their fear of women's dominance. Much sexual violence is rooted in men's sense of psychological weakness toward women. It takes many men to deal with one woman. Woman's voracity is a persistent motif. Clara Bow, it was rumored, took on the USC football team on weekends. Marilyn Monroe, singing "Diamonds Are a Girl's Best Friend," rules a conga line of men in tuxes. Half-clad Cher, in the video for "If I Could Turn Back Time," deranges a battleship of screaming sailors and straddles a pink-lit cannon. Feminism, coveting social power, is blind to woman's cosmic sexual power.

To understand rape, you must study the past. There never was and never will be sexual harmony. Every woman must take personal responsibility for her sexuality, which is nature's red flame. She must be prudent and cautious about where she goes and with whom. When she makes a mistake, she must accept the consequences and, through self-criticism, resolve never to make that mistake again. Running to Mommy and Daddy or the campus grievance committee is unworthy of strong women. Posting lists of guilty men in the toilet is cowardly, infantile stuff.

The Italian philosophy of life espouses high-energy confrontation. A male student makes a vulgar remark about your breasts? Don't slink off to whimper and simper with the campus shrinking violets. Deal with it. On the spot. Say, "Shut up, you jerk! And crawl back to the barnyard where you belong!" In general, women who project this take-charge attitude toward life get harassed less often. I see too many dopey, immature, self-pitying women walking around like melting sticks of butter. It's the Yvette Mimieux syndrome: Make me happy. And listen to me weep when I'm not.

The date-rape debate is already smothering in propaganda churned out by the expensive Northeastern colleges and universities, with their overconcentration of boring, uptight academic feminists and spoiled, affluent students. Beware of the deep manipulativeness of rich students who were neglected by their parents. They love to turn the campus into hysterical psychodramas of sexual transgression, followed by assertions of parental authority and concern. And don't look for sexual enlightenment from academe, which spews out mountains of books but never looks at life directly.

As a fan of football and rock music, I see in the simple, swaggering masculinity of the jock and in the noisy posturing of the heavy-metal guitarist certain fundamental, unchanging truths about sex. Masculinity is aggressive, unstable, combustible. It is also the most creative cultural force in history. Women must reorient themselves toward the elemental powers of sex, which can strengthen or destroy.

The only solution to date rape is female self-awareness and self control. A woman's number one line of defense is herself. When a real rape occurs, she should report it to the police. Complaining to college committees because the courts "take too long" is ridiculous. College administrations are not a branch of the judiciary. They are not equipped or trained for legal inquiry. Colleges must alert incoming students to the problems and dangers of adulthood. Then colleges must stand back and get out of the sex game.

ON THE NET

Critical Thinking Across the Curriculum Project: Resources in Critical Thinking. Longview Community College (Missouri). This is an extensive site that discusses, among other topics, arguments, premises, and fallacies.
<http://mcckc.edu/longview/ctac/toc.htm>

Argument Analysis: Identifying Arguments. Department of Philosophy, The University of Hong Kong. This site includes sections, with exercises, on Identifying Arguments, Validity and

Soundness, and Patterns of Valid Arguments, among others.
<http://philosophy.hku.hk/think/arg/arg.php>

Rational Appeal: "*Logos translates into 'word' or 'reason.'* In rhetoric, logos refers to systems of reasoning." Daniel Kies, College of DuPage, discusses Developing Logos, Kinds of Logic, and Syllogisms and Enthymemes: The Processes of *Logos.*
<http://papyr.com/hypertextbooks/comp1/logos.htm>

Informal Logic. Stanford Encyclopedia of Philosophy. This site contains a number of entries related to the study and use of informal logic, such as a History, Components of Informal Logic, an example of the Ad Hominem fallacy, and A Visual Argument.
<http://plato.stanford.edu/entries/logic-informal/>

EXERCISES

Inductive Reasoning

Assume you are a detective. Based on what you find listed below in the garbage can of a family, determine the type of inhabitants in the house. How many people live in the house? What are their approximate ages and interests? Explain your findings/conclusions in a well-structured paragraph, providing sufficient evidence to support your conclusion.

Grocery Receipts
Styling gel
Clearasil
Oil of Olay
Diet sodas
AAA batteries
Jell-O
Gummy Bears
Tuna
Polo cologne
Decaf coffee
Lean Cuisine
Sugar-coated cereal
Bran flakes
Donuts
Case of beer
Low-cholesterol products
Ulcer medicine

Discarded Mail
College recruitments
Military recruitments
University alumni magazines from private and public universities
Stockholder reports

Magazines
Field and Stream
Cosmopolitan
Rolling Stone
Better Homes and Gardens
TV Guide
Sassy
Golf Digest
Vogue

<u>Canceled Checks</u>
Dance lessons
The Gap
2 County Sheriff's Dept. Traffic Div. citations
Neiman Marcus
Hair Salon
Orthodontist
Country Club
Car insurance (3 cars)
Clinique Cosmetics
Alimony Checks to Mrs. "Ex"

<u>Paycheck Stubs</u>
Mega Energy Corp
McDonalds

Deductive Reasoning

I. Syllogisms. Consider each of the following syllogisms and write valid or invalid, true or not true in the space to the right of each.

1. **Major Premise (MP):** All persons will die.
   Minor Premise (mp): Dr. Deek is a person.
   Conclusion (C): Dr. Deek will die.

2. All Baptists are Protestants.
   All Methodists are Protestants.
   All Baptists are Methodists.

3. Free speech is protected under the Constitution.
   Flag burning is an expression of free speech.
   Flag burning is protected under the Constitution.

4. Tyranny deserves no loyalty.
   King George III is a tyrant.
   King George III deserves no loyalty

5. All rabbits have red eyes.
   Gomer is a rabbit.
   Therefore, Gomer has red eyes.

6. Policemen who commit a crime should be punished severely.

   Those policemen just beat a man to death.

   Those policemen should be punished severely.

II. Enthymemes. Write in the first blank what the assumed premise in each of the following is; in the second blank write valid or not valid, true or not true.

1. Those students are not serious about school because they always sit at the back of the classroom.

   a. _____

   b. _____

2. Percy Pinkus must be an atheist since he opposes organized religion.

   a. _____

   b. _____

III. Validity. Evaluate the following deductive arguments as either valid or invalid. Among those which are valid, can you identify any that are sound as well?

1. The only way to manage a company effectively is to instill fear in your workers. Either you treat your employees kindly and they take advantage of you or goof off, or you are tough on them and they work hard for you.

   _____

   _____

2. I had a bad time with my first two husbands. From these experiences I have learned that men are egotistical, inconsiderate philanderers who just want to score with as many "chicks" as possible.

   _____

   _____

3. Rodney has always been a supporter of minimum wage laws, but we shouldn't pay any attention to his arguments. He has a couple of illegal aliens tending to his kids, and he pays them only two dollars an hour.

_____

_____

Arguments

Identify and underline the conclusion of each of the following arguments:

1. Former Warsaw pact nations should be offered a limited "partnership" in NATO rather than full membership, inasmuch as full membership would fuel Russian phobias about invasion from Eastern Europe.

2. Philosophy is the best subject in which to major because it teaches one to reason, an essential skill for a good life.

3. Cutting wage rates may enable one employer to hire more workers, but cutting the wages of all workers may lead to fewer jobs, not more, since workers would have less to spend on goods.

4. The human mind is not the same thing as the human brain. The human body, including the brain, is a material thing. The human mind is a spiritual thing. Nothing is both a material thing and a spiritual thing.

5. All 70 students who ate dinner at the fraternity house on Friday became ill during the night. None of the students who live at the house but didn't dine there that night became ill, so the illness must have been food poisoning caused by something served for dinner at the house on Friday.

6. The investigation of supernatural phenomena lies outside the realm of science. Therefore, science can neither prove nor disprove the existence of God.

7. Moreover, cutting Social Security will not help the deficit problem. As Edward P. Lazear, chairman of the Council of Economic Advisors, has noted, Social Security is funded by separate payroll taxes and contributes not a cent to the deficit.

8. But the particular evil of silencing the expression of an opinion is, that it is robbing the human race; posterity as well as the existing generation; those who dissent from the opinion, still more than those who hold it. If the opinion is right, they are deprived of the opportunity of exchanging error for truth: if wrong, they lose what is almost as great a benefit, the clearer perception and livelier impression of truth, produced by its collision with error.

9. In England under the blasphemy laws it is illegal to express disbelief in the Christian religion. It is also illegal to teach what Christ taught us on the subject of nonresistance. . . [W]hoever wishes to avoid being a criminal must profess to agree with Christ's teaching but must avoid saying what that teaching was.

10. A coin has been tossed twelve times and has shown a head every time. The next time it is tossed, it will also show a head.

13 Research

In many college courses you will be asked to write the dreaded "research paper." The reasons for writing a research paper are threefold. First, you will learn or further develop your expertise in the research process. Learning how to do research is a valuable skill in itself, one you will employ in almost any field you enter or profession you pursue. Next, you will learn in depth about a specific topic in the course you are taking. Most courses, particularly on the freshman and sophomore levels, are general introductions to a particular discipline. Doing research gives you the chance to go into detail and more fully explore one corner of that discipline. Finally, writing a research paper gives you valuable experience in gathering and digesting information, arguing a point, and organizing the numerous detailed evidence that go into the final paper.

There are six major steps you need to take to complete a written research project. You must:

Choose A Topic
Find and Evaluate Sources
Organize Your Source Material
Use Your Sources Properly
Write Your Paper
Cite Your Sources
Format Your Paper

CHOOSING A TOPIC

Many times it will not be difficult for you to come up with a topic—you will be assigned one. Your professor will take that problem off your plate. However, a lot of times professors will assign general subjects and will leave it up to you to decide on a specific topic. For example, in a freshman composition class you may be asked to research and write a paper on a current issue, such as abortion, global warming, or the death penalty. In choosing a topic, you must consider several different things. First, you will want to choose a topic in which you have some interest. Spending weeks on a subject you hate is no fun. Next, a less obvious consideration is not to choose a topic about which you have strong feelings. If, for instance, you believe abortion or the death penalty to be murder, do not write on those topics. If you feel so strongly about an issue that you cannot understand how people of good will and good morals could be on the opposite side, you will not be open-minded or unbiased in your consideration of the evidence as you research your topic. You should choose a topic that you have not already prejudged. Finally, it is always good to pick several topics you are interested in at first, for you may find very little material on the first topic and lots of material on the second. The first topic may be so recent that not a lot has been said about it. Whether to ban cell phones in automobiles, for example, might be so recent that not much has been written on it.

Search Terms

Once you have chosen two topics that you are interested in but are not strongly biased toward, you need to read a general exposition of each. Simply go to the internet and read, for example, the Wikipedia or Encarta article on it. Your purpose here is to get a general idea of the breadth and depth of the subject. As you read, you should begin to develop a list of search terms. Search terms are words and phrases you will use in catalogs, databases, and search engines to find relevant sources for your research project. For example, let us say that you have chosen "legalizing marijuana" and "euthanasia" as your topics. As you read about these, develop a list of alternative and synonymous terms (and sometimes alternative spellings). You might come up with the following:

Legalizing Marijuana (Marihuana)	Euthanasia
Cannabis, Weed, Mary Jane	Assisted Suicide
Drugs	Active vs. Passive Euthanasia
Illegal Drugs	Euthanasia and Law
Medical Marijuana	Jack Kevorkian
Effects of Marijuana	Hemlock Society
Marijuana Laws	Right to Die

Now you have several terms with which to begin your research. As you conduct your research, always be on the lookout for other terms mentioned in the titles, descriptions, or text of the material you find. For example, in the library catalog description of the book *Death & Dying: Who Decides?*, the following subjects are listed: Terminal Care, Euthanasia—Moral and Ethical Aspects, Death—Psychological Aspects, and Suicide. Some terms might lead to a dead end; others will lead to more sources than you could possibly read in the time you have.

Finding Sources

Our age is awash in information. We have literally hundreds of channels on cable TV, twenty-four-hour news channels, billions of pages on the internet, constantly updated blogs, podcasts, thousands of word-and-phrase searchable electronic books, and cell phones capable of flashing images instantaneously around the world—to name some of the modern "information channels." For students today, the problem is not "finding enough sources" to write a research paper, but rather finding solid and appropriate sources amid the constant onslaught of sound and sight. For students faced with the task of writing a research paper, it can seem overwhelming. It need not be. There are two highways you must travel down in order adequately to research any topic. The first is the electronic highway, consisting of electronic source material in digital form, and the second is the older but still relevant hard-copy, paper highway.

Electronic Source Material

The first and newest highway you will want to travel is the electronic highway, where you will find information in digital form. This highway branches off into three main arteries that can be accessed from any computer, yours at home or the ones on your campus.

The Library's Online Catalog. A library's online catalog contains a list of its books, government documents, audio-visual materials and even electronic sources, such as electronic books and web sites. Once you have located sources in the catalog (unless they are web sites or electronic books), a physical trip to the library is required to obtain the hard-copy, paper resources, which are not themselves in electronic form.

Online Databases. Databases contain information, generally magazine and journal articles, in electronic form that your library has bought from different services, such as EBSCOhost, CQ Researcher, Facts.com, and ProQuest. These databases contain Full-Text Articles, Citations to Articles, and Electronic Books.

Full-text articles are the complete digital copies of articles as they were printed in the original magazine or journal. You can take notes from them, print them, download them, or send them as an e-mail attachment to your home computer.

Some articles, however, may only be listed as citations (a list of authors, titles and publications only). To find the actual articles you must first check to see if your library subscribes to these periodicals. If it does, then you must make a trip to the library's shelves where it keeps current issues or to its microfilm/microfiche section and its reader/copiers to actually read or print out the article.

Thousands of electronic books are also available in digital form. Your library may have a database, such as NetLibrary, that will allow you to read electronic copies of books.

The Open Internet. The internet contains millions of pages that can be searched by using various search engines. Libraries (including the Library of Congress), encyclopedias (including *Encyclopedia Britannica*), government agencies (including the Census Bureau), and just about anything else you can imagine are now all online.

Remember that all three of these arteries on the Electronic Highway can be accessed from your school computer or from your home computer.

Hard-Copy Paper Sources

The second pathway to research, which parallels the Electronic Highway, should not be neglected simply because it is not easily available in electronic form. The Hard-Copy Paper Source path was the only means of research for over two thousand years; it remains a major, if somewhat neglected, highway. It is comprised of reference sources, such as encyclopedias, thousands of books, and, at some libraries, government documents; it also includes paper indexes containing citations to magazine and journal articles. These sources can be found only in the actual library itself.

Books. Books on every imaginable topic are shelved in the library. Most academic libraries follow the Library of Congress Classification System. The Library of Congress, in Washington, D. C., is the research institution of the federal government. It was initially established by Congress in 1800. After the library was burnt by the British in 1814, Thomas Jefferson donated his own extensive collection of books. The Library of Congress contains over 130 million items and, by law, receives two copies of every copyrighted book published in the United States. The LC System is arranged alphabetically from A to Z, with each letter containing books on specific subjects.

The main classes of the LC System are:

> A - GENERAL WORKS
> B - PHILOSOPHY. PSYCHOLOGY. RELIGION
> C - AUXILIARY SCIENCES OF HISTORY
> D - WORLD HISTORY AND HISTORY OF EUROPE, ASIA, AFRICA,
>   AUSTRALIA, NEW ZEALAND, etc.
> E - HISTORY OF THE AMERICAS
> F - HISTORY OF THE AMERICAS
> G - GEOGRAPHY. ANTHROPOLOGY. RECREATION
> H - SOCIAL SCIENCES
> J - POLITICAL SCIENCE
> K - LAW
> L - EDUCATION
> M - MUSIC AND BOOKS ON MUSIC
> N - FINE ARTS
> P - LANGUAGE AND LITERATURE
> Q - SCIENCE
> R - MEDICINE
> S - AGRICULTURE
> T - TECHNOLOGY

U - MILITARY SCIENCE
V - NAVAL SCIENCE
Z - BIBLIOGRAPHY. LIBRARY SCIENCE. INFORMATION RESOURCES
   (GENERAL)

Each of these classes is subdivided by further letters and numbers. To find a book on the library shelf, all you do is find the book in the **Online Catalog,** look up its **Call Number,** and then follow the letters and numbers on the sides of the shelves in the library until you find the book. For example, the book *Animal Rights: Current Debates and New Directions,* has the call number **HV4708.A56 2006**. Once you find this book, be sure to scan the shelves around it; you will find a number of other books on that same subject with additional information.

The best way to check these books to see if they have information you can use is first to look at the **Contents** page for the key words and terms you have already developed. In addition, check the **Index** at the back of the book (if it has one) for the same terms.

Series. There are a number of books in the library that belong to a single series, published by the same company. There may be 25-50 books in such a series, each on a specific topic. Major series titles associated with controversial topics, for example, are the following:

Current Controversies
Contemporary World Issues
Information Series on Current Topics
Opposing Viewpoints
Taking Sides
At Issue

Each book in these series is on a specific topic: Animal Rights, Abortion, Marijuana, and Pollution, for example. In each book, you will generally find background articles as well as articles on different sides of the issue, some written specifically for the book and some reprinted from magazine and journal articles.

Paper Indexes. The library has a number of indexes, or guides, such as the *Reader's Guide to Periodical Literature,* to periodical essays that are not in electronic form. Particularly if you need periodical information from the past—over fifteen years ago—you need to consult these indexes.

EVALUATING SOURCES

As you locate sources on your topic, you need to evaluate them. Not all sources are created equal. For example, as you already know, just about anyone can post anything on the internet. If you just grab something from the net, how do you know it is appropriate or even true? For that matter, how do you know that the book you checked out from the library contains information you will need to help you write your paper? Does it matter what information you use as long as you have those six sources your English professor requires? You will soon find, if you have not already, that just like the people you know, the products you buy, and the commercials you watch on television, neither everyone nor everything can be trusted to have your best interest in mind. You must always go through a process to determine that what you see, read, or hear is true and will actually help you achieve your goals. Likewise, you must evaluate the sources you find to determine their truthfulness and relevance to the research project you have been required to do.

The information you find in your library's databases—magazine and journal articles, electronic books, and government documents—as well as the information in its books and paper documents, must be chosen carefully if you are to write a credible research paper. In reviewing these electronic resources, always keep the following four criteria in mind:

Is the source **Relevant?**

That is, does it address the specific topic you are working on; does it match one of the Search Terms you developed earlier? As you sort through your sources, you will find new and sometimes more revealing topics that will help you focus on a narrower topic within the general topic you have chosen to research. This is all to the good. The quicker you can narrow your topic, the easier your search will become; you will switch from looking for sources to weeding out sources that are not relevant to your narrowed topic. For example, let us say that you have chosen the broad topic of euthanasia for your paper. Looking at the search terms you developed for this topic (above), you begin your search. After scanning several articles, the debate on physician-assisted suicide gets your attention. You find that there is ample information on this topic, on both sides of the issue, and you remember how difficult the last year of your grandmother's life was as she wasted away from cancer. So you decide to narrow your topic to physician-assisted suicide. Now you can concentrate your research on this subtopic and develop an even narrower list of search terms: Definition, Ethics, Methods, Right to Die, Death with Dignity, Legal Issues. After another session scanning articles on these topics, you decide to write your paper on the ethical or legal issues surrounding physician-assisted suicide. You have now developed a narrower, much more focused topic than you had at the beginning of the project.

Is the source **Current?**

All things being equal, the more current or up to date your sources are, the better. That is because things are constantly discovered, constantly change, are constantly updated, and constantly reinterpreted in light of new findings. However, depending on your topic and approach, older sources may still be relevant and even preferred to more-current information. For example, if you provide background information in your paper (to help your audience better understand the importance of your topic), you may need an older source to help you provide historical background. Or, if you are doing research in the humanities, for example, older interpretations and analyses of literary and artistic works are as good, and sometimes better, than some more current ones.

Is the source **Reputable?**

Does the source you have found indicate who wrote it and what this person's qualifications are? Is the author an expert in the field of expertise he is writing about—would you really want to use as a source a book on automobile engines written by a professor of English? What credentials does the author have—does she have an advanced degree in the subject? If it is an article, was it published in a peer-reviewed journal? If it is a magazine or newspaper article, does the source provide information on the author's credentials? Can you find reviews or critiques of the source? The old advice, "Consider the source," is always relevant in research. If you are researching climate change, for example, which source would you consider more credible, *Newsweek* or *The National Enquirer?*

Is the source **Representative?**

As with people and their opinions, sources can be objective and balanced, while others can be extreme. Some sources are mainly factual, present both sides of an issue, and are within "the main stream." Others take a decidedly unorthodox position, present only one side of an issue, and are "out in left field." For example, there are many research institutes, generally known as "think-tanks," that publish enormous quantities of papers and books. Many of these have decidedly conservative or liberal biases. To determine how representative of the thinking and opinions within a given field a source is, you must read enough to get a general idea of the topic you have chosen to research.

Finally, special care must be taken if you use open internet sources. When asked a question we do not know the answer to, we all almost automatically "Google" it. For example, suppose one of the topics you have been given is Genetically Modified Food. The first three Google results are: "Genetically Modified Food—Wikipedia, the free encyclopedia," "Genetically Modified Food: Harmful or Helpful?" and "Genetically Modified Foods and Organisms—HGP Ethical, Legal, and . . . ." Are these all solid sources? To determine if these are useful, you must look at each carefully. Scrolling the Wikipedia article, you will find considerable information organized according to the Contents at the top of the page. There is a section on "Debate around the world," as well as "Political and economic effects," many cross-references to other sites, a number of footnotes and external links, and a list of suggested readings. There is a date at the bottom, stating "last modified on 23 September 2008," but no author, since Wikipedia articles can be written and modified by many people. It appears to be a good source, but keep in mind that we have no idea who actually wrote it, and it is a "general reference" encyclopedia article. Further, keep in mind that these results will change over time; what you find may be different the next time you Google the same term.

The second article on Google's list is a ProQuest Discovery Guide. It lists an author, Deborah B. Whitman, and allows you to click on her name and see her credentials, allowing you to e-mail her as well. The article briefly defines what genetically-modified foods are, their advantages, and criticisms against GM foods. One possible problem is the date given at the top: April 2000.

The third article on the above list is from the Human Genome Project, a government sponsored site under the Department of Energy Office of Science. It has a brief introduction to GM foods and lists the benefits and controversies surrounding this subject. It gives links to other sources on the net and has a current date.

All three of these articles appear to be good sources, but keep in mind that they are "general introductions" to the topic, we don't know who wrote the first one, and the second one is not current.

To refine a web search, you might want to click on the "Advanced Search" option on the Google page. When you do that, you can specify a certain file type (PDF, PowerPoint, or MS Word for example), a specific domain address (.edu or .gov for example), and a date (any time, past year, or past month, for instance). The domain filter is particularly helpful in focusing on college and university produced material, as well as material from government sources such as the National Institutes of Health (NIH), which, in general, are much more reputable than open internet sources.

ORGANIZING SOURCE MATERIAL

Once you have found a number of sources, you will need to organize that material. The traditional way to organize source material is first to develop a preliminary bibliography, or list of sources you have found, in alphabetical order by author (with all the information you will need to generate its Works Cited entry). Once the list is established, you can then begin taking notes from the sources on 3 × 5 index cards, with one note on each card and a reference to the author of the source at the bottom and a subject at the top. Once you have taken a number of notes—which can include facts, paraphrases, and direct quotations—you can sort the cards into separate piles according to specific subjects. For example, if you are working on the topic of immigration, you might have separate notes on the pros and cons of immigration in general, specific proposals on what to do about illegal immigration, and various amnesty proposals. Once sorted, these piles can help you develop a preliminary outline for your paper. Further, organizing research in this manner will help you in other ways. First, it will help you clarify the issues involved in the subject; next, it will help you decide on a more specific thesis that will allow you to do more focused reading and note taking; finally, it will make writing the rough draft much easier.

Researchers today, however, with the availability of multiple electronic devices and access to seemingly limitless information, may want to pursue a slightly different approach. The goal is still to be able to sort and keep track of the sources of information you will use in your paper in order to make the actual writing easier. For instance, since many instructors will require you to "turn in" your actual sources along with your paper, you might want to print out the articles you find in databases and on the internet and copy pages from the books you use. Alternatively, use a specific flash drive to save all the electronic material you think you might use and later print out what you actually find useful. Another option is to email your sources to yourself and print them out of your email account. A good way to separate the topics your sources cover is to color-code them. For example, use a high-lighter pen to mark all the sources on a specific sub-topic. This procedure will make it easier to arrange your sources into piles when you get ready to write your paper—all the sources with a blue mark at the top have strong arguments against assisted suicide, while all those with a red mark are for it, for example. Once you have copies, you can highlight passages and make notes in the margins or on separate sheets of paper you attach to the article. Be sure to **keep all of your research in one folder (and on one flash drive)** so that you do not misplace or lose information.

A third way of taking notes is to use the traditional note-card method, but do it electronically on your computer. There are a number of software programs that allow you to take and sort notes electronically: *Microsoft OneNote, NoteScribe*, and *ndx cards* for example. All allow you to write notes, paraphrases, and summaries, as well as to paste quotations directly from electronic sources. You can then sort these electronic notes according to subject. Most also allow you to generate an outline directly from the notes.

Whatever system you use, you must be sure to understand and digest the material you will use in your paper. Keep in mind a general rule of thumb that says that not more than 20% of your paper should come directly from your sources as paraphrases or quotations.

USING SOURCES

You must use sources properly in order to give credit to those who have gone before you and to enhance the credibility of your own paper. Simply "dumping" material from a source into your own paper, uncritically and undigested, does not add to the credibility of your paper nor show that you have mastered or even understood the sources you have used. Therefore, you must learn to integrate **summaries, paraphrases,** and **direct quotations** from sources that enhance and advance the argument of your paper.

Summary. A summary of a passage, whether a paragraph or several pages, distills or boils down the original to its facts and essential ideas. The summary should include a statement of thesis (or a topic sentence) and a summary of the essential facts, ideas, and conclusions of the original. Before writing a summary, read the selection to determine its basic points. Indicate these major points by using Roman numerals in the margin, or by making an outline on paper. Now strike out or ignore introductory, summary, or illustrative paragraphs and write a summary of the main points you have outlined, beginning with a thesis statement (or topic sentence) and ending with the major conclusions of the article or paragraph. Next, go back over what you have written and delete any nonessential words or phrases. Finally, compare your summary with the original to be sure that you have an accurate condensation of it. Further, make sure your summary is written in complete sentences and organized paragraphs. According to the MLA, without being obscure or cryptic, a summary should be as compact and concise as possible. It should be specific and include only directly significant details. Peripheral comments, generalizations, background information, and, ordinarily, references to previous work should be omitted. The language of the summary should echo the style of the article or report. Key words from the document can be incorporated in the summary (in quotation marks), but direct quotations should be avoided.

Paraphrase. *Merriam-Webster's Collegiate Dictionary*, 10th edition, defines a paraphrase as "a restatement of a text, passage, or work giving the meaning in another form." Thus a paraphrase, like a summary, allows you to restate an author's idea but in your own words. Unlike a summary, however, a paraphrase is restricted to a sentence or two and follows the original in style as well as idea. For example, consider the following source and paraphrase. In *Collapse: How Societies Choose to Fail or Succeed,* Jared Diamond says, "Our world society is presently on a non-sustainable course, and any of our 12 problems of non-sustainability that we have just summarized would suffice to limit our lifestyle within the next several decades"(498). A paraphrase might put it this way: Jared Diamond states that our current global society cannot be sustained, and any one of the twelve problems he has discussed will surely limit our lifestyle in the decades to come (498). Always be sure to introduce the paraphrase with the author's name and follow it with a page number reference, thus avoiding plagiarism. A final caution: it is best not to paraphrase the arguments of those opposed to your position; go ahead and quote them directly. If you paraphrase them, you may be open to charges of "misrepresenting" their arguments.

Direct Quotation. Direct quotations should be used when a summary or paraphrase will not clearly and accurately reflect the ideas of the author you are citing, when the words of the author are distinctive or stylistically important, or when the author's words cannot be disentangled from the ideas he is writing about. The following rules for integrating sources, particularly direct quotations, into your paper are based on MLA guidelines.

1. **Always** introduce quotations, summaries, and paraphrased material so that the reader will know that the material is being drawn from another source— that it is not yours.

Direct Quotation. According to Paula Larocque: "Many writers routinely, and incorrectly, place commas between all adjectives preceding nouns. But we correctly place commas only between adjectives that are equally important and offer similar kinds of information" (30).

Paraphrase. Paula Larocque says that many writers incorrectly place commas between all adjectives before nouns; however, commas should only be placed between adjectives that are equal and convey similar information (30).

2. **Always** make sure that all quotations are exact, and that paraphrases are indeed paraphrases and not simply direct quotations with one or two words changed (see above).

3. Be sure to **integrate phrasal quotations** into your sentences properly so that ungrammatical sentences are not created. You may change words in a quotation so that it can be incorporated grammatically into your sentence, but you should always enclose such changes in brackets. Keep such changes to a minimum.

Source: A common goal of argument is to convince an audience that existing circumstances need to be changed. Some *recommendations* seek only to gain an audience's agreement with an idea or decision, but others have a more practical (and ambitious) purpose: they try to convince their audience to take a particular action or, more modestly, to convince an audience that a particular action should be taken by others.

Direct Quotation: Katherine J. Mayberry states that "a common goal of argument is to convince an audience that existing circumstances need to be changed" (31).

Direct Quotation with Word Changes: Speaking of how arguments affect us, Katherine J. Mayberry says that "some *recommendations* seek only to gain [our] agreement with an idea or decision"; on the other hand, some "try to convince [us] that a particular action should be taken by others" (31).

4. Use ellipses (three spaced dots) to indicate omissions in quotations so that you do not misquote your source. When integrating a quotation into your sentence, you need not indicate omissions at the beginning or end of your quotation.

Source: You can see then that arguments for the critical thinker are not like arm-twisting attempts to make other people accept a particular position. They are not bullying orders to see things one way rather than another. Instead, they set up reasons in such a way that, if you accept those reasons, you are likely to be persuaded of a particular position.

Direct Quotation with Ellipses. "You can see then that arguments . . . are not like arm-twisting attempts to make other people accept a particular position. . . . Instead, they set up reasons in such a way that, if you accept those reasons, you are likely to be persuaded of a particular position" (Van den Brink 10).

Ellipses not needed. Roy Van den Brink further says that arguments are not "bullying orders to see things one way rather than another" (323).

5. Use a colon to introduce a quotation that is independent from the structure of the main sentence; however, use a comma after a verb, such as *says, exclaims,* or *notes:*

   Source: When everyone agrees, there is no need to argue. Since the observation that every morning the sun appears first in the east is uncontroversial, no one has to make an elaborate argument to defend it. That the earth rotates around the sun, however, is not so easy to observe and was once controversial enough to need support. What is arguable changes in different times and places, but the essential structure of argument does not change. Arguments consist of *claims, reasons, evidence,* and *assumptions.*

   Use of colon. A current textbook puts it this way: "When everyone agrees, there is no need to argue. . . . [T]he essential structure of argument does not change. Arguments consist of *claims, reasons, evidence,* and *assumptions*" (Ferster 148).

   Use of comma. As Judith Ferster says, "When everyone agrees, there is no need to argue. . . . . The essential structure of argument does not change. Arguments consist of *claims, reasons, evidence,* and *assumptions*" (148).

6. Follow quotations or paraphrased material with parenthetical documentation giving the exact page number of the source from which material has been taken. If the name of the author has not been given in the introduction to the material, the author's last name must also be included in the parenthesis. Do not include the word *page,* or the abbreviation *p.* See the examples under number 5 above.

7. When you want to quote the words of a person that you find quoted in a source, you should introduce the quotation by giving the name of the author of the quotation and follow the quotation with parenthetical reference to the source preceded by **qtd. in** (quoted in).

   Robert Frost once said that "to learn to write is to learn to have ideas" (qtd. in Barnet 10).

8. If a quotation is a long one, running **over four lines of text,** set it off by indenting it one inch or two tabs (10 spaces) from the left margin and dropping the quotation marks.

In "Reports, Inferences, Judgments," S. I. Hayakawa maintains that most student papers are filled with judgments:

> A judgment ("He is a fine boy," "It was a beautiful service," "Baseball is a healthful sport," "She is an awful bore") is a conclusion, summing up a large number of previously observed facts. The reader is probably familiar with the fact that students almost always have difficulty in writing themes of the required length because their ideas give out after a paragraph or two. The reason for this is that there is little left to be said. When the conclusions are carefully excluded, however, and observed facts are given instead, there is never any trouble about the length of papers; in fact, they tend to become too long, since inexperienced writers, when told to give facts, often give far more than are necessary, because they lack discrimination between the important and the trivial. (122)

9. When quoting or paraphrasing material from a **database** or the **open internet,** follow the rules listed above. However, since such sources usually do not indicate page numbers, the MLA says to omit them.

According to "Constructing an Argument," produced by the University of Central Florida's Writing Center, " The major claim of an argumentative essay is the thesis statement. All other claims in the essay should relate to and elaborate upon the thesis statement."

The following Works Cited entries include all of the sources used in the above examples.

Works Cited

Barnet, Sylvan, and Hugo Bedau. *Current Issues and Enduring Questions: A Guide to Critical Thinking and Argument, with Readings.* Boston: Bedford/St. Martins, 2005. Print.

"Constructing an Argument." *The University Writing Center.* The University of Central Florida. Web. 3 April 2009.

Ferster, Judith. *Arguing Through Literature: A Thematic Anthology and Guide to Academic Writing.* Boston: McGraw Hill, 2005. Print.

Hayakawa, S.I. "Reports, Inferences, Judgments." *Language in Thought and Action.* 4th ed.
New York: Harcourt, 1978. Rpt. in Sally de Witt Spurgin. *The Power to Persuade.* 2nd ed.
Englewood Cliffs: Prentice, 1989. 117-22. Print.

Larocque, Paula. "Use Comma Sense When Constructing Stories." *The Quill* 96.2 (2008): 30.
Proquest. Web. 3 Apr. 2009.

Mayberry, Katherine J. *For Argument's Sake: A Guide to Writing Effective Arguments.* 3rd ed.
New York: Longman, 1999. Print.

Van den Brink, Roy. *Critical Thinking for Students.* Rev. 3rd ed. Oxford: How To Books, 2000.
NetLibrary. Web. 3 Apr. 2009.

PLAGIARISM

According to the *MLA Handbook,* 7th ed., Plagiarism is "derived from the Latin word *plagiarius* ('kidnapper')." It is copying someone else's ideas or words and claiming them as your own. Fundamentally, then, plagiarism refers to the unauthorized, not cited, or incorrectly cited use of another person's work. Plagiarism is fraud. There are two types of plagiarism:

Intentional plagiarism is committed "with malice aforethought." The student engaging in this blatant fraud has simply downloaded a paper from the internet, copied all or a substantial part of the paper from another source, or had the paper written or substantially rewritten by another person. Such fraud is unethical and can have serious consequences. Such a fraudulent paper can receive a "0" and may result in a failing grade in the class.

Unintentional plagiarism occurs when quotation marks are inadvertently omitted around words taken directly from a source, when quotations are not properly introduced or cited, and when paraphrases are too close to direct quotations. Whether motivated by panic, dishonesty, or carelessness, such plagiarism will count against the grade of a paper; if it is extensive, it can also result in a "0." The following list constitutes plagiarism in the eyes of all instructors:

1. Copying or using another person's work without any citation (the most flagrant violation). It is unethical and fraudulent to copy or use a paper, report, web document, or part of a published book and submit it as your own.

2. Having someone else write or substantially rewrite your paper. A parent, friend, or tutor, for example, may not rewrite sentences for you correcting

errors in sentence structure and punctuation. He or she may point out that grammatical errors exist in the paper, explain the rules, and recheck your corrections; point out stylistic problems and explain why clarity is affected; point out deficiencies in your thesis or organizational pattern.

3. Copying the exact words of someone else and using them without documentation. Do not, under any circumstances, copy onto your notes or your paper a direct quotation without providing quotation marks and crediting the source.

4. Borrowing a phrase, using an idea, or paraphrasing material without properly introducing and documenting that material. Included in this category of plagiarism is merely rearranging phrases from the original into a new pattern without proper documentation.

5. Inadequately or inaccurately documenting your sources. This form of plagiarism includes copying the words of a source with no quotation marks even though correct parenthetical notes are included, citing a source correctly within the body of the paper but not providing a works-cited entry, including paraphrases of material from a source with no documentation in the paper but including the source on the works-cited list, and including paraphrases of material from a source but giving misleading or inadequate parenthetical credit.

If the material you use may be considered common knowledge—that is, if it can be found in a number of sources and is not specifically the author's—there is no need to document it. For example, there is no need to document the following fact: Sacramento is the capital of California, but it is not the state's largest city. If you are unsure about whether to document an idea, check with your instructor before the assignment is due.

WRITING YOUR PAPER

Once you have chosen a topic, developed search terms, found and evaluated sources, set up a working bibliography, and taken and organized notes, you are ready to begin writing your research paper. Your paper might be an expository one, where you report the results of your research—for example, a report on the latest findings on intelligence for a psychology course—or an argument paper where you take sides on a controversial issue, such as euthanasia. Whichever paper you have been asked to write, you should first develop a preliminary outline to guide you. The preliminary outline will be based on the notes you have taken from your sources and whatever ideas you have developed in the course of your research. If you are writing an expository paper, you should refer to **Part Two (Chapters Four through Eleven)** to see which expository mode, or combination of modes, best suits your topic. If your paper is an argument, refer to

Chapter Twelve. No matter what kind of paper you are writing, be sure to develop a clear thesis that you can develop or defend. Refer to **Chapter Two** for appropriate ways to develop a thesis statement.

A good way to begin is to write your paper in sections based on your preliminary outline. Don't try to start at the beginning and work your way through to the end of five or ten pages. Pick a section that really interests you and on which you have a lot of information. As you begin writing this section, other ideas will occur to you for other parts of the paper. Note these down! Move from the most engaging to the least interesting of the parts of your paper. Leave the introduction and the conclusion for last. As you write, you may find that the preliminary outline needs to be changed, so don't worry about moving parts or sections of your paper around. Don't try to write the entire paper in one sitting (get started well before the paper's deadline). If you have a certain block of time set aside for writing, be sure to take a break every hour, and don't try to do other things at the same time, such as cruising the internet or chatting with friends. You must focus your attention, writing without distractions! Finally, when you are near the end of the time you have set aside for writing, find a stopping place that will allow you to jump right in the next time. Don't quit when you have run out of ideas,; quit when you are in the middle of an idea. If you do that, you will quickly be able to begin writing the next time.

CITING SOURCES

The information and advice given to you so far in this chapter, as well as the citation examples that follow, are based on the Modern Language Association's *Handbook for Writers of Research Papers* 7th ed. The Modern Language Association is a national community of scholars in the humanities. The advice and rules that it gives in its handbook, the *MLA Handbook for Writers of Research Papers*, govern the production of research papers for publication in literally hundreds of journals across the United States, as well the submission of papers, masters' theses and doctoral dissertations in colleges and universities. However, the procedures outlined in the *MLA Handbook* are not the only ones used. In fact, besides the MLA guidelines, there are other major "style sheets" governing the production and submission of research: *The Chicago Manual of Style*, APA (American Psychological Association) Style, CSE (Council of Scientific Editors) Style, and Kate Turabian's *A Manual for Writers of Term Papers*. Before you begin writing your research paper, be sure to find out which of these styles your instructor wants you to use. Links to sites that explain these other styles (as well as to MLA style itself) can be found in the "On the Net" section at the end of this chapter.

Common MLA Citation Examples. All entries on a Works Cited page are arranged alphabetically by the last name of the author, or, if there is no author, by titles (excluding *A*, *An*, and *The*); further, they are **double-spaced** throughout. In addition, second and third lines of an entry are indented one-half inch (five spaces) or one tab space. There are software packages, such as *WorksCited4you* and *easybib.com* that generate proper Works Cited pages. However, if you use any of these programs you must be sure that you have all the required information you will need. Examples of proper citations are listed below. These examples are single-spaced, but in your paper remember you must **always double-space them.**

Books

Single Author: Print

> Diamond, Jared. Collapse: *How Societies Choose to Fail or Succeed.* New York: Viking, 2005. Print.

Two or Three Authors: Print

> Miller, Robert, Cher Brock, and Steve Sansom. *Discovering A Voice: A Rhetoric for Writers.* Southlake, TX: Fountainhead, 2008. Print.

> *Note:* For more than three authors, use the first author's name + et al.

Electronic Books

> Ticciati, Laura, and Robin Ticciati. *Genetically Engineered Foods: Are they Safe? You Decide.* New Canaan, CT: Contemporary, 1998. NetLibrary. Web. 13 Nov. 2006.

> Scruton, Roger. *Animal Rights and Wrongs.* UK: Demos, 1998. *Google Book Search.* Web. 16 Nov. 2006

An Edited Collection in a Series: Print

> Wekesser, Carol, ed. *Genetic Engineering: Opposing Viewpoints.* San Diego: Greenhaven, 1996. Print. Opposing Viewpoints.

An Article Reprinted in an Edited Collection: Print

> Singer, Peter. "Xenotransplantation and Speciesism." *Transplantation Proceedings* 24 (1992): 728-32. Rpt. in *Taking Sides: Clashing Views on Controversial Bioethical Issues.* Ed. Carol Levine. Guilford: Dushkin, 1993. 232-38. Print.

Magazine and Journal Articles

Magazine Article: Print

> Horgan, John. "The God Experiments: Five Researchers Take Science Where it Has Never Gone Before." *Discover* Dec. 2006: 52-57. Print.

Magazine Article: Database

> Goldberg, Alan M., and Thomas Hartung. "Protecting More Than Animals." *Scientific American* Jan. 2006: 84-91. Academic Search Complete. Web. 27 Apr. 2006.

Magazine Article: Online

> Tumulty, Karen, and James Carney. "Stem Cells: Bush's Fuzzy Science?" *Time Online Edition.* 2 Sept. 2001. Web. 21 Mar. 2006.

Journal Article: Database

> Frey, R. G. "Pain, Vivisection, and the Value of Life." *Journal of Medical Ethics* 31(2005): 202-04. *JME Online. Academic Search Complete.* Web. 4 April 2006.

Journal Article: Online:

> Patz, J. A., et al. "Global Climate Change and Emerging Infectious Diseases." *JAMA* 275.3 (1996): 217-23. American Medical Association. Web. 16 Nov. 2006.

> *Note:* If no page numbers are given for an online article, use n. pag., for no page numbers.

Newspaper Articles

Newspaper Article: Print

> Tanner, Lindsey. "A Sci-Fi Advance May Aid the Heart." *Houston Chronicle* 16 Nov. 2006: B2. Print.

Newspaper Article: Database

Crary, David. "Nationwide, Voters Deny Conservatives' Hoped-For Initiatives / Measures to Ban Abortion, Same-sex Marriage Fail; Stem Cell Effort Passes." *Houston Chronicle* 9 Nov. 2006: 24. *ProQuest Newspapers. ProQuest.* Web. 16 Nov. 2006.

Newspaper Article: Online

Robbins, Maro. "Court: Bush Overstepped in Capital Cases." *Houston Chronicle*, 16 Nov. 2006. Web. 16 Nov. 2006.

Web Sites

"What is a Designer Baby?" *BIONET.* 2002. Web. 16 Nov. 2006.

"Women's Rights." *Human Rights Watch.* 2006. Web. 21 Nov. 2006.

"Arguments in Support of Assisted Suicide." *End-of-Life Issues and Care: Assisted Suicide. APA Online.* 2001. Web. 21 Nov. 2006.

Note: If you can find no date on the site, use n.d., for no date. If no sponsor or publisher of the site is listed, use N.p. for no publisher.

Government Documents

Government Document: Print

United States. Dept. of Commerce, Bureau of the Census; Dept of Agriculture, Economic Research Service. *Residents of Farms and Rural Areas.* Washington: GPO, 1990. Print.

Government Document: Online

United States. U. S. Census Bureau. Population Division, Population Projections Branch. *About Population Projections.* 2 Aug. 2002. Web. 16 Nov. 2006.

FORMATTING YOUR PAPER

Merriam-Webster's Collegiate Dictionary (10th edition) defines *format* as "the shape, size, and general makeup (as of something printed)." Before you submit your research paper to your professor for evaluation, be sure you follow precisely any format requirements he has given you. The following format recommendations are based on the requirements of the *MLA Handbook for Writers of Research Papers.*

Margins. Allow margins of 1" on top, bottom, and sides.

Font and Type Size. Times New Roman, 12.

Title Page. Submit a title page only if your professor requires one, or if you are required to submit an outline with your paper. Center the title of your paper, followed by your name, the class, your professor's name, and the date, as follows:

Genetically Modified Food:
The Future of Agriculture

Amelia Goodstudent

English 1301.1008

Professor John Wordsworth

5 May 2009

Outline. If you are required to submit an outline with your paper (make sure you know if your professor requires a topic or a sentence outline), center the title of your paper at the top, double space, and begin typing your outline (see Chapter Two for correct outline form).

First Page. If you include a title page, simply center your title at the top of this page, double space, and begin typing your paper, as follows:

Genetically Modified Food: The Future of Agriculture

Genetically modified food, known as GM food, has been sold in the United States for many years. However, the US cannot export GM food to Europe where it is known as "Frankenfood."

If you do **not** include a title page, put your name, the name of your professor, the class name, and the date at the top left-hand corner of the first page of your paper (within the one-inch margin), and double space it, as follows:

Amelia Goodstudent

Professor John Wordsworth

English 1301.11008

12 May 2009

Genetically Modified Food: The Future of Agriculture

Genetically modified food, known as GM food, has been sold in the United States for many years. However, the US cannot export

---

Works Cited Page. Simply center the words Works Cited at the top of this page, double space, and type your entries as noted under Citing Sources above.

Pagination. MLA says to number your pages in the upper right-hand corner of your paper one-half inch from the top and flush with the right margin. It also suggests that you include your last name with the page number, like this: Smith 5. Do not put a comma after your name or the word *page* or the abbreviation *p*. Most word processors will automatically paginate your paper.

Finally, if you are working in MS Word, save the title page, the outline, and the paper itself (including the Works Cited page) in **separate** files. Doing this will make it easier to paginate each section properly.

◆

CHECK LIST FOR THE RESEARCH PAPER

Did you:

1. Summarize and paraphrase correctly?
2. Integrate quotations correctly into your paper?
3. State a clear thesis?
4. Adequately develop that thesis?
5. Set up your Works Cited page correctly?
6. Make sure that the citations in your paper match the works on the Works Cited page?
7. Format your paper as required by your professor?
8. Include an outline and copies of sources if required?
9. Did you edit carefully, checking for major grammatical and spelling errors?

An example of a complete student research paper is included on page 230 of this text.

ON THE NET

Sources for Writing and Organizing Your Research Paper

Writing a Research Paper. Sarah Hamid. The OWL at Purdue.
<http://owl.english.purdue.edu/workshops/hypertext/ResearchW/>.

Organizing Research with Computers. Study Guides and Strategies.
<http://www.studygs.net/plagiarism.htm>.

Organizing Research: The Note Card System. Study Guides and Strategies.
<http://www.studygs.net/wrtstr5.htm>.

Three Ways to Organize Research
<http://newarkwww.rutgers.edu/guides/threeways.htm>.

How to Organize a Research Paper and Document It with MLA Citations. GeoCities.
<http://www.geocities.com/athens/Oracle/4184/>.

Model Papers. Sample student-written papers formatted in MLA, APA, and Chicago styles.
Diana Hacker. A Writer's Reference.
<http://bcs.bedfordstmartins.com/writersref6e/Player/Pages/Main.aspx>.

Documenting Sources

Documenting Sources. Diane Hacker.
    <http://www.dianahacker.com/resdoc/>.

MLA Formatting and Style Guide. Purdue OWL.
    <http://owl.english.purdue.edu/owl/resource/557/01/>.

A Guide for Writing Research Papers Based on Modern Language Association (MLA) Guidelines.
    Capital Community College.
    <http://www.ccc.commnet.edu/mla/index.shtml>.

*A Guide for Writing Research Papers Based on Styles Recommended by The American Psychological
    Association.* Capital Community College.
    <http://webster.commnet.edu/apa/>.

Chicago/Turabian Documentation. The Writing Center. The University of Wisconsin at Madison.
    <http://www.wisc.edu/writing/Handbook/DocChicago.html>.

Turabian Samples for a Bibliography. Ithaca College Library.
    <http://www.ithaca.edu/library/course/turabian.html>.

The Chicago Manual of Style Online, Fifteenth Edition.
    <http://www.chicagomanualofstyle.org/home.html>.

A Research and Reference Guide (MLA). Perspectives in American Literature. Appendix I.
    <http://www.csustan.edu/english/reuben/pal/append/AXI.HTML>.

MLA Style Citations. University of California, Berkeley.
    <http://www.lib.berkeley.edu/instruct/guides/mlastyle.pdf>.

MLA Documentation. Wilson College. PowerPoint.
    <http://www.wilson.edu/wilson/uploadedfiles/offices/academic_affairs/learning_
    resource_ctr/MLA Documentation(2).pdf>.

Assembling a List of Works Cited in Your Paper. Duke University Libraries.
    <http://library.duke.edu/research/citing/workscited/>.

MLA Works Cited Documentation. Studyguide.org.
    <http://www.studyguide.org/MLAdocumentation.htm>.

Create Your Works Cited.
    <workscited4you.com>.

Easy Bib: The Free AutomaticBibliography Composer. esaasybib.com.
    <http://www.easybib.com/>.

Exercises

I. Read the following passage:

"For thousands of years farmers have used a process of selection and cross breeding to continually improve the quality of crops. Even in nature, plants and animals selectively breed, thus ensuring the optimum gene pool for future generations. Traditional breeding methods are slow, requiring intensive labor: while trying to get a desirable trait in a bred species, undesirable traits will appear and breeders must continue the process over and over again until all the undesirables are bred out.

In contrast, organisms acquire one specific gene or a few genes together through genetic modification, without other traits included and within a single generation. However, this technology too is inherently unpredictable and some scientists believe it can produce potentially dangerous results unless better testing methods are developed."

Kerryn Sakko. "The Debate over Genetically Modified Foods." *ActionBioScience.org.* May 2002. Web. 2 Mar. 2009.

1. Write a summary of the above paragraphs. Do not exceed 75 words.

2. Using a proper method of introduction and quotation, integrate pertinent information from paragraph one into several sentences of your own.

II. Take the information given in each of the following and set up a proper Works Cited list:

1. **Article Title.** "Consumer acceptance and labeling of GMOs in food products: a study of fluid milk demand." **Authors.** Kristin Kiesel, David Buschena, Vincent Smith. **Book Title.** Consumer Acceptance of Genetically Modified Food. **Editors.** Robert E. Evenson and Vittorio Santaniello. **Copyright.** 2004. **Publisher.** CABIPub. **Place of Publication.** Wallingford, Oxon, UK. **Article Pagination.** 37-42.

2. **Article Title.** "Is GM food the future for Africa?" **Author.** Khadja Sharife. **Magazine Title.** New African. **Date.** January 2009. **Pages.** 8-13. **Data Base.** Academic Search Complete.

3. **Article Title.** "An Open Mind Wants More: Opinion Strength and the Desire for Genetically Modified Food Labeling Policy." **Authors.** Sonja Radas, Mario

F. Teisl, Brian Roe. **Journal Title.** Journal of Consumer Affairs. **Date.** Fall 2008. **Volume and Issue.** 42.3. **Pages.** 335-61. **Data Base.** Academic Search Complete.

4. **Article Title.** "Frankenfoods will save the world from starvation." **Author.** Melanie Peters. **Newspaper.** The Weekend Argus (South Africa). **Date.** October 5, 2008. **Pages.** 11. **Data Base.** InfoTrac Newspapers.

5. **Article Title.** How Do You Make a Transgenic Plant? **Author.** None Listed. **Web Site.** Transgenic Crops: An Introduction and Resource Guide. **Date.** March 11, 2004. **Sponsor.** Colorado State University. **Date Accessed.** March 9, 2009.

6. **Book Title.** *Issues and Dilemmas of Biotechnology: A Reference Guide.* **Author.** Bernice Schacter. **Publisher.** Greenwood Press. **Place of Publication.** Westport, Connecticut. **Copyright Date.** 1999.

III. Rewrite the following student paragraph and Works Cited page correcting the problems in quotation and citation:

A second argument for English-only laws is that Spanish will become the common language if we do nothing. The first problem with this argument is that most immigrant children learn English and forget their ancestors' tongue. For example, Ericka Mellon reports, "Researchers found...that third generation Americans are rarely fluent in their immigrant ancestors' native tongue." (A10) In addition, what is wrong with speaking Spanish? According to Michigan State University, English and Spanish have about the same number of speakers in the world. (1) Thus, there should be no problem with all of us speaking Spanish. Granted, certain things, such as the United States Constitution, which is written in English, might cause some problems, but if Spanish overcomes such barriers then it would prove to be a superior language, and we would be better off speaking it; if it is inferior to English, then it will not succeed, and the problem will go away.

Work Cited

Ericka Mellon. "Study Says English is Alive and Well" *Houston Chronicle.* 14 Aug.2006: A10

Michigan State University. "Spanish" Nov. 25, 2008

<https://www.msu.edu/user/saullost/spanish.htm>

PART III

FURTHER READINGS

PROFESSIONAL MODELS
(Expository Essays)

NONE OF THIS IS FAIR

Richard Rodriguez

My plan to become a professor of English—my ambition during long years in college at Stanford, then in graduate school at Columbia and Berkeley—was complicated by feelings of embarrassment and guilt. So many times I would see other Mexican-Americans and know we were alike only in race. And yet, simply because our race was the same, I was, during the last years of my schooling, the beneficiary of their situation. Affirmative Action programs had made it all possible. The disadvantages of others permitted my promotion; the absence of many Mexican-Americans from academic life allowed my designation as a "minority student."

For me opportunities had been extravagant. There were fellowships, summer research grants, and teaching assistantships. After only two years in graduate school, I was offered teaching jobs by several colleges. Invitations to Washington conferences arrived and I had the chance to travel abroad as a "Mexican-American representative." The benefits were often, however, too gaudy to please. In three published essays, in conversations with teachers, in letters to politicians and at conferences, I worried about the issue of Affirmative Action. Often I proposed contradictory opinions, though consistent was the admission that—because of an early, excellent education—I was no longer a principal victim of racism or any other social oppression. I said that but still I continued to indicate on applications for financial aid that I was a Hispanic-American. It didn't really occur to me to say anything else, or to leave the question unanswered.

Thus I complied with and encouraged the odd bureaucratic logic of Affirmative Action. I let government officials treat the disadvantaged condition of many Mexican-Americans with my advancement. Each fall my presence was noted by Health, Education, and Welfare department statisticians. As I pursued advanced literary studies and learned the skill of reading Spenser and Wordsworth and Empson, I would hear myself numbered among the culturally disadvantaged. Still, silent, I didn't object.

But the irony cut deep. And guilt would not be evaded by averting my glance when I confronted a face like my own in a crowd. By late 1975, nearing the completion of my graduate studies at Berkeley, I was so wary of the benefits of Affirmative Action that I feared my inevitable success as an applicant for a teaching position. The months of fall—traditionally that time of academic job-searching—passed without my applying to a single school. When one of my professors chanced to learn this in late November, he was astonished, then furious. He yelled at me: Did I think that because I was a minority student jobs would just come looking for me? What was I thinking? Did I realize that he and several other faculty members had already written letters on my behalf? Was

I going to start acting like some other minority students he had known? They struggled for success and then, when it was almost within reach, grew strangely afraid and let it pass. Was that it? Was I determined to fail?

I did not respond to his questions. I didn't want to admit to him, and thus to myself, the reason I delayed.

I merely agreed to write to several schools. (In my letter I wrote: "I cannot claim to represent disadvantaged Mexican-Americans. The very fact that I am in a position to apply for this job should make that clear.") After two or three days, there were telegrams and phone calls, invitations to interviews, then airplane trips. A blur of faces and the murmur of their soft questions. And, over someone's shoulder, the sight of campus buildings shadowing pictures I had seen years before when I leafed through Ivy League catalogues with great expectations. At the end of each visit, interviewers would smile and wonder if I had any questions. A few times I quietly wondered what advantage my race had given me over other applicants. But that was an impossible question for them to answer without embarrassing me. Quickly, several persons insisted that my ethnic identity had given me no more than a "foot inside the door"; at most, I had a "slight edge" over other applicants. "We just looked at your dossier with extra care and we like what we saw. There was never any question of having to alter our standards. You can be certain of that."

In the early part of January, offers arrived on stiffly elegant stationery. Most schools promised terms appropriate for any new assistant professor. A few made matters worse—and almost more tempting by offering more: the use of university housing; an unusually large starting salary; a reduced teaching schedule. As the stack of letters mounted, my hesitation increased. I started calling department chairmen to ask for another week, then 10 more days—"more time to reach a decision" – to avoid the decision I would need to make.

At school, meantime, some students hadn't received a single job offer. One man, probably the best student in the department, did not even get a request for his dossier. He and I met outside a classroom one day and he asked about my opportunities. He seemed happy for me. Faculty members beamed. They said they had expected it. "After all, not many schools are going to pass up getting a Chicano with a Ph.D. in Renaissance literature," somebody said laughing. Friends wanted to know which of the offers I was going to accept. But I couldn't make up my mind. February came and I was running out of time and excuses. (One chairman guessed my delay was a bargaining ploy and increased his offer with each of my calls.) I had to promise a decision by the 10th; the 12th at the very latest.

On the 18th of February, late in the afternoon, I was in the office I shared with several other teaching assistants. Another graduate student was sitting across the room at his desk. When I got up to leave, he looked over to say in an uneventful voice that he had some big news. He had finally decided to accept a position at a faraway university. It was not a job he especially wanted, he admitted. But he had to take it because there hadn't been any other offers. He felt trapped, and depressed, since his job would separate him from his young daughter.

I tried to encourage him by remarking that he was lucky at least to have found a job. So many others hadn't been able to get anything. But before I finished speaking I realized that I had said the wrong thing. And I anticipated his next question.

"What are your plans?" he wanted to know. "Is it true you've gotten an offer from Yale?" I said that it was. "Only, I still haven't made up my mind."

He stared at me as I put on my jacket. And smiling, then unsmiling, he asked if I knew that he too had written to Yale. In his case, however, no one had bothered to acknowledge his letter with even a postcard. What did I think of that?

He gave me no time to answer.

"Damn!" he said sharply and his chair rasped the floor as he pushed himself back. Suddenly, it was to me that he was complaining. "It's just not right, Richard. None of this is fair. You've done some good work, but so have I. I'll bet our records are just about equal. But when we look for jobs this year, it's a different story. You get all of the breaks."

To evade his criticism, I wanted to side with him. I was about to admit the injustice of Affirmative Action. But he went on, his voice hard with accusation. "It's all very simple this year. You're a Chicano. And I am a Jew. That's the only real difference between us."

His words stung me: there was nothing he was telling me that I didn't know. I had admitted everything already. But to hear someone else say these things, and in such an accusing tone, was suddenly hard to take. In a deceptively calm voice, I responded that he had simplified the whole issue. The phrases came like bubbles to the tip of my tongue: "new blood"; "the importance of cultural diversity"; "the goal of racial integration." These were all the arguments I had proposed several years ago—and had long since abandoned. Of course the offers were unjustifiable. I knew that. All I was saying amounted to a frantic self-defense. I tried to find an end to a sentence. My voice faltered to a stop.

"Yeah, sure," he said. "I've heard all that before. Nothing you say really changes the fact that Affirmative Action is unfair. You see that, don't you? There isn't any way for me to compete with you. Once there were quotas to keep my parents out of certain schools; now there are quotas to get you in and the effect on me is the same as it was for them."

I listened to every word he spoke. But my mind was really on something else. I knew at that moment that I would reject all of the offers. I stood there silently surprised by what an easy conclusion it was. Having prepared for so many years to teach, having trained myself to do nothing else, I had hesitated out of practical fear. But now that it was made, the decision came with relief. I immediately knew I had made the right choice.

My colleague continued talking and I realized that he was simply right. Affirmative Action programs *are* unfair to white students. But as I listened to him assert his rights, I thought of the seriously disadvantaged. How different they were from white, middle-class students who come armed with the testimony of their grades and aptitude scores and self-confidence to complain about the unequal treatment they now receive. I listen to them. I do not want to be careless about what they say. Their rights are important to protect. But inevitably when I hear them or their lawyers, I think about the most seriously disadvantaged, not simply Mexican-Americans, but of all those who do not ever imagine themselves going to college or becoming doctors: white, black, brown. Always poor. Silent. They are not plaintiffs before the court or against the misdirection of Affirmative Action. They lack the confidence (my confidence!) to assume their right to a good education. They lack the confidence and skills a good primary and secondary education provides and which are prerequisites for informed public life. They remain silent.

The debate drones on and surrounds them in stillness. They are distant, faraway figures like the boys I have seen peering down from freeway overpasses in some other part of town.

THE BROWN WASPS

Loren Eiseley

There is a corner in the waiting room of one of the great Eastern stations where women never sit. It is always in the shadow and overhung by rows of lockers. It is, however, always frequented—not so much by genuine travelers as by the dying. It is here that a certain element of the abandoned poor seeks a refuge out of the weather, clinging for a few hours longer to the city that has fathered them. In a precisely similar manner I have seen, on a sunny day in midwinter, a few old brown wasps creep slowly over an abandoned wasp nest in a thicket. Numbed and forgetful and frost-blackened, the hum of the spring hive still resounded faintly in their sodden tissues. Then the temperature would fall and they would drop away into the white oblivion of the snow. Here in the station it is in no way different save that the city is busy in its snows. But the old ones cling to their seats as though these were symbolic and could not be given up. Now and then they sleep, their gray old heads resting with painful awkwardness on the backs of the benches.

Also they are not at rest. For an hour they may sleep in the gasping exhaustion of the ill-nourished and aged who have to walk in the night. Then a policeman comes by on his round and nudges them upright.

"You can't sleep here," he growls.

A strange ritual then begins. An old man is difficult to waken. After a muttered conversation the policeman presses a coin into his hand and passes fiercely along the benches prodding and gesturing toward the door. In his wake, like birds rising and settling behind the passage of a farmer through a cornfield, the men totter up, move a few paces and subside once more upon the benches.

One man, after a slight, apologetic lurch, does not move at all. Tubercularly thin, he sleeps on steadily. The policeman does not look back. To him, too, this has become a ritual. He will not have to notice it again officially for another hour.

Once in a while one of the sleepers will not awake. Like the brown wasps, he will have had his wish to die in the great droning center of the hive rather than in some lonely room. It is not so bad here with the shuffle of footsteps and the knowledge that there are others who share the bad luck of the world. There are also the whistles and the sounds of everyone, everyone in the world, starting on journeys. Amidst so many journeys somebody is bound to come out all right. Somebody.

Maybe it was on a like thought that the brown wasps fell away from the old paper nest in the thicket. You hold till the last, even if it is only to a public seat in a railroad station. You want your place in the hive more than you want a room or a place where the aged can be eased gently out of the way. It is the place that matters, the place at the heart of things. It is life that you want, that bruises your gray old head with the hard chairs; a man has a right to his place.

But sometimes the place is lost in the years behind us. Or sometimes it is a thing of air, a kind of vaporous distortion above a heap of rubble. We cling to a time and place because without them man is lost, not only man but life. This is why the voices real or unreal, which speak from the floating trumpets at spiritualist séances, are so unnerving. They are voices out of nowhere whose only reality is in their ability to stir the memory of a living person with some fragment of the past. Before the medium's cabinet both the dead and the living revolve endlessly about an episode, a place, an event that has already been engulfed by time.

This feeling runs deep in life; it brings stray cats running over endless miles, and birds homing from the ends of the earth. It is as though all living creatures, and particularly the more intelligent, can survive only by fixing or transforming a bit of time into space or by securing a bit of space with its objects immortalized and made permanent in time. For example, I once saw, on a flower pot in my own living room, the efforts of a field mouse to build a remembered field. I have lived to see this episode repeated in a thousand guises, and since I have spent a large portion of my life in the shade of a nonexistent tree, I think I am entitled to speak for the field mouse.

One day as I cut across the field which at that time extended on one side of our suburban shopping center, I found a giant slug feeding from a runnel of pink ice cream in an abandoned Dixie cup. I could see his eyes telescope and protrude in a kind of dim, uncertain ecstasy as his dark body bunched and elongated in the curve of the cup. Then, as I stood there at the edge of the concrete, contemplating the slug, I began to realize it was like standing on a shore where a different type of life creeps up and fumbles tentatively among the rocks and sea wrack. It knows its place and will only creep so far until something changes. Little by little as I stood there I began to see more of this shore that surrounds the place of man. I looked with sudden care and attention at things I had been running over thoughtlessly for years. I even waded out a short way into the grass and the wild-rose thickets to see more. A huge black-belted bee went droning by and there were some indistinct scurryings in the underbrush.

Then I came to a sign which informed me that this field was to be the site of a new Wanamaker suburban store. Thousands of obscure lives were about to perish, the spores of puffballs would go smoking off to new fields, and the bodies of little white-footed mice would be crunched under the inexorable wheels of the bulldozers. Life disappears or modifies its appearances so fast that everything takes on an aspect of illusion—a momentary fizzing and boiling with smoke rings, like pouring dissident chemicals into a retort. Here man was advancing, but in a few years his plaster and bricks would be disappearing once more into the insatiable maw of the clover.

Being of an archaeological cast of mind, I thought of this fact with an obscure sense of satisfaction and waded back through the rose thickets to the concrete parking lot. As I did so, a mouse scurried ahead of me, frightened of my steps if not of that ominous Wanamaker sign. I saw him vanish in the general direction of my apartment house, his little body quivering with fear in the great open sun on the blazing concrete. Blinded and confused, he was running straight away from his field. In another week scores would follow him.

I forgot the episode then and went home to the quiet of my living room. It was not until a week later, letting myself into the apartment, that I realized I had a visitor. I am fond of plants and had several ferns standing on the floor in pots to avoid the noon glare by the south window.

As I snapped on the light and glanced carelessly around the room, I saw a little heap of earth on the carpet and a scrabble of pebbles that had been kicked merrily over the edge of one of the flower pots. To my astonishment I discovered a full-fledged burrow delving downward among the fern roots. I waited silently. The creature who had made the burrow did not appear. I remembered the wild field then, and the flight of the mice. No house mouse, no *Mus domesticus*, had kicked up this little heap of earth or sought refuge under a fern root in a flower pot. I thought of the desperate little creature I had seen fleeing from the wild-rose thicket. Through intricacies of pipes and attics, he, or one of his fellows, had climbed to this high green solitary room. I could visualize what had occurred. He had an image in his head, a world of seed pods and quiet, of green sheltering leaves in the dim light among the weed stems. It was the only world he knew and it was gone.

Somehow in his flight he had found his way to this room with drawn shades where no one would come till nightfall. And here he had smelled green leaves and run quickly up the flower pot to dabble his paws in common earth. He had even struggled half the afternoon to carry his burrow-deeper and had failed. I examined the hole, but no whiskered twitching face appeared. He was gone. I gathered up the earth and refilled the burrow. I did not expect to find traces of him again.

Yet for three nights thereafter I came home to the darkened room and my ferns to find the dirt kicked gaily about the rug and the burrow reopened, though I was never able to catch the field mouse within it. I dropped a little food about the mouth of the burrow, but it was never touched. I looked under beds or sat reading with one ear cocked for rustlings in the ferns. It was all in vain; I never saw him. Probably he ended in a trap in some other tenant's room.

But before he disappeared I had come to look hopefully for his evening burrow. About my ferns there had begun to linger the insubstantial vapor of an autumn field, the distilled essence, as it were, of a mouse brain in exile from its home. It was a small dream, like our dreams, carried a long and weary journey along pipes and through spider webs, past holes over which loomed the shadows of waiting cats, and finally, desperately, into this room where he had played in the shuttered daylight for an hour among the green ferns on the floor. Every day these invisible dreams pass us on the street, or rise from beneath our feet, or look out upon us from beneath a bush.

Some years ago the old elevated railway in Philadelphia was torn down and replaced by a subway system. This ancient El with its barnlike stations containing nut-vending machines and scattered food scraps had, for generations, been the favorite feeding ground of flocks of pigeons, generally one flock to a station along the route of the El. Hundreds of pigeons were dependent upon the system. They flapped in and out of its stanchions and steel work or gathered in watchful little audiences about the feet of anyone who rattled the peanut-vending machines. They even watched people who jingled change in their hands, and prospected for food under the feet of the crowds who gathered between trains. Probably very few among the waiting people who tossed a crumb to an eager pigeon realized that this El was like a food-bearing river, and that the life which haunted its banks was dependent upon the running of the trains with their human freight.

I saw the river stop.

The time came when the underground tubes were ready; the traffic was transferred to a realm unreachable by pigeons. It was like a great river sub-siding suddenly into desert sands. For a day, for two days, pigeons continued to circle over the El or stand close to the red vending machines. They were patient birds, and surely this great river which had flowed through the lives of unnumbered generations was merely suffering from some momentary drought. They listened for the familiar vibrations that had always heralded an approaching train; they flapped hopefully about the head of an occasional workman walking along the steel runways. They passed from one empty-station to another, all the while growing hungrier. Finally they flew away.

I thought I had seen the last of them about the El, but there was a revival and it provided a curious instance of the memory of living things for a way of life or a locality that has long been cherished. Some weeks after the El was abandoned workmen began to tear it down. I went to work every morning by one particular station, and the time came when the demolition crews readied this spot. Acetalene torches showered passersby with sparks, pneumatic drills hammered at the base of the structure, and a blind man who, like the pigeons, had clung with his cup to a stairway leading to the change booth, was forced to give up his place.

It was then, strangely, momentarily, one morning that I witnessed the return of a little band of the familiar pigeons. I even recognized one or two members of the flock that had lived around this particular station before they were dispersed into the streets. They flew bravely in and out among the sparks and the hammers and the shouting workmen. They had returned—and they had returned because the hubbub of the wreckers had convinced them that the river was about to flow once more. For several hours they flapped in and out through the empty windows, nodding their heads and watching the fall of girders with attentive little eyes. By the following morning the station was reduced to some burned-off stanchions in the street. My bird friends had gone. It was plain, however, that they retained a memory for an insubstantial structure now compounded of air and time. Even the blind man clung to it. Someone had provided him with a chair, and he sat at the same corner staring sightlessly at an invisible stairway where, so far as he was concerned, the crowds were still ascending to the trains.

I have said my life has been passed in the shade of a nonexistent tree, so that such sights do not offend me. Prematurely I am one of the brown wasps and I often sit with them in the great droning hive of the station, dreaming sometimes of a certain tree. It was planted sixty years ago by a boy with a bucket and a toy spade in a little Nebraska town. That boy was myself. It was a cottonwood sapling and the boy remembered it because of some words spoken by his father and because everyone died or moved away who was supposed to wait and grow old under its shade. The boy was passed from hand to hand, but the tree for some intangible reason had taken root in his mind. It was under its branches that he sheltered; it was from this tree that his memories, which are my memories, led away into the world.

After sixty-years the mood of the brown wasps grows heavier upon one. During a long inward struggle I thought it would do me good to go and look upon that actual tree. I found a rational excuse in which to clothe this madness. I purchased a ticket and at the end of two thousand miles I walked another mile to an address that was still the same. The house had not been altered.

I came close to the white picket fence and reluctantly, with great effort, looked down the long vista of the yard. There was nothing there to see. For sixty years that cottonwood had been growing in my mind. Season by season its seeds had been floating farther on the hot prairie winds. We had planted it lovingly there, my father and I, because he had a great hunger for soil and live things growing, and because none of these things had long been ours to protect. We had planted the little sapling and watered it faithfully, and I remembered that I had run out with my small bucket to drench its roots the day we moved away. And all the years since it had been growing in my mind, a huge tree that somehow stood for my father and the love I bore him. I took a grasp on the picket fence and forced myself to look again.

A boy with the hard bird eye of youth pedaled a tricycle slowly up beside me.

"What'cha lookin' at?" he asked curiously.

"A tree," I said.

"What for?" he said.

"It isn't there," I said, to myself mostly, and began to walk away at a pace just slow enough not to seem to be running.

"What isn't there?" the boy asked. I didn't answer. It was obvious I was attached by a thread to a thing that had never been there, or certainly not for long. Something that had to be held in the air, or sustained in the mind, because it was part of my orientation in the universe and I could not survive without it. There was more than an animal's attachment to a place. There was something else, the attachment of the spirit to a grouping of events in time; it was part of our mortality.

So I had come home at last, driven by a memory in the brain as surely as the field mouse who had delved long ago into my flower pot or the pigeons flying forever amidst the rattle of nut-vending machines. These, the burrow under the greenery in my living room and the red-bellied bowls of peanuts now hovering in midair in the minds of pigeons, were all part of an elusive world that existed nowhere and yet everywhere. I looked once at the real world about me while the persistent boy pedaled at my heels.

It was without meaning, though my feet took a remembered path. In sixty years the house and street had rotted out of my mind. But the tree, the tree that no longer was, that had perished in its first season, bloomed on in my individual mind, unblemished as my father's words. "We'll plant a tree here, son, and we're not going to move any more. And when you're an old, old man you can sit under it and think how we planted it here, you and me, together."

I began to outpace the boy on the tricycle.

"Do you live here, Mister?" he shouted after me suspiciously. I took a firm grasp on airy nothing—to be precise, on the bole of a great tree. "I do," I said. I spoke for myself, one field mouse, and several pigeons. We were all out of touch but somehow permanent. It was the world that had changed.

OF YOUTH AND AGE

Francis Bacon

A man that is young in years may be old in hours, if he have lost no time. But that happeneth rarely. Generally, youth is like the first cogitations, not so wise as the second. For there is a youth in thoughts as well as in ages. And yet the invention of young men is more lively than that of old, and imaginations stream into their minds better, and as it were more divinely. Natures that have much heat, and great and violent desires and perturbations, are not ripe for action till they have passed the meridian of their years: as it was with Julius Caesar, and Septimius Severus. Of the latter of whom it is said, *Juventutem egit erroribus, imo furoribus, plenam* ["He passed a youth full of folly, or rather of madness," —Spartianus *(Life of Severus)*]; and yet he was the ablest emperor, almost, of all the list. But reposed natures may do well in youth. As it is seen in Augustus Caesar, Cosmus, Duke of Florence, Gaston de Foix, and others. On the other side, heat and vivacity in age is an excellent composition for business. Young men are fitter to invent than to judge, fitter for execution than for counsel, and fitter for new projects than for settled business. For the experience of age, in things that fall within the compass of it, directeth them, but in new things abuseth them. The errors of young men are the ruin of business; but the errors of aged men amount but to this, that more might have been done, or sooner. Young men, in the conduct and manage of actions, embrace more than they can hold; stir more than they can quiet; fly to the end, without consideration of the means and degrees; pursue some few principles which they have chanced upon absurdly; care not to innovate, which draws unknown inconveniences; use extreme remedies at first; and, that which doubleth all errors, will not acknowledge or retract them; like an unready horse that will neither stop nor turn. Men of age object too much, consult too long, adventure too little, repent too soon, and seldom drive business home to the full period, but content themselves with a mediocrity of success. Certainly it is good to compound employments of both, for that will be good for the present, because the virtues of either age may correct the defects of both; and good for succession, that young men may be learners while men in age are actors; and, lastly, good for extern accidents, because authority followeth old men, and favour and popularity youth. But for the moral part, perhaps youth will have the pre-eminence, as age hath for the politic. A Certain rabbin, upon the text, Your young men shall see visions, and your old men shall dream dreams [Joel 2:28], inferreth that young men are admitted nearer to God than old, because vision is a clearer revelation than a dream. And certainly, the more a man drinketh of the world, the more it intoxicateth; and age doth profit rather in the powers of understanding than in the virtues of the will and affections. There be some have an over-early ripeness in their years, which fadeth betimes. These are, first, such as have brittle wits, and edge whereof is soon turned; such as was Hermogenes the rhetorician, whose books are exceeding subtle, who afterwards waxed stupid. A second sort is of those that have some natural dispositions which have better grace in youth than in age, such as is a fluent and luxuriant speech, which becomes youth well, but not age: so Tully saith of Hortensius, *Idem manebat, neque idem docebat* ["He remained the same when the same style no longer became him" (Cicero, *Brutus*)]. The third is of such as take too high a strain at the first, and are magnanimous more than tract of years can uphold. As was Scipio Africanus, of whom Livy saith in effect, *Ultima primis cedebant* ["His last actions were not the equal of his first" (Heroides 9)].

GRANT AND LEE: A STUDY IN CONTRAST

Bruce Catton

When Ulysses S. Grant and Robert E. Lee met in the parlor of a modest house at Appomattox Court House, Virginia, on April 9, 1865, to work out the terms for the surrender of Lee's Army of Northern Virginia, a great chapter in American life came to a close, and a great new chapter began.

These men were bringing the Civil War to its virtual finish. To be sure, other armies had yet to surrender, and for a few days the fugitive Confederate government would struggle desperately and vainly, trying to find some way to go on living now that its chief support was gone. But in effect it was all over when Grant and Lee signed the papers, and the little room where they wrote out the terms was the scene of one of the poignant, dramatic contrasts in American History.

They were two strong men, these oddly different generals, and they represented the strengths of two conflicting currents that, through them, had come into final collision.

Back of Robert E. Lee was the notion that the old aristocratic concept might somehow survive and be dominant in American life.

Lee was tidewater Virginia, and in his background were family, culture, and tradition … the age of chivalry transplanted to a New World which was making its own legends and its own myths. He embodied a way of life that had come down through the age of knighthood and the English country squire. America was a land that was beginning all over again, dedicated to nothing much more complicated than the rather hazy belief that all men had equal rights and should have an equal chance in the world. In such a land Lee stood for the feeling that it was somehow of advantage to human society to have a pronounced inequality in the social structure. There should be a leisure class, backed by ownership of land; in turn, society itself should be keyed to the land as the chief source of wealth and influence. It would bring forth (according to this ideal) a class of men with a strong sense of obligation to the community; men who lived not to gain advantage for themselves, but to meet the solemn obligations which had been laid on them by the very fact that they were privileged. From them the country would get its leadership; to them it could look for the higher values—of thought, of conduct, or personal deportment—to give it strength and virtue.

Lee embodied the noblest elements of this aristocratic ideal. Through him, the landed nobility justified itself. For four years, the Southern states had fought a desperate war to uphold the ideals for which Lee stood. In the end, it almost seemed as if the Confederacy fought for Lee; as if he himself was the Confederacy. . .the best thing that the way of life for which the confederacy stood could ever have to offer. He had passed into legend before Appomattox. Thousands of tired, underfed, poorly clothed Confederate soldiers, long since past the simple enthusiasm of the early days of the struggle, somehow considered Lee the symbol of everything for which they had been willing to die. But they could not quite put this feeling into words. If the Lost Cause, sanctified by so much heroism and so many deaths, had a living justification, its justification was General Lee.

Grant, the son of a tanner on the Western frontier, was everything Lee was not. He had come up the hard way and embodied nothing in particular except the eternal toughness and sinewy fiber of the men who grew up beyond the mountains. He was one of a body of men who owed reverence and obeisance to no one, who were self-reliant to a fault, who cared hardly anything for the past but who had a sharp eye for the future.

These frontier men were the precise opposites of the tidewater aristocrats. Back of them in the great surge that had taken people over the Alleghenies and into the opening Western country, there was a deep, implicit dissatisfaction with a past that had settled into grooves. They stood for democracy, not from any reasoned conclusion about the proper ordering of human society, but simply because they had grown up in the middle of democracy and knew how it worked. Their society might have privileges, but they would be privileges each man had won for himself. Forms and patterns meant nothing. No man was born to anything, except perhaps to a chance to show how far he could rise. Life was competition.

Yet along with this feeling had come a deep sense of belonging to a national community. The Westerner who developed a farm, opened a shop, or set up in business as a trader could hope to prosper only as his own community prospered—and this community ran from the Atlantic to the Pacific and from Canada down to Mexico. If the land was settled, with towns and highways and accessible markets, he could better himself. He saw his fate in terms of the nation's own destiny. As its horizons expanded, so did his. He had, in other words, an acute dollars-and-cents stake in the continued growth and development of his country.

And that, perhaps, is where the contrast between Grant and Lee becomes most striking. The Virginia aristocrat, inevitably, saw himself in relation to his own region. He lived in a static society which could endure almost anything except change. Instinctively, his first loyalty would go to the locality in which that society existed. He would fight to the limit of endurance to defend it, because in defending it he was defending everything that gave his own life its deepest meaning.

The Westerner, on the other hand, would fight with an equal tenacity for the broader concept of society. He fought so because everything he lived by was tied to growth, expansion, and a constantly widening horizon. What he lived by would survive or fall with the nation itself. He could not possibly stand by unmoved in the face of an attempt to destroy the Union. He would combat it with everything he had, because he could only see it as an effort to cut the ground out from under his feet.

So Grant and Lee were in complete contrast, representing two diametrically opposed elements in American life. Grant was the modern man emerging; beyond him, ready to come on the stage, was the great age of steel and machinery, of crowded cities and restless burgeoning vitality. Lee might have ridden down from the old age of chivalry, lance in hand, silken banner fluttering over his head. Each man was the perfect champion of his cause, drawing both his strengths and his weaknesses from the people he led.

Yet it was not all contrast, after all. Different as they were—in background, in personality, in underlying aspiration—these two great soldiers had much in common. Under everything else, they were marvelous fighters. Furthermore, their fighting qualities were really very much alike.

Each man had, to begin with, the great virtue of utter tenacity and fidelity. Grant fought his way down the Mississippi Valley in spite of acute personal discouragements and profound military handicaps. Lee hung on in the trenches at Petersburg after hope itself had died. In each man there was an indomitable quality ... the born fighter's refusal to give up as long as he can still remain on his feet and lift his two fists.

Daring and resourcefulness they had, too: the ability to think faster and move faster than the enemy. These were the qualities which gave Lee the dazzling campaigns of Second Manassas and Chancellorsville and won Vicksburg for Grant.

Lastly, and perhaps greatest of all, there was the ability, at the end, to turn quickly from war to peace once the fighting was over. Out of the way these two men behaved at Appomattox came the possibility of a peace of reconciliation. It was a possibility not wholly realized, in the years to come, but which did, in the end, help the two sections to become one nation again ... after a war whose bitterness might have seemed to make such a reunion wholly impossible. No part of either man's life became him more than the part he played in their brief meeting in the McLean house at Appomattox. Their behavior there put all succeeding generations of Americans in their debt. Two great Americans, Grant and Lee—very different, yet under everything very much alike. Their encounter at Appomattox was one of the great moments of American History.

DIOGENES AND ALEXANDER

Gilbert Highet

Lying on the bare earth, shoeless, bearded, half-naked, he looked like a beggar or a lunatic. He was one, but not the other. He had opened his eyes with the sun at dawn, scratched, done his business like a dog at the roadside, washed at the public fountain, begged a piece of breakfast bread and a few olives, eaten them squatting on the ground, and washed them down with a few handfuls of water scooped from the spring. (Long ago he had owned a rough wooden cup, but he threw it away when he saw a boy drinking out of his hollowed hands.) Having no work to go to and no family to provide for, he was free. As the market place filled up with shoppers and merchants and gossipers and sharpers and slaves and foreigners, he had strolled through it for an hour or two. Everybody knew him, or knew of him. They would throw sharp questions at him and get sharper answers. Sometimes they threw jeers, and got jibes; sometimes bits of food, and got scant thanks; sometimes a mischievous pebble, and got a shower of stones and abuse. They were not quite sure whether he was mad or not. He knew they were mad, each in a different way; they amused him. Now he was back at his home.

It was not a house, not even a squatter's hut. He thought everybody lived far too elaborately, expensively, anxiously. What good is a house? No one needs privacy; natural acts are not shameful; we all do the same things, and need not hide them. No one needs beds and chairs and such furniture: the animals live healthy lives and sleep on the ground. All we require, since nature did not dress us properly, is one garment to keep us warm, and some shelter from rain and wind. So he had one blanket—to dress him in the daytime and cover him at night—and he slept in a cask. His name was Diogenes. He was the founder of the creed called Cynicism (the word means "doggishness"); he spent much of his life in the rich, lazy, corrupt Greek city of Corinth, mocking and satirizing its people, and occasionally converting one of them.

His home was not a barrel made of wood: too expensive. It was a storage jar made of earthenware, something like a modern fuel tank—no doubt discarded because a break had made it useless. He was not the first to inhabit such a thing: the refugees driven into Athens by the Spartan invasion had been forced to sleep in casks. But he was the first who ever did so by choice, out of principle.

Diogenes was not a degenerate or a maniac. He was a philosopher who wrote plays and poems and essays expounding his doctrine; he talked to those who cared to listen; he had pupils who admired him. But he taught chiefly by example. All should live naturally, he said, for what is natural is normal and cannot possibly be evil or shameful. Live without conventions, which are artificial and false; escape complexities and superfluities and extravagances: only so can you live a free life. The rich man believes he possesses his big house with its many rooms and its elaborate furniture, his pictures and his expensive clothes, his horses and his servants and his bank accounts. He does not. He depends on them, he worries about them, he spends most of his life's energy looking after them; the thought of losing them makes him sick with anxiety. They possess him. He is their slave. In order to produce a quantity of false, perishable goods he has sold the only true, lasting good, his own independence.

There have been many men who grew tired of human society with its complications, and went away to live simply—on a small farm, in a quiet village, in a hermit's cave, or in the darkness of anonymity. Not so Diogenes. He was a not a recluse, or a stylite, or a beatnik. He was a missionary. His life's aim was clear to him: it was "to restamp the currency." (He and his father had once been convicted for counterfeiting, long before he turned to philosophy, and this phrase was Diogenes's bold, unembarrassed joke on the subject.) To restamp the currency: to take the clean metal of human life, to erase the old false conventional markings, and to imprint it with its true values.

The other great philosophers of the fourth century before Christ taught mainly their own private pupils. In the shady groves and cool sanctuaries of the Academy, Plato discoursed to a chosen few on the unreality of this contingent existence. Aristotle, among the books and instruments and specimens and archives and research-workers of his Lyceum, pursued investigations and gave lectures that were rightly named *esoteric* "for those within the walls." But for Diogenes, laboratory and specimens and lecture halls and pupils were all to be found in a crowd of ordinary people. Therefore he chose to live in Athens or in the rich city of Corinth, where travelers from all over the Mediterranean world constantly came and went. And, by design, he publicly behaved in such ways as to show people what real life was. He would constantly take up their spiritual coin, ring it on a stone, and laugh at its false superscription.

He thought most people were only half-alive, most men only half-men. At bright noonday he walked through the market place carrying a lighted lamp and inspecting the face of everyone he met. They asked him why. Diogenes answered, "I am trying to find a man."

To a gentleman whose servant was putting on his shoes for him, Diogenes said, "You won't be really happy until he wipes your nose for you: that will come after you lose the use of your hands."

Once there was a war scare so serious that it stirred even the lazy, profit-happy Corinthians. They began to drill, clean their weapons, and rebuild their neglected fortifications. Diogenes took his old cask and began to roll it up and down, back and forward. "When you are all so busy," he said, "I feel I ought to do *something!*"

And so he lived—like a dog, some said, because he cared nothing for privacy and other human conventions, and because he showed his teeth and barked at those whom he disliked. Now he was lying in the sunlight, as contented as a dog on the warm ground, happier (he himself used to boast) than the Shah of Persia. Although he knew he was going to have an important visitor, he would not move.

The little square began to fill with people. Page boys elegantly dressed, spearmen speaking a rough foreign dialect, discreet secretaries, hard-browed officers, suave diplomats, they all gradually formed a circle centered on Diogenes. He looked them over, as a sober man looks at a crowd of tottering drunks, and shook his head. He knew who they were. They were the attendants of the conqueror of Greece, the servants of Alexander, the Macedonian king, who was visiting his newly subdued realm.

Only twenty, Alexander was far older and wiser than his years. Like all Macedonians he loved drinking, but he could usually handle it; and toward women he was nobly restrained and chivalrous. Like Macedonians he loved fighting; he was a magnificent commander, but he was not merely a military automaton. He could think. At thirteen he had become a pupil of the greatest mind in Greece, Aristotle. No exact record of his schooling survives. It is clear, though, that Aristotle took the passionate, half-barbarous boy and gave him the best of Greek culture. He taught Alexander poetry: the young prince slept with the *Iliad* under his pillow and longed to emulate Achilles, who brought the mighty power of Asia to ruin. He taught him philosophy, in particular the shapes and uses of political power: a few years later Alexander was to create a supranational empire that was not merely a power system but a vehicle for the exchange of Greek and Middle Eastern cultures.

Aristotle taught him the principles of scientific research: during his invasion of the Persian domains Alexander took with him a large corps of scientists, and shipped hundreds of zoological specimens back to Greece for study. Indeed, it was from Aristotle that Alexander learned to seek out everything strange which might be instructive. Jugglers and stunt artists and virtuosos of the absurd he dismissed with a shrug; but on reaching India he was to spend hours discussing the problems of life and death with naked Hindu mystics, and later to see one demonstrate Yoga self-command by burning himself impassively to death.

Now, Alexander was in Corinth to take command of the League of Greek States which, after conquering them, his father Philip had created as a disguise for the New Macedonian Order. He was welcomed and honored and flattered. He was the man of the hour, of the century: he was unanimously appointed commander-in-chief of a new expedition against old, rich, corrupt Asia. Nearly everyone crowded to Corinth in order to congratulate him, to seek employment with him, even simply to see him: soldiers and statesmen, artists and merchants, poets and philosophers. He received their compliments graciously. Only Diogenes, although he lived in Corinth, did not visit the new monarch. With that generosity which Aristotle had taught him was a quality of the truly magnanimous man, Alexander determined to call upon Diogenes. Surely Diogenes, the God-born, would acknowledge the conqueror's power by some gift of hoarded wisdom.

With his handsome face, his fiery glance, his strong supple body, his purple and gold cloak, and his air of destiny, he moved through the parting crowd, toward the Dog's kennel. When a king approaches, all rise in respect. Diogenes did not rise, he merely sat up on one elbow. When a monarch enters a precinct, all greet him with a bow or an acclamation. Diogenes said nothing.

There was a silence. Some years later Alexander speared his best friend to the wall, for objecting to the exaggerated honors paid to His Majesty; but now he was still young and civil. He spoke first, with a kindly greeting. Looking at the poor broken cask, the single ragged garment, and the rough figure lying on the ground, he said: "Is there anything I can do for you, Diogenes?"

"Yes," said the Dog. "Stand to one side. You're blocking the sunlight."

There was silence, not the ominous silence preceding a burst of fury, but a hush of amazement. Slowly, Alexander turned away. A titter broke out from the elegant Greeks, who were already beginning to make jokes about the cur that looked at the King. The Macedonian officers, after deciding that Diogenes was not worth the trouble of kicking, were starting to guffaw and nudge one another. Alexander was still silent. To those nearest him he said quietly, "If I were not Alexander, I should be Diogenes." They took it as a paradox, designed to close the awkward little scene with a polite curtain line. But Alexander meant it. He understood cynicism as the others could not. Later he took one of Diogenes's pupils with him to India as a philosophical interpreter (it was he who spoke to the naked *saddhus*). He was what Diogenes called himself, a *cosmopolites*, "citizen of the world." Like Diogenes, he admired the heroic figure of Hercules, the mighty conqueror who labors to help mankind while all others toil and sweat only for themselves. He knew that of all men then alive in the world only Alexander the conqueror and Diogenes the beggar were truly free.

WHY WE FALL IN LOVE

M. Scott Peck

Of all the misconceptions about love the most powerful and pervasive is the belief that "falling in love" is love or at least one of the manifestations of love. It is a potent misconception because falling in love is subjectively experienced in a very powerful fashion as an experience of love. When a person falls in love what he or she certainly feels is "I love him" or "I love her," but two problems are immediately apparent. The first is that the experience of falling in love is specifically a sex-linked erotic experience. We do not fall in love with our children though we may love them very deeply. We do not fall in love with our friends of the same sex—unless we are homosexually oriented—even though we may care for them greatly. We fall in love only when we are consciously or unconsciously sexually motivated. The second problem is that the experience of falling in love is invariably temporary. No matter whom we fall in love with, we sooner or later fall out of love if the relationship continues long enough. This is not to say that we invariably cease loving the person with whom we fell in love. But it is to say that the feeling of ecstatic lovingness that characterizes the experience of falling in love always passes. The honeymoon always ends. The bloom of romance always fades.

To understand the nature of the phenomenon of falling in love and the inevitability of its ending, it is necessary to examine the nature of what psychiatrists call ego boundaries. From what we can ascertain by indirect evidence, it appears that the newborn infant during the first few months of its life does not distinguish between itself and the rest of the universe. When it moves its arms and legs, the world is moving. When it is hungry, the world is hungry. When it sees its mother move, it is as if it is moving. When its mother sings, the baby does not know that it is itself not making the sound. It cannot distinguish itself from the crib, the room and its parents. The animate and inanimate are the same. There is no distinction yet between I and thou. It and the world are one. There are no boundaries, no separations. There is no identity.

But with experience the child begins to experience itself—namely, as an entity separate from the rest of the world. When it is hungry, mother doesn't always appear to feed it. When it is playful, mother doesn't always want to play. The child then has the experience of its wishes not being its mother's command. Its will is experienced as something separate from its mother's behavior. A sense of the "me" begins to develop. This interaction between the infant and the mother is believed to be the ground out of which the child's sense of identity begins to grow. When there is no mother, no satisfactory mother substitute or when because of her own mental illness the mother is totally uncaring or uninterested—then the infant grows into a child or adult whose sense of identity is grossly defective in the most basic ways.

As the infant recognizes its will to be its own and not that of the universe, it begins to make other distinctions between itself and the world. When it wills movement, its arm waves before its eyes, but neither the crib nor the ceiling move. Thus the child learns that its arm and its will are connected, and therefore that its arm is its and not something or someone else's. In this manner, during the first year of life, we learn the fundamentals of who we are and who we are not, what we are and what we are not. By the end of our first year we know that this is my arm, my foot, my head, my tongue, my eyes and even my viewpoint, my voice, my thoughts, my stomachache, and my feelings. We know our size and our physical limits. These limits are our boundaries. The knowledge of these limits inside our minds is what is meant by ego boundaries.

The development of ego boundaries is a process that continues through childhood into adolescence and even into adulthood, but the boundaries established later are more psychic than physical. For instance, the age between two and three is typically a time when the child comes to terms with the limits of its power. While before this time the child has learned that its wish is not necessarily its mother's command, it still clings to the possibility that its wish might be its mother's command and the feeling that its wish would be her command. It is because of this hope and feeling that the two-year-old usually attempts to act like a tyrant and autocrat, trying to give orders to its parents, siblings and family pets as if they were menials in its own private army, and responds with regal fury when they won't be dictated to. Thus parents speak of this age as "the terrible twos." By the age of three the child has usually become more tractable and mellow as a result of an acceptance of the reality of its own relative powerlessness. Still, the possibility of omnipotence is such a sweet, sweet dream that it cannot be completely given up even after several years of very painful confrontation with one's own impotence. Although the child of three has come to accept the reality of the boundaries of its power, it will continue to escape occasionally for some years to come into a world of fantasy in which the possibility of omnipotence (particularly its own) still exists. This is the world of Superman and Captain Marvel. Yet gradually even the superheroes are given up, and by the time of mid-adolescence, young people know that they are individuals, confined to the boundaries of their flesh and the limits of their power, each one a relatively frail and impotent organism, existing only by cooperation within a group of fellow organisms called society. Within this group they are not particularly distinguished, yet they are isolated from others by their individuals identities, boundaries and limits.

It is lonely behind these boundaries. Some people—particularly those whom psychiatrists call schizoid—because of unpleasant, traumatizing experiences in childhood, perceive the world outside of themselves as unredeemably dangerous, hostile, confusing and un-nurturing. Such people feel their boundaries to be protecting and comforting and find a sense of safety in their loneliness. But most of us feel our loneliness to be painful and yearn to escape from behind the walls of our individual identities to a condition in which we can be more unified with the world outside of ourselves. The experience of falling in love allows us this escape—temporarily. The essence of the phenomenon of falling in love is a sudden collapse of a section of an individual's ego boundaries, permitting one to merge his or her identity with that of another person. The sudden release of oneself from oneself, the explosive pouring out of oneself into the beloved, and the dramatic surcease of loneliness accompanying this collapse of ego boundaries is experienced by most of us as ecstatic. We and our beloved are one! Loneliness is no more!

In some respects (but certainly not in all) the act of falling in love is an act of regression. The experience of merging with the loved one has in it echoes from the time when we were merged with our mothers in infancy. Along with the merging we also re-experience the sense of omnipotence which we had to give up in our journey out of childhood. All things seem possible! United with our beloved we feel we can conquer all obstacles. We believe that the strength of our love will cause the forces of opposition to bow down in submission and melt away into the darkness. All problems will be overcome. The future will be all light. The unreality of these feelings when we have fallen in love is essentially the same as the unreality of the two-year-old who feels itself to be king of the family and the world with power unlimited.

Just as reality intrudes upon the two-year-old's fantasy of omnipotence so does reality intrude upon the fantastic unity of the couple who have fallen in love. Sooner or later, in response to the problems of daily living, individual will reasserts itself. He wants to have sex; she doesn't. She wants to go to the movies; he doesn't. He wants to put money in the bank; she wants a dishwasher. She wants to talk about her job; he wants to talk about his. She doesn't like his friends; he doesn't like hers. So both of them, in the privacy of their hearts, begin to come to the sickening realization that they are not one with the beloved, that the beloved has and will continue to have his or her own desires, tastes, prejudices and timing different from the other's. One by one, gradually or suddenly, the ego boundaries snap back into place; gradually or suddenly, they fall out of love. Once again they are two separate individuals. At this point they begin either to dissolve the ties of their relationship or to initiate the work of real loving.

By my use of the word "real" I am implying that the perception that we are loving when we fall in love is a false perception—that our subjective sense of lovingness is an illusion. Full elaboration of real love will be deferred until later in this section. However, by stating that it is when a couple falls out of love they may begin to really love I am also implying that real love does not have its roots in a feeling of love. To the contrary, real love often occurs in a context in which the feeling of love is lacking, when we act lovingly despite the fact that we don't feel loving. Assuming the reality of the definition of love with which we started, the experience of "falling in love" is not real love for the several reasons that follow.

Falling in love is not an act of will. It is not a conscious choice. No matter how open to or eager for it we may be, the experience may still elude us. Contrarily, the experience may capture us at times when we are definitely not seeking it, when it is inconvenient and undesirable. We are as likely to fall in love with someone with whom we are obviously ill matched as with someone more suitable. Indeed, we may not even like or admire the object of our passion, yet, try as we might, we may not be able to fall in love with a person whom we deeply respect and with whom a deep relationship would be in all ways desirable. This is not to say that the experience of falling in love is immune to discipline. Psychiatrists, for instance, frequently fall in love with their patients, just as their patients fall in love with them, yet out of duty to the patient and their role they are usually able to abort the collapse of their ego boundaries and give up the patient as a romantic object. The struggle and suffering of the discipline involved may be enormous. But discipline and will can only control the experience; they cannot create it. We can choose how to respond to the experience of falling in love, but we cannot choose the experience itself.

Falling in love is not an extension of one's limits or boundaries; it is a partial and temporary collapse of them. The extension of one's limits requires effort; falling in love is effortless. Lazy and undisciplined individuals are as likely to fall in love as energetic and dedicated ones. Once the precious moment of falling in love has passed and the boundaries have snapped back into place, the individual may be disillusioned, but is usually none the larger for the experience. When limits are extended or stretched, however, they tend to stay stretched. Real love is a permanently self-enlarging experience. Falling in love is not.

Falling in love has little to do with purposively nurturing one's spiritual development. If we have any purpose in mind when we fall in love it is to terminate our own loneliness and perhaps insure this result through marriage. Certainly we are not thinking of spiritual development. To the contrary, we perceive him or her as perfect, as having been perfected. If we see any faults in our beloved, we perceive them as insignificant—little quirks or darling eccentricities that only add color and charm.

If falling in love is not love, then what is it other than temporary and partial collapse of ego boundaries? I do not know, but the sexual specificity of the phenomenon leads me to suspect that it is a genetically determined instinctual component of mating behavior. In other words, the temporary collapse of ego boundaries that constitutes falling in love is a stereotypic response of human beings to a configuration of internal sexual drives and external sexual stimuli, which serves to increase the probability of sexual pairing and bonding so as to enhance the survival of the species. Or to put it in another, rather crass way, falling in love is a trick that our genes pull on our otherwise perceptive mind to hoodwink or trap us into marriage. Frequently the trick goes awry one way or another, as when the sexual drives and stimuli are homosexual or when other forces—parental interference, mental illness, conflicting responsibilities or mature self-discipline—supervene to prevent the bonding. On the other hand, without this trick, this illusory and inevitably temporary (it would not be practical were it not temporary) regression to infantile merging and omnipotence, many of us who are happily or unhappily married today would have retreated in wholehearted terror from the realism of the marriage vows.

WHO KILLED BENNY PARET?

Norman Cousins

Sometime about 1935 or 1936 I had an interview with Mike Jacobs, the prize-fight promoter. I was a fledgling newspaper reporter at that time; my beat was education, but during the vacation season I found myself on varied assignments, all the way from ship news to sports reporting. In this way I found myself sitting opposite the most powerful figure in the boxing world.

There was nothing spectacular in Mr. Jacobs's manner or appearance, but when he spoke about prizefights, he was no longer a bland little man but a colossus who sounded the way Napoleon must have sounded when he reviewed a battle. You knew you were listening to Number One. His saying something made it true.

We discussed what to him was the only important element in successful promotion—how to please the crowd. So far as he was concerned, there was no mystery to it. You put killers in the ring and the people filled your arena. You hire boxing artists—men who are adroit at feinting, parrying, weaving, jabbing, and dancing, but who don't pack dynamite in their fists—and you wind up counting your empty seats. So you searched for the killers and sluggers and maulers—fellows who could hit with the force of a baseball bat.

I asked Mr. Jacobs if he was speaking literally when he said people came out to see the killer.

"They don't come out to see a tea party," he said evenly. "They come out to see the knockout. They come out to see a man hurt. If they think anything else, they're kidding themselves."

Recently a young man by the name of Benny Paret was killed in the ring. The killing was seen by millions; it was on television. In the twelfth round he was hit hard in the head several times, went down, was counted out, and never came out of the coma.

The Paret fight produced a flurry of investigations. Governor Rockefeller was shocked by what happened and appointed a committee to assess the responsibility. The New York State Boxing Commission decided to find out what was wrong. The District Attorney's office expressed its concern. One question that was solemnly studied in all three probes concerned the action of the referee. Did he act in time to stop the fight? Another question had to do with role of the examining doctors who certified the physical fitness of the fighters before the bout. Still another question involved Mr. Paret's manager; did he rush his boy into the fight without adequate time to recuperate from the previous one?

In short, the investigators looked into every possible cause except the real one. Benny Paret was killed because the human fist delivers enough impact, when directed against the head, to produce a massive hemorrhage in the brain. The human brain is the most delicate and complex mechanism in all creation. It has a lacework of millions of highly fragile nerve connections. Nature attempts to protect this exquisitely intricate machinery by encasing it in a hard shell. Fortunately, the shell is thick enough to withstand a great deal of pounding. Nature, however, can protect man against everything except man himself. Not every blow to the head will kill a man—but there is always the risk of concussion and damage to the brain. A prizefighter may be able to survive even repeated brain concussions and go on fighting, but the damage to his brain may be permanent.

In any event, it is futile to investigate the referee's role and seek to determine whether he should have intervened to stop the fight earlier. This is not where the primary responsibility lies. The primary responsibility lies with the people who pay to see a man hurt. The referee who stops a fight too soon from the crowd's viewpoint can expect to be booed. The crowd wants the knockout; it wants to see a man stretched out on the canvas. This is the supreme moment in boxing. It is nonsense to talk about prize fighting as a test of boxing skills. No crowd was ever brought to its feet screaming and cheering at the sight of two men beautifully dodging and weaving out of each other's jabs. The time the crowd comes alive is when a man is hit hard over the heart or the head, when his mouthpiece flies out, when blood squirts out of his nose or eyes, when he wobbles under the attack and his pursuer continues to smash at him with poleax impact.

Don't blame it on the referee. Don't even blame it on the fight managers. Put the blame where it belongs—on the prevailing mores that regard prize fighting as a perfectly proper enterprise and vehicle of entertainment. No one doubts that many people enjoy prize fighting and will miss it if it should be thrown out. And that is precisely the point.

WHY MEN MARRY

George Gilder

Men marry for love. But what does this mean beyond what they got in their lives as single men: the flash of a new face, new flesh across a room. The glimpse of breasts shifting softly in a silken blouse. The open sesame of a missing ring. The excited pursuit, the misunderstood meanings, the charged meetings. The telling touch of hands. The eyes welling open to the gaze. The scent of surrender. The pillowed splash of unbound hair. The ecstatic slipping between new sheets. The race. The winning. The chase and the conquest . . . and back on the road. Definitely back on the road. Free again. Strong again. For new women, new pursuit. What more is there in life—in love—than this?

Marriage means giving it all up. Giving up love? That is how it seems to the single man, and that is why he fears it. He must give up his hunter's heart, forgo the getaway Honda growl, shear off his shaggy hair, restrict his random eye, hang up his handgun, bow down and enter the cage. At bottom, what he is is a hunter. No way he will be hubby.

And yet, he will. For years he lunges at women's surfaces, but as time passes he learns of a deeper promise. For years he may not know the reasons or believe them or care. The heart, it is said, has its reasons. They spring from the primal predicament of man throughout the history of the race: the need to choose a particular woman and stay by her and provide for her if he is to know his children and they are to love him and call him father.

In procreative love, both partners consciously or unconsciously glimpse a future infant—precarious in the womb, vulnerable in the world, and in need of nurture and protection. In the swelter of their bodies together, in the shape and softness of the woman, in the protective support of the man, the couple senses the outlines of a realm that can endure and perpetuate their union: a pattern of differences and complements that goes beyond the momentary pleasures of reciprocal sex.

Marriage asks men to give their essential sexuality only as part of a clear scheme for replacing it with new, far more important, and ultimately far more sexual roles: husband and father. Without these roles, a woman can bear a child, but the man is able only to screw. He can do it a lot, but after his first years it will only get him unthreaded, and in the end he is disconnected and alone. In his shallow heats and frustrations, he all too often becomes a menace to himself and his community.

There are millions of single men, unlinked to any promising reality, dissipating their lives by the years, moving from job to job, woman to woman, illusion to embitterment. Yet they are not hopeless. Many more millions have passed through the same sloughs, incurred the same boozy dreams, marijuana highs, cocaine crashes, sex diseases, job vapors, legal scrapes, wanderings. They follow the entire syndrome and then break out of it. Normally they do not escape through psychiatrists' offices, sex-education courses, VISTA or Peace Corps programs, reformatories, or guidance-counseling uplift. What happens, most of the time—the only effective thing that happens, the only process that reaches the sources of motivation and character—is falling in love.

Love is effective because it works at a deeper, more instinctual level than the other modes of education and change. Love does not teach or persuade. It possesses and transforms. It is not just an intelligent appraisal of his circumstances that transforms the single man. It is not merely a desire for companionship or "growth." It is a deeper alchemy of change, flowing from a primal source. It seeps slowly into the flesh, the memory, the spirit; it rises through a life, until it can ignite. It is a perilous process, full of chances for misfire and mistake—or for an ever more mildewed middle age. It is not entirely understood. But we have seen it work, and so have we seen love. Love unifies reason and experience with the power to change a man caught in a morbid present into a man passionately engaged with the future.

The change that leads to love often comes slowly. Many of the girls a man finds will not help. They tend to go along with him and affirm his single life. But one morning he turns to the stranger sleeping next to him, who came to him as easily as a whiskey too many, and left him as heavy-headed, and decides he must seek a better way to live. One day he looks across the room over a pile of dirty dishes and cigarette butts and beer cans and sex magazines and bills and filthy laundry, and he does not see the evidence of happy carousing and bachelor freedom; he sees a trap closing in upon him more grimly than any marriage. One day while joking with friends about the latest of his acquaintances to be caught and caged, he silently wonders, for a moment, whether he really wishes it were he.

Suddenly he has a new glimpse of himself. His body is beginning to decline, grow weaker and slower, even if he keeps it fit. His body, which once measured out his few advantages over females, is beginning to intimate its terrible plan to become as weak as an older woman's. His aggressiveness, which burst in fitful storms throughout his young life but never seemed to cleanse him—his aggression for which he could so rarely find the adequate battle, the harmonious chase—is souring now. His job, so below his measure as a man, so out of tune with his body and his inspiration, now stretches ahead without joy or relief.

His sex, the force that drove the flower of his youth, drives still, drives again and again the same hard bargain—for which there are fewer and fewer takers, in a sexual arena with no final achievement for the single man, in which sex itself becomes work that is never done.

The single man is caught on a reef and the tide is running out. He is being biologically stranded and he has a hopeless dream. Studs Terkel's book *Working* registers again and again men's desire to be remembered. Yet who in this world is much remembered. Yet who in this world is much remembered for his job?

Stuck with what he may sense as a choice between being trapped and being stranded, he still may respond by trying one more fling. The biological predicament can be warded off for a time, like Hemingway's hyena. Death often appears in the guise of eternal youth, at the ever-infatuating fountains: alcohol, drugs, hallucinogenic sex. For a while he may believe in the disguise. But the hyena returns and there is mortality in the air—diseases, accidents, concealed suicides, the whole range of the single man's aggression, turned at last against himself.

But where there is death, there is hope. For the man who is in touch with his mortality, but not in the grips of it, is also in touch with the sources of his love. He is in contact with the elements—the natural fires and storms so often used as metaphors for his passions. He is a man who can be deeply and effectively changed. He can find his age, his relation to the world, his maturity, his future. He can burn his signature into the covenant of a specific life.

The man has found a vital energy and a possibility of durable change. It has assumed the shape of a woman. It is the same form that has caught his eye and roiled his body all these years. But now there will be depths below the pleasing surfaces, meanings beyond the momentary ruttings. There will be a sense that this vessel contains the secrets of new life, that the womb and breasts bear a message of immortality. There will be a knowledge that to treat this treasure as an object—mere flesh like his own, a mere matrix of his pleasure—is to defile life itself. It is this recognition that she offers a higher possibility—it is this consciousness that he has to struggle to be worthy of her—that finally issues the spark. And then arises the fire that purges and changes him as it consumes his own death. His children ... they will remember. It is the only hope.

The man's love begins in a knowledge of inferiority, but it offers a promise of dignity and purpose. For he then has to create, by dint of his own effort, and without the miracle of a womb, a life that a woman should choose. Thus are released and formed the energies of civilized society. He provides, and he does it for a lifetime, for a life.

PROFESSIONAL MODELS
(Argumentation)

I BELIEVE IN GOD

Gerald Kennedy

I never met an atheist. I have met a few people who claimed they were atheists. But when we talked it over, it always seemed to me they were objecting to someone else's idea of God rather than insisting that there was no God. There is a story about a man at a convention of atheists who became annoyed because he thought the other delegates were backing down from their atheism. He made a speech against this compromising attitude and ended by saying, "I am a real atheist, thank God!"

WE CANNOT LIVE WITHOUT GOD

There are people who will insist they are atheists. For them the words of Tolstoy are the point. He said that God is he without whom we cannot live. If some people insist there is no God and yet go on living, how shall we explain it? Let us say they go on living because they act as if they had not said it. Tolstoy was right. If a man really did not believe in God, he could not go on living as a man. We have to live as if we believe there is something in this universe that gives our life meaning. And when we face this basic fact in living as men, God has found us.

I do not see how anyone in a day like ours can doubt that God is real. We have been trying to get along without him for some time, and look at the sorry shape our world is in. We have felt that we ourselves could solve all our problems. We have set ourselves up high and worshipped gods made by our own hands—gods named Science, Progress, Money, Power, Prosperity, Pleasure, Reason, Education, Success. For a while these gods seemed to take the place of the God of our fathers well enough. But they have proved to be false gods. Worshipping them is superstition and not religion. Sometimes they turn their worshipers into monsters, madmen, or dull robots. If we follow them farther, we plunge into the abyss. God is he without whom men cannot live.

The point is that God is not a matter of choice; he is a matter of necessity. We cannot do as we please, cannot take him or leave him. When we go our own way, we go wrong. When we try to build a life or a society without coming to terms with him, we build on the sand. A civilization is always built on a religion. Once men begin to doubt their faith in God, they are on the way down. Experience shows that God is the reality on which life is built. Let a man doubt that he himself is real if he must, but never let him doubt that God is real.

It takes less effort to believe the most difficult doctrines of Christianity than it does to believe the universe began by chance. Men who accept that idea show more willingness to believe the unlikely than the most conservative of Christians. To put blind force in place of God calls for more blind credulity than a thinking man can muster. We turn from such nonsense to the opening words of Genesis, "In the beginning God. . ." The simple words shine in their own light and speak with conviction.

HOW SHALL WE DESCRIBE GOD?

I cannot undertake a profound, philosophical, exhaustive discussion of the nature of God. I am simply writing as a witness, telling what I believe about God. To the lazy, indifferent Christian people of our time I would like to say, "Why don't you take the time to find out what Christianity says about God? You would be ashamed to know as little about how your car operates as you know about what the great Christian thinkers have said about God." Christian people should not be content to take their ideas about God from experts in other fields—who mean well but do not know what the Church has been teaching.

Surely God has left enough signs of his presence to show plain men some things about his nature. For one thing, God is an artist who has given us beauty on every side. Painters, poets, and musicians know we can live in a world that is beyond the world our minds can grasp. It is the world of beauty. Sometimes we need help to see and hear, but you and I have enough appreciation in us to respond to the wonder of God's presence in Nature.

We remember autumn woods, mountains at sunrise, sunsets by the sea, forest groves at noontime, valleys by moonlight. Every place and every season has its special beauty for us. We cannot be a part of it without feeling our hearts rise up in worship. Admiral Byrd in his book *Alone* described his feelings as he watched a day die at the South Pole. He wrote: "The conviction came that that rhythm was too orderly, too harmonious, too perfect to be a product of blind chance—that, therefore, there must be purpose in the whole and that man was part of that whole and not an accidental offshoot."

GOD IS MIND

We cannot look at the wonders of the natural world without seeing a great Mind at work. Whether we think of the miracle of the atom or try vainly to understand what billions of light years mean, we cannot escape this conviction: the world reveals a Mind that makes our own minds count for something only as they can recognize this greater Mind. We do not create; we only discover. Most of our thinking is seeing and appreciating the marvels that prove a vast Intelligence at work. The glory of science is that it can reveal this truth. The weakness of science is its pride that assumes these marvels of nature are no longer God's because men have understood them. Nature's laws were not set up by men. They were operating a long time before man appeared.

The greatest scientists recognize how little their minds are beside the Mind revealed in the world of nature. They speak of "thinking the thoughts of God after him." They speak of standing on the ocean shore with a few shells in their hands while the great mystery of God stretches out before them. They speak of the universe as being not a great machine but a great thought. Men are growing dissatisfied with the nineteenth-century theory that nature is a substitute for God. They are driven at last to confess that nature is clear proof of a mighty Mind at work. In the words of Shakespeare, man increasingly

> Finds tongues in trees, books in the running brooks,
> Sermons in stones.

GOD IS RIGHTEOUSNESS

Beside the laws of nature there is the moral law. This would seem to say that God is the champion of the right. He has established an order that holds up good and tears down evil. Any man who is not an idiot knows that the sense of right and wrong is real.

The Court of last appeal is the sense of "I ought." Against this we cannot argue, nor can we explain it apart from God. Some people have tried to make conscience out as merely social custom, but for his conscience's sake many a man defies social custom and goes against public opinion. Some people would say conscience is only a matter of education and home training. But every man recognizes the demands of conscience and sees them much alike no matter what his home training or cultural background has been. Every man has a conscience, and every man's conscience tells him he should do what is right and not do what is wrong.

Where does conscience come from? It comes from the God who created the world and men. We have a sense of owing something to the one who made us. Even when no man knows of our fault and there is no chance that any man will ever find it out, still we are guilty in our own eyes. We are guilty because we know there is Another who also knows all about it. How often a sensitive man who shrinks from an unpleasant duty says to himself: "If only God would leave me alone! If only he would let me be comfortable!" But God will not let us alone. When it comes to putting his demands upon us, God neither slumbers nor sleeps.

The moral law shows in the history of nations and societies. The children of Israel discovered it early. In Deborah's song of joy over the fall of an oppressor she says:

> From heaven fought the stars,
> from their courses they fought against Sisera.
>
> —*Judg.* 5:20

She knew that the universe itself is against wrong. Israel's prophets saw this so clearly that God became real to them in every event of history He was the deciding force in battles, in social life, in politics. We can be sure of one thing: no nation founded on injustice can long endure. When men or nations do wrong, they will be punished. In the words of the Old Testament:

> Righteousness exalteth a nation;
> But sin is a reproach to any people.
>
> —*Prov.* 14:34

None of this makes sense if we have a blind machine for a world. It makes sense only when we see that back of all our affairs there is God, who protects the good and destroys evil.

GOD IS A PERSON

The Christian truth that takes first place and includes all I have been saying is this: God is a person. This troubles a good many people. They suppose Christians are childish folk who think of God as if he were only a man. Such people prefer to talk about God as a "principle," or an "idea."

Let me make clear what I am *not* saying. I am not making God an old man with a long white beard. The Gospel of John saves us from that mistake by insisting that "God is a Spirit."

But I am saying God is a person. By this I mean he has will, mind, purpose, freedom, self-consciousness. The highest creation we know in the world is a person. The climax of the whole process of creation is a personality. Persons tower over nature and the animal kingdom. We must say God is at least a person, or we would be making him something of less value than a man. Principles and ideas do not mean as much as persons. God may be more than personal; but since we do not know anything that is more, we shall go as high as we know.

GOD FACES MEN

All of this becomes clear in the Christian experience of being found by God. When God finds a man, that man meets a Divine Person who faces him with personal claims. The man has to do much more than heed a moral principle or adjust his life to the law of right and wrong. He has to go through a personal experience. It is like David's experience when Nathan pointed to him and said, "Thou art the man." It is like Jesus' experience when he heard a voice from out the heavens say, "Thou art my beloved Son."

Until a man finds God and is found by God, he begins at no beginning and he works to no end. In other words, God is not one of the elective courses in the school of life; he is the one required course. Without this course we cannot pass our final examinations. There is nothing to take the place of God. Everything goes wrong without him. Nothing fits into place until a man has put God at the center of his thought and action.

Life has no purpose without God, and no generation should understand that better than ours. For we have most of the things we thought we wanted. We can travel swiftly; we can send messages over vast distances; we can produce more comforts of life than our fathers could imagine. Today the poor can enjoy things which would have been luxuries to the ancient kings. Yet something has gone wrong. We are no longer thrilled to think we will soon produce still more goods, more comforts. All our trinkets have not brought us peace of mind. In spite of our heroic conquests over nature, the feeling haunts us that we spend our time on toys and trivialities, and we are moved by no mighty purposes.

Only God can keep our sense of values straight. William Temple, late Archbishop of Canterbury, once said that the world is like a shop window where some prankster has gone in and changed all the price tags. On the expensive articles he has put the low prices, and on the cheap articles he has put the high prices. We pay more than we should for what does not satisfy us, and we neglect the things we really need. Isaiah's question is for us: "Wherefore do ye spend money for that which is not bread? and your labor for that which satisfieth not?" (Isa. 55:2). People who forget God also forget what is worth striving for.

Without God we cannot have human brotherhood, which is the recognition of each man's worth. If you can rob men of their belief that they are the sons of God, you pave the way for tyranny. This is not just somebody's opinion. This is history. We have only one bulwark against the cheapening of human life. It is to maintain at all costs the Christian belief that God created each man and made him a son of God. Like coins, men have value, not in themselves, but because they bear the stamp of the King.

We can find freedom only in God. God's demands often seem severe, yet they free us more than anything we know. When we try to get away from his demands, we end up as slaves to ourselves or to other men. But when we decide we must obey God rather than men, we feel we have been set free. It is like escaping from a prison. In God's service we find perfect freedom.

All the things that make us men have their roots in God. He is like the air we breathe and the water we drink. Eddie Rickenbacker, the famous flyer, drifted around on a life raft for twenty-one days, hopelessly lost in the Pacific. A friend later asked him what lesson he had learned. "The biggest lesson I learned from that experience," he said, "was that if you have all the fresh water you want to drink and all the food you want to eat, you ought never to complain about anything." So it is with the man who has lost God. He comes to know that God is man's one necessary possession.

I believe in God because he has faced men and laid his claims upon me. Just as a man knows it when he falls in love, or knows it when he thrills to the beauty of nature, so he knows it when God places his demand upon him. Maybe he cannot be as precise as John Wesley and say that it happened about a quarter of nine. But he knows that once he was lost and now he is found, his life is changed. The experience makes him humble. He may have learned enough about God to live by, but he now finds the ruling passion of his life is to learn *more* about him.

That is the hope of every Christian. It is the worthiest goal for any man's life. When we have gone far enough to be able to say, "I believe in God," we stand at the beginning of life's great adventure.

WHY I AM AN AGNOSTIC

Clarence Darrow

An agnostic is a doubter. The word is generally applied to those who doubt the verity of accepted religious creeds or faiths. Everyone is an agnostic as to the beliefs or creeds they do not accept. Catholics are agnostic to the Protestant creeds, and the Protestants are agnostic to the Catholic creed. Anyone who thinks is an agnostic about something, otherwise he must believe that he is possessed of all knowledge. And the proper place for such a person is in the madhouse or the home for the feeble-minded. In a popular way, in the western world, an agnostic is one who doubts or disbelieves the main tenets of the Christian faith.

I would say that belief in at least three tenets is necessary to the faith of a Christian; a belief in God, a belief in immortality, and a belief in a supernatural book. Various Christian sects require much more, but it is difficult to imagine that one could be a Christian, under any intelligent meaning of the word, with less. Yet there are some people who claim to be Christians who do not accept the literal interpretation of all the Bible, and who give more credence to some portions of the book than to others.

I am an agnostic as to the question of God. I think that it is impossible for the human mind to believe in an object or thing unless it can form a mental picture of such object or thing. Since man ceased to worship openly an anthropomorphic God and talked vaguely and not intelligently about some force in the universe, he cannot be said to believe in God. One cannot believe in a force excepting as a force that pervades matter and is not an individual entity. To believe in a thing, an image of the thing must be stamped on the mind. If one is asked if he believes in such an animal as a camel, there immediately arises in his mind an image of the camel. This image has come from experience or knowledge of the animal gathered in some way or other. No such image comes, or can come, with the idea of a God who is described as a force.

Man has always speculated upon the origin of the universe, including himself. I feel, with Herbert Spencer, that whether the universe had an origin—and if it had—what the origin is will never be known by man. The Christian says that the universe could not make itself; that there must have been some higher power to call it into being. Christians have been obsessed for many years by Paley's argument that if a person passing through a desert should find a watch and examine its spring, its hands, its case and its crystal, he would at once be satisfied that some intelligent being capable of design had made the watch. The reason he would not doubt it is because he is familiar with watches and other appliances made by man. The savage was once unfamiliar with a watch and would have had no idea upon the subject. There are plenty of crystals and rock of natural formation that are as intricate as a watch, but even to intelligent man they carry no implication that some intelligent power must have made them. They carry no such implication because no one has any knowledge or experience of someone having made these natural objects which everywhere abound.

To say that God made the universe gives us no explanation of the beginnings of things. If we are told that God made the universe, the question immediately arises: Who made God? Did he always exist, or was there some power back of that? Did he create matter out of nothing, or is his existence coextensive with matter? The problem is still there. What is the origin of it all? If, on the other hand, one says that the universe was not made by God, that it always existed, he has the same difficulty to confront. To say that the universe was here last year, or millions of years ago, does not explain its origin. This is still a mystery. As to the question of the origin of things, man can only wonder and doubt and guess.

As to the existence of the soul, all people may either believe or disbelieve. Everyone knows the origin of the human being. They know that it came from a single cell in the body of the mother, and that the cell was one out of ten thousand in the mother's body. Before gestation the cell must have been fertilized by a spermatozoon from the body of the father. This was one out of perhaps a billion spermatozoa that was the capacity of the father. When the cell is fertilized a chemical process begins. The cell divides and multiplies and increases into millions of cells, and finally a child is born. Cells die and are born during the life of the individual until they finally drop apart, and this is death.

If there is a soul, what is it, and where did it come from, and where does it go? Can anyone who is guided by his reason possibly imagine a soul independent of a body, or other place of its residence, or the character of it, or anything concerning it? If man is justified in any belief or disbelief on any subject, he is warranted in the disbelief in a soul. Not one scrap of evidence exists to prove any such impossible thing.

Many Christians base the belief of a soul and God upon the Bible. Strictly speaking, there is no such book. To make the Bible, sixty-six books are bound into one volume. These books were written by many people at different times, and no one knows the time or the identity of any author. Some of the books were written by several authors at various times. These books contain all sorts of contradictory concepts of life and morals and the origin of things. Between the first and last nearly a thousand years intervened, a longer time than has passed since the discovery of America by Columbus.

When I was a boy the theologians used to assert that the proof of the divine inspiration of the Bible rested on miracles and prophecies. But a miracle means a violation of a natural law, and there can be no proof imagined that could be sufficient to show the violation of a natural law; even though proof seemed to show violation, it would only show that we were not acquainted with all natural laws. One believes in the truthfulness of a man because of his long experience with the man, and because the man has always told a consistent story. But no man has told so consistent a story as nature. If one should say that the sun did not rise, to use the ordinary expression, on the day before, his hearer would not believe it, even though he had slept all day and knew that his informant was a man of the strictest veracity. He would not believe it because the story is inconsistent with the conduct of the sun in all the ages past.

Primitive and even civilized people have grown so accustomed to believing in miracles that they often attribute the simplest manifestations of nature to agencies of which they know nothing. They do this when the belief is utterly inconsistent with knowledge and logic. They believe in old miracles and new ones. Preachers pray for rain, knowing full well that no such prayer was ever answered. When a politician is sick, they pray for God to cure him, and the politician almost invariably dies. The modern clergyman who prays for rain and for the health of the politician is no more intelligent in this matter than the primitive man who saw a separate miracle in the rising and setting of the sun, in the birth of an individual, in the growth of a plant, in the stroke of lightning, in the flood, in every manifestation of nature and life.

As to prophecies, intelligent writers gave them up long ago. In all prophecies facts are made to suit the prophecy, or the prophecy was made after the facts, or the events have no relation to the prophecy. Weird and strange and unreasonable interpretations are used to explain simple statements, that a prophecy may be claimed.

Can any rational person believe that the Bible is anything but a human document? We now know pretty well where the various books came from, and about when they were written. We know that they were written by human beings who had no knowledge of science, little knowledge of life, and were influenced by the barbarous morality of primitive times, and were grossly ignorant of most things that men know today. For instance, Genesis says that God made the earth, and he made the sun to light the day and the moon to light the night, and in one clause disposes of the stars by saying that "he made the stars also." This was plainly written by someone who had no conception of the stars. Man, by the aid of his telescope looking further into the heavens, only discovers more and more worlds and suns and systems in the endless reaches of space. The men who wrote Genesis believed, of course, that this tiny speck of mud that we call the earth was the center of the universe, the only world in space and made for man, who was the only being worth considering. These men believed that the stars were only a little way above the earth, and were set in the firmament for man to look at, and for nothing else. Everyone today knows that this conception is not true.

The origin of the human race is not as blind a subject as it once was. Let alone God creating Adam out of hand, from the dust of the earth, does anyone believe that Eve was made from Adam's rib—that the snake walked and spoke in the Garden of Eden—that he tempted Eve to persuade Adam to eat an apple, and that it is on that account that the whole human race was doomed to hell—that for four thousand years there was no chance for any human to be saved, though none of them had anything whatever to do with the temptation; and that finally men were saved only through God's son dying for them, and that unless human beings believed this silly, impossible and wicked story they were doomed to hell? Can anyone with intelligence really believe that a child born today should be doomed because the snake tempted Eve and Eve tempted Adam? To believe that is not God-worship, it is devil-worship.

Can anyone call this scheme of creation and damnation moral? It defies every principle of morality, as man conceives morality. Can anyone believe today that the whole world was destroyed by flood, save only Noah and his family and a male and female of each species of animal that entered the Ark? There are almost a million species of insects alone. How did

Noah match these up and make sure of getting male and female to reproduce life in the world after the flood had spent its force? And why should all the lower animals have been destroyed? Were they included in the sinning of man? This is a story which could not beguile a fairly bright child of five years of age today.

Do intelligent people believe that the various languages spoken by man on earth came from the confusion of tongues at the Tower of Babel, some four thousand years ago? Human languages were dispersed all over the face of the earth long before that time. Evidences of civilizations are in existence now that were old long before the date that romancers fix for the building of the Tower, and even before the date claimed for the flood.

Do Christians believe that Joshua made the sun stand still, so that the day could be lengthened, that a battle might be finished? What kind of person wrote that story, and what did he know about astronomy? It is perfectly plain that the author thought that the earth was the center of the universe and stood still in the heavens, and that the sun either went around it or was pulled across its path each day, and that the stopping of the sun would lengthen the day. We know now that had the sun stopped when Joshua commanded it, and had it stood still until now, it would not have lengthened the day. We know that the day is determined by the rotation of the earth upon its axis, and not by the movement of the sun. Everyone knows that this story simply is not true, and not many even pretend to believe the childish fable.

What of the tale of Balaam's ass speaking to him, probably in Hebrew? Is it true, or is it a fable? Many asses have spoken, and doubtless some in Hebrew, but they have not been that breed of asses. Is salvation to depend on a belief in a monstrosity like this?

Above all the rest, would any human being today believe that a child was born without a father? Yet this story was not at all unreasonable in the ancient world; at least three or four miraculous births are recorded in the Bible, including John the Baptist and Samson. Immaculate conceptions were common in the Roman world at the time and at the place where Christianity really had its nativity. Women were taken to the temples to be inoculated of God so that their sons might be heroes, which meant, generally, wholesale butchers. Julius Caesar was a miraculous conception—indeed, they were common all over the world. How many miraculous-birth stories is a Christian now expected to believe?

In the days of the formation of the Christian religion, disease meant the possession of human beings by devils. Christ cured a sick man by casting out the devils, who ran into the swine, and the swine ran into the sea. Is there any question but what that was simply the attitude and belief of a primitive people? Does anyone believe that sickness means the possession of the body by devils, and that devils must be cast out of the human being that he may be cured? Does anyone believe that a dead person can come to life? The miracles recorded in the Bible are not the only instances of dead men coming to life. All over the world one finds testimony of such miracles: miracles which no person is expected to believe, unless it is his kind of miracle. Still at Lourdes today, and all over the present world, from New York to Los Angeles and up and down the lands, people believe in miraculous occurrences, and even the return of the dead. Superstition is everywhere prevalent in the world. It has been so from the beginning, and most likely will be so unto the end.

The reasons for agnosticism are abundant and compelling. Fantastic and foolish and impossible consequences are freely claimed for the belief in religion. All the civilization of any period is put down as a result of religion. All the cruelty and error and ignorance of the period has no relation to religion. The truth is that the origin of what we call civilization is not due to religion but to skepticism. So long as men accepted miracles without question, so long as they believed in original sin and the road to salvation, so long as they believed in a hell where man would be kept for eternity on account of Eve, there was no reason whatever for civilization: life was short, and eternity was long, and the business of life was preparation for eternity.

When every event was a miracle, when there was no order or system or law, there was no occasion for studying any subject, or being interested in anything excepting a religion which took care of the soul. As man doubted the primitive conceptions about religion, and no longer accepted the literal, miraculous teachings of ancient books, he set himself to understand nature. We no longer cure disease by casting out devils. Since that time, men have studied the human body, have built hospitals and treated illness in a scientific way. Science is responsible for the building of railroads and bridges, of steamships, of telegraph lines, of cities, towns, large buildings and small, plumbing and sanitation, of the food supply, and the countless thousands of useful things that we now deem necessary to life. Without skepticism and doubt, none of these things could have been given to the world.

The fear of God is not the beginning of wisdom. The fear of God is the death of wisdom. Skepticism and doubt lead to study and investigation, and investigation is the beginning of wisdom.

The modern world is the child of doubt and inquiry, as the ancient world was the child of fear and faith.

DEATH AND JUSTICE

Edward I. Koch

Last December a man named Robert Lee Willie, who had been convicted of raping and murdering an 18-year-old woman, was executed in the Louisiana state prison. In a statement issued several minutes before his death, Mr. Willie said: "Killing people is wrong .... It makes no difference whether it's citizens, countries, or governments. Killing is wrong." Two weeks later in South Carolina, an admitted killer named Joseph Carl Shaw was put to death for murdering two teenagers. In an appeal to the governor for clemency, Mr. Shaw wrote: "Killing is wrong when I did it. Killing is wrong when you do it. I hope you have the courage and moral strength to stop the killing."

It is a curiosity of modern life that we find ourselves being lectured on morality by cold-blooded killers. Mr. Willie previously had been convicted of aggravated rape, aggravated kidnapping, and the murders of a Louisiana deputy and a man from Missouri. Mr. Shaw committed another murder a week before the two for which he was executed, and admitted mutilating the body of the 14-year-old girl he killed. I can't help wondering what prompted these murderers to speak out against killing as they entered the death-house door. Did their new-found reverence for life stem from the realization that they were about to lose their own?

Life is indeed precious, and I believe the death penalty helps to affirm this fact. Had the death penalty been a real possibility in the minds of these murders, they might well have stayed their hand. They might have shown moral awareness before the victims died, and not after. Consider the tragic death of Rosa Velez, who happened to be home when a man named Luis Vera burglarized her apartment in Brooklyn. "Yeah, I shot her," Vera admitted. "She knew me, and I knew I wouldn't go to the chair."

During my 22 years in public service, I have heard the pros and cons of capital punishment expressed with special intensity. As a district leader, councilman, congressman, and mayor, I have represented constituencies generally thought of as liberal. Because I support the death penalty for heinous crimes of murder, I have sometimes been the subject of emotional and outraged attacks by voters who find my position reprehensible or worse. I have listened to their ideas. I have weighed their objections carefully. I still support the death penalty. The reasons I maintain my position can be best understood by examining the arguments most frequently heard in opposition.

1. The death penalty is "barbaric." Sometimes opponents of capital punishment horrify with tales of lingering death on the gallows, of faulty electric chairs, or of agony in the gas chamber. Partly in response to such protests, several states such as North Carolina and Texas switched to execution by lethal injection. The condemned person is put to death painlessly, without ropes, voltage, bullets, or gas. Did this answer the objections of death penalty opponents? Of course not. On June 22, 1984, *The New York Times* published an editorial that sarcastically attacked the new "hygienic" method of death by injection, and stated that "execution can never be made humane through science." So it's not the method that really troubles opponents. It's the death itself they consider barbaric.

Admittedly, capital punishment is not a pleasant topic. However, one does not have to like the death penalty in order to support it any more than one must like radical surgery, radiation, or chemotherapy in order to find necessary these attempts at curing cancer. Ultimately we may learn how to cure cancer with a simple pill. Unfortunately, that day has not yet arrived. Today we are faced with the choice of letting the cancer spread or trying to cure it with the methods available, methods that one day will almost certainly be considered barbaric. But to give up and do nothing would be far more barbaric and would certainly delay the discovery of an eventual cure. The analogy between cancer and murder is imperfect, because murder is not the "disease" we are trying to cure. The disease is injustice. We may not like the death penalty, but it must be available to punish crimes of cold-blooded murder, cases in which any other form of punishment would be inadequate and, therefore, unjust. If we create a society in which injustice is not tolerated, incidents of murder—the most flagrant form of injustice—will diminish.

2. No other major democracy uses the death penalty. No other major democracy—in fact, few other countries of any description—are plagued by a murder rate such as that in the United States. Fewer and fewer Americans can remember the days when unlocked doors were the norm and murder was a rare and terrible offense. In America the murder rate climbed 122 percent between 1963 and 1980. During the same period, the murder rate in New York City increased by almost 400 percent, and the statistics are even worse in many other cities. A study at MIT showed that based on 1970 homicide rates a person who lived in a large American city ran a greater risk of being murdered than an American soldier in World War II ran of being killed in combat. It is not surprising that the laws of each country differ according to differing conditions and traditions. If other countries had our murder problem, the cry for capital punishment would be just as loud as it is here. And I daresay that any other major democracy where 75 percent of the people supported the death penalty would soon enact it into law.

3. An innocent person might be executed by mistake. Consider the work of Adam Bedau, one of the most implacable foes of capital punishment in this country. According to Mr. Bedau, it is "false sentimentality to argue that the death penalty should be abolished because of the abstract possibility than an innocent person might be executed." He cites a study of the 7,000 executions in this country from 1893 to 1971, and concludes that the record fails to show that such cases occur. The main point, however, is this. If government functioned only when the possibility of error didn't exist, government wouldn't function at all. Human life deserves special protection, and one of the best ways to guarantee that protection is to assure that convicted murderers do not kill again. Only the death penalty can accomplish this end. In a recent case in New Jersey, a man named Richard Biegenwald was freed from prison after serving 18 years for murder; since his release he has been convicted of committing four murders. A prisoner named Lemuel

Smith, who, while serving four life sentences for murder (plus two life sentences for kidnapping and robbery) in New York's Green Haven Prison, lured a woman corrections officer into the chaplain's office and strangled her. He then mutilated and dismembered her body. An additional life sentence for Smith is meaningless. Because New York has no death penalty statute, Smith has effectively been given a license to kill.

But the problem of multiple murder is not confined to the nation's penitentiaries. In 1981, 91 police officers were killed in the line of duty in this country. Seven percent of those arrested in the cases that have been solved had a previous arrest for murder. In New York City in 1976 and 1977, 85 persons arrested for homicide had a previous arrest for murder. Six of these individuals had two previous arrests for murder, and one had four previous murder arrests. During those two years the New York police were arresting for murder persons with a previous arrest for murder on the average one every 8.5 days. This is not surprising when we learn that in 1975, for example, the median time served in Massachusetts for homicide was less than two-and-a half years. In 1976 a study sponsored by the Twentieth Century Fund found that the average time served in the United States for first-degree murder is ten years. The median time served may be considerably lower.

4. Capital punishment cheapens the value of human life. On the contrary, it can be easily demonstrated that the death penalty strengthens the value of human life. If the penalty for rape were lowered, clearly it would signal a lessened regard for the victims' suffering, humiliation, and personal integrity. It would cheapen their horrible experience, and expose them to an increased danger of recurrence. When we lower the penalty for murder, it signals a lessened regard for the value of the victim's life. Some critics of capital punishment, such as columnist Jimmy Breslin, have suggested that a life sentence is actually a harsher penalty for murder than death. This is sophistic nonsense. A few killers may decide not to appeal a death sentence, but the overwhelming majority make every effort to stay alive. It is by exacting the highest penalty for the taking of human life that we affirm the highest value of human life.

5. The death penalty is applied in a discriminatory manner. This factor no longer seems to be the problem it once was. The appeals process for a condemned prisoner is lengthy and painstaking. Every effort is made to see that the verdict and sentence were fairly arrived at. However, assertions of discrimination are not an argument for ending the death penalty but for extending it. It is not justice to exclude everyone from the penalty of the law if a few are found to be so favored. Justice requires that the law be applied equally to all.

6. Thou shalt not kill. The bible is our greatest source of moral inspiration. Opponents of the death penalty frequently cite the sixth of the Ten Commandments in an attempt to prove the capital punishment is divinely proscribed. In the original Hebrew, however, the Sixth Commandment reads "Thou Shalt Not Commit Murder," and the Torah specifies capital punishment for a variety of offenses. The biblical viewpoint has been upheld by philosophers throughout history. The greatest thinkers of the 19th century—Kant, Locke, Hobbs, Rousseau,

Montesquieu, and Mill—agreed that natural law properly authorizes the sovereign to take life in order to vindicate justice. Only Jeremy Bentham was ambivalent. Washington, Jefferson, and Franklin endorsed it. Abraham Lincoln authorized executions for deserters in wartime. Alexis de Tocqueville, who expressed profound respect for American institutions, believed that the death penalty was indispensable to the support of social order. The United States Constitution, widely admired as one of the seminal achievements in the history of humanity, condemns cruel and inhuman punishment, but does not condemn capital punishment.

7. ***The death penalty is state-sanctioned murder.*** This is the defense with which Messrs. Willie and Shaw hoped to soften the resolve of those who sentenced them to death. By saying in effect, "You're no better than I am," the murderer seeks to bring his accusers down to his own level. It is also a popular argument among opponents of capital punishment, but a transparently false one. Simply put, the state has rights that the private individual does not. In a democracy, those rights are given to the state by the electorate. The execution of a lawfully condemned killer is no more an act of murder than is legal imprisonment an act of kidnapping. If an individual forces a neighbor to pay him money under threat of punishment, it's called extortion. If the state does it, it's called taxation. Rights and responsibilities surrendered by the individual are what give the state its power to govern. This contract is the foundation of civilization itself.

Everyone wants his or her rights, and will defend them jealously. Not everyone, however, wants responsibilities, especially the painful responsibilities that come with law enforcement. Twenty-one years ago a woman named Kitty Genovese was assaulted and murdered on a street in New York. Dozens of neighbors heard her cries for help but did nothing to assist her. They didn't even call the police. In such a climate the criminal understandably grows bolder. In the presence of moral cowardice, he lectures us on our supposed failings and tries to equate his crimes with our quest for justice.

The death of anyone—even a convicted killer—diminishes us all. But we are diminished even more by a justice system that fails to function. It is an illusion to let ourselves believe that doing away with capital punishment removes the murderer's deed from our conscience. The rights of society are paramount. When we protect guilty lives, we give up innocent lives in exchange. When opponents of capital punishment say to the state: "I will not let you kill in my name," they are also saying to murderers: "You can kill in your own name as long as I have an excuse for not getting involved."

It is hard to imagine anything worse than being murdered while neighbors do nothing. But something worse exists. When those same neighbors shrink back from justly punishing the murderer, the victim dies twice.

THE CASE AGAINST
THE DEATH PENALTY

Hugo Adam Bedau

Hugo Adam Bedau is Fletcher Professor of Philosophy at Tufts University. He has written and edited a number of books on political philosophy and on capital punishment, including *Death is Different* (1987) and *The Death Penalty in America*, 3rd edition (1982). He gratefully acknowledges the assistance of Henry Schwarzschild, Director Emeritus of the ACLU Capital Punishment Project.

The American Civil Liberties Union holds that the death penalty inherently violates the constitutional ban against cruel and unusual punishment and the guarantee of due process of law and the equal protection of the laws. The imposition of the death penalty is inconsistent with fundamental values of our democratic system. The state should not arrogate unto itself the right to kill human beings, especially when it kills with premeditation and ceremony, under color of law, in our names, and when it does so in an arbitrary and discriminatory fashion. In the judgment of the ACLU, capital punishment is an intolerable denial of civil liberties. We shall therefore continue to seek to prevent executions and to abolish capital punishment by litigation, legislation , commutation, or by the weight of a renewed public outcry against this brutal and brutalizing institution.

INTRODUCTION

In 1972, the Supreme Court declared that under then existing laws "the imposition and carrying out of the death penalty … constitutes cruel and unusual punishment in violation of the Eighth and Fourteenth Amendments." (*Furman v. Georgia*, 408 U.S.238) The majority of the Court concentrated its objections on the way death-penalty laws had been applied, finding the result so "harsh, freakish, and arbitrary" as to be constitutionally unacceptable. Making the nationwide impact of its decision unmistakable, the Court summarily reversed death sentences in the many cases then before it, which involved a wide range of state statutes, crimes, and factual situations.

But within four years after the *Furman decision*, more than 600 persons had been sentenced to death under new capital-punishment statutes that provided guidance for the jury's sentencing discretion. These statutes typically require a bifurcated (two-stage) trial procedure, in which the jury first determines guilt or innocence and then chooses imprisonment or death in the light of aggravating or mitigating circumstances.

In July 1976, the Supreme Court moved in the opposite direction, holding that "the punishment of death does not invariably violate the Constitution." The Court ruled that these new statutes contained "objective standards to guide, regularize, and make rationally reviewable the process for imposing the sentence of death." (*Gregg v. Georgia*, 428 U.S.153) Thus the states as well as Congress have had for some years constitutionally valid statutory models for death-penalty laws, and more than three dozen state legislatures have enacted death penalty statutes patterned after those the Court upheld in *Gregg*. In recent years, Congress has enacted death penalty statutes for peacetime espionage by military personnel and for drug-related murders.

Executions resumed in 1977, and by the early 1990s nearly three thousand persons were under sentence of death and more than 180 had been executed.

* * * * *

DETERENCE

The argument most often cited in support of capital punishment is that the threat of executions deters capital crimes more effectively than imprisonment. This claim is plausible, but the facts do not support it. The death penalty fails as a deterrent for several reasons.

1. Any punishment can be an effective deterrent only if it is consistently and promptly employed. Capital punishment cannot be administered to meet these conditions.

Only a small proportion of first-degree murderers is sentenced to death, and even fewer are executed. Although death sentences since 1980 have increased in number to about 250 per year,[1] this is still only 1 per cent of all homicides known to the police.[2] Of all those convicted on a charge of criminal homicide, only 2 percent—about 1 in 50—are eventually sentenced to death.[3]

The possibility of increasing the number of convicted murderers sentenced to death and executed by enacting mandatory death penalty laws was ruled unconstitutional in 1976 (*Woodson v. North Carolina*, 428 U.S. 280).

Considerable delay in carrying out the death sentence is unavoidable, given the procedural safeguards required by the courts in capital cases. Starting with empanelling the trial jury, murder trials take far longer when the death penalty is involved. Post-conviction appeals in death-penalty cases are far more frequent as well. All these factors increase the time and cost of administering criminal justice.

The sobering lesson is that we can reduce such delay and costs only by abandoning the procedural safeguards and constitutional rights of suspects, defendants, and convicts, with the attendant high risk of convicting the wrong person and executing the innocent.

2. Persons who commit murder and other crimes of personal violence either premeditate them or they do not. If the crime is premeditated, the criminal ordinarily concentrates on escaping detection, arrest, and conviction. The threat of even the severest punishment will not deter those who expect to escape detection and arrest. If the crime is not premeditated, then it is impossible to imagine how the threat of any punishment could deter it. Most capital crimes are committed during moments of great emotional stress or under the influence of drugs or alcohol, when logical thinking has been suspended. Impulsive or expressive violence is inflicted by persons heedless of the consequences to themselves as well as to others.

Gangland killings, air piracy, drive-by shootings, and kidnapping for ransom are among the graver felonies that continue to be committed because some individuals think they are too clever to get caught. Political terrorism is usually committed in the name of an ideology that honors its martyrs; trying to cope with it by threatening death for terrorists is futile. Such threats leave untouched the underlying causes and ignore the many political and diplomatic sanctions (such as treaties against asylum for international terrorists) that could appreciably lower the incidence of terrorism.

The attempt to reduce murders in the illegal drug trade by the threat of severe punishment ignores this fact: Anyone trafficking in illegal drugs is already betting his life in violent competition with other dealers. It is irrational to think that the death penalty—a remote threat at best—will deter murders committed in drug turf wars or by street-level dealers.

3. If, however, severe punishment can deter crime, then long term imprisonment is severe enough to cause any rational person not to commit violent crimes. The vast preponderance of the evidence shows that the death penalty is no more effective than imprisonment in deterring murder and that it may even be an incitement to criminal violence in certain cases.

- Death-penalty states as a group do not have lower rates of criminal homicide than non-death penalty states. During the 1980s, death-penalty states averaged an annual rate of 7.5 criminal homicides per 100,000 of population; abolition states averaged a rate of 7.4.[4]

- Use of the death penalty in a given state may increase the subsequent rate of criminal homicide in that state. In New York, for example, between 1907 and 1964, 692 executions were carried out. On the average, over this 57-year period, one or more executions in a given month aided a net increase of two homicides to the total committed in the next month.[5]

- In neighboring states—one with the death penalty and the others without it—the one with the death penalty does not show a consistently lower rate of criminal homicide. For example, between 1972 and 1990, the homicide rate in Michigan (which has no death penalty) was generally as low as or lower than the neighboring state of Indiana, which restored the death penalty in 1973 and since then has sentenced 70 persons to death and carried out 2 executions.[6]

- Police officers on duty do not suffer a higher rate of criminal assault and homicide in states that have abolished the death penalty than they do in death-penalty states. Between 1973 and 1984, for example, lethal assaults against police were not significantly more or less frequent in abolition states than in death-penalty states. There is "no support for the view that the death penalty provides a more effective deterrent to police homicides than alternative sanctions. Not for a single year was evidence found that police are safer in jurisdictions that provide for capital punishment."[7]

■ Prisoners and prison personnel do not suffer a higher rate of criminal assault and homicide from life-term prisoners in abolition states than they do in death-penalty states.[8] Between 1984 and 1989, seventeen prison staff were murdered by prisoners in ten states; of these murders, 88 percent (15 of 17) occurred in death penalty jurisdictions—just as about 88 percent of all the prisoners in those ten states were in death penalty jurisdictions.[9] Evidently, the threat of the death penalty "does not even exert an incremental deterrent effect over the threat of a lesser punishment in the abolitionist state."[10]

* * * * *

It must, of course, be conceded that inflicting the death penalty guarantees that the condemned person will commit no further crimes. This is an incapacitative, not a deterrent, effect of executions. Furthermore, it is too high a price to pay when studies show that very few convicted murderers ever commit another crime of violence.[15] A recent study examined the prison and post-release records of 533 prisoners on death row in 1972 whose sentences were reduced to life by the Supreme Court's ruling in Furman. The research showed that 6 had committed another murder. But the same study showed that in 4 other cases, an innocent man had been sentenced to death.[16]

Actual experience establishes these conclusions beyond a reasonable doubt. No comparable body of evidence contradicts them.

* * * * *

UNFAIRNESS

Constitutional due process as well as elementary justice require that the judicial functions of trial and sentencing be conducted with fundamental fairness, especially where the irreversible sanction of the death penalty is involved. In murder cases (since 1930, 99 percent of all executions have been for this crime), there has been substantial evidence to show that courts have been arbitrary, racially biased, and unfair in the way in which they have sentenced some persons to prison but others to death.

Racial discrimination was one of the grounds on which the Supreme Court relied in *Furman* in ruling the death penalty unconstitutional. Half a century ago, Gunnar Myrdal, in his classic *American Dilemma* (1944), reported that "the South makes the widest application of the death penalty, and Negro criminals come in for much more than their share of the executions." Statistics confirm this discrimination, only it is not confined to the South. Between 1930 and 1990, 4,016 persons were executed in the United States. Of these, 2,129 (or 53 percent) were black. For the crime of murder, 3,343 were executed; 1,693 (or 51 percent) were black.[17] During these years African-Americans were about 12 per cent of the nation's population.

The nation's death rows have always had a disproportionately large population of African-Americans, relative to their fraction of the total population. Over the past century, black offenders, as compared with white, were often executed for crimes less often receiving the death penalty, such as rape and burglary. (Between 1930 and 1976, 455 men were executed for rape, of whom 405 (or 90 percent) were black.) A higher percentage of the blacks who were executed were juveniles; and blacks were more often executed than were whites without having their conviction reviewed by any higher court.[18]

In recent years, it has been widely believed that such flagrant discrimination is a thing of the past. Since the revival of the death penalty in the mid-1970s, about half of those on death row at any given time have been black[19]—a disproportionately large fraction given the black/white ratio of the total population, but not so obviously unfair if judged by the fact that roughly 50 percent of all those arrested for murder were also black.[20] Nevertheless, when those under death sentence are examined more closely, it turns out that race is a decisive factor after all.

An exhaustive statistical study of racial discrimination in capital cases in Georgia, for example, showed that "the average odds of receiving a death sentence among all indicted cases were 4.3 times higher in cases with white victims."[21] In 1987 these data were placed before the Supreme Court in *McCleskey v. Kemp* and the Court did not dispute the statistical evidence. The Court did hold, however, that the evidence failed to show that there was "a constitutionally significant risk of racial bias [...]" (481 U.S. 279).

In 1990, the U.S. General Accounting Office reported to the Congress the results of its review of empirical studies on racism and the death penalty. The GAO concluded: "Our synthesis of the 28 studies shows a pattern of evidence indicating racial disparities in the charging, sentencing, and imposition of the death penalty after the Furman decision" and that "race of victim influence was found at all stages of the criminal justice system process[...]."

These results cannot be explained away by relevant non-racial factors (such as prior criminal record or type of crime), and they lead to a very unsavory conclusion: In the trial courts of this nation, even at the present time, the killing of a white is treated much more severely than the killing of a black. Of the 168 persons executed between January 1977 and April 1992, only 29 had been convicted of the killing of a non-white, and only one of these 29 was himself white.[23] Where the death penalty is involved, our criminal justice system essentially reserves the death penalty for murderers (regardless of their race) who kill white victims.

Both sex and socio-economic class are also factors that enter into determining who receives a death sentence and who is executed. During the 1980s and aerially 1990s, only about 1 percent of all those on death row were women,[24] even though women commit about 15 percent of all criminal homicides.[25] A third or more of the women under death sentence were guilty of killing men who had victimized them with years of violent abuse.[26] Since 1930, only 33 women (12 of them black) have been executed in the United States.[27]

* * * * *

Thoughtful citizens, who in contemplating capital punishment in the abstract might support it, must condemn it in actual practice.

INEVITABILITY OF ERROR

Unlike all other criminal punishments, the death penalty is uniquely irrevocable. Speaking to the French Chamber of Deputies in 1830, years after the excesses of the French Revolution, which he had witnessed, the Marquis de Lafayette said, "I shall ask for the abolition of the punishment of death until I have the infallibility of human judgment demonstrated to me."[31] Although some proponents of capital punishment would argue that its merits are worth the occasional execution of innocent people, most would also insist that there is little likelihood of the innocent being executed. Yet a large body of evidence shows that innocent people are often convicted of crimes, including capital crimes and that some of them have been executed.

Since 1900, in this country, there have been on the average more than four cases per year in which an entirely innocent person was convicted of murder. Scores of these persons were sentenced to death. In many cases, a reprieve or commutation arrived just hours, or even minutes, before the scheduled execution. These erroneous convictions have occurred in virtually every jurisdiction from one end of the nation to the other. Nor have they declined in recent years, despite the new death penalty statutes approved by the Supreme Court.[32] Consider this handful of representative cases:

■ In 1975, only a year before the Supreme Court affirmed the constitutionality of capital punishment, two African-American men in Florida, Freddie Pitts and Wilbert Lee, were released from prison after twelve years awaiting execution for the murder of two white men. Their convictions were the result of coerced confessions, erroneous testimony of an alleged eyewitness, and incompetent defense counsel. Though a white man eventually admitted his guilt, a nine-year legal battle was required before the governor would grant Pitts and Lee a pardon.[33] Had their execution not been stayed while the constitutional status of the death penalty was argued in the courts, these two innocent men probably would not be alive today.

* * * * *

■ In 1989, Texas authorities decided not to retry Randall Dale Adams after the appellate court reversed his conviction for murder. Adams had spent more than three years on death row for the murder of a Dallas police officer. He was convicted on the perjured testimony of a 16-year-old youth who was the real killer. Adams's plight was vividly presented in the 1988 docudrama, *The Thin Blue Line*, which convincingly told the true story of the crime and exposed the errors that resulted in his conviction.[36]

■ Another case in Texas from the 1980s tells an even more sordid story. In 1980 a black high school janitor, Clarence Brandley, and his white co-worker found the body of a missing 15-year-old white schoolgirl. Interrogated by the police, they were told, "One of you two is going to hang for this." Looking at Brandley, the officer said, "Since you're the nigger, you're elected." In a classic case of rush to judgment, Brandley was tried, convicted, and sentenced to death. The circumstantial evidence against him was thin, other leads were ignored by the police, and the courtroom atmosphere reeked of racism. In 1986 Centurion Ministries—a volunteer group devoted to freeing wrongly convicted prisoners—came to Brandley's aid. Evidence had meanwhile emerged that another man had committed the murder for which Brandley was awaiting execution. Brandley was not released until 1990.[37]

Each of the five stories told above has a reassuring ending: The innocent prisoner is saved from execution and is released. But when prisoners are executed, no legal forum exists in which unanswered questions about their guilt can be resolved. In May 1992, Roger Keith Coleman was executed in Virginia despite widely publicized doubts surrounding his guilt and evidence that pointed to another person as the murderer—evidence that was never submitted at his trial. Not until late in the appeal process did anyone take seriously the possibility that the state was about to kill an innocent man, and then efforts to delay or nullify his execution failed. Was Coleman really innocent? At the time of his execution, his case was marked with many of the features found in other cases where the defendant was eventually cleared. Were Coleman still in prison, his friends and attorneys would have a strong incentive to resolve these questions. But with Coleman dead, further inquiry into the facts of the crime for which he was convicted is unlikely.

Overzealous prosecution, mistaken or perjured testimony, faulty police work, coerced confessions, the defendant's previous criminal record, inept defense counsel, seemingly conclusive circumstantial evidence, community pressure for a conviction—such factors help explain why the judicial system cannot guarantee that justice will never miscarry. And when it does miscarry, volunteers outside the criminal justice system—newspaper reporters, for example—and not the police or prosecutors are the ones who rectify the errors. To retain the death penalty in the face of the demonstrable failures of the system is unacceptable, especially as there are no strong counterbalancing factors in favor of the death penalty.

BARBARITY

The traditional mode of execution, still available in a few states, is hanging. Death on the gallows is easily bungled: If the drop is too short, there will be a slow and agonizing death by strangulation. If the drop is too long, the head will be torn off.

Two states, Idaho and Utah, still authorize the firing squad. The prisoner is strapped into a chair, and hooded. A target is pinned to the chest. Five marksmen, one with blanks, take aim and fire.

Electrocution has been the most widely used form of execution in this country in this century. The condemned prisoner is led—or dragged—into the death chamber, strapped into the chair, and electrodes are fastened to head and legs. When the switch is thrown the body strains, jolting as the voltage is raised and lowered. Often smoke rises from the head. There is the awful odor of burning flesh. No one knows how long electrocuted individuals retain consciousness.

* * * * *

The latest mode of inflicting the death penalty, enacted into law by nearly two dozen states, is lethal injection, first used in Texas in 1982. It is easy to overstate the humaneness and efficacy of this method. There is no way of knowing that it is really painless. As the U.S. Court of

Appeals observed, there is "substantial and uncontroverted evidence ... that execution by lethal injection poses a serious risk of cruel, protracted death.... Even a slight error in dosage or administration can leave a prisoner conscious but paralyzed while dying, a sentient witness of his or her own asphyxiation" (*Chaney v. Heckler*, 718 F.2d 1174 [1983]).

Nor does the execution always proceed smoothly as planned. In 1985 "the authorities repeatedly jabbed needles into ... Stephen Morin, when they had trouble finding a usable vein because he had been a drug abuser."[40] In 1988, during the execution of Raymond Landry, "a tube attached to a needle inside the inmate's right arm began leaking, sending the lethal mixture shooting across the death chamber toward witnesses."[41]

Indeed, by its veneer of decency and by subtle analogy with life-saving medical practice, death by lethal injection makes killing as punishment more acceptable to the public. Even when it prevents the struggles of the condemned person and avoids maiming the body, it is no different from hanging or shooting as an expression of the absolute power of the state over the helpless individual.

* * * * *

RETRIBUTION

Justice, it is often insisted, requires the death penalty as the only suitable retribution for heinous crimes. This claim will not bear scrutiny. All punishment by its nature is retributive, not only the death penalty. Whatever legitimacy, therefore, is to be found in punishment as just retribution can in principle be satisfied without recourse to executions.

It is also obvious that the death penalty could be defended on narrowly retributive grounds only for the crime of murder, and not for any of the many other crimes that have frequently been made subject to this mode of punishment (rape, kidnapping, espionage, treason, drug king-pins). Few defenders of the death penalty are willing to confine themselves consistently to the narrow scope afforded by retribution. In any case, execution is more than a punishment exacted in retribution for the taking of a life.

As Camus wrote, "For there to be equivalence, the death penalty would have to punish a criminal who had warned his victim of the date at which he would inflict a horrible death on him and who, from that moment onward, had confined him at his mercy for months. Such a monster is not encountered in private life."[46]

It is also often argued that death is what murderers deserve, and that those who oppose the death penalty violate the fundamental principle that criminals should be punished according to their deserts—"making the punishment fit the crime."

If this principle is understood to require that punishments are unjust unless they are like the crime itself, then the principle is unacceptable. It would require us to rape rapists, torture torturers, and inflict other horrible and degrading punishments on offenders. It would require us to betray traitors and kill multiple murderers again and again, punishments impossible to inflict. Since we cannot reasonably aim to punish all crimes according to this principle, it is arbitrary to invoke it as a requirement of justice in the punishment of murderers.

If, however, the principle of just deserts is understood to require that the severity of punishments must be proportional to the gravity of the crime, and that murder being the gravest crime deserves the severest punishment, then the principle is no doubt sound. But it does not compel support for the death penalty. What it does require is that crimes other than murder be punished with terms of imprisonment or other deprivations less severe than those used in the punishment of murder.

Criminals no doubt deserve to be punished, and punished with severity appropriate to their culpability and the harm they have caused to the innocent. But severity of punishment has its limits—imposed both by justice and our common human dignity. Governments that respect these limits do not use premeditated, violent homicide as an instrument of social policy.

Some whose loved one was a murder victim believe that they cannot rest until the murderer is executed. But the feeling is by no means universal. Coretta Scott King has observed, "As one whose husband and mother-in-law have died the victims of murder assassination, I stand firmly and unequivocally opposed to the death penalty for those convicted of capital offenses. An evil deed is not redeemed by an evil deed of retaliation. Justice is never advanced in the taking of a human life. Morality is never upheld by a legalized murder."[47]

Kerry Kennedy, daughter of the slain Senator Robert Kennedy, has written: "I was eight years old when my father was murdered. It is almost impossible to describe the pain of losing a parent to a senseless murder [...] But even as a child one thing was clear to me: I didn't want the killer, in turn, to be killed. I remember lying in bed and praying, 'Please, God. Please don't take his life, too.' I saw nothing that could be accomplished in the loss of one life being answered with the loss of another. And I knew, far too vividly, the anguish that would spread through another family—another set of parents, children, brothers, and sisters thrown into grief."[48]

FINANCIAL COSTS

It is sometimes suggested that abolishing capital punishment is unfair to the taxpayer, as though life imprisonment were obviously more expensive than executions. If one takes into account all the relevant costs, the reverse is true. "The death penalty is not now, nor has it ever been, a more economical alternative to life imprisonment."[49]

A murder trial normally takes much longer when the death penalty is at issue than when it is not. Litigation costs—including the time of judges, prosecutors, public defenders, and court reporters, and the high costs of briefs—are all borne by the taxpayer.

A 1982 study showed that were the death penalty to be reintroduced in New York, the cost of the capital trial alone would be more than double the cost of a life term in prison.[50]

In Maryland, a comparison of capital trial costs with and without the death penalty for the years 1979-1984 concluded that a death penalty case costs "approximately 42 percent more than a case resulting in a non-death sentence."[51] In 1988 and 1989 the Kansas legislature voted against reinstating the death penalty after it was informed that reintroduction would involve a first-year cost of "more than $ 11 million."[52] Florida, with one of the nation's largest death rows, has estimated that the true cost of each execution is approximately $3.2 million, or approximately six times the cost of a life-imprisonment sentence.[53]

The only way to make the death penalty a "better buy" than imprisonment is to weaken due process and curtail appellate review, which are the defendant's (and society's) only protections against the grossest miscarriages of justice. The savings in dollars would be at the cost of justice: In nearly half of the death-penalty cases given review under federal habeas corpus, the conviction is overturned.[54]

PUBLIC OPINION

The media commonly report that the American public overwhelmingly supports the death penalty. More careful analysis of public attitudes, however, reveals that most Americans would oppose the death penalty if convicted murderers were sentenced to life without parole and were required to make some form of financial restitution. In California, for example, a Field Institute survey showed that in 1990, 82 percent approved in principle of the death penalty. But when asked to choose between the death penalty and life imprisonment plus restitution, only a small minority—26 percent—continued to favor executions.[55]

A comparable change in attitude toward the death penalty has been verified in many other states and contradicted in none.

ABOLITION TRENDS

The death penalty in the United States needs to be put into international perspective. In 1962, it was reported to the Council of Europe that "the facts clearly show that the death penalty is regarded in Europe as something of an anachronism [...]."[56]

Today, 28 European countries have abolished the death penalty either in law or in practice. In Great Britain, it was abolished (except for treason) in 1971; France abolished it in 1981. Canada abolished it in 1976. The United Nations General Assembly affirmed in a formal resolution that, throughout the world, it is desirable to "progressively restrict the number of offenses for which the death penalty might be imposed, with a view to the desirability of abolishing this punishment."[57]

Conspicuous by their indifference to these recommendations are nations generally known for their disregard for the human rights of their citizens: China, Iraq, Iran, South Africa, and the former Soviet Union.[58] Americans ought to be embarrassed to find themselves linked with the governments of such nations in retaining execution as a method of crime control.

Opposition to the death penalty in the United States is widespread and diverse. Catholic, Jewish, and Protestant religious groups, national organizations representing people of color, and public-interest law groups are among the more than fifty national organizations that constitute the National Coalition to Abolish the Death Penalty.

Once in use everywhere and for a wide variety of crimes, the death penalty today is generally forbidden by law and widely abandoned in practice. The unmistakable worldwide trend is toward the complete abolition of capital punishment.

Notes

[1] See U.S. Dept. Justice, *Capital Punishment*, annually, 1980 et seq.

[2] See *Uniform Crime Reports*, annually, 1980 et seq.

[3] See *Uniform Crime Reports*.

[4] *Uniform Crime Reports*, annually, 1980-1989.

[5] Bowers and Pierce, "Deterrence or Brutalization," in *Crime & Delinquency* (1980).

[6] U.S. Dept. Justice, *Capital Punishment*, 1972-1990; *Uniform Crime Reports*, annually, 1972-1990; and NAACP Legal Defense and Educational Fund, "Death Row, USA," Spring 1992.

[7] Bailey and Peterson, in *Criminology* (1987), p. 22.

[8] *Sourcebook of Criminal Justice Statistics*—1990.

[9] Bureau of Justice Statistics, *Prisons and Prisoners in the United States* (1992), p. 1.

[10] Wolfson, in Bedau, ed., *The Death Penalty in America*, 3rd ed. (1982), p. 167

[11] Ehrlich, in *American Economic Review* (1974); Phillips, in *American Journal of Sociology* (1980); and Layson, in *Southern Economic Journal* (1985)

[12] Lempert, in *Crime & Delinquency* (1983); Peterson and Bailey in Chambliss, ed., *Criminal Law in Action*, 2nd ed. (1984); Bowers, in Hasse and Inciardi, eds., *Challenging Capital Punishment* (1988); Peterson and Cello, in *Social Forces* (1988); and Fox and Radelet, in *Loyola of Los Angeles Law Review* (1989).

[13] Blumstein, Cohen, and Nagin, eds., *Deterrence and Incapacitation* (1975), p. 358.

[14] West, Solomon, and Diamond, in Bedau and Pierce, eds., *Capital Punishment in the United States* (1976).

[15] Bedau, "Recidivism, Parole, and Deterrence," in Bedau, ed., *Death Penalty in America*, 3rd ed.

[16] Marquart and Sorensen, in *Loyola of Los Angeles Law Review* (1989).

[17] U.S. Bureau of Justice Statistics, "Capital Punishment," 1977, and NAACP LDF, "Death Row, USA," Spring 1992.

[18] Bowers, *Legal Homicide* (1984); Streib, *Death Penalty for Juveniles* (1987).

[19] "Death Row, USA," 1976 *et seq.*

[20] *Uniform Crime Reports*, 1972-1990.

[21] Baldus, Woodworth, and Pulaski, *Equal Justice and The Death Penalty* (1990), p. 401.

[22] U.S. General Accounting Office, "Death Penalty Sentencing" (1990), pp.5, 6.

[23] "Death Row, USA," Spring 1992; and *Sourcebook of Criminal Justice Statistics*—1990.

[24] U.S. Bureau of Justice Statistics, "Capital Punishment," 1980-1990.

[25] *Uniform Crime Reports*, 1980-1990.

[26] Memorandum, National Coalition to Abolish the Death Penalty, January 1991.

[27] U.S. Bureau of Justice Statistics, "Capital Punishment," 1979; NAACP LDF, "Death Row, USA," Spring 1992.

[28] Tabak, in *Loyola of Los Angeles Law Review* (1989).

[29] Gross and Mauro, *Death and Discrimination* (1989), p. 224.

[30] Black, *Capital Punishment. The Inevitability of Caprice and Mistake.* 2nd ed. (1982).

31 *Lucas Recueil des debats* ... (1831) pt. II, p. 32.

32 Radelet, Bedau, and Putnam, *In Spite of Innocence* (1992); Bedau and Radelet, Miscarriages of Justice in Potentially Capital Cases, *Stanford Law Review* (1987).

33 Miller, *Invitation to a Lynching* (1975); also *The New York Times*, Sept 10, 1975, p.1.

34 "Capital Punishment" Senate Hearings (1981) pp. 713-20

35 *Atlanta Weekly*, May 30, 1982.

36 Adams, Hoffer, and Hoffer, *Adams v. Texas* (1991).

37 Davies, *White Lies* (1991).

38 (*Glass v. Louisiana*, 471 U.S. 1080 (1985).

39 *Boston Globe*, April 24, 1983, p. 24.

40 *The New York Times*, December 14, 1988, p. A29.

41 Ibid.

42 *Los Angeles Times*, March 24, 1985, Pt IV, p. 5.

43 Lawes, *Life and Death in Sing Sing* (1928).

44 Teeters, in *Journal of the Lancaster County Historical Society* (1960).

45 *Boston Globe*, August 16, 1976, p. 17

46 Camus, "Reflections on the Guillotine," in *Resistance, Rebellion and Death* (1960).

47 Speech to National Coalition to Abolish the Death Penalty, Washington, D.C., September 26, 1981.

48 Foreword to Gray and Stanley, *A Punishment in Search of A Crime* (1989).

49 Spangenberg and Walsh, in *Loyola of Los Angeles Law Review* (1989), p. 47

50 N. Y. State Defenders Assn., *Capital Losses* (1982).

51 U S. Govt. Accounting Office, *Limited Data Available on Costs of Death Sentences* (1989), p. 50.

52 Cited in Spangenberg and Walsh, note 49.

53 *Miami Herald*, July 10, 1988.

54 *New York Times*, Sept. 22, 1989

55 *New York Times*, May 28, 1990; and Fox, Radelet, and Bonsteel, in *N.Y.U. Review of Law and Social Change* (1990-91).

56 Ancel, *The Death Penalty in European Countries* (1962), p 55.

57 UN, Ecosoc, Official Records 58th Sess. (1971), Supl. 1, p.36.

58 Hood, *The Death Penalty: A World-Wide Perspective* (1989); Amnesty International, *When The State Kills...* (1989).

A MODEST PROPOSAL

Jonathan Swift

For Preventing the Children of Poor People in Ireland
from Being a Burden to Their Parents or Country,
and for Making Them Beneficial to the Public.

It is a melancholy object to those who walk through this great town[1] or travel in the country, when they see the streets, the roads, and cabin doors, crowded with beggars of the female sex, followed by three, four, or six children, all in rags and importuning every passenger for an alms. These mothers, instead of being able to work for their honest livelihood, are forced to employ all their time in strolling to beg sustenance for their helpless infants: who as they grow up either turn thieves for want of work, or leave their dear native country to fight for the pretender in Spain,[2] or sell themselves to the Barbadoes.[3]

I think it is agreed by all parties that this prodigious number of children in the arms, or on the backs, or at the heels of their mothers, and frequently of their fathers, is in the present deplorable state of the kingdom a very great additional grievance; and, therefore, whoever could find out a fair, cheap, and easy method of making these children sound, useful members of the commonwealth, would deserve so well of the public as to have his statue set up for a preserver of the nation.

But my intention is very far from being confined to provide only for the children of professed beggars; it is of a much greater extent, and shall take in the whole number of infants at a certain age who are born of parents in effect as little able to support them as those who demand our charity in the streets.

As to my own part, having turned my thoughts for many years upon this important subject, and maturely weighed the several schemes of our projectors,[4] I have always found them grossly mistaken in their computation. It is true, a child just dropped from its dam may be supported by her milk for a solar year, with little other nourishment; at most not above the value of 2s.,[5] which the mother may certainly get, or the value in scraps, by her lawful occupation of begging; and it is exactly at one year old that I propose to provide for them in such a manner as

---

[1] **this great town:** Dublin.—EDS

[2] **pretender in Spain:** James Stuart (1688-1766); exiled in Spain, he laid claim to the English crown and had the support of many Irishmen who had joined an army hoping to restore him to the throne.—EDS.

[3] **the Barbadoes:** Inhabitants of the British colony in the Caribbean where Irishmen emigrated to work as indentured servants in exchange for their passage.—EDS.

[4] **projectors:** Planners.—EDS.

[5] **2s.:** Two shillings; in Swift's time one shilling was worth less than twenty-five cents. Other monetary references in the essay are to pounds sterling ("£"), pence ("d"), a crown, and a groat. A pound consisted of twenty shillings; a shilling of twelve pence; a crown was five shillings; a groat was worth a few cents.—EDS.

instead of being a charge upon their parents or the parish, or wanting food and raiment for the rest of their lives, they shall on the contrary contribute to the feeding, and partly to the clothing, of many thousands.

There is likewise another great advantage in my scheme, that it will prevent those voluntary abortions, and that horrid practice of women murdering their bastard children, alas! too frequent among us! sacrificing the poor innocent babes I doubt more to avoid the expense than the shame, which would move tears and pity in the most savage and inhuman breast.

The number of souls in this kingdom being usually reckoned one million and a half, of these I calculate there may be about 200,000 couple whose wives are breeders; from which number I subtract 30,000 couples who are able to maintain their own children (although I apprehend there cannot be so many, under the present distress of the kingdom); but this being granted, there will remain 170,000 breeders. I again subtract 50,000 for those women who miscarry, or whose children die by accident or disease within the year. There only remain 120,000 children of poor parents annually born. The question therefore is, how this number shall be reared and provided for? which, as I have already said, under the present situation of affairs, is utterly impossible by all the methods hitherto proposed. For we can neither employ them in handicraft or agriculture; we neither build houses (I mean in the country) nor cultivate land; they can very seldom pick up a livelihood by stealing, till they arrive at six years old, except where they are of towardly parts;[6] although I confess they learn the rudiments much earlier; during which time they can, however, be properly looked upon only as probationers; as I have been informed by a principal gentleman in the county of Cavan, who protested to me that he never knew above one or two instances under the age of six, even in a part of the kingdom so renowned for the quickest proficiency in that art.

I am assured by our merchants, that a boy or a girl before twelve years old is no salable commodity; and even when they come to this age they will not yield above 3£. or 3£. 2s. 3d. at most on the exchange; which cannot turn to account either to the parents or kingdom, the charge of nutriment and rags having been at least four times that value.

I shall now therefore humbly propose my own thoughts, which I hope will not be liable to the least objection.

I have been assured by a very knowing American of my acquaintance in London, that a young healthy child well nursed is at a year old a most delicious, nourishing, and wholesome food, whether stewed, roasted, baked, or broiled; and I make no doubt that it will equally serve in a fricassee or a ragout.[7]

I do therefore humbly offer it to public consideration that of the 120,000 children already computed 20,000 may be reserved for breed, whereof only one-fourth part to be males; which is more than we allow to sheep, black cattle, or swine; and my reason is, that these children are seldom the fruits of marriage, a circumstance not much regarded by our savages; therefore one

---

[6] **towardly parts:** Natural abilities.—EDS.

[7] **ragout:** A stew.—EDS.

male will be sufficient to serve four females. That the remaining 100,000 may, at a year old, be offered in sale to the persons of quality and fortune through the kingdom; always advising the mother to let them suck plentifully in the last month, so as to render them plump and fat for a good table. A child will make two dishes at an entertainment for friends; and when the family dines alone, the fore and hind quarter will make a reasonable dish, and seasoned with a little pepper or salt will be very good boiled on the fourth day, especially in winter.

I have reckoned upon a medium, that a child just born will weigh 12 pounds, and in a solar year, if tolerably nursed, will increase to 28 pounds.

I grant this food will be somewhat dear, and therefore very proper for landlords, who, as they have already devoured most of the parents, seem to have the best title to the children.

Infants' flesh will be in season throughout the year, but more plentiful in March, and a little before and after: for we are told by a grave author, an eminent French physician,[8] that fish being a prolific diet, there are more children born in Roman Catholic countries about nine months after Lent than at any other season; therefore, reckoning a year after Lent, the markets will be more glutted than usual, because the number of popish infants is at least three to one in this kingdom: and therefore it will have one other collateral advantage, by lessening the number of papists among us.

I have already computed the charge of nursing a beggar's child (in which list I reckon all cottagers, laborers, and four-fifths of the farmers) to be about 2s. per annum, rags included; and I believe no gentleman would repine to give 10s. for the carcass of a good fat child, which, as I have said, will make four dishes of excellent nutritive meat, when he has only some particular friend or his own family to dine with him. Thus the squire will learn to be a good landlord, and grow popular among the tenants; the mother will have 8s. net profit, and be fit for work till she produces another child.

Those who are more thrifty (as I must confess the times require) may flay the carcass; the skin of which artificially[9] dressed will make admirable gloves for ladies, and summer boots for fine gentlemen.

As to our city of Dublin, shambles[10] may be appointed for this purpose in the most convenient parts of it, and butchers we may be assured will not be wanting: although I rather recommend buying the children alive, and dressing them hot from the knife as we do roasting pigs.

A very worthy person, a true lover of his country, and whose virtues I highly esteem, was lately pleased in discoursing on this matter to offer a refinement upon my scheme. He said that many gentlemen of this kingdom, having of late destroyed their deer, he conceived that the want of venison might be well supplied by the bodies of young lads and maidens, not exceeding fourteen years of age nor under twelve; so great a number of both sexes in every country being now ready to starve for want of work and service; and these to be disposed of by their

---

[8] **French physician:** François Rabelais (c. 1494-1553), the great Renaissance humanist and author of the comic masterpiece *Gargantua and Pantagruel.* Swift is being ironic in calling Rabelais "grave."—EDS.

[9] **artifically:** Artfully.—EDS.

[10] **shambles:** Slaughterhouses.—EDS.

parents, if alive, or otherwise by their nearest relations. But with due deference to so excellent a friend and so deserving a patriot, I cannot be altogether in his sentiments; for as to the males, my American acquaintance assured me from frequent experience that their flesh was generally tough and lean, like that of our schoolboys by continual exercise, and their taste disagreeable; and to fatten them would not answer the charge. Then as to the females, it would, I think, with humble submission be a loss to the public, because they soon would become breeders themselves: and besides, it is not improbable that some scrupulous people might be apt to censure such a practice (although indeed very unjustly), as a little bordering upon cruelty; which, I confess, has always been with me the strongest objection against any project, how well soever intended.

But in order to justify my friend, he confessed that this expedient was put into his head by the famous Psalmanazar,[11] a native of the island Formosa, who came from thence to London about twenty years ago: and in conversation told my friend, that in his country when any young person happened to be put to death, the executioner sold the carcass to persons of quality as a prime dainty; and that in his time the body of a plump girl of fifteen, who was crucified for an attempt to poison the emperor, was sold to his imperial majesty's prime minister of state, and other great mandarins of the court, in joints from the gibbet, at 400 crowns. Neither indeed can I deny, that if the same use were made of several plump young girls in this town, who without one single groat to their fortunes cannot stir abroad without a chair,[12] and appear at the playhouse and assemblies in foreign fineries which they never will pay for, the kingdom would not be the worse.

Some persons of a desponding spirit are in great concern about the vast number of poor people, who are aged, diseased, or maimed, and I have been desired to employ my thoughts what course may be taken to ease the nation of so grievous an encumbrance. But I am not in the least pain upon the matter, because it is very well known that they are every day dying and rotting by cold and famine, and filth and vermin, as fast as can be reasonably expected. And as to the young laborers, they are now in as hopeful a condition: They cannot get work, and consequently pine away for want of nourishment, to a degree that if at any time they are accidentally hired to common labor, they have not strength to perform it; and thus the country and themselves are happily delivered from the evils to come.

I have too long digressed, and therefore shall return to my subject. I think the advantages by the proposal which I have made are obvious and many, as well as of the highest importance.

For first, as I have already observed, it would greatly lessen the number of papists, with whom we are yearly overrun, being the principal breeders of the nation as well as our most dangerous enemies; and who stay at home on purpose to deliver the kingdom to the Pretender, hoping to take their advantage by the absence of so many good Protestants, who have chosen

---

[11] **Psalmanazar:** George Psalmanazar (c. 1679-1763) was a Frenchman who tricked London society into believing he was a native of Formosa (now Taiwan).—EDS.

[12] **a chair:** A sedan chair in which one is carried about.—EDS.

rather to leave their country than stay at home and pay tithes against their conscience to an Episcopal curate.

Secondly, The poor tenants will have something valuable of their own, which by law may be made liable to distress[13] and help to pay their landlord's rent, their corn and cattle being already seized, and money a thing unknown.

Thirdly, Whereas the maintenance of 100,000 children from two years old and upward, cannot be computed at less than 10s. a-piece per annum, the nation's stock will be thereby increased £50,000 per annum, beside the profit of a new dish introduced to the tables of all gentlemen of fortune in the kingdom who have any refinement in taste. And the money will circulate among ourselves, the goods being entirely of our own growth and manufacture.

Fourthly, The constant breeders beside the gain of 8s. sterling per annum by the sale of their children, will be rid of the charge of maintaining them after the first year.

Fifthly, This food would likewise bring great custom to taverns, where the vintners will certainly be so prudent as to procure the best receipts[14] for dressing it to perfection, and consequently have their houses frequented by all the fine gentlemen, who justly value themselves upon their knowledge in good eating; and a skillful cook who understands how to oblige his guests, will contrive to make it as expensive as they please.

Sixthly, This would be a great inducement to marriage, which all wise nations have either encouraged by rewards or enforced by laws and penalties. It would increase the care and tenderness of mothers toward their children, when they were sure of a settlement for life to the poor babes, provided in some sort by the public, to their annual profit instead of expense. We should see an honest emulation among the married women, which of them would bring the fattest child to the market. Men would become as fond of their wives during the time of their pregnancy as they are now of their mares in foal, their cows in calf, their sows when they are ready to farrow; nor offer to beat or kick them (as is too frequent a practice) for fear of a miscarriage.

Many other advantages might be enumerated. For instance, the addition of some thousand carcasses in our exportation of barreled beef, the propagation of swine's flesh, and improvement in the art of making good bacon, so much wanted among us by the great destruction of pigs, too frequent at our table; which are no way comparable in taste or magnificence to a well-grown, fat, yearling child, which roasted whole will make a considerable figure at a lord mayor's feast or any other public entertainment. But this and many others I omit, being studious of brevity.

Supposing that 1,000 families in this city would be constant customers for infants' flesh, besides others who might have it at merry-meetings, particularly at weddings and christenings, I compute that Dublin would take off annually about 20,000 carcasses; and the rest of the kingdom (where probably they will be sold somewhat cheaper) the remaining 80,000.

I can think of no one objection that will possibly be raised against this proposal, unless it should be urged that the number of people will be thereby much lessened in the kingdom.

---

[13] **distress:** Seizure of payment of debt.—EDS.

[14] **receipts:** Recipes.—EDS.

This I freely own, and it was indeed one principal design in offering it to the world. I desire the reader will observe, that I calculate my remedy for this one individual kingdom of Ireland and for no other that ever was, is, or I think ever can be upon earth. Therefore let no man talk to me of other expedients: of taxing our absentees at 5s. a pound: of using neither clothes nor household furniture except what is our own growth and manufacture: of utterly rejecting the materials and instruments that promote foreign luxury: of curing the expensiveness of pride, vanity, idleness, and gaming in our women: of introducing a vein of parsimony, prudence, and temperance: of learning to love our country, in the want of which we differ even from Laplanders and the inhabitants of Topinamboo:[15] of quitting our animosities and factions, nor acting any longer like the Jews, who were murdering one another at the very moment their city was taken:[16] of being a little cautious not to sell our country and conscience for nothing: of teaching landlords to have at least one degree of mercy toward their tenants: lastly, of putting a spirit of honesty, industry, and skill into our shopkeepers; who, if a resolution could now be taken to buy only our native goods, would immediately unite to cheat and exact upon us in the price the measure, and the goodness, nor could ever yet be brought to make one fair proposal of just dealing, though often and earnestly invited to it.

Therefore I repeat, let no man talk to me of these and the like expedients, till he has at least some glimpse of hope that there will be ever some hearty and sincere attempt to put them in practice.

But as to myself, having been wearied out for many years with offering vain, idle, visionary thoughts, and at length utterly despairing of success, I fortunately fell upon this proposal; which, as it is wholly new, so it has something solid and real, of no expense and little trouble, full in our power, and whereby we can incur no danger in disobliging England. For this kind of commodity will not bear exportation, the flesh being of too tender a consistence to admit a long continuance in salt, although perhaps I could name a country which would be glad to eat up our whole nation without it.

After all, I am not so violently bent upon my own opinion as to reject any offer proposed by wise men, which shall be found equally innocent, cheap, easy, and effectual. But before something of that kind shall be advanced in contradiction to my scheme, and offering a better, I desire the author or authors will be pleased maturely to consider two points. First, as things now stand, how they will be able to find food and raiment for 100,000 useless mouths and backs. And secondly, there being a round million creatures in human figure throughout this kingdom, whose subsistence put into a common stock would leave them in debt 2,000,000£. sterling, adding those who are beggars by profession to the bulk of farmers, cottagers, and laborers, with the wives and children who are beggars in effect; I desire those politicians who dislike my overture, and may perhaps be so bold as to attempt an answer, that they will first ask the parents of these mortals, whether they would not at this day think it a great happiness to have been

---

[15] **Laplanders and the inhabitants of Topinamboo:** Lapland is the area of Scandanavia above the Artic Circle; Topinamboo, in Brazil, was known in Swift's time for the savagery of its tribes.—EDS.

[16] **was taken:** A reference to the Roman seizure of Jerusalem (A.D. 70).—EDS.

sold for food at a year old in the manner I prescribe, and thereby have avoided such a perpetual scene of misfortunes as they have since gone through by the oppression of landlords, the impossibility of paying rent without money or trade, the want of common sustenance, with neither house nor clothes to cover them from the inclemencies of the weather, and the most inevitable prospect of entailing the like or greater miseries upon their breed for ever.

I profess, in the sincerity of my heart, that I have not the least personal interest in endeavoring to promote this necessary work, having no other motive than the public good of my country, by advancing our trade, providing for infants, relieving the poor, and giving some pleasure to the rich. I have no children by which I can propose to get a single penny; the youngest being nine years old, and my wife past childbearing. (1729)

JUST BE NICE

Stephen Carter

When I was a child, attending grade school in Washington, D.C., we took classroom time to study manners. Not only the magic words we have already discussed ("please" and "thank you") but more complicated etiquette questions, like how to answer the telephone ("Carter residence, Stephen speaking") and how to set the table (we were quizzed on whether knife blades point in or out). And somehow nobody—no children, no parents—objected to what nowadays would surely be viewed as indoctrination.

Today instruction of this sort is so rare that when a school tries to teach manners to children, it makes news. So when the magazine *U.S. News & World Report* ran a story in 1996 about the decline of civility, it opened with what it must have considered the man-bites-dog vignette—an account of a classroom where young people were taught to be polite. Ironically, this newsworthy curriculum evidently teaches a good deal less about etiquette than we learned back at Margaret M. Amidon Elementary School in the sixties, but that is still a good deal more than children learn in most places. Deportment classes are long gone. Now and then the schools teach some norms of conduct, but almost always about sex, and never the most important ones: *Do not engage in harassment* and *Always use a condom* seem to be the outer limits of their moral capacity. The idea that sex, as a unique human activity, might require a unique morality, different from the general moral rules against physical harm to others and harm to the self, is not one that public schools are prepared to entertain.

Respect for rules of conduct has been lost in the deafening and essentially empty rights-talk of our age. Following a rule of good manners may mean doing something you do not want to do, and the weird rhetoric of our self-indulgent age resists the idea that we have such things as obligations to others. We suffer from what James Q. Wilson has described as the elevation of self-expression over self-control. So when a black student at a Connecticut high school was disciplined in 1996 for wearing pants that drooped (exposing his underwear), not only did he claim a right to wear what he liked, but some community leaders hinted at racism, on the theory that many young African American males dress this way. (The fact that the style is copied from prison garb, which lacks a belt, evidently makes no impression on these particular defenders of the race.)

When I was a child, had my school sought to discipline me, my parents would have assumed the school had good reason. And they probably would have punished me further at home. Unlike many of today's parents, they would not have begun by challenging the teacher or principal who thought I had done wrong. To the student of civility, the relevant difference between that era and the present is the collapse of trust, particularly trust in strangers and in institutions. My parents would have trusted the school's judgment—and thus trusted the school to punish me appropriately—but trust of that kind has largely dissolved. Trust (along with generosity) is at the heart of civility. But cynicism has replaced the healthier emotion of trust.

Cynicism is the enemy of civility: It suggests a deep distrust of the motives of our fellow passengers, a distrust that ruins any project that rests, as civility does, on trusting others even when there is risk. And so, because we no longer trust each other, we place our trust in the vague and conversation-stifling language of "rights" instead.

Consider again the boy with the droopy pants. To talk about wearing a particular set of clothes as a "right" is demeaning to the bloody struggles for such basic rights as the vote and an unsegregated education. But the illusion that all desires are rights continues its insidious spread. At about the same time, a fired waitress at a restaurant not far from Yale, where I teach, announced a "right" to pierce her face with as many studs and rings as she wishes. And, not long ago, a television program featured an interview with a woman who insisted on the "right" to be as fat as she likes. Rights that are purchased at relatively low cost stand a fair chance of being abused, simply because there is no history behind them, and thus little pressure to use them responsibly—in short, because nobody knows why the right exists. But even a right that possesses a grimly instructive history—a right like freedom of speech—may fall subject to abuse when we forget where it came from.

This proposition helps explain *Cohen v. California*, a 1971 decision in which the Supreme Court overturned the conviction of a young man who wore on his jacket the benign legend F _ _ _ THE DRAFT. The case arose as the public language grew vulgar. The 19th and early 20th centuries offered a tradition of public insults that were witty, pointed, occasionally cruel, but not obscene or particularly offensive. Politicians and other public figures competed to demonstrate their cleverness in repartee. (One of my favorites is Benjamin Disraeli's explanation of the difference between a misfortune and a calamity: "If Gladstone fell into the Thames, that would be a misfortune. And if anyone pulled him out, that would be a calamity.") Nowadays the tradition of barbed wit has given way to a witless barbarism, our lazier conversational habit of reaching for the first bit of profanity that comes to mind. The restraint and forethought that are necessary to be clever, even in insult, are what a sacrificial civility demands. When we are lazy about our words, we tell those at whom our vulgarity is directed that they are so far beneath us that they are not worth the effort of stopping to think how best to insult them; we prefer, animal-like, to make the first sound that comes to mind.

In *Cohen v. California*, the justices were unfortunately correct that what the dissenters called "Cohen's absurd and immature antic" was protected by the freedom of speech. But it is important to add that when the framers of the Constitution envisioned the rough-and-tumble world of public argument, they almost certainly imagined heated disagreements against a background of broadly shared values; certainly that was the model offered by John Locke, by then a kind of political folk hero. It is unlikely that the framers imagined a world in which I might feel (morally) free to say the first thing that came into my head. I do think *Cohen* was rightly decided, but the danger deserves emphasis: When offensiveness becomes a constitutional right, it is a right without any tradition behind it, and consequently we have no norms to govern its use.

Consider once more the fired waitress. I do not deny that the piercing of one's body conveys, in many cultures, information of great significance. But in America, we have no tradition to serve as guide. No elder stands behind our young to say, "Folks have fought and died for your right to pierce your face, so do it right"; no community exists that can model for a young person the responsible use of the "right"; for the right, even if called self-expression, comes from no source other than desire. If we fail to distinguish desire from right, we will not understand that rights are sensible and wise only within particular contexts that give them meaning. The Constitution protects a variety of rights, but our moral norms provide the discipline in their exercise. Sometimes what the moral norm of civility demands is that we restrain our self-expression for the sake of our community. That is why Isaac Peebles in the nineteenth century thought it wrong for people to sing during a train ride; and why it is wrong to race our cars through the streets, stereos cranked high enough to be sure that everyone we pass has the opportunity to enjoy the music we happen to like; and why it was wrong for Cohen to wear his jacket; and why it is wrong for racists to burn crosses (another harmful act of self-expression that the courts have protected under the First Amendment). And it is why a waitress who encounters the dining public every day in her work must consider the interest of that public as she mulls the proper form of self-expression.

Consequently, our celebration of Howard Stern, Don Imus, and other heroes of "shock radio" might be evidence of a certain loss of moral focus. The proposition that all speech must be protected should not be confused with the very different proposition that all speech must be celebrated. When radio station WABC in New York dismissed a popular talk show host, Bob Grant, who refused to stop making racist remarks on the air, some of his colleagues complained that he was being censored. Lost in the brouhaha was the simple fact that Grant's comments and conduct were reprehensible, and that his abuse of our precious freedoms was nothing to be celebrated.

The point is not that we should rule the offensive illegal, which is why the courts are correct to strike down efforts to regulate speech that some people do not like, and even most speech that hurts; the advantages of yielding to the government so much power over what we say have never been shown to outweigh the dangers. Yet we should recognize the terrible damage that free speech can do if people are unwilling to adhere to the basic precept of civility, that we must sometimes rein in our own impulses—including our impulses to speak hurtful words—for the sake of those who are making the democratic journey with us. The Proverb tells us, "Death and life are in the power of the tongue" (Proverbs 18:21). The implication is that the choice of how to use the tongue, for good or for evil, is ours.

Words are magic. We conjure with them. We send messages, we paint images. With words we report the news, profess undying love, and preserve our religious traditions. Words at their best are the tools of morality, of progress, of hope. But words at their worst can wound. And wounds fester. Consequently, the way we use words matters. This explains why many traditional rules of etiquette, from Erasmus's handbook in the sixteenth century to the explosion of guides to good manners during the Victorian era, were designed to govern how words—those marvelous, dangerous words—should be used. Even the controversial limits on sexual harassment and "hate speech" that have sprouted in our era, limits that often carry the force of law, are really just more rules of civility, more efforts, in a morally bereft age, to encourage us to discipline our desires.

My point is not to tell us how to speak. My point is to argue that how we speak is simply one point on a continuum of right and wrong ways to treat one another. And how we treat one another is what civility is about.

ON BEING A BLACK MAN
AND MIDDLE CLASS

Shelby Steele

Not long ago, a friend of mine, black like myself, said to me that the term "black middle class" was actually a contradiction in terms. Race, he insisted, blurred class distinctions among blacks. If you were black, you were just black and that was that. When I argued, he let his eyes roll at my naivete. Then he went on. For us, as black professionals, it was an exercise in self-flattery, a pathetic pretension, to give meaning to such a distinction. Worse, the very idea of class threatened the unity that was vital to the black community as a whole. After all, since when had white America taken note of anything but color when it came to blacks? He then reminded me of an old Malcolm X line that had been popular in the sixties. Question: What is a black man with a Ph.D.? Answer: A nigger.

For many years I had been on my friend's side of this argument. Much of my conscious thinking on the old conundrum of race and class was shaped during my high school and college years in the race-charged sixties, when the fact of my race took on an almost religious significance. Progressively, from the mid-sixties on, more and more aspects of my life found their explanation, their justification, and their motivation in race. My youthful concerns about career, romance, money, values, and even styles of dress became a subject to consultation with various oracular sources of racial wisdom. And these ranged from a figure as ennobling as Martin Luther King, Jr., to the underworld elegance of dress I found in jazz clubs on the South Side of Chicago. Everywhere there were signals, and in those days I considered myself so blessed with clarity and direction that I pitied my white classmates who found more embarrassment than guidance in the fact of their race. In I 968, inflated by my new power, I took a mischievous delight in calling them culturally disadvantaged.

But now, hearing my friend's comment was like hearing a priest from a church I'd grown disenchanted with. I understood him, but my faith was weak. What had sustained me in the sixties sounded monotonous and off the mark in the eighties. For me, race had lost much of its juju, its singular capacity to conjure meaning. And today, when I honestly look at my life and the lives of many other middle-class blacks I know, I can see that race never fully explained our situation in American society. Black though I may be, it is impossible for me to sit in my single-family house with two cars in the driveway and a swing set in the back yard and not see the role class has played in my life. And how can my friend, similarly raised and I , similarly situated, not see it?

Yet despite my certainty I felt a sharp tug of guilt as I tried to explain myself over my friend's skepticism. He is a man of many comedic facial expressions and, as I spoke, his brow lifted in extreme moral alarm as if I were uttering the unspeakable. His clear implication was that I was being elitist and possibly (dare he suggest?) anti-black—crimes for which there might well be no redemption. He pretended to fear for me. I chuckled along with him, but inwardly I did wonder at myself. Though I never doubted the validity of what I was saying, I felt guilty saying it. Why?

After he left (to retrieve his daughter from a dance lesson) I realized that the trap I felt myself in had a tiresome familiarity and, in a sort of slow-motion epiphany, I began to see its outline. It was like the suddenly sharp vision one has at the end of a burdensome marriage when all the long-repressed incompatibilities come undeniably to light.

What became clear to me is that people like myself, my friend, and middle-class blacks generally are caught in a very specific double bind that keeps two equally powerful elements of our identity at odds with each other. The middle-class values by which we were raised—the work ethic, the importance of education, the value of property ownership, of respectability, of "getting ahead," of stable family life, of initiative, of self-reliance, etc.—are, in themselves, race-less and even assimilationist. They urge us toward participation in the American mainstream, toward integration, toward a strong identification with the society—and toward the entire constellation of qualities that are implied in the word "individualism. These values are almost rules for how to prosper in a democratic, free-enterprise society that admires and rewards individual effort. They tell us to work hard for ourselves and our families and to seek our opportunities whenever they appear, inside or outside the confines—of whatever ethnic group we may belong to.

But the particular pattern of racial identification that emerged in the sixties and that still prevails today urges middle-class blacks (and all blacks) in the opposite direction. This pattern asks us to see ourselves as an embattled minority, and it urges an adversarial stance toward the mainstream, an emphasis on ethnic consciousness over individualism. It is organized around an implied separatism.

The opposing thrust of these two parts of our identity results in the double bind of middle-class blacks. There is no forward movement on either plane that does not constitute backward movement on the other. This was the familiar trap I felt myself in while talking with my friend. As I spoke about class, his eyes reminded me that I was betraying race. Clearly, the two indispensable parts of my identity were a threat to each other.

Of course, when you think about it, class and race are both similar in some ways and also naturally opposed. They are two forms of collective identity with boundaries that intersect. But whether they clash or peacefully coexist has much to do with how they are defined. Being both black and middle class becomes a double bind when class and race are defined in sharply antagonistic terms, so that one must be repressed to appease the other.

But what is the "substance" of these two identities, and how does each establish itself in an individual's overall identity? It seems to me that when we identify with any collective we are basically identifying with images that tell us what it means to be a member of that collective. Identity is not the same thing as the fact of membership in a collective: it is, rather, a form of self-definition, facilitated by images of what we wish our membership in the collective to mean. In this sense, the images we identify with may reflect the aspirations of the collective more than they reflect reality, and their content can vary with shifts in those aspirations. But the process of identification is usually dialectical. It is just as necessary to say what we are not as it is to say what we are—so that finally identification comes about by embracing a polarity of positive and negative images. To identify as middle class, for example, I must have both positive and negative images of what being middle class entails; then I will know what I should and should not be doing in order to be middle class. The same goes for racial identity.

In the racially turbulent sixties the polarity of images that came to define racial identification was very antagonistic to the polarity that defined middle-class identification. One might say that the positive images of one lined up with the negative images of the other, so that to identify with both required either a contortionist's flexibility or a dangerous splitting of the self. The double bind of the black middle class was in place....

The black middle class has always defined its class identity by means of positive images gleaned from middle- and upper-class white society, and by means of negative images of lower-class blacks. This habit goes back to the institution of slavery itself, when "house" slaves both mimicked the whites they served and held themselves above the "field" slaves. But in the sixties the old bourgeois impulse to dissociate from the lower classes (the "we-they" distinction) backfired when racial identity suddenly called for the celebration of this same black lower class. One of the qualities of a double bind is that one feels it more than sees it, and I distinctly remember the tension and strange sense of dishonesty I felt in those days as I moved back and forth like a bigamist between the demands of class and race.

Though my father was born poor, he achieved middle-class standing through much hard work and sacrifice (one of his favorite words) and by identifying fully with solid middle-class values mainly hard work, family life, property ownership, and education for his children (all four of whom have advanced degrees). In his mind these were not so much values as laws of nature. People who embodied them made up the positive images in his class polarity. The negative images came largely from the blacks he had left behind because they were "going nowhere."

No one in my family remembers how it happened, but as time went on, the negative images congealed into an imaginary character named Sam, who, from the extensive service we put him to, quickly grew to mythic proportions. In our family lore he was sometimes a trickster, sometimes a boob, but always possessed of a catalogue of sly faults that gave up graphic images of everything we should not be. On sacrifice: "Sam never thinks about tomorrow. He wants it now or he doesn't care about it." On work: "Sam doesn't favor it too much." On children: "Sam likes to have them but not to raise them." On money: "Sam drinks it up and pisses it out." On fidelity: "Sam has to have two or three women." On clothes: "Sam features loud clothes. He likes to see and be seen." And so on. Sam's persona amounted to a negative instruction manual in class identity.

I don't think that any of us believed Sam's faults were accurate representations of lower-class black life. He was an instrument of self-definition, not of sociological accuracy. It never occurred to us that he looked very much like the white racist stereotype of blacks, or that he might have been a manifestation of our own racial self-hatred. He simply gave us a counterpoint against which to express our aspirations. If self-hatred was a factor, it was not, for us, a matter of hating lower-class blacks but of hating what we did not want to be.

Still, hate or love aside, it is fundamentally true that my middle-class identity involved a dissociation from images of lower-class black life and a corresponding identification with values and patterns of responsibility that are common to the middle class everywhere. These values sent me a clear message: be both an individual and a responsible citizen; understand that the quality of your life will approximately reflect the quality of effort you put into it; know that individual responsibility is the basis of freedom and that the limitations imposed by fate (whether fair or unfair) are no excuse for passivity.

Whether I live up to these values or not, I know that my acceptance of them is the result of lifelong conditioning. I know also that I share this conditioning with middle-class people of all races and that I can no more easily be free of it than I can be free of my race. Whether all this got started because the black middle class modeled itself on the white middle class is no longer relevant. For the middle-class black, conditioned by these values from birth, the sense of meaning they provide is as immutable as the color of his skin.

I started the sixties in high school feeling that my class conditioning was the surest way to overcome racial barriers. My racial identity was pretty much taken for granted. After all, it was obvious to the world that I was black. Yet I ended the sixties in graduate school a little embarrassed by my class background and with an almost desperate need to be "black." The tables had turned. I knew very clearly (though I struggled to repress it) that my aspirations and my sense of how to operate in the world came from my class background, yet "being black" required certain attitudes and stances that made me feel secretly a little duplicitous. The inner compatibility of class and race I had known in 1960 was gone.

For blacks, the decade between 1960 and 1969 saw racial identification undergo the same sort of transformation that national identity undergoes in times of war. It became more self-conscious, more narrowly focused, more prescribed, less tolerant of opposition. It spawned an implicit party line, which tended to disallow competing forms of identity. Race-as-identity was lifted from the relative slumber it knew in the fifties and pressed into service in a social and political war against oppression. It was redefined along sharp adversarial lines and directed toward the goal of mobilizing the great mass of black Americans in this warlike effort. It was imbued with a strong moral authority, useful for denouncing those who opposed it and for celebrating those who honored it as a positive achievement rather than as a mere birthright.

The form of racial identification that quickly evolved to meet this challenge presented blacks as a racial monolith, a singular people with a common experience of oppression. Differences within the race, no matter how ineradicable, had to be minimized. Class distinctions were one of the first such differences to be sacrificed, since they not only threatened racial unity but also seemed to stand in contradiction to the principle of equality which was the announced goal of the movement for racial progress. The discomfort I felt in 1969, the vague but relentless sense of duplicity, was the result of a historical necessity that put my race and class at odds, that was asking me to cast aside the distinction of my class and identify with a monolithic view of my race.

If the form of this racial identity was the monolith, its substance was victimization. The civil rights movement and the more radical splinter groups of the late sixties were all dedicated to ending racial victimization, and the form of black identity that emerged to facilitate this goal made blackness and victimization virtually synonymous. Since it was our victimization more than any other variable that identified and unified us, moreover, it followed logically that the purest black was the poor black. It was images of him that clustered around the positive pole of the race polarity; all other blacks were, in effect, required to identify with him in order to confirm their own blackness.

Certainly there were more dimensions to the black experience than victimization, but no other had the same capacity to fire the indignation needed for war. So, again out of historical necessity, victimization became the overriding focus of racial identity. But this only deepened the double bind for middle-class blacks like me.

When it came to class we were accustomed to defining ourselves against lower-class blacks and identifying with at least the values of middle-class whites; when it came to race we were now being asked to identify with images of lower-class blacks and to see whites, middle class or otherwise, as victimizers. Negative lining up with positive, we were called upon to reject what we had previously embraced and to embrace what we had previously rejected. To put it still more personally, the Sam figure I had been raised to define myself against had now become the "real" black I was expected to identify with.

The fact that the poor black's new status was only passively earned by the condition of his victimization, not by assertive, positive action, made little difference. Status was status apart from the means by which it was achieved, and along with it came a certain power—the power to define the terms of access to that status, to say who was black and who was not. If a lower-class black said you were not really "black" a sellout, an Uncle Tom—the judgment was all the more devastating because it carried the authority of his status. And this judgment soon enough came to be accepted by many whites as well.

In graduate school I was once told by a white professor, "Well, but ... you're not really black. I mean, you're not disadvantaged." In his mind my lack of victim status disqualified me from the race itself. More recently I was complimented by a black student for speaking reasonably correct English, proper" English as he put it. "But I don't know if I really want to talk like that," he went on. "Why not?" I asked. "Because then I wouldn't be black no more," he replied without a pause.

To overcome his marginal status, the middle-class black had to identify with a degree of victimization that was beyond his actual experience. In college (and well beyond) we used to play a game called "nap matching." It was a game of one-upmanship, in which we sat around outdoing each other with stories of racial victimization, symbolically measured by the naps of our hair. Most of us were middle-class and so had few personal stories to relate, but if we could not match, naps with our own biographies, we would move on to those legendary tales of victimization that came to us from the public domain.

The single story that sat atop the pinnacle of racial victimization for us was that of Emmett Till, the Northern black teenager who, on a visit to the South in 1955, was killed and grotesquely mutilated for supposedly looking at or whistling at (we were never sure which, though we argued the point endlessly) a white woman. Oh, how we probed his story, finding in his youth and Northern upbringing the quintessential embodiment of black innocence, brought down by a white evil so portentous and apocalyptic, so gnarled and hideous, that it left us with a feeling not far from awe. By telling his story and others like it, we came to feel the immutability of our victimization, its utter indigenousness, as a thing on this earth like dirt or sand or water.

Of course, these sessions were a ritual of group identification, a means by which we, as middle-class blacks, could be at one with our race. But why were we, who had only a moderate experience of victimization (and that offset by opportunities our parents never had), so intent on assimilating or appropriating an identity that in so many ways contradicted our own? Because, I think, the sense of innocence that is always entailed in feeling victimized filled us with a corresponding feeling of entitlement, or even license, that helped us endure our vulnerability on a largely white college campus.

In my junior year in college I rode to a debate tournament with three white students and our faculty coach, an elderly English professor. The experience of being the lone black in a group of whites was so familiar to me that I thought nothing of it as our trip began. But then halfway through the trip the professor casually turned to me and, in an isn't-the-world-funny sort of tone, said that he had just refused to rent an apartment in a house he owned to a "very nice" black couple because their color would "offend" the white couple who lived downstairs. His eyebrows lifted helplessly over his hawkish nose, suggesting that he too, like me, was a victim of America's racial farce. His look assumed a kind of comradeship: he and I were above this grimy business of race, though for expediency we had occasionally to concede the world its madness.

My vulnerability in this situation came not so much from the professor's blindness to his own racism as from his assumption that I would participate in it, that I would conspire with him against my own race so that he might remain comfortably blind. Why did he think I would be amenable to this? I can only guess that he assumed my middle-class identity was so complete and all-encompassing that I would see his action as nothing more than a trifling concession to the folkways of our land, that I would in fact applaud his decision not to disturb propriety. Blind to both his own racism and to me—one blindness serving the other—he could not recognize that he was asking me to betray my race in the name of my class.

His blindness made me feel vulnerable because it threatened to expose my own repressed ambivalence. His comment pressured me to choose between my class identification, which had contributed to my being a college student and a member of the debating team, and my desperate desire to be "black." I could have one but not both; I was double-bound.

Because double binds are repressed there is always an element of terror in them: the terror of bringing to the conscious mind the buried duplicity, self-deception, and pretense involved in serving two masters. This terror is the stuff of vulnerability, and since vulnerability is one of the least tolerable of all human feelings, we usually transform it into an emotion that seems to restore the control of which it has robbed us; most often, that emotion is anger. And so, before the professor had even finished his little story, I had become a furnace of rage. The year was 1967, and I had been primed by endless hours of nap-matching to feel, at least consciously, completely at one with the victim-focused black identity. This identity gave me the license, and the impunity, to unleash upon this professor one of those volcanic eruptions of racial indignation familiar to us from the novels of Richard Wright. Like Cross Damon in *Outsider*, who kills in perfectly righteous anger, I tried to annihilate the man. I punished him not according to the measure of his crime but according to the measure of my vulnerability, a measure set by the cumulative tension of years of repressed terror. Soon I saw the terror in *his* face, as he stared hollow-eyed at the road ahead. My white friends in the back seat, knowing no conflict between their own class and race, were astonished that someone they had taken to be so much like themselves could harbor a rage that for all the world looked murderous.

Though my rage was triggered by the professor's comment, it was deepened and sustained by a complex of need, conflict, and repression in myself of which I had been wholly unaware. Out of my racial vulnerability I had developed the strong need of an identity with which to defend myself. The only such identity available was that of me as victim, him as victimizer. Once in the grip of this paradigm, I began to do far more damage to myself than he had done.

Seeing myself as a victim meant that I clung all the harder to my racial identity, which, in turn, meant that I suppressed my class identity. This cut me off from all the resources my class values might have offered me. In those values, for instance, I might have found the means to a more dispassionate response, the response less of a victim attacked by a victimizer than of an individual offended by a foolish old man. As an individual I might have reported this professor to the college dean. Or I might have calmly tried to reveal his blindness to him, and possibly won a convert. (The flagrancy of his remark suggested a hidden guilt and even self-recognition on which I might have capitalized. Doesn't confession usually signal a willingness to face oneself?) Or I might have simply chuckled and then let my silence serve as an answer to his provocation. Would not my composure, in any form it might take, deflect into his own heart the arrow he'd shot at me?

Instead, my anger, itself the hair-trigger expression of a long-repressed double bind, not only cut me off from the best of my own resources, it also distorted the nature of my true racial problem. The right-eousness of this anger and the easy catharsis it brought buoyed the delusion of my victimization and left me as blind as the professor himself.

As a middle-class black I have often felt myself *contriving* to be "black." And I have noticed this same contrivance in others—a certain stretching away from the natural flow of one's life to align oneself with a victim-focused black identity. Our particular needs are out of sync with the form of identity available to meet those needs. Middle-class blacks need to identify racially; it is better to think of ourselves as black and victimized than not black at all; so we contrive (more unconsciously than consciously) to fit ourselves into an identity that denies our class and fails to address the true source of our vulnerability.

For me this once meant spending inordinate amounts of time at black faculty meetings, though these meetings had little to do with my real racial anxieties or my professional life. I was new to the university, one of two blacks in an English department of over seventy, and I felt a little isolated and vulnerable, though I did not admit it to myself. But at these meetings we discussed the problems of black faculty and students within a framework of victimization. The real vulnerability we felt was covered over by all the adversarial drama the victim/victimized polarity inspired, and hence went unseen and unassuaged. And this, I think, explains our rather chronic ineffectiveness as a group. Since victimization was not our primary problem—the university had long ago opened its doors to us—we had to contrive to make it so, and there is not much energy in contrivance. What I got at these meetings was ultimately an object lesson in how fruitless struggle can be when it is not grounded in actual need.

At our black faculty meetings, the old equation of blackness with victimization was ever present-to be black was to be a victim; therefore, not to be a victim was not to be black. As we contrived to meet the terms of this formula there was an inevitable distortion of both ourselves and the larger university. Through the prism of victimization the university seemed more impenetrable than it actually was, and we more limited in our powers. We fell prey to the victim's myopia, making the university an institution from which we could seek redress but which we could never fully join. And this mind-set often led us to look more for compensations for our supposed victimization than for opportunities we could pursue as individuals.

The discomfort and vulnerability felt by middle-class blacks in the sixties, it could be argued, was a worthwhile price to pay considering the progress achieved during that time of racial confrontation. But what may have been tolerable then is intolerable now. Though changes in American society have made it an anachronism, the monolithic form of racial identification that came out of the sixties is still very much with us. It may be more loosely held, and its power to punish heretics has probably diminished, but it continues to catch middle-class blacks in a double bind, thus impeding not only their own advancement but even, I would contend, that of blacks as a group.

The victim-focused black identity encourages the individual to feel that his advancement depends almost entirely on that of the group. Thus he loses sight not only of his own possibilities but of the inextricable connection between individual effort and individual advancement. This is a profound encumbrance today, when there is more opportunity for blacks than ever before, for it reimposes limitations that can have the same oppressive effect as those the society has only recently begun to remove.

It was the emphasis on mass action in the sixties that made the victim-focused black identity a necessity. But in the eighties and beyond, when racial advancement will come only through a multitude of individual advancements, this form of identity inadvertently adds itself to the forces that hold us back. Hard work, education, individual initiative, stable family life, property ownership—these have always been the means by which ethnic groups have moved ahead in America. Regardless of past or present victimization, these "laws" of advancement apply absolutely to black Americans also. There is no getting around this. What we need is a form of racial identity that energizes the individual by putting him in touch with both his possibilities and his responsibilities.

It has always annoyed me to hear from the mouths of certain arbiters of blackness that middle-class blacks should "reach back" and pull up those blacks less fortunate than they—as though middle-class status were an unearned and essentially passive condition in which one needed a large measure of noblesse oblige to occupy one's time. My own image is of reaching back from a moving train to lift on board those who have no tickets. A noble enough sentiment –but might it not be wiser to show them the entire structure of principles, efforts, and sacrifice that puts one in a position to buy a ticket any time one likes? This, I think, is something members of the black middle class can realistically offer to other blacks. Their example is not only a testament to possibility but also a lesson in method. But they cannot lead by example until they are released from a black identity that regards that example as suspect, that sees them as "marginally" black, indeed that holds *them* back by catching them in a double bind.

To move beyond the victim-focused black identity we must learn to make a difficult but crucial distinction: between actual victimization, which we must resist with every resource, and identification with the victim's status. Until we do this we will continue to wrestle more with ourselves than with the new opportunities which so many paid so dearly to win.

THE SHATTERER OF WORLDS

Kildare Dobbs

Before that morning in 1945 only a few conventional bombs, none of which did any great damage, had fallen on the city. Fleets of U. S. bombers had, however, devastated many cities round about, and Hiroshima had begun a program of evacuation which had reduced its population from 380,000 to some 245,000. Among the evacuees were Emiko and her family.

"We were moved out to Otake, a town about an hour's train-ride out of the city," Emiko told me. She had been a fifteen-year-old student in 1945. Fragile and vivacious, versed in the gentle traditions of the tea ceremony and flower arrangement, Emiko still had an air of the frail school-child when I talked with her. Every day, she and her sister Hideko used to commute into Hiroshima to school. Hideko was thirteen. Their father was an antique-dealer and he owned a house in the city, although it was empty now. Tetsuro, Emiko's thirteen-year-old brother, was at the Manchurian front with the Imperial Army. Her mother was kept busy looking after the children, for her youngest daughter Eiko was sick with heart trouble, and rations were scarce. All of them were undernourished.

The night of August 5, 1945, little Eiko was dangerously ill. She was not expected to live. Everybody took turns watching by her bed, soothing her by massaging her arms and legs. Emiko retired at 8:30 (most Japanese people go to bed early) and at midnight was roused to take her turn with the sick girl. At 2 a.m. she went back to sleep.

While Emiko slept, the *Enola Gay*, a U. S. B-29 carrying the world's first operational atom bomb, was already in the air. She had taken off from the Pacific island of Iwo Jima at 1:45 a.m., and now Captain William Parsons, U. S. N. ordnance expert, was busy in her bomb-hold with the final assembly of Little Boy. Little Boy looked much like an outsize T. N. T. blockbuster but the crew knew there was something different about him. Only Parsons and the pilot, Colonel Paul Tibbets, knew exactly in what manner Little Boy was different. Course was set for Hiroshima.

Emiko slept.

On board the *Enola Gay* co-pilot Captain Robert Lewis was writing up his personal log. "After leaving Iwo," he recorded, "we began to pick up some low stratus and before very long we were flying on top of an under-cast. Outside of a thin, high cirrus and the low stuff, it's a very beautiful day."

Emiko and Hideko were up at six in the morning. They dressed in the uniform of their women's college—white blouse, quilted hat, and black skirt—breakfasted and packed their aluminum lunch-boxes with white rice and eggs. These they stuffed into their shoulder bags as they hurried for the seven-o'clock train to Hiroshima. Today there would be no classes. Along with many women's groups, high school students, and others, the sisters were going to work on demolition. The city had begun a project of clearance to make fire-breaks in its downtown huddle of wood and paper buildings.

It was a lovely morning.

While the two young girls were at breakfast, Captain Lewis, over the Pacific, had made an entry in his log. "We are loaded. The bomb is now alive, and it's a funny feeling knowing it's right in back of you. Knock wood!"

In the train Hideko suddenly said she was hungry. She wanted to eat her lunch. Emiko dissuaded her: she'd be much hungrier later on. The two sisters argued, but Hideko at last agreed to keep her lunch till later. They decided to meet at the main station that afternoon and catch the five-o'clock train home. By now they had arrived at the first of Hiroshima's three stations. This was where Hideko got off, for she was to work in a different area from her sister. "Sayonara!" she called. "Goodbye." Emiko never saw her again.

There had been an air-raid at 7 a.m., but before Emiko arrived at Hiroshima's main station, two stops farther on, the sirens had sounded the all-clear. Just after eight, Emiko stepped off the train, walked through the station, and waited in the morning sunshine for her streetcar.

At about the same moment Lewis was writing in his log. "There'll be a short intermission while we bomb our target."

It was hot in the sun, Emiko saw a classmate and greeted her. Together they moved back into the shade of a high concrete wall to chat. Emiko looked up at the sky and saw, far up in the cloudless blue, a single B-29.

It was exactly 8:10 a.m. The other people waiting for the streetcar saw it too and began to discuss it anxiously. Emiko felt scared. She felt that at all costs she must go on talking to her friend. Just as she was thinking this, there was a tremendous greenish-white flash in the sky. It was far brighter than the sun. Emiko afterwards remembered vaguely that there was a roaring or a rushing sound as well, but she was not sure, for just at that moment she lost consciousness.

"About 15 seconds after the flash," noted Lewis, 30,000 feet high and several miles away, "there were two very distinct slaps on the ship from the blast and the shock wave. That was all the physical effect we felt. We turned the ship so that we could observe the results."

When Emiko came to, she was lying on her face about forty feet away from where she had been standing. She was not aware of any pain. Her first thought was: "I'm alive!" She lifted her head slowly and looked about her. It was growing dark. The air was seething with dust and black smoke. There was a smell of burning. Emiko felt something trickle into her eyes, tested it in her mouth. Gingerly she put a hand to her head, then looked at it. She saw with a shock that it was covered with blood.

She did not give a thought to Hideko. It did not occur to her that her sister who was in another part of the city could possibly have been in danger. Like most of the survivors, Emiko assumed she had been close to a direct hit by a conventional bomb. She thought it had fallen on the post-office next to the station. With a hurt child's panic, Emiko, streaming with blood from gashes in her scalp, ran blindly in search of her mother and father.

The people standing in front of the station had been burned to death instantly (a shadow had saved Emiko from the flash). The people inside the station had been crushed by falling masonry. Emiko heard faint cries, saw hands scrabbling weakly from under the collapsed platform. All around her the maimed survivors were running and stumbling away from the roaring furnace that had been a city. She ran with them toward the mountains that ring the landward side of Hiroshima.

From the *Enola Gay*, the strangers from North America looked down at their handiwork. "There, in front of our eyes," wrote Lewis, "was without a doubt the greatest explosion man had ever witnessed. The city was nine-tenths covered with smoke of a boiling nature, which seemed to indicate buildings blowing up, and a large white cloud which in less than three minutes reached 30,000 feet, then went to at least 50,000 feet."

Far below, on the edge of this cauldron of smoke, at a distance of some 2,500 yards from the blast's epicenter, Emiko ran with the rest of the living. Some who could not run limped or dragged themselves along. Others were carried. Many, hideously burned, were screaming with pain; when they tripped they lay where they had fallen. There was a man whose face had been ripped open from mouth to ear, another whose forehead was a gaping wound. A young soldier was running with a foot-long splinter of bamboo protruding from one eye. But these, like Emiko, were the lightly wounded.

Some of the burned people had been literally roasted. Skin hung from their flesh like sodden tissue paper. They did not bleed but plasma dripped from their seared limbs.

The *Enola Gay*, mission completed, was returning to base. Lewis sought words to express his feelings, the feelings of all the crew. "I might say," he wrote, "I might say 'My God! What have we done?'"

Emiko ran. When she had reached the safety of the mountain she remembered that she still had her shoulder bag. There was a small first-aid kit in it and she applied ointment to her wounds and to a small cut in her left hand. She bandaged her head.

Emiko looked back at the city. It was a lake of fire. All around her the burned fugitives cried out in pain. Some were scorched on one side only. Others, naked and flayed, were burned all over. They were too many to help and most of them were dying. Emiko followed the walking wounded along a back road, still delirious, expecting suddenly to meet her father and mother.

The thousands dying by the roadside called feebly for help or water. Some of the more lightly injured were already walking in the other direction back towards the flames. Others, with hardly any visible wounds, stopped, turned ashy pale, and died within minutes. No one knew then that they were victims of radiation.

Emiko reached the suburb of Nakayama.

Far off in the *Enola Gay*, Lewis, who had seen none of this, had been writing, "If I live a hundred years, I'll never get those few minutes out of my mind. Looking at Captain Parsons, why he is as confounded as the rest, and he is supposed to have known everything and expected this to happen...."

At Nakayama, Emiko stood in line at a depot where rice-balls were being distributed. Though it distressed her that the badly maimed could hardly feed themselves, the child found she was hungry. It was about 6 p.m. now. A little farther on, at Gion, a farmer called her by name. She did not recognize him, but it seemed he came monthly to her home to collect manure. The farmer took Emiko by the hand, led her to his own house, where his wife bathed her and fed her a meal of white rice. Then the child continued on her way. She passed another town where there were hundreds of injured. The dead were being hauled away in trucks. Among the injured a woman of about forty-five was waving frantically and muttering to herself. Emiko brought this woman a little water in a pumpkin leaf. She felt guilty about it; the school girls had been warned not to give water to the seriously wounded. Emiko comforted herself with the thought that the woman would die soon anyway.

At Koi, she found standing-room in a train. It was heading for Otake with a full load of wounded. Many were put off at Ono, where there was a hospital; and two hours later the train rolled into Otake station. It was around 10 p.m.

A great crowd had gathered to look for their relations. It was a nightmare, Emiko remembered years afterwards; people were calling their dear kinfolk by name, searching frantically. It was necessary to call them by name, since most were so disfigured as to be unrecognizable. Doctors in the town council offices stitched Emiko's head-wounds. The place was crowded with casualties lying on the floor. Many died as Emiko watched.

The town council authorities made a strange announcement. They said a new and mysterious kind of bomb had fallen in Hiroshima. People were advised to stay away from the ruins.

Home at midnight, Emiko found her parents so happy to see her that they could not even cry. They could only give thanks that she was safe. Then they asked, "Where is your sister?"

For ten long days, while Emiko walked daily one and a half miles to have her wounds dressed with fresh gauze, her father searched the rubble of Hiroshima for his lost child. He could not have hoped to find her alive. All, as far as the eye could see, was a desolation of charred ashes and wreckage, relieved only by a few jagged ruins and by the seven estuarial rivers that flowed through the waste delta. The banks of these rivers were covered with the dead and in the rising tidal waters floated thousands of corpses. On one broad street in the Hakushima district the crowds who had been thronging there were all naked and scorched cadavers. Of thousands of others there was no trace at all. A fire several times hotter than the surface of the sun had turned them instantly to vapor.

On August 11 came the news that Nagasaki had suffered the same fate as Hiroshima; it was whispered that Japan had attacked the United States mainland with similar mysterious weapons. With the lavish circumstantiality of rumor, it was said that two out of a fleet of six-engined trans-Pacific bombers had failed to return. But on August 15, speaking for the first time over the radio to his people, the Emperor Hirohito announced his country's surrender. Emiko heard him. No more bombs! she thought. No more fear! The family did not learn till June the following year that this very day young Tetsuro had been killed in action in Manchuria.

Emiko's wounds healed slowly. In mid-September they had closed with a thin layer of pinkish skin. There had been a shortage of antiseptics and Emiko was happy to be getting well. Her satisfaction was short-lived. Mysteriously she came down with diarrhea and high fever. The fever continued for a month. Then one day she started to bleed from the gums, her mouth and throat became acutely inflamed, and her hair started to fall out. Through her delirium the child heard the doctors whisper by her pillow that she could not live. By now the doctors must have known that ionizing radiation caused such destruction of the blood's white cells that victims were left with little or no resistance against infection.

Yet Emiko recovered.

The wound on her hand, however, was particularly troublesome and did not heal for a long time.

As she got better, Emiko began to acquire some notion of the fearful scale of the disaster. Few of her friends and acquaintances were still alive. But no one knew precisely how many died in Hiroshima. To this day the claims of various agencies conflict.

According to General Douglas MacArthur's headquarters, there were 78,150 dead and 13,083 missing. The United States Atomic Bomb Casualty Commission claims there were 79,000 dead. Both sets of figures are probably far too low. There's reason to believe that at the time of the surrender Japanese authorities lied about the number of survivors, exaggerating it to get extra medical supplies. The Japanese welfare ministry's figures of 260,000 dead and 163,263 missing may well be too high. But the very order of such discrepancies speaks volumes about the scale of the catastrophe. The dead were literally uncountable.

This appalling toll of human life had been exacted from a city that had been prepared for air attack in a state of full wartime readiness. All civil-defense services had been overwhelmed from the first moment and it was many hours before any sort of organized rescue and relief could be put into effect.

It's true that single raids using so-called conventional weapons on other cities such as Tokyo and Dresden inflicted far greater casualties. And that it could not matter much to a victim whether he was burnt alive by a fire-storm caused by phosphorous, or by napalm or by nuclear fission. Yet in the whole of human history so savage a massacre had never before been inflicted with a single blow. And modern thermonuclear weapons are upwards of 1,000 times more powerful and deadly than the Hiroshima bomb.

The white scar I saw on Emiko's small, fine-boned hand was a tiny metaphor, a faint but eloquent reminder of the scar on humanity's conscience.

THANK GOD FOR THE ATOM BOMB

Paul Fussell

Many years ago in New York I saw on the side of a bus a whiskey ad I've remembered all this time. It's been for me a model of the short poem, and indeed I've come upon few short poems subsequently that exhibited more poetic talent. The ad consisted of two eleven-syllable lines of "verse," thus:

> In life, experience is the great teacher.
> In Scotch, Teacher's is the great experience.

For present purposes we must jettison the second line (licking our lips, to be sure, as it disappears), leaving the first to register a principle whose banality suggests that it enshrines a most useful truth. I bring up the matter because, writing on the forty-second anniversary of the atom-bombing of Hiroshima and Nagasaki, I want to consider something suggested by the long debate about the ethics, if any, of that ghastly affair. Namely, the importance of experience, sheer, vulgar experience, in influencing, if not determining, one's views about that use of the atom bomb.

The experience I'm talking about is having to come to grips, face to face, with an enemy who designs your death. The experience is common to those in the marines and the infantry and even the line navy, to those, in short, who fought the Second World War mindful always that their mission was, as they were repeatedly assured, "to close with the enemy and destroy him." *Destroy*, notice: not hurt, frighten, drive away, or capture. I think there's something to be learned about that war, as well as about the tendency of historical memory unwittingly to resolve ambiguity and generally clean up the premises, by considering the way testimonies emanating from real war experience tend to complicate attitudes about the most cruel ending of that most cruel war.

"What did you do in the Great War, Daddy?" The recruiting poster deserves ridicule and contempt, of course, but here its question is embarrassingly relevant, and the problem is one that touches on the dirty little secret of social class in America. Arthur T. Hadley said recently that those for whom the use of the A-bomb was "wrong" seem to be implying "that it would have been better to allow thousands on thousands of American and Japanese infantrymen to die in honest hand-to-hand combat on the beaches than to drop those two bombs." People holding such views, he notes, "do not come from the ranks of society that produce infantry-men or pilots." And there's an eloquence problem: most of those with firsthand experience of the war at its worst were not elaborately educated people. Relatively inarticulate, most have remained silent about what they know. That is, few of those destined to be blown to pieces if the main Japanese islands had been invaded went on to become our most effective men of letters or impressive ethical theorists or professors of contemporary history or of international law. The testimony of experience has tended to come from rough diamonds—James Jones is an example—who went through the war as enlisted men in the infantry or the Marine Corps.

Anticipating objections from those without such experience, in his book *WWII* Jones carefully prepares for his chapter on the A-bombs by detailing the plans already in motion for the infantry assaults on the home islands of Kyushu (thirteen divisions scheduled to land in November 1945) and ultimately Honshu (sixteen divisions scheduled for March 1946). Planners of the invasion assumed that it would require a full year, to November 1946, for the Japanese to be sufficiently worn down by land-combat attrition to surrender. By that time, one million American casualties was the expected price. Jones observes that the forthcoming invasion of Kyushu "was well into its collecting and stockpiling stages before the war ended." (The island of Saipan was designated a main ammunition and supply base for the invasion, and if you go there today you can see some of the assembled stuff still sitting there.) "The assault troops were chosen and already in training," Jones reminds his readers, and he illuminates by the light of experience what this meant:

> What it must have been like to some old-timer buck sergeant or staff sergeant who had been through Guadalcanal or Bougainville or the Philippines, to stand on some beach and watch this huge war machine beginning to stir and move all around him and know that he very likely had survived this far only to fall dead on the dirt of Japan's home islands, hardly bears thinking about.

Another bright enlisted man, this one an experienced marine destined for the assault on Honshu, adds his testimony. Former Pfc. E. B. Sledge, author of the splendid memoir *With the Old Breed at Peleliu and Okinawa*, noticed at the time that the fighting grew "more vicious the closer we got to Japan," with the carnage of Iwo Jima and Okinawa worse than what had gone before. He points out that

> what we had *experienced* [my emphasis] in fighting the Japs (pardon the expression) on Peleliu and Okinawa caused us to formulate some very definite opinions that the invasion ... would be a ghastly bloodletting .... It would shock the American public and the world. [Every Japanese] soldier, civilian, woman, and child would fight to the death with whatever weapons they had, rifle, grenade, or bamboo spear.

The Japanese pre-invasion patriotic song, "One Hundred Million Souls for the Emperor," says Sledge, "meant just that." Universal national kamikaze was the point. One kamikaze pilot, discouraged by his unit's failure to impede the Americans very much despite the bizarre casualties it caused, wrote before diving his plane onto an American ship, "I see the war situation becoming more desperate. All Japanese must become soldiers and die for the Emperor." Sledge's First Marine Division was to land close to the Yokosuka Naval Base, "one of the most heavily defended sectors of the island." The marines were told, he recalls, that "due to the strong beach defenses, caves, tunnels, and numerous Jap suicide torpedo boats and manned mines, few Marines in the first five assault waves would get ashore alive—my company was scheduled to be in the first and second waves. The veterans in the outfit felt we had already run out of luck anyway .... We viewed the invasion with complete resignation that we would be killed—either on the beach or inland."

And the invasion was going to take place: there's no question about that. It was not theo-retical or merely rumored in order to scare the Japanese. By July 10, 1945, the prelanding naval and aerial bombardment of the coast had begun, and the battleships *Iowa, Missouri, Wis-consin,* and *King George V* were steaming up and down the coast, softening it up with their six-teen-inch shells.

On the other hand, John Kenneth Galbraith is persuaded that the Japanese would have sur-rendered surely by November without an invasion. He thinks the A-bombs were unnecessary and unjustified because the war was ending anyway. The A-bombs meant, he says, "a difference, at most, of two or three weeks." But at the time, with no indication that surrender was on the way, the kamikazes were sinking American vessels; the *Indianapolis* was sunk (880 men killed), and Allied casualties were running to over 7,000 per week. "Two or three weeks," says Gal-braith. Two weeks more means 14,000 more killed and wounded, three weeks more, 21,000. Those weeks mean the world if you're one of those thousands or related to one of them. Dur-ing the time between the dropping of the Nagasaki bomb on August 9 and the actual surren-der on the fifteenth, the war pursued its accustomed course: on the twelfth of August eight captured American fliers were executed (heads chopped off); the fifty-first United States subma-rine, *Bonefish,* was sunk (all aboard drowned); the destroyer *Callaghan* went down, the seventieth to be sunk, and the Destroyer Escort *Underhill* was lost. That's a bit of what happened in six days of the two or three weeks posited by Galbraith. What did he do in the war? He worked in the Office of Price Administration in Washington. I don't demand that he experience having his ass shot off. I merely note that he didn't.

Likewise, the historian Michael Sherry, author of a recent book on the rise of the Ameri-can bombing mystique, *The Creation of Armageddon,* argues that we didn't delay long enough between the test explosion in New Mexico and the mortal explosions in Japan. More delay would have made possible deeper moral considerations and perhaps laudable second thoughts and restraint. "The risks of delaying the bomb's use," he says, "would have been small—not the thousands of casualties expected of invasion but only a few days or weeks of relatively rou-tine operations." While the mass murders represented by these "relatively routine operations" were enacting, Michael Sherry was safe at home. Indeed, when the bombs were dropped he was going on eight months old, in danger only of falling out of his pram. In speaking thus of Galbraith and Sherry, I'm aware of the offensive implications *ad hominem.* But what's at stake in an infantry assault is so entirely unthinkable to those without the experience of one, or sev-eral, or many, even if they possess very wide-ranging imaginations and warm sympathies, that experience is crucial in this case.

In general, the principle is, the farther from the scene of horror, the easier the talk. One young combat naval officer close to the action wrote home in the fall of 1943, just before the marines underwent the agony of Tarawa: "When I read that we will fight the Japs for years if necessary and will sacrifice hundreds of thousands if we must, I always like to check from where he's talking: it's seldom out here." That was Lieutenant (j.g.) John F. Kennedy. And Winston Churchill, with an irony perhaps too broad and easy, noted in Parliament that the people who preferred invasion to A-bombing seemed to have "no intention of proceeding to the Japanese front themselves."

A remoteness from experience like Galbraith's and Sherry's, and a similar rationalistic abstraction from actuality, seem to motivate the reaction of an anonymous reviewer of William Manchester's *Goodbye Darkness: A Memoir of the Pacific War* for *The New York Review of Books*. The reviewer naturally dislikes Manchester's still terming the enemy Nips or Japs, but what really shakes him (her?) is this passage of Manchester's:

> After Biak the enemy withdrew to deep caverns. Rooting them out became a bloody business which reached its ultimate horrors in the last months of the war. You think of the lives which would have been lost in an invasion of Japan's home islands—a staggering number of Americans but millions more of Japanese—and you thank God for the atomic bomb.

Thank God for the atom bomb. From this, "one recoils," says the reviewer. One does, doesn't one?

And not just a staggering number of Americans would have been killed in the invasion. Thousands of British assault troops would have been destroyed too, the anticipated casualties from the almost 200,000 men in the six divisions (the same number used to invade Normandy) assigned to invade the Malay Peninsula on September 9. Aimed at the reconquest of Singapore, this operation was expected to last until about March 1946—that is, seven more months of infantry fighting. "But for the atomic bombs," a British observer intimate with the Japanese defenses notes, "I don't think we would have stood a cat in hell's chance. We would have been murdered in the biggest massacre of the war. They would have annihilated the lot of us."

The Dutchman Laurens van der Post had been a prisoner of the Japanese for three and a half years. He and thousands of his fellows, enfeebled by beriberi and pellagra, were being systematically starved to death, the Japanese rationalizing this treatment not just because the prisoners were white men but because they had allowed themselves to be captured at all and were therefore moral garbage. In the summer of 1945 Field Marshal Terauchi issued a significant order: at the moment the Allies invaded the main islands, all prisoners were to be killed by the prison-camp commanders. But thank God that did not happen. When the A-bombs were dropped, van der Post recalls, "This cataclysm I was certain would make the Japanese feel that they could withdraw from the war without dishonor, because it would strike them, as it had us in the silence of our prison night, as something supernatural."

* * * * *

In an exchange of views not long ago in *The New York Review of Books*, Joseph Alsop and David Joravsky set forth the by now familiar argument on both sides of the debate about the "ethics" of the bomb. It's not hard to guess which side each chose once you know that Alsop experienced capture by the Japanese at Hong Kong early in 1942, while Joravsky came into no deadly contact with the Japanese: a young, combat-innocent soldier, he was on his way to the Pacific when the war ended. The editors of *The New York Review* gave the debate the tendentious title "Was the Hiroshima Bomb Necessary?" surely an unanswerable question (unlike

"Was It Effective?") and one precisely indicating the intellectual difficulties involved in imposing *ex post facto* a rational and even a genteel ethics on this event. In arguing the acceptability
of the bomb, Alsop focuses on the power and fanaticism of War Minister Anami, who insisted
that Japan fight to the bitter end, defending the main islands with the same techniques and
tenacity employed at Iwo and Okinawa. Alsop concludes: "Japanese surrender could never
have been obtained, at any rate without the honor-satisfying bloodbath envisioned by ... Anami,
if the hideous destruction of Hiroshima and Nagasaki had not finally galvanized the peace advocates into tearing up the entire Japanese book of rules." The Japanese plan to deploy the unde-
feated bulk of their ground forces, over two million men, plus 10,000 kamikaze planes, plus
the elderly and all the women and children with sharpened spears they could muster in a suici-
dal defense makes it absurd, says Alsop, to "hold the common view, by now hardly challenged
by anyone, that the decision to drop the two bombs on Japan was wicked in itself, and that President Truman and all others who joined in making or who [like Robert Oppenheimer] assented
to this decision shared in the wickedness." And in explanation of "the two bombs," Alsop adds:
"The true, climactic, and successful effort of the Japanese peace advocates ... did not begin in
deadly earnest until *after* the second bomb had destroyed Nagasaki. The Nagasaki bomb was
thus the trigger to all the developments that led to peace." At this time the army was so unready
for surrender that most looked forward to the forthcoming invasion as an indispensable opportunity to show their mettle, enthusiastically agreeing with the army spokesman who reasoned
early in 1945, "Since the retreat from Guadalcanal, the Army has had little opportunity to
engage the enemy in land battles. But when we meet in Japan proper, our Army will demonstrate its invincible superiority." This possibility foreclosed by the Emperor's post-A-bomb surrender broadcast, the shocked, disappointed officers of one infantry battalion, anticipating a
professionally impressive defense of the beaches, killed themselves in the following numbers:
one major, three captains, ten first lieutenants, and twelve second lieutenants.

David Joravsky, now a professor of history at Northwestern, argued on the other hand
that those who decided to use the A-bombs on cities betray defects of "reason and self-
restraint." It all needn't have happened, he says, "if the U.S. government had been willing to
take a few more days and to be a bit more thoughtful in opening up the age of nuclear warfare." I've already noted what "a few more days" would mean to the luckless troops and sailors
on the spot, and as to being thoughtful when "opening up the age of nuclear warfare," of course
no one was focusing on anything as portentous as that, which reflects a historian's tidy hindsight. The U.S. government was engaged not in that sort of momentous thing but in ending the
war conclusively, as well as irrationally Remembering Pearl Harbor with a vengeance. It didn't
know then what everyone knows now about leukemia and various kinds of carcinoma and birth
defects. Truman was not being sly or coy when he insisted that the bomb was "only another
weapon." History, as Eliot's "Gerontion" notes:

> ... has many cunning passages, contrived corridors
> And issues, deceives with whispering ambitions,
> Guides us by vanities....

                                        Think
        Neither fear nor courage saves us.
        Unnatural vices
        Are fathered by our heroism. Virtues
        Are forced upon us by our impudent crimes.

    Understanding the past requires pretending that you don't know the present. It requires
feeling its own pressure on your pulses without any *ex post facto* illumination. That's a harder
thing to do than Joravsky seems to think.

    The Alsop-Joravsky debate, reduced to a collision between experience and theory, was con-
ducted with a certain civilized respect for evidence. Not so the way the scurrilous, agitprop
New Statesman conceives those justifying the dropping of the bomb and those opposing. They
are, on the one hand, says Bruce Page, "the imperialist class-forces acting through Harry Truman" and, on the other, those representing "the humane, democratic virtues"—in short, "fas-
cists" as opposed to "populists." But ironically the bomb saved the lives not of any imperialists
but only of the low and humble, the quintessentially democratic huddled masses—the con-
scripted enlisted men manning the fated invasion divisions and the sailors crouching at their
gun-mounts in terror of the Kamikazes. When the war ended, Bruce Page was nine years old.
For someone of his experience, phrases like "imperialist class forces" come easily, and the
issues look perfectly clear.

    He's not the only one to have forgotten, if he ever knew, the unspeakable savagery of the
Pacific war. The dramatic postwar Japanese success at hustling and merchandising and tourism
has (happily, in many ways) effaced for most people the vicious assault context in which the
Hiroshima horror should be viewed. It is easy to forget, or not to know, what Japan was like
before it was first destroyed, and then humiliated, tamed, and constitutionalized by the West.
"Implacable, treacherous, barbaric"—those were Admiral Halsey's characterizations of the
enemy, and at the time few facing the Japanese would deny that they fit to a T. One remembers the captured American airmen—the lucky ones who escaped decapitation—locked for years
in packing crates. One remembers the gleeful use of bayonets on civilians, on nurses and the
wounded, in Hong Kong and Singapore. Anyone who actually fought in the Pacific recalls the
Japanese routinely firing on medics, killing the wounded (torturing them first, if possible), and
cutting off the penises of the dead to stick in the corpses' mouths. The degree to which Americans register shock and extraordinary shame about the Hiroshima bomb correlates closely with
lack of information about the Pacific war.

    And of course the brutality was not just on one side. There was much sadism and cruelty,
undeniably racist, on ours. (It's worth noting in passing how few hopes blacks could entertain of desegregation and decent treatment when the U.S. Army itself slandered the enemy
as "the little brown Jap.") Marines and soldiers could augment their view of their own invin-
cibility by possessing a well-washed Japanese skull, and very soon after Guadalcanal it was
common to treat surrendering Japanese as handy rifle targets. Plenty of Japanese gold teeth
were extracted—some from still living mouths—with Marine Corps Ka-Bar Knives, and one

of E. B. Sledge's fellow marines went around with a cut-off Japanese hand. When its smell grew too offensive and Sledge urged him to get rid of it, he defended his possession of this trophy thus: "How many Marines you reckon that hand pulled the trigger on?" (It's hardly necessary to observe that a soldier in the ETO would probably not have dealt that way with a German or Italian—that is, a "white person's"—hand.) In the Pacific the situation grew so public and scandalous that in September 1942, the Commander in Chief of the Pacific Fleet issued this order: "No part of the enemy's body may be used as a souvenir. Unit Commanders will take stern disciplinary action . . . ."

Among Americans it was widely held that the Japanese were really subhuman, little yellow beasts, and popular imagery depicted them as lice, rats, bats, vipers, dogs, and monkeys. What was required, said the Marine Corps journal *The Leatherneck* in May 1945, was "a gigantic task of extermination." The Japanese constituted a "pestilence," and the only appropriate treatment was "annihilation." Some of the marines landing on Iwo Jima had "Rodent Exterminator" written on their helmet covers, and on one American flagship the naval commander had erected a large sign enjoining all to "KILL JAPS! KILL JAPS! KILL MORE JAPS!" Herman Wouk remembers the Pacific war scene correctly while analyzing Ensign Keith in *The Caine Mutiny:* "Like most of the naval executioners of Kwajalein, he seemed to regard the enemy as a species of animal pest . . . ." And the feeling was entirely reciprocal: "From the grim and desperate taciturnity with which the Japanese died, they seemed on their side to believe that they were contending with an invasion of large armed ants." Hiroshima seems to follow in natural sequence: "This obliviousness of both sides to the fact that the opponents were human beings may perhaps be cited as the key to the many massacres of the Pacific war." Since the Jap vermin resist so madly and have killed so many of us, let's pour gasoline into their bunkers and light it and then shoot those afire who try to get out. Why not? Why not blow them all up, with satchel charges or with something stronger? Why not, indeed, drop a new kind of bomb on them, and on the un-uniformed ones too, since the Japanese government has announced that women from ages of seventeen to forty are being called up to repel the invasion? The intelligence officer of the U. S. Fifth Air Force declared on July 21, 1945, that "the entire population of Japan is a proper military target," and he added emphatically, *"There are no civilians in Japan."* Why delay and allow one more American high school kid to see his own intestines blown out of his body and spread before him in the dirt while he screams and screams when with the new bomb we can end the whole thing just like that?

On Okinawa, only weeks before Hiroshima, 123,000 Japanese and Americans *killed* each other. (About 140,000 Japanese died at Hiroshima.) "Just awful" was the comment on the Okinawa slaughter, not of some pacifist but of General MacArthur. On July 14, 1945, General Marshall sadly informed the Combined Chiefs of Staff—he was not trying to scare the Japanese—that it's "now clear . . . that in order to finish with the Japanese quickly, it will be necessary to invade the industrial heart of Japan." The invasion was definitely on, as I know because I was to be in it.

When the atom bomb ended the war, I was in the Forty-fifth Infantry Division, which had been through the European war so thoroughly that it had needed to be reconstituted two or three times. We were in a staging area near Rheims, ready to be shipped back across the United States for refresher training at Fort Lewis, Washington, and then sent on for final preparation in the Philippines. My division, like most of the ones transferred from Europe, was to take part in the invasion of Honshu. (The earlier landing on Kyushu was to be carried out by the 700,000 infantry already in the Pacific, those with whom James Jones has sympathized.) I was a twenty-one-year old second lieutenant of infantry leading a rifle platoon. Although still officially fit for combat, in the German war I had already been wounded in the back and the leg badly enough to be adjudged, after the war, 40 percent disabled. But even if my leg buckled and I fell to the ground whenever I jumped out of the back of a truck, and even if the very idea of more combat made me breathe in gasps and shake all over, my condition was held to be adequate for the next act. When the atom bombs were dropped and news began to circulate that "Operation Olympic" would not, after all, be necessary, when we learned to our astonishment that we would not be obliged in a few months to rush up the beaches near Tokyo assault-firing while being machine-gunned, mortared, shelled, for all the practiced phlegm of our tough façades we broke down and cried with relief and joy. We were going to live. We were going to grow to adulthood after all. The killing was all going to be over, and peace was actually going to be the state of things. When the *Enola Gay* dropped its package, "There were cheers," says John Toland, "over the intercom; it meant the end of the war." Down on the ground the reaction of Sledge's marine buddies when they heard the news was more solemn and complicated. They heard about the end of the war

> with quiet disbelief coupled with an indescribable sense of relief. We thought the Japanese would never surrender. Many refused to believe it .... Sitting in stunned silence, we remembered our dead. So many dead. So many maimed. So many bright futures consigned to the ashes of the past. So many dreams lost in the madness that had engulfed us. Except for a few widely scattered shouts of joy, the survivors of the abyss sat hollow-eyed and silent, trying to comprehend a world without war.

These troops who cried and cheered with relief or who sat stunned by the weight of their experience are very different from the high-minded, guilt-ridden GIs we're told about by J. Glenn Gray in his sensitive book *The Warriors*. During the war in Europe Gray was an interrogator in the Army Counterintelligence Corps, and in that capacity he experienced the war at Division level. There's no denying that Gray's outlook on everything was admirably noble, elevated, and responsible. After the war he became a much-admired professor of philosophy at Colorado College and an esteemed editor of Heidegger. But *The Warriors*, his meditation on the moral and psychological dimensions of modern soldiering, gives every sign of error occasioned by remoteness from experience. Division headquarters is miles—*miles*—behind the line where soldiers experience terror and madness and relieve those pressures by crazy brutality and sadism. Indeed, unless they actually encountered the enemy during the war, most "soldiers" have very little idea what "combat" was like. As William Manchester says, "All who wore uniforms are called veterans, but more than 90 percent of them are as uninformed about the killing zones as those on the home front." Manchester's fellow marine E. B. Sledge thoughtfully and responsibly invokes the terms *drastically* and *totally* to underline the differences in experience between front and rear, and not even the far rear, but the close rear. "Our code of conduct toward the enemy," he notes, "differed drastically from that prevailing back at the division CP." (He's describing gold-tooth extraction from still-living Japanese.) Again he writes: "We existed in an environment totally incomprehensible to men behind the lines ...," even, he would insist, to men as intelligent and sensitive as Glenn Gray, who missed seeing with his own eyes Sledge's marine friends sliding under fire down a shell-pocked ridge slimy with mud and liquid dysentery shit into the maggoty Japanese and USMC corpses at the bottom, vomiting as the maggots burrowed into their own foul clothing. "We didn't talk about such things," says Sledge. "They were too horrible and obscene even for hardened veterans. . . . Nor do authors normally write about such vileness; unless they have seen it with their own eyes, it is too preposterous to think that men could actually live and fight for days and nights on end under such terrible conditions and not be driven insane." And Sledge has added a comment on such experience and the insulation provided by even a short distance: "Often people just behind our rifle companies couldn't understand what we knew." Glenn Gray was not in a rifle company, or even just behind one. "When the news of the atomic bombing of Hiroshima and Nagasaki came," he asks us to believe, "many an American soldier felt shocked and ashamed." Shocked, OK, but why ashamed? Because we'd destroyed civilians? We'd been doing that for years, in raids on Hamburg and Berlin and Cologne and Frankfurt and Mannheim and Dresden, and Tokyo, and besides, the two A-bombs wiped out 10,000 Japanese troops, not often thought of now, John Hersey's kindly physicians and Jesuit priests being more touching. If around division headquarters some of the people Gray talked to felt ashamed, down in the rifle companies no one did, despite Gray's assertions. "The combat soldier," he says, "knew better than did Americans at home what those bombs meant in suffering and injustice. The man of conscience realized intuitively the vast majority of Japanese in both cities were no more, if no less, guilty of the war than were his own parents, sisters, or brothers."

I find this canting nonsense. The purpose of the bombs was not to "punish" people but to stop the war. To intensify the shame Gray insists we feel, he seems willing to fiddle the facts. The Hiroshima bomb, he says, was dropped "without any warning." But actually, two days before, 720,000 leaflets were dropped on the city urging everyone to get out and indicating that the place was going to be (as the Potsdam Declaration had promised) obliterated. Of course few left.

Experience whispers that the pity is not that we used the bomb to end the Japanese war but that it wasn't ready in time to end the German one. If only it could have been rushed into production faster and dropped at the right moment on the Reich Chancellery or Berchtesgaden or Hitler's military headquarters in East Prussia (where Colonel Stauffenberg's July 20 bomb didn't do the job because it wasn't big enough), much of the Nazi hierarchy could have been pulverized immediately, saving not just the embarrassment of the Nuremberg trials but the lives of around four million Jews, Poles, Slavs, and gypsies, not to mention the lives and limbs of millions of Allied and German soldiers. If the bomb had only been ready in time, the young men of my infantry platoon would not have been so cruelly killed and wounded.

* * * * *

All this is not to deny that like the Russian Revolution, the atom-bombing of Japan was a vast historical tragedy, and every passing year magnifies the dilemma into which it has lodged the contemporary world. As with the Russian Revolution, there are two sides—that's why it's a tragedy instead of a disaster—and unless we are, like Bruce Page, simple-mindedly unimaginative and cruel, we will be painfully aware of both sides at once. To observe that from the viewpoint of the war's victims-to-be the bomb seemed precisely the right thing to drop is to purchase no immunity from horror. To experience both sides, one might study the book *Unforgettable Fire: Pictures Drawn by Atomic Bomb Survivors*, which presents a number of amateur drawings and watercolors of the Hiroshima scene made by middle-aged and elderly survivors for a peace exhibition in 1975. In addition to the almost unbearable pictures, the book offers brief moments of memoir not for the weak-stomached:

> While taking my severely wounded wife out to the river bank ..., I was horrified indeed at the sight of a stark naked man standing in the rain with his eyeball in his palm. He looked to be in great pain but there was nothing that I could do for him. I wonder what became of him. Even today, I vividly remember the sight. I was simply miserable.

These childlike drawings and paintings are of skin hanging down, breasts torn off, people bleeding and burning, dying mothers nursing dead babies. A bloody woman holds a bloody child in the ruins of a house, and the artist remembers her calling, "Please help this child! Someone, please help this child. Please help! Someone, please." As Samuel Johnson said of the smothering of Desdemona, the innocent in another tragedy, "It is not to be endured." Nor, it should be noticed, is an infantryman's account of having his arm blown off in the Arno Valley in Italy in 1944:

> I wanted to die and die fast. I wanted to forget this miserable world. I cursed the war, I cursed the people who were responsible for it, I cursed God for putting me here ... to suffer for something I never did or knew anything about.

(A good place to interrupt and remember Glenn Gray's noble but hopelessly one-sided remarks about "injustice," as well as "suffering.")

"For this was hell," the soldier goes on, "and I never imagined anything or anyone could suffer so bitterly. I screamed and cursed. Why? What had I done to deserve this? But no answer came. I yelled for medics, because subconsciously I wanted to live. I tried to apply my right hand over my bleeding stump, but I didn't have the strength to hold it. I looked to the left of me and saw the bloody mess that was once my left arm; its fingers and palm were turned upward, like a flower looking to the sun for its strength."

The future scholar-critic who writes *The History of Canting in the Twentieth Century* will find much to study and interpret in the utterances of those who dilate on the special wickedness of the A-bomb-droppers. He will realize that such utterance can perform for the speaker a valuable double function. First, it can display the fineness of his moral weave. And second, by implication it can also inform the audience that during the war he was not socially so unfortunate as to find himself down there with the ground forces, where he might have had to compromise the purity and clarity of his moral system by the experience of weighing his own life against someone else's. Down there, which is where the other people were, is the place where coarse self-interest is the rule. When the young soldier with the wild eyes comes at you, firing, do you shoot him in the foot, hoping he'll be hurt badly enough to drop or mis-aim the gun with which he's going to kill you, or do you shoot him in the chest (or, if you're a prime shot, in the head) and make certain that you and not he will be the survivor of that mortal moment?

It would be not just stupid but would betray a lamentable want of human experience to expect soldiers to be very sensitive humanitarians. The Glenn Grays of this world need to have their attention directed to the testimony of those who know, like, say, Admiral of the Fleet Lord Fisher, who said, "Moderation in war is imbecility," or Sir Arthur Harris, director of the admittedly wicked aerial-bombing campaign designed, as Churchill put it, to "de-house" the German civilian population, who observed that "War is immoral," or our own General W. T. Sherman: "War is cruelty, and you cannot refine it." Lord Louis Mountbatten, trying to say something sensible about the dropping of the A-bomb, came up only with "War is crazy." Or rather, it requires choices among crazinesses. "It would seem even more crazy," he went on, "if we were to have more casualties on our side to save the Japanese." One of the unpleasant facts for anyone in the ground armies during the war was that you had to become pro tem a subordinate of the very uncivilian George S. Patton and respond somehow to his unremitting insistence that you embrace his view of things. But in one of his effusions he was right, and his observation tends to suggest the experimental dubiousness of the concept of "just wars." "War is not a contest with gloves," he perceived. "It is resorted to only when laws, which are rules, have failed." Soldiers being like that, only the barest decencies should be expected of them. They did not start the war, except in the terrible sense hinted at in Frederic Manning's observation based on his front-line experience in the Great War: "War is waged by men; not by beasts, or by gods. It is a peculiarly human activity. To call it a crime against mankind is to miss at least half its significance; it is also the punishment of a crime." Knowing that unflattering truth by experience, soldiers have every motive for wanting a war stopped, by any means.

* * * * *

The stupidity, parochialism, and greed in the international mismanagement of the whole nuclear challenge should not tempt us to misimagine the circumstances of the bomb's first "use." Nor should our well-justified fears and suspicions occasioned by the capture of the nuclear-power trade by the inept and the mendacious (who have fucked up the works at Three Mile Island, Chernobyl, etc.) tempt us to infer retrospectively extraordinary corruption, imbecility, or motiveless malignity in those who decided, all things considered, to drop the bomb. Times change. Harry Truman knew war, and he knew better than some of his critics then and now what he was doing and why he was doing it. "Having found the bomb," he said, "we have used it .... We have used it to shorten the agony of young Americans."

The past, which as always did not know the future, acted in ways that ask to be imagined before they are condemned. Or even simplified.

THE TYRANNY OF THE MAJORITY

Lani Guinier

I have always wanted to be a civil rights lawyer. This lifelong ambition is based on a deep-seated commitment to democratic fair play—to playing by the rules as long as the rules are fair. When the rules seem unfair, I have worked to change them, not subvert them. When I was eight years old, I was a Brownie. I was especially proud of my uniform, which represented a commitment to good citizenship and good deeds. But one day, when my Brownie group staged a hat-making contest, I realized that uniforms are only as honorable as the people who wear them. The contest was rigged. The winner was assisted by her milliner mother, who actually made the winning entry in full view of all the participants. At the time, I was too young to be able to change the rules, but I was old enough to resign, which I promptly did.

To me, fair play means that the rules encourage everyone to play. They should reward those who win, but they must be acceptable to those who lose. The central theme of my academic writing is that not all rules lead to elemental fair play. Some even commonplace rules work against it.

The professional milliner competing with amateur Brownies stands as an example of rules that are patently rigged or patently subverted. Yet, sometimes, even when rules are perfectly fair in form, they serve in practice to exclude particular groups from meaningful participation. When they do not encourage everyone to play, or when, over the long haul, they do not make the losers feel as good about the outcomes as the winners, they can seem as unfair as the milliner who makes the winning hat for her daughter.

Sometimes, too, we construct rules that force us to be divided into winners and losers when we might have otherwise joined together. This idea was cogently expressed by my son, Nikolas, when he was four years old, far exceeding the thoughtfulness of his mother when she was an eight-year-old Brownie. While I was writing one of my law journal articles, Nikolas and I had a conversation about voting prompted by a Sesame Street Magazine exercise. The magazine pictured six children: four children had raised their hands because they wanted to play tag; two had their hands down because they wanted to play hide-and-seek. The magazine asked its readers to count the number of children whose hands were raised and then decide what game the children would play.

Nikolas quite realistically replied, "They will play both. First they will play tag. Then they will play hide-and-seek." Despite the magazine's "rules," he was right. To children, it is natural to take turns. The winner may get to play first or more often, but even the "loser" gets something. His was a positive-sum solution that many adult rule-makers ignore.

The traditional answer to the magazine's problem would have been a zero-sum solution: "The children—all the children—will play tag, and only tag." As a zero-sum solution, everything is seen in terms of "I win; you lose." The conventional answer relies on winner-take-all majority rule, in which the tag players, as the majority, win the right to decide for all the children what game to play. The hide-and-seek preference becomes irrelevant. The numerically more powerful majority choice simply subsumes minority preferences.

In the conventional case, the majority that rules gains all the power and the minority that loses gets none. For example, two years ago Brother Rice High School in Chicago held two senior proms. It was not planned that way. The prom committee at Brother Rice, a boys' Catholic high school, expected just one prom when it hired a disc jockey, picked a rock band, and selected music for the prom by consulting student preferences. Each senior was asked to list his three favorite songs, and the band would play the songs that appeared most frequently on the lists.

Seems attractively democratic. But Brother Rice is predominantly white, and the prom committee was all white. That's how they got two proms. The black seniors at Brother Rice felt so shut out by the "democratic process" that they organized their own prom. As one black student put it: "For every vote we had, there were eight votes for what they wanted . . . . [W]ith us being in the minority we're always outvoted. It's as if we don't count."

Some embittered white seniors saw things differently. They complained that the black students should have gone along with the majority: "The majority makes a decision. That's the way it works."

In a way, both groups were right. From the white students' perspective, this was ordinary decision-making. To the black students, majority rule sent the message: "we don't count" is the "way it works" for minorities. In a racially divided society, majority rule may be perceived as majority tyranny.

That is a large claim, and I do not rest my case for it solely on the actions of the prom committee in one Chicago high school. To expand the range of the argument, I first consider the ideal of majority rule itself, particularly as reflected in the writings of James Madison and other founding members of our Republic. These early democrats explored the relationship between majority rule and democracy. James Madison warned, "If a majority be united by a common interest, the rights of the minority will be insecure." The tyranny of the majority, according to Madison, requires safeguards to protect "one part of the society against the injustice of the other part."

For Madison, majority tyranny represented the great danger to our early constitutional democracy. Although the American revolution was fought against the tyranny of the British monarch, it soon became clear that there was another tyranny to be avoided. The accumulations of all powers in the same hands, Madison warned, "whether of one, a few, or many, and whether hereditary, self-appointed, or elective, may justly be pronounced the very definition of tyranny."

As another colonist suggested in papers published in Philadelphia, "We have been so long habituated to a jealousy of tyranny from monarchy and aristocracy, that we have yet to learn the dangers of it from democracy." Despotism had to be opposed "whether it came from Kings, Lords or the people."

The debate about majority tyranny reflected Madison's concern that the majority may not represent the whole. In a homogeneous society, the interest of the majority would likely be that of the minority also. But in a heterogeneous community, the majority may not represent all competing interests. The majority is likely to be self-interested and ignorant or indifferent to the concerns of the minority. In such case, Madison observed, the assumption that the majority represents the minority is "altogether fictitious."

Yet even a self-interested majority can govern fairly if it cooperates with the minority. One reason for such cooperation is that the self-interested majority values the principle of reciprocity. The self-interested majority worries that the minority may attract defectors from the majority and become the next governing majority. The Golden Rule principle of reciprocity functions to check the tendency of a self-interested majority to act tyrannically.

So the argument for the majority principle connects it with the value of reciprocity: You cooperate when you lose in part because members of the current majority will cooperate when they lose. The conventional case for the fairness of majority rule is that it is not really the rule of a fixed group—The Majority—on all issues; instead it is the rule of shifting majorities, as the losers at one time or on one issue join with others and become part of the governing coalition at another time or on another issue. The result will be a fair system of mutually beneficial cooperation. I call a majority that rules but does not dominate a Madisonian Majority.

The problem of majority tyranny arises, however, when the self-interested majority does not need to worry about defections. When the majority is fixed and permanent, there are no checks on its ability to be overbearing. A majority that does not worry about defectors is a majority with total power.

In such a case, Madison's concern about majority tyranny arises. In a heterogeneous community, any faction with total power might subject "the minority to the caprice and arbitrary decisions of the majority, who instead of consulting the interest of the whole community collectively, attend sometimes to partial and local advantages."

"What remedy can be found in a republican Government, where the majority must ultimately decide," argued Madison, but to ensure "that no one common interest or passion will be likely to unite a majority of the whole number in an unjust pursuit." The answer was to disaggregate the majority to ensure checks and balances or fluid, rotating interests. The minority needed protection against an overbearing majority, or that "a common sentiment is less likely to be felt, and the requisite concert less likely to be formed, by a majority of the whole."

Political struggles would not be simply a contest between rulers and people; the political struggles would be among the people themselves. The work of government was not to transcend different interests but to reconcile them. In an ideal democracy, the people would rule, but the minorities would also be protected against the power of majorities. Again, where the rules of decisionmaking protect the minority, the Madisonian Majority rules without dominating.

But if a group is unfairly treated, for example, when it forms a racial minority, and if the problems of unfairness are not cured by conventional assumptions about majority rule, then what is to be done? The answer is that we may need an *alternative* to winner-take-all majoritarianism. In this book, a collection of my law review articles, I describe the alternative, which, with Nikolas's help, I now call the "principle of taking turns." In a racially divided society, this principle does better than simple majority rule if it accommodates the values of self-government, fairness, deliberation, compromise, and consensus that lie at the heart of the democratic ideal.

In my legal writing, I follow the caveat of James Madison and other early American democrats. I explore decisionmaking rules that might work in a multi-racial society to ensure that majority rule does not become majority tyranny. I pursue voting systems that might disaggregate

The Majority so that it does not exercise power unfairly or tyrannically. I aspire to a more cooperative political style of decision making to enable all of the students at Brother Rice to feel comfortable attending the same prom. In looking to create Madisonian Majorities, I pursue a positive-sum, taking-turns solution.

Structuring decision making to allow the minority "a turn" may be necessary to restore the reciprocity ideal when a fixed majority refuses to cooperate with the minority. If the fixed majority loses its incentive to follow the Golden Rule principle of shifting majorities, the minority never gets to take a turn. Giving the minority a turn does not mean the minority gets to rule; what it does mean is that the minority gets to influence decision making and the majority rules more legitimately.

Instead of automatically rewarding the preferences of the monolithic majority, a taking-turns approach anticipates that the majority rules, but is not overbearing. Because those with 51 percent of the votes are not assured 100 percent of the power, the majority cooperates with, or at least does not tyrannize, the minority.

The sports analogy of "I win; you lose" competition within a political hierarchy makes sense when only one team can win; Nikolas's intuition that it is often possible to take turns suggests an alternative approach. Take family decision making, for example. It utilizes a taking-turns approach. When parents sit around the kitchen table deciding on a vacation destination or activities for a rainy day, often they do not simply rely on a show of hands, especially if that means that the older children always prevail or if affinity groups among the children (those who prefer movies to video games, or those who prefer baseball to playing cards) never get to play their activity of choice. Instead of allowing the majority simply to rule, the parents may propose that everyone take turns, going to the movies one night and playing video games the next. Or as Nikolas proposes, they might do both on a given night.

Taking turns attempts to build consensus while recognizing political or social differences, and it encourages everyone to play. The taking-turns approach gives those with the most support more turns, but it also legitimates the outcome from each individual's perspective, including those whose views are shared only by a minority.

In the end, I do not believe that democracy should encourage rule by the powerful—even a powerful majority. Instead, the idea of democracy promises a fair discussion among self-defined equals about how to achieve our common aspirations. To redeem that promise, we need to put the idea of taking turns and disaggregating the majority at the center of our conception of representation. Particularly as we move into the twenty-first century as a more highly diversified citizenry, it is essential that we consider the ways in which voting and representational systems succeed or fail at encouraging Madisonian Majorities.

To use Nikolas's terminology, "it is no fair" if a fixed, tyrannical majority excludes or alienates the minority. It is no fair if a fixed, tyrannical majority monopolizes all the power all the time. It is no fair if we engage in the periodic ritual of elections, but only the permanent majority gets to choose who is elected. Where we have tyranny by The Majority, we do not have genuine democracy.

IN DEFENSE OF PREJUDICE

Jonathan Rauch

The war on prejudice is now, in all likelihood, the most uncontroversial social movement in America. Opposition to "hate speech," formerly identified with the liberal left, has become a bipartisan piety. In the past year, groups and factions that agree on nothing else have agreed that the public expression of any and all prejudices must be forbidden. On the left, protesters and editorialists have insisted that Francis L. Lawrence resign as president of Rutgers University for describing blacks as a "disadvantaged population that doesn't have that genetic, hereditary background to have a higher average." On the other side of the ideological divide, Ralph Reed, the executive director of the Christian Coalition, responded to criticism of the religious right by calling a press conference to denounce a supposed outbreak of "name-calling, scapegoating, and religious bigotry." Craig Rogers, an evangelical Christian student at California State University, recently filed a $2.5 million sexual-harassment suit against a lesbian professor of psychology, claiming that anti-male bias in one of her lectures violated campus rules and left him feeling "raped and trapped."

In universities and on Capitol Hill, in workplaces and newsrooms, authorities are declaring that there is no place for racism, sexism, homophobia, Christian-bashing, and other forms of prejudice in public debate or even in private thought. "Only when racism and other forms of prejudice are expunged," say the crusaders for sweetness and light, "can minorities be safe and society be fair." So sweet, this dream of a world without prejudice. But the very last thing society should do is seek to utterly eradicate racism and other forms of prejudice.

I suppose I should say, in the customary I-hope-I-don't-sound-too-defensive tone, that I am not a racist and that this is not an article favoring racism or any other particular prejudice. It is an article favoring intellectual pluralism, which permits the expression of various forms of bigotry and always will. Although we like to hope that a time will come when no one will believe that people come in types and that each type belongs with its own kind, I doubt such a day will ever arrive. By all indications, Homo sapiens is a tribal species for whom "us versus them" comes naturally and must be continually pushed back. Where there is genuine freedom of expression, there will be racist expression. There will also be people who believe that homosexuals are sick or threaten children or—especially among teenagers—are rightful targets of manly savagery. Homosexuality will always be incomprehensible to most people, and what is incomprehensible is feared. As for anti-Semitism, it appears to be a hardier virus than influenza. If you want pluralism, then you get racism and sexism and homophobia, and communism and fascism and xenophobia and tribalism, and that is just for a start. If you want to believe in intellectual freedom and the progress of knowledge and the advancement of science and all those other good things, then you must swallow hard and accept this: for as thickheaded and wayward an animal as us, the realistic question is how to make the best of prejudice, not how to eradicate it.

Indeed, "eradicating prejudice" is so vague a proposition as to be meaningless. Distinguishing prejudice reliably and nonpolitically from non-prejudice, or even defining it crisply, is quite hopeless. We all feel we know prejudice when we see it. But do we? At the University of Michigan, a student said in a classroom discussion that he considered homosexuality a disease treatable with therapy. He was summoned to a formal disciplinary hearing for violating the school's policy against speech that "victimizes" people based on "sexual orientation." Now, the evidence is abundant that that particular hypothesis is wrong, and any American homosexual can attest to the harm that the student's hypothesis has inflicted on many real people. But was it a statement of prejudice or of misguided belief? Hate speech or hypothesis? Many Americans who do not regard themselves as bigots or haters believe that homosexuality is a treatable disease. They may be wrong, but are they all bigots? I am unwilling to say so, and if you are willing, beware. The line between a prejudiced belief and a merely controversial one is elusive, and the harder you look the more elusive it becomes. "God hates homosexuals" is a statement of fact, not of bias, to those who believe it; "American criminals are disproportionately black" is a statement of bias, not of fact, to those who disbelieve it.

Who is right? You may decide, and so may others, and there is no need to agree. That is the great innovation of intellectual pluralism (which is to say, of post-Enlightenment science, broadly defined). We cannot know in advance or for sure which belief is prejudice and which is truth, but to advance knowledge we don't need to know. The genius of intellectual pluralism lies not in doing away with prejudices and dogmas but in channeling them—making them socially productive by pitting prejudice against prejudice and dogma against dogma, exposing all to withering public criticism. What survives at the end of the day is our base of knowledge.

* * * * *

What they told us in high school about this process is very largely a lie. The Enlightenment tradition taught us that science is orderly, antiseptic, rational, the province of detached experimenters and high-minded logicians. In the popular view, science stands for reason against prejudice, open-mindedness against dogma, calm consideration against passionate attachment—all personified by pop-science icons like the magisterially deductive Sherlock Holmes, the coolly analytic Mr. Spock, the genially authoritative Mr. Science (from our junior-high science films). Yet one of science's dirty secrets is that although science as a whole is as unbiased as anything human can be, scientists are just as biased as anyone else, sometimes more so. "One of the strengths of science," writes the philosopher of science David L. Hull, "is that it does not require that scientists be unbiased, only that different scientists have different biases." Another dirty secret is that, no less than the rest of us, scientists can be dogmatic and pigheaded. "Although this pigheadedness often damages the careers of individual scientists," says Hull, "it is beneficial for the manifest goal of science," which relies on people to invest years in their ideas and defend them passionately. And the dirtiest secret of all, if you believe in the antiseptic popular view of science, is that this most ostensibly rational of enterprises depends on the most irrational of motives—ambition, narcissism, animus, even revenge. "Scientists acknowledge that among their motivations are natural curiosity, the love of truth, and the desire to help humanity, but other inducements exist as well, and one of them is to 'get that son of a bitch,'" says Hull. "Time and again, scientists whom I interviewed described the powerful spur that 'showing that son of a bitch' supplied to their own research."

Many people, I think, are bewildered by this unvarnished and all too human view of science. They believe that for a system to be unprejudiced, the people in it must also be unprejudiced. In fact, the opposite is true. Far from eradicating ugly or stupid ideas and coarse or unpleasant motives, intellectual pluralism relies upon them to excite intellectual passion and redouble scientific effort. I know of no modern idea more ugly and stupid than that the Holocaust never happened, nor any idea more viciously motivated. Yet the deniers' claims that the Auschwitz gas chambers could not have worked led to closer study and, in 1993, research showing, at last, how they actually did work. Thanks to prejudice and stupidity, another opening for doubt has been shut.

An enlightening and efficient intellectual regime lets a million prejudices bloom, including many that you or I may regard as hateful or grotesque. It avoids any attempt to stamp out prejudice, because stamping out prejudice really means forcing everyone to share the same prejudice, namely that of whoever is in authority. The great American philosopher Charles Sanders Peirce wrote in 1877: "When complete agreement could not otherwise be reached, a general massacre of all who have not thought in a certain way has proved a very effective means of settling opinion in a country." In speaking of "settling opinion," Peirce was writing about one of the two or three most fundamental problems that any human society must confront and solve. For most societies down through the centuries, this problem was dealt with in the manner he described: errors were identified by the authorities—priests, politburos, dictators—or by mass opinion, and then the error-makers were eliminated along with their putative mistakes. "Let all men who reject the established belief be terrified into silence," wrote Peirce, describing this system. "This method has, from the earliest times, been one of the chief means of upholding correct theological and political doctrines."

Intellectual pluralism substitutes a radically different doctrine: we kill our mistakes rather than each other. Here I draw on another great philosopher, the late Karl Popper, who pointed out that the critical method of science "consists in letting our hypotheses die in our stead." Those who are in error are not (or are not supposed to be) banished or excommunicated or forced to sign a renunciation or required to submit to "rehabilitation" or sent for psychological counseling. It is the error we punish, not the errant. By letting people make errors—even mischievous, spiteful errors (as, for instance, Galileo's insistence on Copernicanism was taken to be in 1633)—pluralism creates room to challenge orthodoxy, think imaginatively, experiment boldly. Brilliance and bigotry are empowered in the same stroke.

Pluralism is the principle that protects and makes a place in human company for that loneliest and most vulnerable of all minorities, the minority who is hounded and despised among blacks and whites, gays and straights, who is suspect or criminal among every tribe and in every nation of the world, and yet on whom progress depends: the dissident. I am not saying that dissent is always or even usually enlightened. Most of the time it is foolish and self-serving. No dissident has the right to be taken seriously, and the fact that Aryan Nation racists or Nation of Islam anti-Semites are unorthodox does not entitle them to respect. But what goes around comes around. As a supporter of gay marriage, for example, I reject the majority's view of family, and as a Jew I reject its view of God. I try to be civil, but the fact is that most Americans regard my views on marriage as a reckless assault on the most fundamental of all institutions, and many people are more than a little discomfited by the statement, "Jesus Christ was no more divine than anybody else" (which is why so few people ever say it). Trap the racists and anti-Semites, and you lay a trap for me too. Hunt for them with eradication in your mind, and you have brought dissent itself within your sights.

The new crusade against prejudice waves aside such warnings. Like earlier crusades against antisocial ideas, the mission is fueled by good (if cocksure) intentions and a genuine sense of urgency. Some kinds of error are held to be intolerable, like pollutants that even in small traces poison the water for a whole town. Some errors are so pernicious as to damage real people's lives, so wrongheaded that no person of right mind or goodwill could support them. Like their forebears of other stripe—the Church in its campaigns against heretics, the McCarthyites in their campaigns against Communists—the modern anti-racist and anti-sexist and anti-homophobic campaigners are totalists, demanding not that misguided ideas and ugly expressions be corrected or criticized but that they be eradicated. They make war not on errors but on error, and like other totalists they act in the name of public safety, especially, or minorities.

* * * * *

The sweeping implications of this challenge to pluralism are not, I think, well enough understood by the public at large. Indeed, the new brand of totalism has yet even to be properly named. "Multiculturalism," for instance, is much too broad. "Political correctness" comes much closer but is too trendy and snide. For lack of anything else, I will call the new anti-pluralism "purism," since its major tenet is that society cannot be just until the last traces of invidious prejudice have been scrubbed away. Whatever you call it, the purists' way of seeing things has spread through American intellectual life with remarkable speed, so much so that many people will blink at you uncomprehendingly or even call you a racist (or sexist or homophobe, etc.) if you suggest that expressions of racism should be tolerated or that prejudice has its part to play.

The new purism sets out, to begin with, on a campaign against words, for words are the currency of prejudice, and if prejudice is hurtful then so must be prejudiced words. "We are not safe when these violent words are among us," wrote Mari Matsuda, then a UCLA law professor. Here one imagines gangs of racist words swinging chains and smashing heads in back alleys. To suppress bigoted language seems, at first blush, reasonable, but it quickly leads to a curious result. A peculiar kind of verbal shamanism takes root, as though certain expressions, like curses or magical incantations, carry in themselves the power to hurt or heal—as though words were bigoted rather than people. "Context is everything," people have always said. The use of the word "nigger" in *Huckleberry Finn* does not make the book an "act" of hate speech—or does it? In the new view, this is no longer so clear. The very utterance of the word "nigger" (at least by a non-black) is a racist act. When a *Sacramento Bee* cartoonist put the word "nigger" mockingly in the mouth of a white supremacist, there were howls of protest and 1,400 canceled subscriptions and an editorial apology, even though the word was plainly being invoked against racists, not against blacks.

Faced with escalating demands of verbal absolutism, newspapers issue lists of forbidden words. The expressions "gyp" (derived from "Gypsy") and "Dutch treat" were among the dozens of terms stricken as "offensive" in a much-ridiculed (and later withdrawn) *Los Angeles Times* speech code. The University of Missouri journalism school issued a *Dictionary of Cautionary Words and Phrases,* which included "Buxom: Offensive reference to a woman's chest. Do not use. See 'Woman.' Codger: Offensive reference to a senior citizen."

As was bound to happen, purists soon discovered that chasing around after words like "gyp" or "buxom" hardly goes to the roots of the problem. As long as they remain bigoted, bigots will simply find other words. If they can't call you a kike then they will say Jewboy, Judas, or Hebe, and when all those are banned they will press words like "oven" and "lampshade" into their service. The vocabulary of hate is potentially as rich as your dictionary, and all you do by banning language used by cretins is to let them decide what the rest of us may say. The problem, some purists have concluded, must therefore go much deeper than laws: it must go to the deeper level of ideas. Racism, sexism, homophobia, and the rest must be built into the very structure of American society and American patterns of thought, so pervasive yet so insidious that, like water to a fish, they are both omnipresent and unseen. The mere existence of prejudice constructs a society whose very nature is prejudiced.

This line of thinking was pioneered by feminists, who argued that pornography, more than just being expressive, is an act by which men construct an oppressive society. Racial activists quickly picked up the argument. Racist expressions are themselves acts of oppression, they said. "All racist speech constructs the social reality that constrains the liberty of nonwhites because of their race," wrote Charles R. Lawrence III, then a law professor at Stanford. From the purist point of view, a society with even one racist is a racist society, because the idea itself threatens and demeans its targets. They cannot feel wholly safe or wholly welcome as long as racism is present. Pluralism says: There will always be some racists. Marginalize them, ignore them, exploit them, ridicule them, take pains to make their policies illegal, but otherwise leave them alone. Purists say: That's not enough. Society cannot be just until these pervasive and oppressive ideas are searched out and eradicated.

And so what is now under way is a growing drive to eliminate prejudice from every corner of society. I doubt that many people have noticed how far-reaching this anti-pluralist movement is becoming.

In universities: Dozens of universities have adopted codes proscribing speech or other expression that (this is from Stanford's policy, which is more or less representative) "is intended to insult or stigmatize an individual or a small number of individuals on the basis of their sex, race, color, handicap, religion, sexual orientation or national and ethnic origin." Some codes punish only persistent harassment of a targeted individual, but many, following the purist doctrine that even one racist is too many, go much further. At Penn, an administrator declared: "We at the University of Pennsylvania have guaranteed students and the community that they can live in a community free of sexism, racism, and homophobia." Here is the purism that gives "political correctness" its distinctive combination of puffy high-mindedness and authoritarian zeal.

In school curricula: "More fundamental than eliminating racial segregation has to be the removal of racist thinking, assumptions, symbols, and materials in the curriculum," writes theorist Molefi Kete Asante. In practice, the effort to "remove racist thinking" goes well beyond striking egregious references from textbooks. In many cases it becomes a kind of mental engineering in which students are encouraged to see prejudice.

Ah, but the task of scouring minds clean is Augean. "Nobody escapes," said a Rutgers University report on campus prejudice. Bias and prejudice, it found, cross every conceivable line, from sex to race to politics: "No matter who you are, no matter what the color of your skin, no matter what your gender or sexual orientation, no matter what you believe, no matter how you behave, there is somebody out there who doesn't like people of your kind." Charles Lawrence writes: "Racism is ubiquitous. We are all racists." If he means that most of us think racist thoughts of some sort at one time or another, he is right. If we are going to "eliminate prejudices and biases from our society," then the work of the prejudice police is unending. They are doomed to hunt and hunt, scour and scour and scour.

* * * * *

What is especially dismaying is that the purists pursue prejudice in the name of protecting minorities. In order to protect people like me (homosexual), they must pursue people like me (dissident). In order to bolster minority self-esteem, they suppress minority opinion. There are, of course, all kinds of practical and legal problems with the purists' campaign: the incursions against the First Amendment; the inevitable abuses by prosecutors and activists who define as "hateful" or "violent" whatever speech they dislike or can score points off of; the lack of any evidence that repressing prejudice eliminates rather than inflames it. But minorities, or all people, ought to remember that by definition we cannot prevail by numbers, and we generally cannot prevail by force. Against the power of ignorant mass opinion and group prejudice and superstition, we have only our voices. If you doubt that minorities' voices are powerful weapons, think of the lengths to which Southern officials went to silence the Reverend Martin Luther King Jr. (recall that the city commissioner of Montgomery, Alabama, won a $500,000 libel suit, later overturned in *New York Times v. Sullivan* [1964], regarding an advertisement in the *Times* placed by civil-rights leaders who denounced the Montgomery police). Think of how much gay people have improved their lot over twenty-five years simply by refusing to remain silent. Recall the Michigan student who was prosecuted for saying that homosexuality is a treatable disease, and notice that he was black. Under that Michigan speech code, more than twenty blacks were charged with racist speech, while no instance of racist speech by whites was punished. In Florida, the hate-speech law was invoked against a black man who called a policeman a "white cracker"; not so surprisingly, in the first hate-crimes case to reach the Supreme Court, the victim was white and the defendant black.

In the escalating war against "prejudice," the right is already learning to play by the rules that were pioneered by the purist activists of the left. Last year leading Democrats, including the President, criticized the Republican Party for being increasingly in the thrall of the Christian right. Some of the rhetoric was harsh ("fire-breathing Christian radical right"), but it wasn't vicious or even clearly wrong. Never mind: when Democratic Representative Vic Fazio said Republicans were "being forced to the fringes by the aggressive political tactics of the religious right," the chairman of the Republican National Committee, Haley Barbour, said, "Christian-bashing" was "the left's preferred form of religious bigotry." Bigotry! Prejudice! "Christians active in politics are now on the receiving end of an extraordinary campaign of bias and prejudice," said the conservative leader William J. Bennett. One discerns, here, where the new purism leads. Eventually, any criticism of any group will be "prejudice."

Here is the ultimate irony of the new purism: words, which pluralists hope can be substituted for violence, are redefined by purists as violence. "The experience of being called 'nigger,' 'spic,' 'Jap,' or 'kike' is like receiving a slap in the face," Charles Lawrence wrote in 1990. "Psychic injury is no less an injury than being struck in the face, and it often is far more severe." This kind of talk is commonplace today. Epithets, insults, often even polite expressions of what's taken to be prejudice are called by purists "assaultive speech," "words that wound," "verbal violence." "To me, racial epithets are not speech," one University of Michigan law professor said. "They are bullets." In her speech accepting the 1993 Nobel Prize for Literature in Stockholm, Sweden, the author Toni Morrison said this: "Oppressive language does more than represent violence; it is violence."

It is not violence. I am thinking back to a moment on the subway in Washington, a little thing. I was riding home late one night and a squad of noisy kids, maybe seventeen or eighteen years old, noisily piled into the car. They yelled across the car and a girl said, "Where do we get off?"

A boy said, "Farragut North."

The girl: "Faggot North!"

The boy: "Yeah! Faggot North!"

General hilarity.

First, before the intellect resumes control, there is a moment of fear, an animal moment. Who are they? How many of them? How dangerous? Where is the way out? All of these things are noted preverbally and assessed by the gut. Then the brain begins an assessment; they are sober, this is probably too public a place for them to do it, there are more girls than boys, they were just talking, it is probably nothing.

They didn't notice me and there was no incident. The teenage babble flowed on, leaving me to think. I became interested in my own reaction: the jump of fear out of nowhere like an alert animal, the sense for a brief time that one is naked and alone and should hide or run away. For a time, one ceases to be a human being and becomes instead a faggot.

The fear engendered by these words is real. The remedy is as clear and as imperfect as ever: protect citizens against violence. This, I grant, is something that American society has never done very well and now does quite poorly. It is no solution to define words as violence or prejudice as oppression, and then by cracking down on words or thoughts pretend that we are doing something about violence and oppression. No doubt it is easier to pass a speech code or hate-crimes law and proclaim the streets safer than actually to make the streets safer, but the one must never be confused with the other. Every cop or prosecutor chasing words is one fewer chasing criminals. In a world rife with real violence and oppression, full of Rwandas and Bosnias and eleven-year-olds spraying bullets at children in Chicago and in turn being executed by gang lords, it is odious of Toni Morrison to say that words are violence.

Indeed, equating "verbal violence" with physical violence is a treacherous, mischievous business. Not long ago a writer was charged with viciously and gratuitously wounding the feelings and dignity of millions of people. He was charged, in effect, with exhibiting flagrant prejudice against Muslims and outrageously slandering their beliefs. "What is freedom of expression?" mused Salman Rushdie a year after the ayatollahs sentenced him to death and put a price on his head. "Without the freedom to offend, it ceases to exist." I can think of nothing sadder than that minority activists, in their haste to make the world better, should be the ones to forget the lesson of Rushdie's plight: for minorities, pluralism, not purism, is the answer. The campaigns to eradicate prejudice—all of them, the speech codes and workplace restrictions and mandatory therapy for accused bigots and all the rest—should stop, now. The whole objective of eradicating prejudice, as opposed to correcting and criticizing it, should be repudiated as a fool's errand. Salman Rushdie is right, Toni Morrison wrong, and minorities belong at his side, not hers.

THE CASE FOR THE USE OF ANIMALS
IN BIOMEDICAL RESEARCH

Carl Cohen

Using animals as research subjects in medical investigations is widely condemned on two grounds: first, because it wrongly violates the rights of animals, and second, because it wrongly imposes on sentient creatures much avoidable suffering. Neither of these arguments is sound. The first relies on a mistaken understanding of rights; the second relies on a mistaken calculation of consequences. Both deserve definitive dismissal.

WHY ANIMALS HAVE NO RIGHTS

A right, properly understood, is a claim, or potential claim, that one party may exercise against another. The target against whom such a claim may be registered can be a single person, a group, a community, or (perhaps) all humankind. The content of rights claims also varies greatly: repayment of loans, nondiscrimination by employers, noninterference by the state, and so on. To comprehend any genuine right fully, therefore, we must know who holds the right, against whom it is held, and *to what it is a right*.

Alternative sources of rights add complexity. Some rights are grounded in constitution and law (e.g., the right of an accused to trial by jury); some rights are moral but give no legal claims (e.g., my right to your keeping the promise you gave me); and some rights (e.g., against theft or assault) are rooted both in morals and in law.

The different targets, contents, and sources of rights, and their inevitable conflict, together weave a tangled web. Notwithstanding all such complications, this much is clear about rights in general: they are in every case claims, or potential claims, within a community of moral agents. Rights arise, and can be intelligibly defended, only among beings who actually do, or can, make moral claims against one another. Whatever else rights may be, therefore, they are necessarily human; their possessors are persons, human beings.

The attributes of human beings from which this moral capability arises have been described variously by philosophers, both ancient and modern: the inner consciousness of a free will (Saint Augustine); the grasp, by human reason, of the binding character of moral law (Saint Thomas); the self-conscious participation of human beings in an objective ethical order (Hegel); human membership in an organic moral community (Bradley); the development of the human self through the consciousness of other moral selves (Mead); and the underivative, intuitive cognition of the rightness of an action (Prichard). Most influential has been Immanuel Kant's emphasis on the universal human possession of a uniquely moral will and the autonomy its use entails. Humans confront choices that are purely moral; humans—but certainly not dogs or mice—lay down moral laws, for others and for themselves. Human beings are self-legislative, morally *autonomous*.

Animals (that is, nonhuman animals, the ordinary sense of that word) lack this capacity' for free moral judgment. They are not beings of a kind capable of exercising or responding to moral claims. Animals therefore have no rights, and they can have none. This is the core of the argument about the alleged rights of animals. The holders of rights must have the capacity to comprehend rules of duty, governing all including themselves. In applying such rules, the holders of rights must recognize possible conflicts between what is in their own interest and what is just. Only in a community of beings capable of self-restricting moral judgments can the concept of a right be correctly invoked.

Humans have such moral capacities. They are in this sense self-legislative, are members of communities governed by moral rules, and do possess rights. Animals do not have such moral capacities. They are not morally self legislative, cannot possibly be members of a truly moral community, and therefore cannot possess rights. In conducting research on animal subjects, therefore, we do not violate their rights, because they have none to violate.

To animate life, even in its simplest forms, we give a certain natural reverence. But the possession of rights presupposes a moral status not attained by the vast majority of living things. We must not infer, therefore, that a live being has, simply in being alive, a "right" to its life. The assertion that all animals, only because they are alive and have interests, also possess the "right to life" is an abuse of that phrase, and wholly without warrant.

It does not follow from this, however, that we are morally free to do anything we please to animals. Certainly not. In our dealings with animals, as in our dealings with other human beings, we have obligations that do not arise from claims against us based on rights. Rights entail obligations, but many of the things one ought to do are in no way tied to another's entitlement. Rights and obligations are not reciprocals of one another, and it is a serious mistake to suppose that they are.

Illustrations are helpful. Obligations may arise from internal commitments made: physicians have obligations to their patients not grounded merely in their patients' rights. Teachers have such obligations to their students, shepherds to their dogs, and cowboys to their horses. Obligations may arise from differences of status: adults owe special care when playing with young children, and children owe special care when playing with young pets. Obligations may arise from special relationships: the payment of my son's college tuition is something to which he may have no right, although it may be my obligation to bear the burden if I reasonably can; my dog has no right to daily exercise and veterinary care, but I do have the obligation to provide these things for her. Obligations may arise from particular acts or circumstances: one may be obliged to another for a special kindness done, or obliged to put an animal out of its misery in view of its condition—although neither the human benefactor nor the dying animal may have had a claim of right.

Plainly, the grounds of our obligations to humans and to animals are manifold and cannot be formulated simply. Some hold that there is a general obligation to do no gratuitous harm to sentient creatures (the principle of nonmaleficence); some hold that there is a general obligation to do good to sentient creatures when that is reasonably within one's power (the principle of beneficence). In our dealings with animals, few will deny that we are at least obliged to act humanely—that is, to treat them with the decency and concern that we owe, as sensitive human beings, to other sentient creatures. To treat animals humanely, however, is not to treat them as humans or as the holders of rights.

A common objection, which deserves a response, may be paraphrased as follows:

> If having rights requires being able to make moral claims, to grasp and apply moral laws, then many humans—the brain-damaged, the comatose, the senile—who plainly lack those capacities must be without rights. But that is absurd. This proves [the critic concludes] that rights do not depend on the presence of moral capacities.

This objection fails; it mistakenly treats an essential feature of humanity as though it were a screen for sorting humans. The capacity for moral judgment that distinguishes humans from animals is not a test to be administered to human beings one by one. Persons who are unable, because of some disability, to perform the full moral functions natural to human beings are certainly not for that reason ejected from the moral community. The issue is one of kind. Humans are of such a kind that they may be the subject of experiments only with their voluntary consent. The choices they make freely must be respected. Animals are of such a kind that it is impossible for them, in principle, to give or withhold voluntary consent or to make a moral choice. What humans retain when disabled, animals have never had.

A second objection, also often made, may be paraphrased as follows:

> Capacities will not succeed in distinguishing humans from the other animals. Animals also reason; animals also communicate with one another; animals also care passionately for their young; animals also exhibit desires and preferences. Features of moral relevance—rationality, interdependence, and love—are not exhibited uniquely by human beings. Therefore [this critic concludes], there can be no solid moral distinction between humans and other animals.

This criticism misses the central point. It is not the ability to communicate or to reason, or dependence on one another, or care for the young, or the exhibition of preference, or any such behavior that marks the critical divide. Analogies between human families and those of monkeys, or between human communities and those of wolves, and the like, are entirely beside the point. Patterns of conduct are not at issue. Animals do indeed exhibit remarkable behavior at times. Conditioning, fear, instinct, and intelligence all contribute to species survival. Membership in a community of moral agents nevertheless remains impossible for them. Actors subject to moral judgment must be capable of grasping the generality of an ethical premise in a practical syllogism. Humans act immorally often enough, but only they—never wolves or monkeys—can discern, by applying some moral rule to the facts of a case, that a given act ought or ought not to be performed. The moral restraints imposed by humans on themselves are thus highly abstract and are often in conflict with the self-interest of the agent. Communal behavior among animals, even when most intelligent and most endearing, does not approach autonomous morality in this fundamental sense.

Genuinely moral acts have an internal as well as an external dimension. Thus, in law, an act can be criminal only when the guilty deed, the *actus reus*, is done with a guilty mind, *mens rea*. No animal can ever commit a crime; bringing animals to criminal trial is the mark of primitive ignorance. The claims of moral right are similarly inapplicable to them. Does a lion have a right to eat a baby zebra? Does a baby zebra have a right not to be eaten? Such questions, mistakenly invoking the concept of right where it does not belong, do not make good sense. Those who condemn biomedical research because it violates "animal rights" commit the same blunder.

IN DEFENSE OF "SPECIESISM"

Abandoning reliance on animal rights, some critics resort instead to animal sentience—their feelings of pain and distress. We ought to desist from imposition of pain insofar as we can. Since all or nearly all experimentation on animals does impose pain and could be readily forgone, say these critics, it should be stopped. The ends sought may be worthy, but those ends do not justify imposing agonies on humans, and by animals the agonies are felt no less. The laboratory use of animals (these critics conclude) must therefore be ended—or at least very sharply curtailed.

Argument of this variety is essentially utilitarian, often expressly so; it is based on the calculation of the net product, in pains and pleasures, resulting from experiments on animals. Jeremy Bentham, comparing horses and dogs with other sentient creatures, is thus commonly quoted: "The question is not Can they reason? nor, Can they talk? but, Can they suffer?"

Animals certainly can suffer and surely ought not to be made to suffer needlessly. But in inferring, from these uncontroversial premises, that biomedical research causing animal distress is largely (or wholly) wrong, the critic commits two serious errors.

The first error is the assumption, often explicitly defended, that all sentient animals have equal moral standing. Between a dog and a human being, according to this view, there is no moral difference; hence the pains suffered by dogs must be weighed no differently from the pains suffered by humans. To deny such equality, according to this critic, is to give unjust preference to one species over another; it is "Speciesism." The most influential statement of this moral equality of species was made by Peter Singer:

> The racist violates the principle of equality by giving greater weight to the interests of members of his own race when there is a clash between their interests and the interests of those of another race. The sexist violates the principle of equality by favoring the interests of his own sex. Similarly the speciesist allows the interests of his own species to override the greater interests of members of other species. The pattern is identical in each case.

This argument is worse than unsound; it is atrocious. It draws an offensive moral conclusion from a deliberately devised verbal parallelism that is utterly specious. Racism has no rational ground whatever. Differing degrees of respect or concern for humans for no other reason than that they are members of different races is an injustice totally without foundation in the nature of the races themselves. Racists, even if acting on the basis of mistaken factual beliefs, do grave moral wrong precisely because there is no morally relevant distinction among the races. The supposition of such differences has led to outright horror. The same is true of the sexes, neither sex being entitled by right to greater respect or concern than the other. No dispute here.

Between species of animate life, however—between (for example) humans on the one hand and cats or rats on the other—the morally relevant differences are enormous, and almost universally appreciated. Humans engage in moral reflection; humans are morally autonomous; humans are members of moral communities, recognizing just claims against their own interest. Human beings do have rights; theirs is a moral status very different from that of cats or rats.

I am a speciesist. Speciesism is not merely plausible; it is essential for right conduct, because those who will not make the morally relevant distinctions among species are almost certain, in consequence, to misapprehend their true obligations. The analogy between speciesism and racism is insidious. Every sensitive moral judgment requires that the differing natures of the beings to whom obligations are owed be considered. If all forms of animate life—or vertebrate animal life?—must be treated equally, and if therefore in evaluating a research program the pains of a rodent count equally with the pains of a human, we are forced to conclude (1) that neither humans nor rodents possess rights, or (2) that rodents possess all the rights that humans possess. Both alternatives are absurd. Yet one or the other must be swallowed if the moral equality of all species is to be defended.

Humans owe to other humans a degree of moral regard that cannot be owed to animals. Some humans take on the obligation to support and heal others, both humans and animals, as a principal duty in their lives; the fulfillment of that duty may require the sacrifice of many animals. If biomedical investigators abandon the effective pursuit of their professional objectives because they are convinced that they may not do to animals what the service of humans requires, they will fail, objectively, to do their duty. Refusing to recognize the moral differences among species is a sure path to calamity. (The largest animal rights group in the country is People for the Ethical Treatment of Animals; its codirector, Ingrid Newkirk, calls research using animal subjects "fascism" and "supremacism." "Animal liberationists do not separate out the *human animal,*" she says, "so there is no rational basis for saying that a human being has special rights. A rat is a pig is a dog is a boy. They're all mammals."

Those who claim to base their objection to the use of animals in biomedical research on their reckoning of the net pleasures and pains produced make a second error, equally grave. Even if it were true—as it is surely not—that the pains of all animal beings must be counted equally, a cogent utilitarian calculation requires that we weigh all the consequences of the use, and of the nonuse, of animals in laboratory research. Critics relying (however mistakenly) on animal rights may claim to ignore the beneficial results of such research, rights being trump cards to which interest and advantage must give way. But an argument that is explicitly framed in terms of interest and benefit for all over the long run must attend also to the disadvantageous consequences of not using animals in research, and to all the achievements attained and attainable only through their use. The sum of the benefits of their use is utterly beyond quantification. The elimination of horrible disease, the increase of longevity, the avoidance of great pain, the saving of lives, and the improvement of the quality of lives (for humans and for animals) achieved through research using animals is so incalculably great that the argument of these critics, systematically pursued, establishes not their conclusion but its reverse: to refrain from using animals in biomedical research is, on utilitarian grounds, morally wrong.

When balancing the pleasures and pains resulting from the use of animals in research, we must not fail to place on the scales the terrible pains that would have resulted, would be suffered now, and would long continue had animals not been used. Every disease eliminated, every vaccine developed, every method of pain relief devised, every surgical procedure invented, every prosthetic device implanted—indeed, virtually every modern medical therapy is due, in part or in whole, to experimentation using animals. Nor may we ignore, in the balancing process, the predictable gains in human (and animal) well-being that are probably achievable in the future but that will not be achieved if the decision is made now to desist from such research or to curtail it.

Medical investigators are seldom insensitive to the distress their work may cause animal subjects. Opponents of research using animals are frequently insensitive to the cruelty of the results of the restrictions they would impose. Untold numbers of human beings—real persons, although not now identifiable—would suffer grievously as the consequence of this well-meaning but shortsighted tenderness. If the morally relevant differences between humans and animals are borne in mind, and if all relevant considerations are weighed, the calculation of long-term consequences must give overwhelming support for biomedical research using animals.

CONCLUDING REMARKS

Substitution. The humane treatment of animals requires that we desist from experimenting on them if we can accomplish the same result using alternative methods—in vitro experimentation, computer simulation, or others. Critics of some experiments using animals rightly make this point.

It would be a serious error to suppose, however, that alternative techniques could soon be used in most research now using live animal subjects. No other methods now on the horizon—or perhaps ever to be available—can fully replace the testing of a drug, a procedure, or a vaccine, in live organisms. The flood of new medical possibilities being opened by the successes of recombinant DNA technology will turn to a trickle if testing on live animals is forbidden. When initial trials entail great risks, there may be no forward movement whatever without the use of live animal subjects. In seeking knowledge that may prove critical in later clinical applications, the unavailability of animals for inquiry may spell complete stymie. In the United States, federal regulations require the testing of new drugs and other products on animals, for efficacy and safety, before human beings are exposed to them. We would not want it otherwise.

Every new advance in medicine—every new drug, new operation, new therapy of any kind—must sooner or later be tried on a living being for the first time. That trial, controlled or uncontrolled, will be an experiment. The subject of that experiment, if it is not an animal, will be a human being. Prohibiting the use of live animals in biomedical research, therefore, or sharply restricting it, must result either in the blockage of much valuable research or in the replacement of animal subjects with human subjects. These are the consequences—unacceptable to most reasonable persons—of not using animals in research.

Reduction. Should we not at least reduce the use of animals in biomedical research? No, we should increase it, to avoid when feasible the use of humans as experimental subjects. Medical investigations putting human subjects at some risk are numerous and greatly varied. The risks run in such experiments are usually unavoidable, and (thanks to earlier experiments on animals) most such risks are minimal or moderate. But some experimental risks are substantial.

When an experimental protocol that entails substantial risk to humans comes before an institutional review board, what response is appropriate? The investigation, we may suppose, is promising and deserves support, so long as its human subjects are protected against unnecessary dangers. May not the investigators be fairly asked, Have you done all that you can do to eliminate risk to humans by the extensive testing of that drug, that procedure, or that device on animals? To achieve maximal safety for humans we are right to require thorough experimentation on animal subjects before humans are involved.

Opportunities to increase human safety in this way are commonly missed; trials in which risks may be shifted from humans to animals are often not devised, sometimes not even considered. Why? For the investigator, the use of animals as subjects is often more expensive, in money and time, than the use of human subjects. Access to suitable human subjects is often quick and convenient, whereas access to appropriate animal subjects may be awkward, costly, and burdened with red tape. Physician-investigators have often had more experience working with human beings and know precisely where the needed pool of subjects is to be found and how they may be enlisted. Animals, and the procedures for their use, are often less familiar to these investigators. Moreover, the use of animals in place of humans is now more likely to be the target of zealous protests from without. The upshot is that humans are sometimes subjected to risks that animals could have borne, and should have borne, in their place. To maximize the protection of human subjects, I conclude, the wide and imaginative use of live animal subjects should be encouraged rather than discouraged. This enlargement in the use of animals is our obligation.

Consistency. Finally, inconsistency between the profession and the practice of many who oppose research using animals deserves comment. This frankly *ad hominem* observation aims chiefly to show that a coherent position rejecting the use of animals in medical research imposes costs so high as to be intolerable even to the critics themselves.

One cannot coherently object to the killing of animals in biomedical investigations while continuing to eat them. Anesthetics and thoughtful animal husbandry render the level of actual animal distress in the laboratory generally lower than that in the abattoir. So long as death and discomfort do not substantially differ in the two contexts, the consistent objector must not only refrain from all eating of animals but also protest as vehemently against others eating them as against others experimenting on them. No less vigorously must the critic object to the wearing of animal hides in coats and shoes, to employment in any industrial enterprise that uses animal parts, and to any commercial development that will cause death or distress to animals.

Killing animals to meet human needs for food, clothing, and shelter is judged entirely reasonable by most persons. The ubiquity of these uses and the virtual universality of moral support for them confront the opponent of research using animals with an inescapable difficulty. How can the many common uses of animals be judged morally worthy, while their use in scientific investigation is judged unworthy?

The number of animals used in research is but the tiniest fraction of the total used to satisfy assorted human appetites. That these appetites, often base and satisfiable in other ways, morally justify the far larger consumption of animals, whereas the quest for improved human health and understanding cannot justify the far smaller, is wholly implausible. Aside from the numbers of animals involved, the distinction in terms of worthiness of use, drawn with regard to any single animal, is not defensible. A given sheep is surely not more justifiably used to put lamb chops on the supermarket counter than to serve in testing a new contraceptive or a new prosthetic device. The needless killing of animals is wrong; if the common killing of them for our food or convenience is right, the less common but more humane uses of animals in the service of medical science are certainly not less right.

Scrupulous vegetarianism, in matters of food, clothing, shelter, commerce, and recreation, and in all other spheres, is the only fully coherent position the critic may adopt. At great human cost, the lives of fish and crustaceans must also be protected, with equal vigor, if Speciesism has been forsworn. A very few consistent critics adopt this position. It is the *reductio ad absurdum* of the rejection of moral distinctions between animals and human beings.

Opposition to the use of animals in research is based on arguments of two different kinds—those relying on the alleged rights of animals and those relying on the consequences for animals. I have argued that arguments of both kinds must fail. We surely do have obligations to animals, but they have, and can have, no rights against us on which research can infringe. In calculating the consequences of animal research, we must weigh all the long-term benefits of the results achieved—to animals and to humans—and in that calculation we must not assume the moral equality of all animate species.

SOME THOUGHTS ON THE EXPLOITATION OF NON-HUMAN ANIMALS

Jane Goodall

The more we learn of the true nature of non-human animals, especially those with complex brains and correspondingly complex social behavior, the more ethical concerns are raised regarding their use in the service of man—whether this be in entertainment, as "pets," for food, in research laboratories or any of the other uses to which we subject them. This concern is sharpened when the usage in question leads to intense physical or mental suffering—as is so often true with regard to vivisection.

Biomedical research involving the use of living animals began in an era when the man in the street, while believing that animals felt pain (and other emotions) was not, for the most part, much concerned by their suffering. Subsequently, scientists were much influenced by the Behaviorists, a school of psychologists which maintained that animals were little more than machines, incapable of feeling pain or any humanlike feelings or emotions. Thus it was not considered important, or even necessary, to cater to the wants and needs of experimental animals. There was, at that time, no understanding of the effect of stress on the endocrine and nervous systems, no inkling of the fact that the use of a stressed animal could affect the results of an experiment. Thus the conditions in which animals were kept—size and furnishings of cage, solitary versus social confinement—were designed to make the life of the caretaker and experimenter as easy as possible. The smaller the cage the cheaper it was to make, the easier to clean, and the simpler the task of handling its inmate. Thus it was hardly surprising that research animals were kept in tiny sterile cages, stacked one on top of the other, usually one animal per cage. And ethical concern for the animal subjects was kept firmly outside the (locked) doors.

As time went on, the use of non-human animals in the laboratories increased, particularly as certain kinds of clinical research and testing on *human* animals became, for ethical reasons, more difficult to carry out legally. Animal research was increasingly perceived, by scientists and the general public, as being crucial to all medical progress. Today it is, by and large, taken for granted—the accepted way of gaining new knowledge about disease, its treatment and prevention. And, too, the accepted way of testing all manner of products, destined for human use, before they go on the market.

At the same time, thanks to a growing number of studies into the nature and mechanisms of animals' perceptions and intelligence, most people now believe that all except the most primitive of non-human animals experience pain, and that the "higher" animals have emotions similar to the human emotions we label pleasure or sadness, fear or despair. How is it, then, that scientists, at least when they put on their white coats and close the lab doors behind them, can continue to treat experimental animals as mere "things"? How can we, the citizens of civilized, western countries, tolerate laboratories which—from the point of view of animal inmates—are not unlike concentration camps? I think it is mainly because most people, even in these enlightened times, have little idea as to what goes on behind the closed doors of the laboratories, down in the basements. And even those who do have some knowledge, or those who are disturbed by the reports of cruelty that are occasionally released by animal rights organizations, believe that all animal research is essential to human health and progress in medicine and that the suffering so often involved is a necessary part of the research.

This is not true. Sadly, while some research is undertaken with a clearly defined objective that could lead to a medical breakthrough, a good many projects, some of which cause extreme suffering to the animals used, are of absolutely no value to human (or animal) health. Additionally, many experiments simply duplicate previous experiments. Finally, some research is carried out for the sake of gaining knowledge for its own sake. And while this is one of our more sophisticated intellectual abilities, should we be pursuing this goal at the expense of other living beings whom, unfortunately for them, we are able to dominate and control? Is it not an arrogant assumption that we have the *right* to (for example) cut up, probe, inject, drug and implant electrodes into animals of all species simply in our attempt to learn more about what makes them tick? Or what effect certain chemicals might have on them? And so on.

We may agree that the general public is largely ignorant of what is going on in the labs, and the reasons behind the research there, rather as the German people were mostly uninformed about the Nazi concentration camps. But what about the animal technicians, the veterinarians and the research scientists, those who are actually working in the labs and who know exactly what is going on? Are all those who use living animals as part of standard laboratory apparatus, heartless monsters?

Of course not. There may be some—there are occasional sadists in all walks of life. But they must be in the minority. The problem, as I see it, lies in the way we train young people in our society. They are victims of a kind of brainwashing that starts, only too often, in school and is intensified, in all but a few pioneering colleges and universities, throughout higher science education courses. By and large, students are taught that it is ethically acceptable to perpetrate, in the name of science, what, from the point of view of the animals, would certainly qualify as torture. They are encouraged to suppress their natural empathy for animals, and persuaded that animal pain and feelings are utterly different from our own—if, indeed, they exist at all. By the time they arrive in the labs these young people have been programmed to accept the suffering around them. And it is only too easy for them to justify this suffering on the grounds that the work being done is for the good of humanity. For the good of one animal species which has evolved a sophisticated capacity for empathy, compassion and understanding, attributes which we proudly acclaim as the hallmarks of humanity. I have been described as a "rabid anti-vivisectionist." But my own mother is alive today because her clogged aortic valve was removed and replaced by that of a pig. The valve in question—a "bioplasticized" one, apparently—came, we were told, from a commercially slaughtered hog. In other words, the pig would have died anyway. This, however, does not eliminate my feeling of concern for that particular pig—I have always had a special fondness for pigs. The suffering of laboratory pigs and those who are raised in intensive farming units has become a special concern of mine. I am writing a book, *An Anthology of the Pig*, which, I hope, will help to raise public awareness regarding the plight of those intelligent animals.

Of course I should like to see the lab cages standing empty. So would every caring, compassionate human, including most of those who work with animals in biomedical research. But if all use of animals in the laboratory was *abruptly* stopped there would probably, for a while anyway, be a great deal of confusion, and many lines of inquiry would be brought to a sudden halt. This would inevitably lead to an increase in human suffering. This means that, until alternatives to the use of live animals in the research labs are widely available and, moreover, researchers and drug companies are legally compelled to use them, society will demand—and accept—the continued abuse of animals on its behalf.

Already, in many fields of research and testing, the growing concern for animal suffering has led to major advances in the development of techniques such as tissue culture, *in vitro* testing, computer simulation and so on. The day will eventually come when it will no longer be necessary to use animals at all. It must. But much more pressure should be brought to bear for the speedy development of additional techniques. We should put far more money into the research, and give due acknowledgment and acclaim to those who make new breakthroughs—at the very least a series of Nobel prizes. It is necessary to attract the brightest in the field. Moreover, steps should be taken to insist on the use of techniques already developed and proven. In the meantime, it is imperative that the numbers of animals used be reduced drastically. Unnecessary duplication of research must be avoided. There should be more stringent rules regarding what animals may and may not be used for. They should be used only for the most pressing projects that have clear-cut health benefits for many people, and contribute significantly to the alleviation of human suffering. Other use of animals in the labs should be stopped *immediately*, including the testing of cosmetics and household products. Finally, so long as animals are used in our labs, for any reason whatsoever, they should be given the most humane treatment possible, and the best possible living conditions.

Why is it that only relatively few scientists are prepared to back those who are insisting on better, more humane conditions for laboratory animals? The usual answer is that changes of this sort would cost so much that all progress in medical knowledge would come to an end. This is not true. Essential research would continue—the cost of building new cages and instigating better care-giving programmes would be considerable, but negligible, I am assured, when compared with the cost of sophisticated equipment used by research scientists today. Unfortunately, though, many projects are poorly conceived and often totally unnecessary. They might indeed suffer if the costs of maintaining the research animals are increased. People making their living from them would lose their jobs.

When people complain about the cost of introducing humane living conditions, my response is: "Look at your life-style, your house, your car, your clothes. Think of the administrative buildings in which you work, your salary, your expenses, the holidays you take. And, after thinking about those things, *then* tell me that we should begrudge the extra dollars spent in making a little less grim the lives of the animals used to reduce human suffering."

Surely it should be a matter of moral responsibility that we humans, differing from other animals mainly by virtue of our more highly developed intellect and, with it, our greater capacity for understanding and compassion, ensure that medical progress speedily detaches its roots from the manure of non-human animal suffering and despair. Particularly when this involves the servitude of our closest relatives.

In the United States, federal law still requires that every batch of hepatitis B vaccine be tested on a chimpanzee before it is released for human use. In addition, chimpanzees are still used in some highly inappropriate research—such as the effect on them of certain addictive drugs. There are no chimpanzees in the labs in Britain—British scientists use chimpanzees in the United States, or at the TNO Primate Centre in Holland where EEC funding has recently gone into a new chimpanzee facility. (British scientists do, of course, make massive use of other non-human primates and thousands of dogs, cats, rodents, and so forth.)

The chimpanzee is more like us than any other living being. Physiological similarities have been enthusiastically described by scientists for many years, and have led to the use of chimpanzees as "models" for the study of certain infectious diseases to which most non-human animals are resistant. There are, of course, equally striking similarities between humans and chimpanzees in the anatomy of the brain and nervous system, and—although many have been reluctant to admit to these—in social behavior, cognition and emotionality. Because chimpanzees show intellectual abilities once thought unique to our own species, the line between humans and the rest of the animal kingdom, once thought to be so clear, has become blurred. Chimpanzees bridge the gap between "us" and "them."

Let us hope that this new understanding of the chimpanzees' place in nature will bring some relief to the hundreds who presently live out their lives as prisoners, in bondage to Man. Let us hope that our knowledge of their capacity for affection and enjoyment and fun, for fear and sadness and suffering, will lead us to treat them with the same compassion that we would show towards fellow humans. Let us hope that while medical science continues to use chimpanzees for painful or psychologically distressing experiments, we shall have the honesty to label such research for what, from the chimpanzees' point of view, it certainly is—the infliction of torture on innocent victims.

And let us hope that our understanding of the chimpanzee will lead also to a better understanding of the nature of other non-human animals, a new attitude towards the other species with which we share this planet. For, as Albert Schweitzer said, "We need a boundless ethic that includes animals too." And at the present time our ethic, where non-human animals are concerned, is limited and confused.

If we, in the western world, see a peasant beating an emaciated old donkey, forcing it to pull an oversize load, almost beyond its strength, we are shocked and outraged. That is cruelty. But taking an infant chimpanzee from his mother's arms, locking him into the bleak world of the laboratory, injecting him with human diseases—this, if done in the name of Science, is not regarded as cruelty. Yet in the final analysis, both donkey and chimpanzee are being exploited and misused for the benefit of humans. Why is one any more cruel that the other? Only because science has come to be venerated, and because scientists are assumed to be acting for the good of mankind, while the peasant is selfishly punishing a poor animal for his own gain. In fact, much animal research is self-serving too—many experiments are designed in order to keep the grant money coming in.

And let us not forget that we, in the West, incarcerate millions of domestic animals in intensive farm units in order to turn vegetable protein into animal protein for the table. While this is usually excused on grounds of economic necessity, or even regarded by some as sound animal husbandry, it is just as cruel as the beating of the donkey, the imprisonment of the chimpanzee. So are the fur farms. So is the abandonment of pets. And the illegal puppy farms. And fox hunting. And much that goes on behind the scenes when animals are trained to perform for our entertainment. The list could get very long.

Often I am asked whether I do not feel that it is unethical to devote time to the welfare of "animals" when so many human beings are suffering. Would it not be more appropriate to help starving children, battered wives, the homeless? Fortunately, there are hundreds of people addressing their considerable talents, humanitarian principles and fund-raising abilities to such causes. My own particular energies are not needed there. Cruelty is surely the very worst of human sins. To fight cruelty, in any shape or form—whether it be towards other human beings or non-human beings—brings us into direct conflict with that unfortunate streak of *inhumanity* that lurks in all of us. If only we could overcome cruelty with compassion we should be well on the way to creating a new and boundless ethic—one that would respect all living beings. We should stand at the threshold of a new era in human evolution—the realization, at last, of our most unique quality: humanity.

COMMON DECENCY

Susan Jacoby

She was deeply in love with a man who was treating her badly. To assuage her wounded ego (and to prove to herself that she could get along nicely without him), she invited another man, an old boyfriend, to a dinner *a deux* in her apartment. They were on their way to the bedroom when, having realized that she wanted only the man who wasn't there, she changed her mind. Her ex-boyfriend was understandably angry. He left her apartment with a not-so-politely phrased request that she leave him out of any future plans.

And that is the end of the story—except for the fact that he was eventually kind enough to accept her apology for what was surely a classic case of "mixed signals."

I often recall this incident, in which I was the embarrassed female participant, as the controversy over "date rape" ... heats up across the nation. What seems clear to me is that those who place acquaintance rape in a different category from "stranger rape"—those who excuse friendly social rapists on grounds that they are too dumb to understand when "no" means no— are being even more insulting to men than to women.

These apologists for date rape—and some of them are women—are really saying that the average man cannot be trusted to exercise any impulse control. Men are nasty and men are brutes—and a woman must be constantly on her guard to avoid giving a man any excuse to give way to his baser instincts.

If this view were accurate, few women would manage to get through life without being raped, and few men would fail to commit rape. For the reality is that all of us, men as well as women, send and receive innumerable mixed signals in the course of our sexual lives—and that is as true in marital beds at age 50 as in the back seats of cars at age 15.

Most men somehow manage to decode these signals without using superior physical strength to force themselves on their partners. And most women manage to handle conflicting male signals without, say, picking up carving knives to demonstrate their displeasure at sexual rejection. This is called civilization.

Civilized is exactly what my old boyfriend was being when he didn't use my muddle-headed emotional distress as an excuse to rape me. But I don't owe him excessive gratitude for his decent behavior—any more than he would have owed me special thanks for not stabbing him through the heart if our situations had been reversed. Most date rapes do not happen because a man honestly mistakes a woman's "no" for a "yes" or a "maybe." They occur because a minority of men—an ugly minority to be sure—can't stand to take "no" for an answer.

This minority behavior—and a culture that excuses it on grounds that boys will be boys —is the target of the movement against date rape that has surfaced on many campuses during the past year.

It's not surprising that date rape is an issue of particular importance to college-age women. The campus concentration of large numbers of young people, in an unsupervised environment that encourages drinking and partying, tends to promote sexual aggression and discourage inhibition. Drunken young men who rape a woman at a party can always claim they didn't know what they were doing—and a great many people will blame the victim for having been there in the first place.

That is the line adopted by antifeminists like Camille Paglia, author of the *Controversial Sexual Personae: Art and Decadence from Nefertiti to Emily Dickinson*. Paglia, whose views strongly resemble those expounded 20 years ago by Norman Mailer in *The Prisoner of Sex*, argues that feminists have deluded women by telling them they can go anywhere and do anything without fear of rape. Feminism, in this view, is both naive and antisexual because it ignores the power of women to incite uncontrollable male passions.

Just to make sure there is no doubt about a woman's place, Paglia also links the male sexual aggression that leads to rape with the creative energy of art. "There is no female Mozart," she has declared, "because there is no female Jack the Ripper." According to this "logic," one might expect to discover the next generation of composers in fraternity houses and dorms that have been singled out as sites of brutal gang rapes.

This type of unsubtle analysis makes no distinction between sex as an expression of the will to power and sex as a source of pleasure. When domination is seen as an inevitable component of sex, the act of rape is defined not by a man's actions but by a woman's signals.

It is true, of course, that some women (especially the young) initially resist sex not out of real conviction but as part of the elaborate persuasion and seduction rituals accompanying what was once called courtship. And it is true that many men (again, especially the young) take pride in the ability to coax a woman a step further than she intended to go.

But these mating rituals do not justify or even explain date rape. Even the most callow youth is capable of understanding the difference between resistance and genuine fear; between a halfhearted "no, we shouldn't" and tears or screams; between a woman who is physically free to leave a room and one who is being physically restrained.

The immorality and absurdity of using mixed signals as an excuse for rape is cast in high relief when the assault involves one woman and a group of men. In cases of gang rape in a social setting (usually during or after a party), the defendants and their lawyers frequently claim that group sex took place but no force was involved. These upright young men, so the defense invariably contends, were confused because the girl had voluntarily gone to a party with them. Why she may have even displayed sexual interest in one of them. How could they have been expected to understand that she didn't wish to have sex with the whole group.

The very existence of the term "date rape" attests to a slow change in women's consciousness that began with the feminist movement of the late 1960's. Implicit in this consciousness is the conviction that a woman has the right to say no at any point in the process leading to sexual intercourse—and that a man who fails to respect her wishes should incur serious legal and social consequences.

The other, equally important half of the equation is respect for men. If mixed signals are the real cause of sexual assault, it behooves every woman to regard every man as a potential rapist.

In such a benighted universe, it would be impossible for a woman and, let us not forget, for a man to engage in the tentative emotional and physical exploration that eventually produces a mature erotic life. She would have to make up her mind right from the start in order to prevent a rampaging male from misreading her intentions.

Fortunately for everyone, neither the character of men nor the general quality of relations between the sexes is that crude. By censuring the minority of men who use ordinary socializing as an excuse for rape, feminists insist on sex as a source of pure pleasure rather than as a means of social control. Real men want an eager sexual partner—not a woman who is quaking with fear or even one who is ambivalent. Real men don't rape.

BLATTIPHOBIA

Penny Brown

A great wave of fear filters through the body at the thought of creatures that slither and crawl. Of all the bugs, snakes, and spiders in this vast universe, the appearance, feel, and behavior of the tree roach can induce a panic as intense as a heart attack.

The appearance of a roach is fearful in itself. One of the frightening things about a roach is its shape. It is scary to think how aerodynamic its body is. The roach can flatten its body like a pancake, making it appear to move through walls. The "V" shaped antennae appear to be picking up human emotions, especially fear. The size of a roach can send my heart into my throat. I have seen roaches on my countertop two and one half inches long. The host of a late night talk show once had an African variety on his show that was three inches long. It's frightening to think roaches are so big that Raid had to create a motel for them. Seeing a roach crawling in filthy places reminds us of the germs it carries. My body shudders when I see a roach in the toilet. Roaches love to crawl in the grime under the kitchen sink. I once saw a roach bouncing in the dirt of one of my potted plants as if it were a puppy who had just received a bath.

Fear can turn into convulsions as actual contact with a roach is made. Every nerve fires at the same time when a roach crawls on one's skin. I became physically ill with fear when a roach ran up my bare leg. Once one jumped from a box into my lap, and all my extremities thrashed about while trying to remove the bug from my skin. The ultimate contact was when the roach ran across my face; I wanted to die! Getting a roach caught in my hair was frightening—no, traumatic. A romantic evening on the porch turned into a scene out of "Psycho" when a roach dropped on my hair. Dinner was ruined when a roach dropped down the back of my dress at an outdoor restaurant. Momentary skin contact with a roach is bad; stepping on one spells phobia. The crunch of a big roach as it is stepped on sends waves up my spine. I get sick when I see the mess on the bottom of my shoe. I am afraid to step on something that big; it really needs to be run over by a car.

I fear most the behavior of the roach. The unpredictable movements of the roach are to be seriously feared. Roaches can move at warp speed; even sci-fi heroes would be envious. I have crept into the garage where roaches are running in all directions at the same time. I have frantically waved newspapers at a roach, hoping it would run the opposite direction only to have it race toward me. A roach without wings is bad enough, but Satan himself must have created the flying roach. My blood seems to drain from my body when I see a roach fly across the room. The first time a roach flew at me something snatched my breath, and I began to hyperventilate. I fear most not knowing where they are going to land once they start to fly. Likewise, I fear the eating habits of the roach. They eat human skin! I have even seen a roach eat dog food that the dog wouldn't eat. I am afraid of anything that has a diet ranging from human skin to sawdust.

As one can see, the appearance, feel, and behavior of the tree roach make this a creature to be feared. Other bugs, snakes, and spiders have been on earth for a long time. Roaches have been around since the dinosaurs, but I fear they will not meet with the same fate.

BAD TEACHERS

Silas Tomkyn Comberbacke

One of the normal topics of conversation in a college cafeteria or Student Union is teachers. Students enjoy talking about their instructors as much as elderly people enjoy talking about their ailments. After all, everybody likes to complain. If one learns to recognize and avoid three basic kinds of bad teachers—the boring, the incomprehensible, and the demanding— that form the subject of most of this student conversation, his college days will be much more pleasant.

The first kind of bad teacher is exemplified by Dr. Lackluster. His kind tends to concentrate in subject areas that require lists and facts. One may find him in a scientific lecture course, pointing out the details of the Periodic Table of the Elements or discussing the major dates and rulers of the Byzantine Empire in a history class. Wherever one finds him, Dr. Lackluster is recognizable by the quality of his instruction and by his effect on his students. His voice is high, monotonous, and droning, and he speaks at a regular pace, his gaze fixed on a corner of the ceiling at the back of the room. He uses yellowed, crumbling lecture notes he compiled his first year of teaching forty years earlier, but they serve as props, since he has given the same lecture so many times he could do it in his sleep—and often does. The effect of his delivery on his students is unmistakable. They slump in their seats, resigned, glassy-eyed, or they simply turn their ball caps around backwards and instantly go to sleep. The gentle hum of suppressed snoring provides harmony for the professor's dreary lists. The single student ever known to gain anything from Dr. Lackluster's class was a compulsive doodler who filled 141 notebook pages with pen drawings in one semester. The Museum of Modern Art has given an exhibition of the drawings (entitled "Ode to Tedium"), and the young artist was launched on a promising career by his unknowing instructor. It is Dr. Lackluster's single triumph in a long teaching career.

The second kind of bad teacher, exemplified by Professor Fervor, is almost the opposite of Dr. Lackluster. Professor Fervor is usually found in the humanities—philosophy, English, or languages. She is frantic in her love of her subject and her enthusiasm for it. Her lectures resound down the halls, crashing and clanging with the apostolic vigor of an intellectual barroom brawl. Her eyes light with ecstasy as she describes the more arcane subtleties of Spinoza's *Tractatus Theologico–Politicus* or plurisgination in *Beowulf*. The problem is that she is completely incomprehensible to anyone lacking a Ph.D. in her field (and maybe to the Ph.D.s, too, although they refuse to admit it). A look at her students confirms the diagnosis: there is a vast scratching of heads and tugging at ears; muttered conferences ("What does 'infrangible nominalism' mean?"); gestures of pain and dismay. The lady is intelligent, cultured, enthusiastic, and genuinely devoted to her subject. Unfortunately, she is also disorganized, unintelligible, and ultimately of no use to any of her students.

The third kind of bad teacher is Dr. Adamantine. He combines the virtues (such as they are) of the two preceding and has none of their vices. He is organized, systematic, and understandable; he is also enthusiastic, interesting, witty, and intelligent. He has the profile of a Greek god, flashing white teeth, a deep tan, and a BMW 740i. He was captain of the football team at Princeton, was a Rhodes Scholar, and beats the Academic Dean regularly at tennis. In his classes students are ignited by his delivery and by his grasp of the subject, and they remain alert and questing for knowledge throughout the class period. And yet Dr. Adamantine, too, is the subject of scathing remarks and moans of despair in the cafeteria and snack bar. The problem is that he is a hard grader and demands a great deal from his students. This is the final disaster, the cruelest blow of all. One can get an A from Dr. Lackluster by coming to class (he takes roll) and secreting a chart of the Periodic Table or the Byzantine Empire in one's sleeve at exams. One can get an A from Professor Fervor by staying after class once a week and saying, "I was really interested in your discussion of Schopenhauer today, Professor. Are there any books in the library I could read to assuage my burning thirst for knowledge about him?" But to get an A from Dr. Adamantine it is necessary to work for it. And what student in his right mind would go to such an extreme?

These three kinds of college teachers give college a bad name. In fact, if we could get rid of teachers altogether, then there would be no problem, *etc.* ...

PUMPERS

Jade Whelihan

There are many types of people who purchase gasoline, but three types are easy to spot. All three have an obvious physical appearance which sets them apart from other gas purchasers. Each also has a distinctive pumping technique and freely vocalizes his opinion. Finally, each type has a particular way of annoying every other patron at the same location.

The first type of gas purchaser is Leisure Lou. He can be identified immediately by his appearance. He drives a station wagon with wooden side panels and a bumper sticker that tells the world that he is retired. His Hawaiian print shirt captures everyone's attention. He wears Bermuda shorts and black socks with sandals. On his head sits a fly fisherman's hat which is his obvious display of a continuous state of leisure. His pumping technique also sets him apart from the normal crowd. When he parks his car, he stops at the first pump, preventing the use of the pump in front of him. He always pays for his gas in advance so that the attendant can preset the pump, and he will not have to worry about stopping the pump himself. He activates the pump before opening the access door and unscrewing the tank lid. He tucks the hose under his elbow and spills gas on his hip while opening the tank. As Leisure Lou leans against the side of his car, he pumps his gas absent-mindedly, confident that the pump will stop before gas pours onto the ground. Once the pump stops, he replaces the hose and screws on the tank lid but forgets to close the access door. Leisure Lou even vocalizes his not-a-care-in-the-world attitude. He whistles some melodic tune from *The Sound of Music* while pumping his gas. When inside the convenience store, he tells everyone how wonderful retirement is. But Leisure Lou can be a tremendous annoyance. He blocks the use of two pumps while he performs a number of time-consuming tasks. First he browses through the store with no intention of making a purchase. Then he washes his car's windshield. Next he visits the restroom to wash his hands and looks at the stain on his hip. Last, he walks his dog around the small patches of grass that serve as land-scaping. Leisure Lou is a man who cannot be ignored.

The second type of gasoline purchaser is Strictly–Business Betty. Her physical appear-ance is also very distinctive. She drives an economical, imported car that has a lock on the access door so that she can safely hide a spare key inside. She wears closed-toe pumps instead of flirty sandals. Her skirt and blazer are of a classical line with no frills. Strictly-Business Betty's pump-ing technique is equally distinctive. She unscrews the lid to her tank before removing the hose from the pump. She pumps her gas until the tank is nearly full and then slows the volume to pre-vent the gas from spewing from the tank. Next she turns off the pump and gives the handle a final squeeze to empty the hose. Finally, she replaces the hose, seals the tank, and closes the access door as if following instructions. Now Strictly-Business Betty's most tell-tale character-istic is voiced. She announces to the cashier that she must have a legible receipt for her expense-account report. Then she preaches about the economic virtues of owning an import. Finally she distinguishes herself in a way that annoys everyone. She spends more than her fair share of time at the cashier's counter but pays no attention to the amount of purchase because she plans to pay with a credit card. But when the cashier announces the price, Strictly-Business Betty has to double check the accuracy of the computer. Then she borrows a calculator to check the gas mileage that she has received from her last tank. In the end no one has missed Strictly-Business Betty's presence, but the other customers hope they miss her the next time she purchases gas.

The last type of gas purchaser is Lawnmower Larry. He can generally be recognized by his physical appearance. He drives a pickup truck that has a dented fender with a red and yellow gas can in the bed. He wears a sweat-stained shirt and jeans that sag to his hips. Glaring over the waistband of his jeans is his underwear. He has on a baseball cap to protect his face from the sun and stuffed in his pocket is a red shop rag. He has a streak of grease across his brow where he has obviously wiped his sweat off with a dirty hand. Also unique is Lawnmower Larry's pumping technique. He pays his two dollars in advance but always overpumps the gas by one cent or two. He has no change and borrows the needed pennies from the courtesy jar on the cashier's counter. Lawnmower Larry can be distinguished from the other patrons by his conversation. He complains about the difficulty he has trying to get that blankety-blank lawnmower started. Also, now that the mower is running, it is too hot to mow. Lawnmower Larry's annoyances are only two, but they distinctly identify him. First, he leaves sweat on the counter where he has leaned. Second, he always returns later in the day for more gas and repeats his earlier routine. While sympathetic to his plight, the normal patrons do not miss Lawnmower Larry when he has gone.

In conclusion, these three types of patrons can add more frustration to the life of the average patron than the price of gas. While somewhat humorous, these three could test the patience of a saint. Most people can identify with one or two characteristics of each type, but these are extreme characters. If any patron misses Leisure Lou, Strictly–Business Betty, or Lawnmower Larry, he should consider himself lucky.

PTA VOLUNTEERS

Christine Wagner

Many public institutions rely on the generosity and help of volunteers in order to run smoothly. One of the more important institutions is the school, and one of the most visible volunteers in the school is the PTA volunteer. These volunteers fulfill a necessary role, especially for the elementary schools, by augmenting the work of the principal and teachers with extras that the school ordinarily could not have. The people who do the volunteer work are varied, but the PTA seems to act as a magnet for three types of personalities: the power seeker, the eager beaver, and the dependable worker.

Dominating Dora, the "power seeker," usually starts off as a committee chairman and almost always ends up as the PTA president. She feels she must run the PTA her way because only she knows the best way to do it. She calls board meetings often and is incensed and hurt if someone misses the meeting. All jobs must be done her way, and she frequently organizes half of the job before it is delegated. She then checks to see if it is being done precisely as she organized it. On the other hand, she may not delegate anything at all, preferring to do most of the work herself. Not delegating the work ensures that it will be done properly, namely her way. Dominating Dora usually follows an unacknowledged personal agenda to gain status, prestige, influence, and authority; she often has no idea that she is following a personal agenda. The school personnel are wary of her since she is very bossy in her dealings with everyone. She even goes so far as to tell the principal and teachers how to go about their own jobs. Dominating Dora also promotes programs within the PTA that the principal often does not want. For example, her idea of painting cute rainbows and stars down the hallways may not seem reasonable to a cost-conscious principal who has just had the school hallways painted a fresh coat of creamy white. Dominating Dora may pursue the issue anyway until there is a showdown with the principal, who usually has the last word on these things. Unfortunately, this disagreement causes bad feelings which many times costs her votes at the next election of officers. Dominating Dora always sees that her name is prominently displayed on anything that has to do with the PTA. This recognition is her payment for all that she has done, and she glories in it. She makes sure that she is always available for any awards or plaques or other recognition certificates, often missing out on her children's activities. A "power seeker" like Dominating Dora burns out in about two years, or she is pushed out sooner by her fellow volunteers who do not care for her leadership. Of course, she could not have accomplished any of her myriad of activities without the "eager beaver."

Rarin'-to-go Rita is an "eager beaver" who agrees with everything Dominating Dora says. She goes to all the board meetings and would never dream of missing one. She does everything she is told to do. She volunteers to do every job and is delegated to as many as she can handle plus one more for good measure. Rarin'-to-go Rita is usually the volunteer with all the PTA files stored in her dining room. Her family has not eaten in the dining room since she joined the PTA. Rarin'-to-go Rita is also the one who makes all the cute prizes for game day and designs and fashions the charming centerpieces for the PTA banquet. She thinks nothing of staying up until all hours getting them done. Rarin'-to-go Rita also has an unacknowledged personal agenda, which is that she wants to be liked, needed, and recognized as a capable person. The school personnel love to have her around because they benefit from her overachievement. Rarin'-to-go Rita does most of Dominating Dora's background work. She is the one who will find out how much the paint will cost for the cute rainbows and stars, will design them, and do the work when the principal gives in to Dominating Dora's verbal storm. Rarin'-to-go Rita does not expect public accolades for her work so much as she needs peer group acceptance and recognition. If she receives public attention, she usually becomes very embarrassed and flustered. "Eager beavers" like Rarin'-to-go Rita usually burn out within two years, but their places are soon taken by new "eager beavers." If a suitable "eager beaver" cannot be found, the work will be done by the "dependable worker."

Normal Nancy is a "dependable worker" who is not interested in running the PTA. She goes to no board meetings. She does not care whose way is right as long as the job gets done. Normal Nancy always signs up to help in any way she can. When handed a job, she does it quickly, efficiently, and without much fuss. As chairman of a committee, she gathers enough help around her to get the job done, delegating as needed. She also has a personal agenda; she wants to improve the educational experience of her own children as well as other people's children. She feels the only way she can improve school is by giving her time when she can. The school personnel like her because she is reliable, does what is required, and does not interfere with the school. Normal Nancy does not get involved in any programs that are controversial. She does not want to be involved in the politics of the PTA; she just wants to make her contribution and go home. Normal Nancy does not seek recognition. In fact, she goes out of her way to avoid it. For example, she may not show up at the PTA Volunteer Recognition Banquet to receive a special plaque because of a scheduling conflict with her daughter's ballet class. After receiving the plaque from a friend, who carries it to her in a plain brown paper bag, she places it in the filing cabinet along with her other plaques and certificates of recognition because they are not that important to her. The "dependable worker" like Normal Nancy does not burn out because she paces herself, works steadily, and fills in the gaps where needed. Doras and Ritas may come and go, but Nancys "keep going and going and going."

The interesting thing about the "power seeker," the "eager beaver," and the "dependable worker" is that they are all necessary to run the PTA organization. Their quirks are what make them important in getting the activities planned, the prizes made, the playground equipment ordered, and the book fair organized. Another noteworthy fact is that, when necessary, any PTA volunteer can become any one of these three types of people. The fact that a "power seeker," an "eager beaver," and a "dependable worker" can fit together like a puzzle to form a bigger picture is the miracle of the PTA volunteer organization.

THE DIETING GAME

Harriet Murray

A sad fact in American society is that thousands of people search for the elusive dream of being thin. On any given day, one finds neighbors, friends, and relatives on some kind of diet. Dieters assume various disguises, but the noteworthy ones are the "bandwagoneer," the "promiser" and the "lethal loser."

Everyone wants to lose weight quickly and effortlessly; therefore, any fad diet promising overnight results becomes the new "call" of the "bandwagoneer." She tries the grapefruit diet or the watermelon diet, but she decides her stomach cannot possibly deal with all that fruit. The next day the television advertises a new wonder pill that allows the user to lose up to ten pounds in one week, and the "bandwagoneer" answers the "call." Although the magic pill does not produce the desired weight loss, she never gives up hope for a new "wagon" to hitch onto. Once again, this dieter is lured by advertisements of instant spot reduction—liposuction. She crosses over the safety line into a danger zone of unknown procedures, performed by unqualified physicians. Some dieters lose their lives in the search for a beautiful body. The stomach staple is another dieting tool that dieters try. The staple yields a large weight loss, but the dieter endangers her health because of excess loss of body fluids. The "bandwagoneer" is always listening for the newest cure on the dieting market.

A family wedding or a special dance is a logical reason for a woman to decide it is time to take off her few, unwanted pounds; however, decisions made in haste are hard to keep, and the "promiser" soon fails in her attempt. She is the dieter with only fifteen pounds to lose, and, as each year flies by, she decides dieting is harder than eating what she wants to, and much less fun! She promises to lose the extra weight for her ten-year class reunion, but her weight-loss pledge is not kept. Some women become "promisers" during their pregnancies, and they broadcast to all within hearing distance that they will lose the extra pounds as soon as the baby is born. The "tomorrow promiser" and the "Monday promiser" are the dieters with whom most people are familiar and whose excuses they know. The "promisers" are always starting their diets tomorrow, after one last, scrumptious dinner—their favorite meal of course! The "Monday promiser" can last through lunch, but by dinner she cannot take her hunger pains any longer. She decides there is always another Monday; furthermore, she eats all week, like a bear preparing for winter hibernation, in preparation for her Monday fast. One is not fooled by the "promiser" but saddened that her attempts at weight loss are unsuccessful.

The most tragic dieters in American society are the "lethal losers," young women following a self-destructive path. Characteristically, this dieter is a young woman with low self-esteem from a middle income family . While in her teens, the young lady decides to shed some unwanted pounds, and, much to her surprise, she loses the extra weight quickly. She attends a party with friends, overeats on junk food and decides to "rid" her body of the excess food by purging in the bathroom; thus the "deceiver" is born. From that moment on, she thinks she is in control of her "new found" diet, but the ultimate "deceiver" is her diet. She sneaks large quantities of food for midnight snacks, and she does not care what she eats, only that she satisfies the yearning deep inside her soul. She faces the beginning of the downward turn of her diet—the binge and purge cycle. Ultimately she loses touch with reality and is treated by a physician in a hospital. The "deceiver" has a companion who is, much like herself, another deadly player in the dieting game. This dieter analyzes the calorie content of every morsel of food on her dinner plate and decides whether or not to eat it; usually she does not, but quietly excuses herself from the table to return to her room. She has lost all sense of the value of food for her body, and she cannot see what she has become—a "sad scarecrow." A scarecrow gains nourishment from her straw stuffing, and the "sad scarecrow" needs food to hold her body together. But this dieter cannot see the "straw" she leaves on the ground when she turns her head away from food; she is beyond all reasoning. Innocently enough, the "deceiver" and "sad scarecrow" start their diets with good intentions; however, along the way some mechanism is triggered, and the "lethal losers" are awakened; their lives are never the same.

All dieters share a common goal, losing weight, but they approach the goal from many different sides. The importance of the dieting game is not the goal, but how one decides to get there. The dieter can choose life or death in her quest for a thin body.

MOTORCYCLE RIDERS

J. Marshall Hinman, Jr.

My first motorcycle was a Kawasaki Eliminator 250 street bike. I consider it to have been my training bike, and it was somewhat generic in the sense that it was not easily identifiable as a member of a specific style of motorcycle. And, more importantly, by associating with other riders, I realized that I was not easily identifiable as a member of a specific class of riders. Riders are a species all their own; and, though there are many sub-classes within a class, observation has shown that three main branches of evolution can account for most riders.

The cruiser *(Homo Draggusanus)* variety is most often seen riding a vintage Harley or Indian-made motorcycle. He rides very low to the ground in a Ralph-Machio-crane-kick-like position—arms high and outstretched, knees bent, feet level with buttocks. Most cruisers are between thirty-five and sixty years old, but they always look fifty. If one is wearing a helmet at all, it is a small, open-faced helmet covering little more than the crown of his head. The helmet may contain a variety of markings, such as skulls with crossbones, or "Freedom" stickers that tend to match tattoos adorning the rider. The cruiser may have several metal objects hanging from various parts of his body, and he usually has matted facial hair that ranges from one-quarter inch to twelve inches in length. Members of this class also wear tattered bandanas, studded leather vests or jackets, "Born to Ride" T-shirts, or leather boots with spikes. Physically, the cruiser is generally unfit, with dark skin that is somehow both wrinkled and taut, and rotting, tobacco-stained teeth. Though most cruisers are docile unless provoked, a permanent scowl serves to warn would-be assailants that they are not ones to tangle with. Cruisers usually ride alone or in large, slow-moving groups and are best observed from a distance. They can most often be seen and heard traveling on deserted highways or socializing in rural cafés or icehouses.

The sportster *(Homo Crotchrocketus)* is a sleek creature that is most often seen riding a Kawasaki Ninja or Suzuki Katana. In order to decrease air resistance, members of this class ride face down in the fetal position. Sportsters are younger than the average cruiser, ranging in age from eighteen to thirty. They move so swiftly that they are very rarely seen; like the firefly, the sportster may be seen in one's peripheral vision, but when one turns to look, the sportster is gone. If an observer is lucky enough to get a good look at one of these creatures, he may see a full-faced helmet with a dark, tinted shield and a torso covered with bright stripes or patches in wild, fluorescent colors. If one were to sneak a peek at a dis-helmeted sportster, he might also see a clean-shaven face, or, maybe, a short, neatly trimmed goatee, relatively short, bleached-blond hair, and gleaming-white teeth. Members of this class usually ride in groups of two or three and are most often seen in urban areas. They stop infrequently to socialize, usually in large, open parking lots where they smile and laugh heartily with other members of the pack. But don't let this frivolity fool you—when approached by an outsider, on or off the road, the sportster's attitude says, "I am a Motorcycle Maven. God of the Gravel. Ruler of the Road. Out of my way!"

Finally, tourers *(Homo Middlageyuppia)* ride monstrous motorcycles such as the Honda Goldwing or Yamaha Ventura, complete with stereo, air conditioning, multiple luggage compartments and optional trailer-trunk. Unlike the cruiser or sportster, tourers ride two to a bike, usually a male driver and a female passenger. The driver sits upright, as if riding a horse, while the passenger sits comfortably between the armrests, in the classic "electric chair" position. Tourers are usually forty to fifty years old with graying, salt-and-pepper hair. Their helmets are usually a solid color and match the color of the motorcycle. They wear jeans and designer shirts that seem one size too small for them, and, whether or not they have facial hair, they are generally neat and clean. This class is the most easily approachable of the three and usually travels in single, male-female pairs. They are always coming or going, just passing through, and rarely know anyone in the area; yet tourers are the most friendly and outgoing of the classes.

When choosing a motorcycle, one is, in effect, choosing into which class of rider he will eventually evolve. I have not yet decided into which class I would like to evolve. For this reason, I have not yet decided what type of motorcycle will be my second. My decision will rest on a careful consideration of the desirable and undesirable qualities of the different classes. Who knows? Maybe I will begin a new branch of evolution and start a completely new class all my own.

MY DECISION TO TEACH

Brenda Linn

There are many reasons people decide to enter the teaching field. Some enter because they enjoy working with people or children, others because they like being off during the summer months, and still others because of their love for a particular subject. Although all these reasons are valid, I feel my reasons are much simpler. The bottom line is that I love kids and enjoy working with them, and my desire to make learning a more positive experience for them has only increased with time.

I knew very early in life that I enjoyed working with children; I am drawn to their eagerness to learn, their trusting nature, and their inquisitive minds. It has always been a joy for me to be around children, who are eager to learn. Children are thrilled when an adult takes time to read to them. After hearing a story only a couple of times, they are like a digital recorder set on replay. Their thirst for knowledge is overwhelming. At the elementary level, children also tend to have a very trusting nature. They rely heavily on their elders for guidance. Most children are very honest with their feelings and don't try to hide them. This is a crucial time in a child's life; it is a time when teachers and parents should be molding them for the future. It seems their minds are always working on something that makes them extremely inquisitive. Their curiosities seem to be insatiable. Children are always asking "Why?" even when they know the answer. The inquisitive child wants to know the how's, when's, and where's of everything.

Because of my early interest in children, I developed a strong desire to teach; consequently, I sought out jobs that allowed me varied experiences with children. My first experience was baby-sitting. Here I quickly learned that children must be told precisely what to do. For example, "Go wash your hands with soap and dry them right now." Or, "You must take your shoes off and then you may get into the bathtub." From the many baby-sitting jobs I had, I soon discovered that if I did not have a plan the day would be total chaos. As early as thirteen I became familiar with the need for structure and creativity when dealing with younger children and found myself loving every minute of it. The challenge of actually teaching came when I volunteered to assist a teacher at our church with a room full of second graders. They were extremely demanding as they all wanted to talk at the same time, and everyone wanted to be a helper. Some of the children could write, draw, and even sing while others barely muttered a sound. Each child was a challenge in his or her own way, which I found exciting. Since money has obviously never been the reason people become teachers, the rewards for me became apparent as I spent some time teaching at a day care center. It is so gratifying when I see children become stronger because of my efforts. It is the satisfaction of being able to help others learn things about the world that they never imagined existed. It is the look of accomplishment when children have mastered writing their names for the first time.

Through these previous experiences with children, my desire to become a teacher was confirmed; now the opportunity to fulfill my dream has come, and it is my desire to make learning a positive experience by promoting creativity, positive attitudes, and a sense of self-worth. Having a son who is about to leave elementary school has shown me the importance of creativity in keeping the interest of students. Children need variety to keep them motivated. They need visuals. They also need "hands on" learning whenever possible. Class participation is vital to keep them focused. Subjects need to be presented in a non-threatening manner so that the student does not become discouraged. For example, one can present material in the form of a game. Subjects can also be presented through art. Next, positive attitudes need to be promoted. Students need to feel that their opinions matter, and it is important to help children set goals so they can see their accomplishments. Finally, a child should be made aware of his self-worth, for it is critical to his development. Positive strokes, something we as individuals never get enough of, are important to a child's social growth. Teachers and parents should be quick to point out the child's strong points and encourage him to use them whenever possible. Most importantly, every child needs to know that he is special.

My decision to become a teacher is based on my enjoyment of working with children, my experiences with children, and my personal desire to make learning a positive experience for children. I get satisfaction and a lot of love from the children I teach. I feel that I can make a difference in somebody's life. I feel God has given all of us a gift to do something; teaching is mine.

A NEW CAREER

Kathy Crosby

I am presently attending college to obtain an Associate Degree in Nursing. There are a number of factors which led me to make this choice such as the great demand for this particular profession as well as the opportunities available in the area medical center. However, there are three important elements that allowed me to make this very important decision. They are the direct observation and personal contact I experienced, the strong desire and ambition I obtained as a result of this contact, and the encouragement and support of others as they became aware of my strong desire to pursue a career outside the home.

The basic and perhaps most subtle factor which brought me to realize a career in nursing was the influence I experienced from the nurses assigned to care for my terminally ill mother. For a period of six months, I had a considerable amount of contact with these very caring people, and I was able to observe many things. All their routine duties were performed with dedication. They encouraged my mother to ask for pain medication whenever necessary, which is very important for the cancer patient. They would spend hours trying to get her temperature down, for she was subject to night fevers. There were no heroics involved. It was done strictly for her comfort. Every night they would come to give her a back rub. She looked forward to these. These same nurses were compassionate and understanding. If time allowed, they would just sit and visit with my mother. I also found them to be sensitive to the needs of the family, allowing us to hope when despair was often present or sometimes just offering their prayers. They provided a sense of humor, which I found to be so necessary for both my mother and our family. Due to the nurses' dedication, many of my mother's fears, along with those of the family, were lessened. As her last months of life were spent with this new family, it was reassuring for all involved to know that her basic needs and comforts were being taken care of. I was grateful to her new friends. They made her last few months bearable. From this steady diet of their daily routines and personal care of this special patient, each day I became more and more interested in doing the same.

As a result of all this exposure, I acquired a strong desire and ambition to pursue a career in nursing. I find this ambition to be an ever-present necessary ingredient and a principal element for success. It is a quiet resolve that does not quit even when it would be convenient to do so. Sometimes I will ask myself, "Why am I doing this? I don't really need a career. Isn't it enough just being a wife and mother?" But I do go on because of my ambition. My conscience tells me I must continue even though I'd rather be doing something else. It is this same conscience telling me, "I must succeed; I will succeed." I am filled with much hope of attaining this success in school, thus allowing me to provide the necessary care needed by so many individuals. I want to make the difference in the quality of patient care. I want to help alleviate fears and anxieties, ease pain and suffering, maybe help someone to smile or laugh, as I so often witnessed with those who surrounded my mother. I find this ambition to be a very necessary factor in pursuing my new career. Moreover, I find that as I am more and more successful in school, my ambition grows. Also, I do believe strongly that my personal experience afforded me the opportunity to attain this ambition.

Subsequently, as my ambition became known, I was deluged with encouragement and support from family and friends. In this particular situation, I believe this to be the most important factor in my decision regarding careers. I experienced some feelings of apprehension, which were alleviated by the presence of this encouragement. It was reassuring to know that others had confidence in me. Their confidence reinforced the little confidence I had in myself. There were some misconceptions I held which were later discounted through this encouragement. I am thankful for this encouragement. It has allowed me to feel comfortable about attending school. I truly believe that without the support and encouragement of my immediate family, I would not be seeking this new career. There are some sacrifices we have all had to make. My husband is very considerate, supportive, and proud of his wife. My two sons think it is great their mom goes to college. The older one can't wait for school to begin so we can study together. The younger one thinks it is great we get to eat out more often. This encouragement and support I receive helps me balance out the juggling act I sometimes feel I'm performing as I balance the duties of wife and mother versus student. Most of all, I'm not made to feel I am neglecting them in any way. I would not be pursuing this career without their support and encouragement.

In summary, I believe the decision I made to become a nurse began with the experience my mother had with her nurses. She was fortunate to have wonderful and caring nurses. I was fortunate to be able to receive something positive from an unfortunate experience. This experience brought forth a strong desire to enter the field of nursing. And as a result, I have been the object of much encouragement and support, which helped me to make my final decision. I will reach my goal eventually. I will become a nurse. My past experience will provide me with the ambition to finish school with the encouragement and support of my family and friends. One day I'll be working in a hospital caring for people who need compassion and dedication, and I will be able to give them just that and more.

BLUEBERRY WHIPPED CREAM PIE

Taseen Tambra

This recipe allows the average cook to create a delicious homemade blueberry whipped cream pie. Instead of having to buy pies and other desserts from the store, now anyone can make them inexpensively at home. Making a blueberry pie may take some time, but the end result is well worth the effort and the wait. The main steps in making a blueberry pie are not complicated, but one should not forget that there are pre-cooking and post-cooking steps that are just as important as the main cooking steps.

Certain things must be done before the cook actually begins to make the pie. First, he must gather all the ingredients that will be needed. The cook will need flour, salt, Crisco shortening, water, one can of whipped cream, and one twenty-one ounce can of blueberry pie filling. In addition to the ingredients, the cook will need some important utensils, including teaspoons, tablespoons, measuring cups, a large bowl, one nine-inch pie pan, a rolling pin, and a rolling board. Any flat surface can be used instead of a rolling board, but a board is much easier and more efficient. Now that the cook has gathered all of the utensils and ingredients, he can do some pre-baking steps to make his job easier. First, he needs to pre-heat the oven to 425°F. He should also flour the rolling pin and surface so that the dough will not stick. The pie pan must also be lightly oiled; otherwise the crust will stick to the pan when the pie is baking. Finally, the cook should measure out all of the ingredients carefully (making sure they are level) as follows: two cups of flour, one teaspoon of salt, three-fourths of a cup of Crisco shortening, and five tablespoons of cold water. Completing all of these pre-cooking steps enables the cook to have an easier and less confusing time when baking.

Now, in the action stage, the cook is ready to put together and bake a beautiful masterpiece in just three steps. The first major step in creating a pie should be making the crust. To prepare the crust, the cook should mix the flour and salt in a large bowl. Now, he should add the Crisco shortening and begin to mix. The cook should sprinkle in the water, all the while continuing to mix and knead the dough. He should now toss the dough lightly until it forms a firm ball. After dividing the dough into two equal parts, the cook should press each part in his hands so that the dough forms five-to-six-inch round "pancakes." The cook can now roll the "pancakes" with the pin, making sure the new size is about one inch bigger than an upside down pie plate. After loosening and removing one "pancake" from the rolling surface, the cook should carefully press the dough into the pie plate. Lastly, the cook should trim the edges of the dough even with the pie plate. The cook can now move on to the second step, which is to finish putting the pie together. First, the cook should add the blueberry filling to the pie shell. Now he can lift the other "pancake" and place it on top of the filled pie. After trimming one-half of an inch beyond the edge of the pie plate, the cook should fold the top edge under the bottom crust. Now he can flute (make grooves with his fingers) the edge of the pie. The last thing the cook should do before proceeding to the next step is to cut slits in the center of the top crust to allow steam to escape. Once all of the other steps have been completed, the cook can move on to the major action step, which is to bake the pie. The cook should carefully place the pie in the pre-heated oven for about thirty minutes or until the pie is golden brown. If all of the above action steps are followed in order and exactly, the cook should be pleased with a delicious outcome.

While waiting for the pie to bake, the cook can take on some post-cooking events to finish up this process. The first thing the cook should do is begin to clean up. The cook should clean up the countertops and wash all dishes and other utensils he may have used. He should also throw away any empty packages and put the unused ingredients in their proper places. The last step in the finishing process is serving the pie. Once the pie is done, the cook should carefully take it out of the oven and place it on a countertop to allow it to cool. After the pie has cooled, the cook can cut it into pieces and place each piece on a plate. The cook can now place a small mound of whipped cream on top of each piece of pie and serve. The entire cooking process is completed, and the cook now becomes a consumer, feasting on the wonderful delicacy he has created.

People have been baking pies for centuries, everyone with his own individual method. Although there is no one way to make a whipped cream blueberry pie, this recipe presents a simple process with a great outcome. This recipe is a wonderful addition to anyone's collection.

WORKS CITED

"Audience Appeal in 'Letter from Birmingham Jail'," Student Essay.

Bacon, Francis. "Of Youth and Age."

"Bad Teachers," Student Essay.

Batt, Matthew. "Lessons from Lockdown: Sometimes Inmates Make the Best College Students," from *Isthmus*, October 4, 2002. Reprinted with permission.

Batt, Matthew. "Objects d'Art," from *Salt Lake, The Magazine for Utah*, April 2003. Reprinted with permission.

Bedau, Hugo Adam. "The Case Against the Death Penalty," *American Civil Liberties Union*, December 31, 1997, http://www.aclu.org/capital/general/10441pub19971231.html. Reprinted by permission of the author.

"Blattiphobia," Student Essay.

"Blueberry Whipped Cream Pie," Student Essay.

Carter, Stephen. "Just be Nice," *Yale Alumni Magazine*, May 1998.

Catton, Bruce. "Grant and Lee: A Study in Contrast," © by the U.S. Capitol Historical Society. All Rights reserved. Reprinted with permission.

Cohen, Carl. "The Case for the Use of Animals in Biomedical Research," *New England Journal of Medicine*, (No. 315, Oct 1986). Reprinted by permission of the *New England Journal of Medicine*.

Cousins, Norman. "Who Killed Benny Paret?" from *Saturday Review Magazine*, May 5, 1961.

Darrow, Clarence. "Why I am an Agnostic," from Arthur and Lila Weinberg, eds., *Verdicts Out of Court*, 1963, © Chicago: Ivan R. Dee, Inc., Elephant Paperbacks, 1989, © Arthur and Lila Weinberg. Reprinted with permission of Lila Weinberg.

Diamond, Jared. "Collision at Cajamarca," from *Guns, Germs, and Steel*, © 1997 by Jared Diamond. Reprinted by permission of W.W. Norton & Co. on behalf of the author.

"The Dieting Game," Student Essay.

Dubus, Andre. "Digging," from *Meditations from a Movable Chair*, © 1999 by Andre Dubus. Reprinted by permission of Vintage Books, a division of Random House on behalf of the author.

Dobbs, Kildare. "The Shatterer of Worlds," from *Reading the Time* by Kildare Dobbs, © 1968. Reprinted by permission.

Durick, Joseph A., et al. "Letter from Clergyman in Birmingham, Alabama to Dr. Martin Luther King, Jr.," © 1963 *Birmingham Post-Herald*.

Eiseley, Loren. "The Brown Wasps," from *The Night Country*, © 1971 Loren Eisely. Reprinted by permission of Simon & Schuster Inc. New York.

Elbow, Peter. "Desperation Writing," from *Writing Without Teachers*, © by Oxford University Press, Inc. All rights reserved.

Ericsson, Stephanie. "The Ways We Lie." *UTNE Reader*, 54 (Nov./dec. 1992), 56-73.

Fussell, Paul. "Thank God for the Atom Bomb," from *Thank God for the Atom Bomb*, © 1990 by Ballantine Publishing Group, USA. Reprinted by permission.

"Getting Sober," Student Essay.

"Going Home," Student Essay.

Gilder, George. "Why Men Marry," from *Men and Marriage*, © 1986 by George Gilder. Used by permission of Pelican Publishing Company, Inc.

Goodall, Jane. "Some Thoughts on the Exploitation of Non-Human Animals," from *Through a Window: My Thirty Years with the Chimpanzees of Gombre* by Jane Goodall, © 1990 by Soko Publications, Ltd. Reprinted with permission of Houghton Mifflin Company.

Guinier, Lani. "The Tyranny of the Majority," from *The Tyranny of the Majority*, © 1974 by The Free Press, a division of Simon & Schuster, Inc.

"Her Hair," Student Essay.

Highet, Gilbert. "Diogenes and Alexander." Reprinted by permission of American Heritage, a division of Forbes, Inc., © Forbes, Inc. 1963.

"Horror Novels as Therapy," Student Essay.

Jacoby, Susan. "Common Decency," from *The New York Times*, May 19, 1991, © 1991. Reprinted by permission.

Jefferson, Thomas, et al. "Declaration of Independence."

Kennedy, Gerald. "I Believe in God," Chapter One from *I Believe*, © 1958 by Abingdon Press, copyright renewal 1986 by Mary Kennedy. Used by permission.

King, Jr., Martin Luther. "Letter from Birmingham Jail," from *Why We Can't Wait*, © 1963. Reprinted by permission of Harper Collins Publishers.

Koch, Edward. "Death and Justice." Reprinted by permission of *The New Republic*, © 1985, The New Republic, Inc.

"Mallory," Student Essay.

"Motorcycle Riders," Student Essay.

"My Decision to Teach," Student Essay.

"A New Career," Student Essay.

Paglia, Camille. "It's a Jungle Out There."

"Pappadeux and Joe's Crab Shack," Student Essay.

Peck, M. Scott. "Why We Fall in Love," from *The Road Less Traveled*, © 1978 by M. Scott Peck, M.D. Reprinted by permission from Simon & Schuster, Inc.

"Planting a Vegetable Garden," Student Essay.

"PTA Volunteers," Student Essay.

"Pumpers," Student Essay.

Rauch, Jonathan. "In Defense of Prejudice," from *Harper's Magazine*, May 1995, © 1995 by *Harper's Magazine*. All rights reserved. Reproduced from the May issue by special permission.

"The Recovering Dysfunctionals," Student Essay.

"The Right to Assisted Suicide," Student Essay.

"Rings to Ruin," Student Essay.

Rodriguez, Richard. "None of This is Fair."

"Save the Animals: Stop Animal Testing," Student Essay.

"A Seasonal Twist," Student Essay.

Shermer, Michael. "Skepticism as a Virtue: An Inquiry into the Original Meaning of the Word 'Skeptic.'" Reprinted with permission. Copyright 2002 by Scientific American, Inc. All rights reserved.

Staples, Brent. "Just Walk on By: A Black Man Ponders His Power to Alter Public Space," from *Parallel Time: Growing Up in Black and White*, © 1994 by Brent Staples. Used by permission of Pantheon Books, a division of Random House, Inc.

Steele, Shelby. "On Being a Black Man and Middle Class," from *The Content of Our Character: A New Vision of Race in America*, © 1998 Harper Collins. Reprinted with permission.

Swift, Jonathan. "A Modest Proposal," 1729.

Tannen, Deborah. "Sex, Lies, and Conversation," from *The Washington Post*, June 24, 1990, © 1990 by *The Washington Post*. Reprinted by permission.

"Weight Lifters," Student Essay.

White, E.B. "Once More to the Lake," from *Essays of E. B. White*, © 1941 by E. B. White. Reprinted by permission of Tilbury House, publishers, Gardiner, Maine.

"Wisdom," Student Essay.

INDEX